Petra Eckhard, Michael Fuchs,
Walter W. Hölbling (Eds.)

Landscapes of Postmodernity

American Studies in Austria

edited by

Astrid M. Fellner
(Saarland University)
Klaus Rieser
(University of Graz)
Hanna Wallinger
(University of Salzburg)

Volume 10

LIT

Landscapes of Postmodernity

Concepts and Paradigms of Critical Theory

edited by

Petra Eckhard, Michael Fuchs,
and Walter W. Hölbling

LIT

Cover Picture: M. C. Escher's Relativity adapted by Andrew Lipson
and Daniel Shiu

Gedruckt mit Unterstützung des Bundesministeriums
für Wissenschaft und Forschung in Wien

Bibliographic information published by the Deutsche Nationalbibliothek
The Deutsche Nationalbibliothek lists this publication in the Deutsche Nationalbibliografie; detailed bibliographic data are available in the Internet at http://dnb.d-nb.de.

ISBN 978-3-643-50201-8

A catalogue record for this book is available from the British Library

Krotenthallergasse 10/8
A-1080 Wien
Tel. +43 (0) 1-409 56 61
Fax +43 (0) 1-409 56 97
e-Mail: wien@lit-verlag.at
http://www.lit-verlag.at

LIT VERLAG Dr. W. Hopf
Berlin 2010
Fresnostr. 2
D-48159 Münster
Tel. +49 (0) 2 51-620 320
Fax +49 (0) 2 51-922 60 99
e-Mail: lit@lit-verlag.de
http://www.lit-verlag.de

Distribution:
In Germany: LIT Verlag Fresnostr. 2, D-48159 Münster
Tel. +49 (0) 2 51-620 32 22, Fax +49 (0) 2 51-922 60 99, e-Mail: vertrieb@lit-verlag.de

In Austria: Medienlogistik Pichler-ÖBZ, e-mail: mlo@medien-logistik.at

In Switzerland: B + M Buch- und Medienvertrieb, e-mail: order@buch-medien.ch

In the UK: Global Book Marketing, e-mail: mo@centralbooks.com

In North America by:

Transaction Publishers
New Brunswick (U.S.A.) and London (U.K.)

Transaction Publishers
Rutgers University
35 Berrue Circle
Piscataway, NJ 08854

Phone: +1 (732) 445 - 2280
Fax: + 1 (732) 445 - 3138
for orders (U. S. only):
toll free (888) 999 - 6778
e-mail: orders@transactionpub.com

PREFACE

Austria's Young Americanists, a network of young scholars of American Studies based in Austria, was officially brought into being in November 2007 in order to facilitate information transfer among Ph.D. students. Since then, AYA has organized three annual workshops: "Approaching Toni Morrison's *Beloved* from all Sides" (Nov. 2007), "Landscapes of Postmodernity" (Sept. 2008), and "Iconic Figures of the 20th Century and Beyond" (Oct. 2009).

As the title suggests, the volume at hand is the outcome of the workshop held back in fall 2008, which was conceptualized as a space that brings together doctoral students who in their research projects approach central ideas of postmodern thought. Unfortunately, we were not able to include essays by all of the workshop participants, but the additional contributions we were offered finally made possible a well-balanced and versatile collection of essays.

We want to acknowledge the support of this book publication by the Department of American Studies at the University of Graz and the Austrian Federal Ministry of Science and Research. Furthermore, we want to express our gratitude to those that made the workshop possible, primarily to Karin Schmid-Gerlich and the U. S. Embassy Vienna as well as the Fulbright Commission for their continued financial support. Secondly, to the city of Graz and especially City Councilor Wolfgang Riedler, who generously provided the premises of the Literaturhaus Graz to conduct the workshop. Finally, to Michael Rozendal for giving the opening talk at the workshop, conducting the discussion and, of course, also for contributing the opening essay to this volume.

We also want to thank the series editors of American Studies in Austria for accepting the project for publication in the series, Susanne Hamscha for writing the introduction to the section "Polymorphous Identities," and Ana Teresa Jardim Reynaud for penning the afterword.

A very big thanks to Gundo Rial y Costas, who not only was the one to suggest the publication of 'workshop proceedings,' but who also was very active in recruiting additional contributors and a great help in the organization of the Transamérica section, to which he also wrote the introduction.

Finally, we want to thank Andrew Lipson for allowing us to use an image of his LEGO adaptation of M.C. Escher's *Relativity* constructed in collaboration with Daniel Shiu on the book cover. You can find Andrew Lipson's work online at http://homepage.ntlworld.com/andrew.lipson.

Petra Eckhard, Michael Fuchs, Walter W. Hölbling

Table of Contents

Polymorphous Subjectivities

Transamérica

Afterthoughts

REMAPPING POSTMODERN EXCHANGES: THEORY *AVANT LA LETTRE*, A TRAVELOGUE

MICHAEL ROZENDAL

> The difference between a writer and its world gives the reason for writing. All mental existence is an expression, a measure of distance.
>
> Kathy Acker, "Notes on Writing"

> What does not change / is the will to change
>
> Charles Olson, "The Kingfishers"

Let us propose a slippery slope as a way into the unstable multiplicity of postmodern exchanges. [1] It is a slope located in the Bavarian Alps not far from the border with Austria where King Ludwig II commissioned his fairytale creampuff of a castle, built between 1869 and 1886 as the first skyscrapers were rising in Chicago and New York. Neuschwanstein, inspired by Wagner's operatic versions of medieval myths and designed by an theatrical set painter, piles layer upon layer of fantasy in testimony to a German identity that it was attempting to fabricate. What is striking about this particular fantasy, however, is that it has become reality. As the most photographed building in Germany, the castle is now emblematic, attracting thousands to its crag: it is and has been a postmodern building from its inception.

Neuschwanstein is in a way unfinished, although it is also somehow complete in its incompletion. The tour through it skips several floors since the master's and servants' levels are the only there, an archaic assertion of social opposites undermined by the procession of the masses through the halls – some 1.3 million per year with as many as 6000 per day when summer swells the tide.[2] The interior architecture wastes nothing on nuance despite being replete with an ornate grotto, throne room, and an opera hall which all sing in support of the exterior's message. Taking photos through the windows of the surrounding landscape may be fair game, but photos of the interior are *verboten*. This is hardly a loss. After all, Neuschwanstein is all about exteriors. Photos in front of the walls or perhaps a matching set of plasticized placemats are the only way to prove that one has

---

1 I would like to thank Professor Christopher Leise for his comments on an early draft of this piece.

2 Bayerische Schlösserverwaltung Neuschwanstein: Schloss Neuschwanstein heute (http://www.neuschwanstein.de/deutsch/schloss/index.htm). Accessed July 21, 2009.

actually been there, that one has had a direct experience of the image, that our collective dreams are actually stones. And then friends may touch the hand that touched the image itself.

Neuschwanstein (literally "New Swan Stone") faces the same problem that postmodernism does – it is a term predicated on another term, a castle that amplifies and displaces the old twelfth-century ruins of Schwanstein that form the foundations of the family castle just around the bend. The nineteenth century neo-gothic Hohenschwangau glowers there in the sun as all the tourists head up the hill to the glamorous unfinished theater piece, with only a few distracted in their pilgrimage to real Germany of Disney.[3] As a castle that was actually completed and lived in for a generation, Hohenschwangau may find itself frustrated that the game has changed so spectacularly. The past – nation, tradition, art – is primarily a fabrication, a very real collective fantasy, and if the actual could keep from getting in the way, all the better. Besides, Hohenschwangau is still occupied occasionally by the heirs of the royal family, a historical curiosity, an anachronism, a remnant of a lost world that can say little to our living fabric of dreams.

Postmodernism was – and may still be – an interaction between European theory and American material, mind and body, raw and cooked, high and low. These were embodied in the journeys that Jean Baudrillard and Umberto Eco took across the brash confident land of hyperreal simulations.[4] For a new generation of cultural critics in this volume, these tensions are the ground for an engagement with theory and culture, dichotomies to be undermined or exploited as seams for conversation. But the scene has changed – the postmodern is already everywhere. Neuschwanstein – mass tourism object and national treasure precisely because it is a mass tourism object which continually fills the national coffers with treasure – offers its layers of image upon image. Europe and the broader Americas are at least as contaminated and liberated by our strange postmodern condition which has infiltrated all pretenses at a steadying history and secure identities. Indeed, the American shopping mall is no longer as avant-garde as Neuschwanstein. The castle does away with selling objects to address desire itself, with enough direct intimacy to let us see eye to eye, at least briefly, with this fantastic I.

The essays in this volume test the cross-currents sweeping through our contemporary moment. We've all slid far enough down this slippery slope that

---

3 While the castle was prosaically referred to as "Neue Burg Hohenschwangau" during Ludwig II's life, it became Neuschwanstein after his death in a stroke of marketing that entirely displaced dowdy old family burg.

4 Jean Baudrillard *America*, translated by Chirs Turner (London: Verso, 1989) and Umberto Eco *Travels in Hyperreality* (Orlando, FL: Harcourt Brace, 1990).

Neuschwanstein is entirely postmodern despite, or even because of, all its nineteenth-century medievalism and nationalism. In a world of logical fallacies, is it possible to reduce or at least recognize the absurdity that we inhabit?

> With all this freedom, I have no voice
> With all this freedom, I have no choice.
>
> Crimpshrine, "Sleep What's That?"

> The mistake is to look for explanations where we should just watch the slow fuse burning.
>
> Rosmarie Waldrop,
> *Lawn of Excluded Middle*

How do we find our bearings in a historical moment that offers immediate gratification, immediate self-identification without the need for self-reflection? While we are far from the fantasy of endless, virtual gratification – see 'globalization,' 'sweat shop,' 'clean coal,' 'factory farm,' or 'Flint, Michigan,' for examples – we are in a time both predicated on change and denying fundamental changes. Even with the long-term mobilizations in the multiple anti-globalization movements, the short-term spasm of financial crisis and glimmerings of hope, most official politics seems mired in the belief that really There Is No Alternative (TINA) to business as usual.

Where the new was the totemic hope and fear of modernity—Make It New vs. The Wasteland, revolution vs. dictatorship, art vs. commodity—now novelty is entirely quotidian. We are flooded with new products, new styles, new ways of communicating, new forms of community that are continually being reintegrated into the logic of capitalism. How did my liberation end up in your iPhone? When did my identity become a market? What can I buy to claw my way back into the ever more youthful target market? The 'Do It Yourself' (DIY) ethos which pushed punks, hipsters, and riot girls to produce their own culture offered, still offers, the hope of less alienated labor, of less instrumentalized expression, of more direct personal connections.[5] But this too can be hollowed out as a style, with high end designers now putting out DIY lines for the already well-off.[6]

---

[5] For more on DIY, see *DIY Culture: Party and Protest in Nineties Britain*, edited by George McKay (Verso 1998), *Notes from Underground: Zines and the Politics of Alternative Culture* by Stephen Duncombe (Verso 1997), and *DIY: The Rise of Lo-Fi Culture* by Amy Spencer (Marion Books 2005). *Riotgrrrl: Revolution Girl Style Now* edited by Nadine Monem (Black Dog 2007) presents a compelling collection of primary and secondary sources on this feminist punk movement.

[6] The sidelining of disruptive cultural movements into a consumable fad is an ongoing, repeated dynamic. Many of the writers in the Harlem Renaissance struggled to find outlets after the vogue

In a moment stripped of mediation, the new is no longer enough. The theoretical engagements in this volume work to fashion spaces of abstraction, moments of reflective distance to address the overwhelming immediacy of an information-saturated present. Communicating what we may share without realizing it requires peeling back some of the particularity of direct experience, intimating communities or coalitions out of the wash of irreconcilable lived difference.[7] This pleasure of recognition, of shared concerns, of reinforcing engagements plays through this volume, linking work across the Americas. After all, the present is far too important, far too serious not to play with it.

Everything That Acts is Actual

Denise Levertov,
"Everything That Acts is Actual"

words, words
as if all
worlds were there.

Robert Creeley, "A Token"

To appreciate Neuschwanstein and postmodernism, perhaps we should wander further back in time or at least a ways down the Danube to Walhalla, not the mythic Norse mead-hall but the neo-Classical edifice of King Ludwig I of Bavaria, the grandfather to our protagonist Ludwig II. Walhalla, something between a temple and a tomb, is a marble monument to the Great Men of Germany that is set overlooking this valley that was once a Roman territory. Intentionally recalling the Parthenon and sporting external friezes of masculine martial success and feminized diplomatic achievement, there is little at first to mark this building as modern except for the fact that it is still so intact.[8] The site seems to yearn to become ruins, to long for that weight of respectability.

of the 20s. Similarly, the working class writers of "proletarian fiction" in the early thirties were quickly diffused as a style instead of a nascent form of identity politics.

7 "Rather than to immersion in mysteries I was only leading you to common ground" (Waldrop 15).

8 Ludwig I's philhellenism extended beyond the contemporary vogue of supporting the Greek War of Independence from the Ottoman Empire as his second son, Otto II, became the unlikely King of the newly liberated Greece in 1832. Eventually deposed in 1862, he was succeeded by the Danish George I whose line was a tumultuous part of Greece's tumultuous twentieth century through 1973. The line's history is perhaps best summarized by the contemporary Athenian saying that "The best king is a dead king." This Republican sentiment claims to trace its roots to a mythic sacrifice to save the city of Athens, giving a sense of the depths of the anti-authoritarian sentiment most recently mobilized in the 2009 student protests.

Set ten kilometers away from Regensburg on the edge of the Bavarian Forest, Walhalla is a place of contemplative pilgrimage that requires the scaling of hundreds of marble steps on several tiers to reach the monumental, recessed metal doors. For those approaching from the Danube, instead of the modern parking lot around the back, this is a bracing transport from the mundane toward the cool certainty of the ideal, a reverent abstraction recalling pagan ceremonies. A sign announces the entrance fee near the bottom of the hill, allowing visitors to weigh the effort against the Euros in their pockets before attempting the ascent. The cashier manning the entrance was probably not part of Walhalla's initial design and reminds us that despite the neoclassical pomp of the place, the display is now firmly framed in the economics of tourism. Even if guests do not have the money to make it through the door, the nearby lavatories are free and equipped with electric eyes to insure that any mark of a visit will be quickly flushed away.

Unlike Neuschwanstein, all of Walhalla's external flourish is merely preparation for the interior where some sixty four commemorative tablets and one hundred and twenty-eight busts forming a secular German canon line the walls. Looking past the current generation toward the eternity that they already occupy, these white figures are an eclectic vision of a loosely Germanic tradition that embraces figures from modern day Austria, Sweden, Holland, Russia, Switzerland, England, and the Baltics, though this is perhaps as much an unintentional comment on the disavowed heterogeneity of all these nation states as a sign of Ludwig's hubris. While the plaques recognize figures preceding portraiture such as Arminius, also known as Hermann der Cherusker, from two millennia ago, the busts memorialize the usual suspects such as Goethe, Beethoven, and Kant. In a period when Germany was still divided into numerous different principalities, a linguistic abstraction more than a political frame, Walhalla is a tactical canon uniting Erasmus, Mozart, and Catherine the Great. All these, along with an ongoing list of figures who have been dead for at least twenty years, gather around the modern Odin or Caesar of Ludwig I himself, sitting enthroned on a pedestal. Fabricating a German identity was a preoccupation of the line. However, Walhalla is more literal-minded in this pursuit than the cotton-candy of Neuschwanstein, crafting a pedantic and usable past from shards of a current world. The nascent modernism of this vision leads one to wonder if T. S. Eliot or Ezra Pound ever toured by this spot.

The political weight of Walhalla sinks in slowly, as it is in no rush and there is almost no narrative documentation at the site unless visitors are willing to spring for the booklet of biographies (€5 German, €6 English). At first, the memorial presents itself as largely self-evident, disdaining the uninitiated. Though construction on Walhalla began in 1830 and was completed in 1842, an inscription on the floor announces that the site was conceived in 1807 by the then Crown

Prince Ludwig. The primacy of the ideal over the fallen world resonates with the hush of the hall, but all this calm seriousness serves to silence and mystify politics.[9] King Ludwig I, named after his godfather King Louis XVI of France, conceived Walhalla when Napoleon was sweeping through Bavaria, and the edifice here attempts to dam the democratic rush of the French Revolution. Unlike the demotic forces that were modernizing Europe, history here is a cold and markedly armless process of contemplation rather than action. Walhalla crafts a narrative parade of individuals as the agents of history – the masses are only allowed entrance at specified times and only as reverent observers. There is a nod toward collective action in the 2003 plaque recognizing German Resistance fighters against Nazism. However, in conception and most of its ongoing practice all groups beyond the occasional bus-loads are explicitly excluded. The marble cushions gracing the benches are for static display, not actual buttocks.

The failure of this hierarchical neo-Classical/proto-Modernist history can be measured in several ways. It was precisely the *collective* national uprisings of 1848 with their tricolor flag inspired by the French Revolution that forced Ludwig I from the throne. All that was marble began melting into air, the embodiment of the canon did more to attest to its absence rather than its ongoing certainty. Ludwig II must have learned from this insult to his favorite grandfather that plaster and display would be more enduring and compelling. But the sting reaches deeper than that as Walhalla itself is hardly a blip now on the German tourist map, a curiosity more than a destination, a good spot for strawberries and champagne or a brief detour from the bike path along the Danube. After all, the real Parthenon is now only a two and a half hour flight from Munich. The slowly expanding canon of Walhalla may have added Albert Einstein and a couple more women like Sophie Scholl of the anti-Nazi White Rose Group, but this has hardly added vitality since inductees must be dead for two decades before being considered. The masses, so antithetical to Ludwig I's vision, have wandered distractedly into their own history and fantasies.

---

9 According to Perry Anderson, "German tradition, famously, tended to separate the world of culture from that of power, as a compensation or sphere superior to it" (25).

> Everyone agrees. It's about to explode.
>
> The Invisible Committee,
> *The Coming Insurrection*

> We can be precise. The factors are
> in the animal and/or the machine the factors
> are
> communication and/or control, both involve
> the message.
>
> Charles Olson, "The Kingfishers"

In creating a mystified order as a compensation for a fallen aristocraticity, Neuschwanstein outdoes Walhalla: Ludwig II's loss was all the more complete, the fantasy all the more compelling, encompassing. Even though he would continue to rule for more than two decades, Ludwig II died as an ideal aristocratic embodiment two years into his reign when he was forced to accept the domination of Prussia and a bitterly constraining position as a constitutional monarch.[10] Is the death of the author really the birth of the castle? Removed from royal agency, Ludwig II became something of a fanboy of the *ancien régime*, an avid reader of his namesake's House of Burbon line. Styling himself as a Moon King reflecting the light of the long-set Sun King,[11] Ludwig II built castles as a form of fan fiction, elaborating the narratives and forms that he had inherited while affirming exhausted impossibility of the truly new.

Ludwig II's triumph in this vein is his unfinished Herrenchiemsee Palace, an amplification of Versailles floating far from disturbances on an island in southeastern Bavaria. Unsatisfied with merely echoing the past, Ludwig II planned to build many of the rooms to larger dimensions, increasing the grandeur of the past while decreasing the number of inhabitants to one as this palace was largely a private play-space to recreate absolutism as a personal liberation from the immediacy of history. To limit interaction with the staff, an elaborate, fully set table could be raised to the king's private dining room from the unfinished kitchens

---

10 The visitor's brochure to Neuschwanstein offers a pop psychology reading of Ludwig II's castles which seems well suited to our age of incessant autobiographies and a string of extreme makeover "reality" TV shows: "No longer a sovereign ruler, he was unable to cope with the role of a constitutional monarch. He created his own alternative world, in which as the reigning king of Bavaria he could live like a king of the Middle Ages or the baroque age of absolutism. This is the idea behind his castles." Castles as message architecture, message as simultaneous individual apotheosis and evanescence.

11 According to some accounts, Ludwig II went so far as to assume a nocturnal cycle, working by night and sleeping by day after 1875.

one storey below – hot dishes had to be rushed over from the ovens of the nearby Augustinian Monastery which Ludwig had bought in 1873, becoming known as the Old Palace, a religious community secularized, even modernized for the self-mythologizing 'Grail King.'

We can see Ludwig II as a practitioner of a strange historical idealism in his Herrenchiemsee Palace; construction on the castle began in 1878 just ten years after the Paris Commune had attempted for two months to establish a much more materialist and broad-based vision of liberation. Like Neuschwanstein, which was "furnished in medieval styles but equipped with what at the time was the latest technology," Ludwig's Versailles followed the dictum that "building in historical styles meant 'perfecting' them" (Visitor Brochure). The inclusion of bathrooms, running water, and a pool-sized, heated bathtub are certainly improvements over the facilities at Versailles, but this strain of idealism is strikingly static, even parodic in its direct translations of *fleur de lis* and some twenty-five portraits of Louis XIV into the late nineteenth century. With two interlacing capital Ls as his crest, Ludwig II interweaves the past of Louis with his own present, achieving union along an axis of divine right, though the grandeur of the Great Hall of Mirrors serves with its *Lost in the Funhouse* refractions to display the intervening decay of king into an increasingly irrelevant 'king function' self-aware of contingency, of cultural construction.[12]

Despite the amplified scale of the plans, Herrenchiemsee Palace seems much smaller than its inspiration, as the two side wings were never completed and were later torn down. Only the central promenade of the gardens was landscaped by the time of Ludwig's actual death, leaving a rough hewn experience of walking from the ferry through forest to arrive at fountains in front of a surprisingly manageable palace that also houses the Ludwig II museum. The idealism at play in the castle attempts to collapse historical distance through performance – the scenes of the Sun King become present through their possible re-enactment, through their ongoing presence as models. At the same time, it spatializes power as a retreat from the polis into its deadening simulacra.

Strangely enough, this aristocratic palace swimming in replicas of a dead past is more central to the post-WWII political institutions of Germany than the spectacular Neuschwanstein. In August of 1948, the West German Grundgesetz was negotiated in the Old and New Palaces, and this Basic Law continued in force with some minor adjustments even after the reunification with the former Eastern Germany. So, Ludwig II is in many ways the absent father of a nation, a

---

[12] A process open to similar interrogation as Michel Foucault's consideration of our contemporary perceptions of authorship in his classic "What is an Author?"

postmodern nation of representation and mediation. Habermas critiques mass-media society as performing a kind of 'refeudalization,' as power is performed in front of people instead of by them.[13] But the game is already redoubled before the media could become involved: refeudalization is at the core of the state but at the distance of a second remove, springing out of Ludwig II's already incomplete attempts. Where does the play of power begin and the power of display end? Is the castle at least as true as the nation? Could a postmodern author have come up with this *mise en abyme*?

> [...] he might even have tried to survive death, as a paranoia; as a pure conspiracy [...]
>
> Thomas Pynchon, *The Crying of Lot 49*

> The egg is magical and mundane, Baal and baloney, it's the all-purpose object of desire, the placeholder for every operation. My kingdom for an egg. Person, place or egg. Egg, therefore I am.
>
> Shelley Jackson, *The Melancholy of Anatomy*

Amassing extravagant bills to fund his castle projects, flaunting bourgeois propriety or at least productivity, Ludwig II ran afoul of the Burghers in Munich, who began plotting to remove him in 1886. Massive debt coupled with numerous uncompleted castles had left Ludwig II's fancy undimmed – his was a practice of process over product, of the repeated titillation of desire rather than its satiation, of bedtime stories of fanciful rooms built around his beds. Indeed, having nearly bankrupted himself, he still pushed to bankrupt the imagination, having broken ground in the 1880s on a new castle Falkenstein while crafting plans for a Byzantine palace in Graswantgal and a Chinese palace in Tyrol. The ever expanding empire of message architecture embraced Orientalism, dreams of seraglios, dynasties reaching back millennia. This prescient daring must leave Las Vegas' planners blushing; after all, even the most absurd of Las Vegas' postmodern pyramids still plans to turn a profit from its concatenation of kitsch and wonder. One can imagine the horror of the ministers at the time, and the regret in the current Tyrolian tourist agency that they cannot lure visitors to slot machines in a glowing edifice of 19th century Chinoiserie.

---

13 Jürgen Habermas *The Structural Transformation of the Public Sphere: An Inquiry into a Category of Bourgeois Society* 158, 231.

Without legal backing for their planned coup, the ministers turned to the newest scientific advances of psychiatry to have Ludwig II declared insane and unfit to rule. It was a brilliant stroke to reduce Ludwig II to a perverse subject requiring state intervention for his own good: this marked the complete fall of the aristocrat who had at first sought to embody the state or at least to castle his way into an enduring monumentality. His attempt to escape politicized modernity is cut short through medical modernity; the individual as author really is dead here, in becoming the object of professionalized knowledge, Ludwig is reduced to a ward of the paternalistic, bureaucratized state. This is a second abstraction, a second remove from direct action that leaves the rationality of the market as the horizon of logic.

It is here that things become strange. What is agreed upon is that Ludwig II was deposed on June 9th among some standoffs between local police and the psychiatrists who had arrived at Neuschwanstein to deliver the deposition. Despite apparent umbrella wielding assaults by a local baroness in support of Ludwig II, he was eventually taken into custody and moved to Lake Starnberg near Munich. It was in these waters that Ludwig II would be discovered on June 13th, floating dead along with the lead psychiatrist who had declared him insane. This would seem to be the definitive end of the story, but in true postmodern fashion, the narrative itself was only a prequel, an excuse for an open ending that raises many more unanswered questions.

Ludwig II has managed to live on, as conspiracy theories around his death have been ongoing fodder for popular fantasies. The body itself was not enough to bring closure to the tale; in fact it is part of the uncertainty: was there water in his lungs? Was he shot attempting to escape? What about the good doctor? This does not even begin to address the question of motivation—murder/suicide? Botched escape? The heirs of the House of Wittelsbach attempting to get their hands on the inheritance before it could all be turned into display? A simple political silencing? Regardless, Ludwig II's end has become an absence that continues to spawn narrative, much like the willful disbelief around the death of Elvis or the dogged search for meaning in the assassination of J.F.K. This is something of a compensation for the almost immediate transformation of Neuschwanstein, Herrenchiemsee Palace, and Schloss Linderhof, as all three were opened to the public only about seven weeks after the death, perhaps trying to tap into the media attention, not to mention the last of the summer travel season. The tourist became the ideal reader of the fragmented aristocratic space, reconstructing its fabrications into coherent narratives or at least pleasing itineraries. Ludwig II's fantasies of connection with a mythic Germany of the grail myths, of an escape into a transcendent religious time, were replaced by much more secular fantasies of connecting to the ostentatious surfaces that Ludwig left behind. The simulacrum does precede the real. Welcome to the desert of Neuschwanstein.

> What Is To Be Done?
>
> Lenin, 1902

> How now brown cow?
>
> Popular American phrase for elocution training

> drive, he sd, for
> christ's sake, look
> our where yr going
>
> Robert Creeley, "I Know a Man"

Having slid this far down the historical and logical slippery slopes, where do we find ourselves? Clearly, we are once again simply at the beginning. The essays in this volume offer soundings of our moment, test our received theoretical narratives against an expanding geography, propose directions of movement that take us from Bavaria to Brazil, from *Moby-Dick* to *Finding Nemo*, perhaps even moving toward communities through increasingly polymorphous subjectivities. With castles, kings, and nations long blurred into a wash of fabrications and performances proposing unstable but seemingly immutable identities, the need for theoretical engagements is all the more pressing, to enunciate the constraints swaddling our tongues, to prepare many different grounds for many different actions.

The ongoing narratives of Neuschwanstein reveal an often unquestioned fabric of lived reality proceeding from fabrication. Even in the nineteenth century heyday of monarchical resurgence coupled with industrial revolution, between the two Ludwigs, we see each attempt at authorial certainty dissolving exactly into its opposite, becoming a not particularly self-aware postmodern act embracing a vicious yet liberating dialectic of modernizing and markets, individual atomization and global connections. The postmodern may be a period that, as Jameson holds, is unable to think historically (ix), but that is in part because it seems to have claimed the history that might have offered an outside. Here, then, let us return to one of the modernists to hold "Let be be finale of seem" (Stevens line 7): perhaps existence itself offers the seams to open up these totalizing semblances. Theoretical framing will be an important element of exploring which roots may still be radical, which branches bear hybrid fruit rather than the strange, violent crop of so much of the twentieth century.

Where the postmodern theorists reacted against the institutionally canonized positions of the modernists, the critics in this volume find themselves at a similar temporal remove, heightened by the geographical shift to a much more plural view of the Americas. Let us hope that these engagements open ongoing conversations.

WORKS CITED

Anderson, Perry. "A New Germany?" *New Left Review* 57 (2009): 5-40. Print.

Jameson, Fredric. *Postmodernism or, the Cultural Logic of Late Capitalism.* Durham, NC: Duke UP, 1991. Print.

"Neuschwanstein Castle." [Visitor Brochure, English] Bayerische Schlösserverwaltung, n.d. Print.

Stevens, Wallace. "The Emperor of Ice-Cream." *The Collected Poems of Wallace Stevens*. New York, NY: Vintage, 1990. 64. Print.

Part I

The Structurality of Poststructure

THE STRUCTURALITY OF POSTSTRUCTURE: THE FOUNDATIONS OF POSTMODERNISM

WALTER W. HÖLBLING & MICHAEL FUCHS

"Postmodernism: does it exist at all and, if so, what does it mean?" (ix) is the opening question in Hal Foster's preface to *The Anti-Aesthetic: Essays on Postmodern Culture* (1983).[1] At first, it may seem rather odd that Foster raised that question some 50 years after the term had found widespread use in the humanities[2], but on closer look, another two and a half decades later, the question can still not be answered satisfactorily. Apart from the fact that due to its philosophical bases, postmodernism cannot but elude being nailed down to a fixed definition, the sheer number of different postmodernisms complicates the enterprise that is defining postmodernism even further. Fredric Jameson remarks:

> [T]here will be as many different forms of postmodernism as there were high mondernisms in place, since the former are at least initially specific and local reactions *against* those models. That obviously does not make the job of describing postmodernism as a coherent thing any easier. (112)

As indicated by Jameson, defining postmodernism is further obfuscated by its relation to modernism, or rather, a number of different modernisms. Does the 'post' simply stand for succession or rather an evolution? A reaction against? Is postmodernism an effect of modernism? How far is postmodernism dependent on modernism? None of these questions can be answered easily – partly resulting from the fact that postmodernist artifacts rather value "the process of negotiating the postmodern contradictions" than "any satisfactorily completed and closed production that results from their resolution" (Hutcheon xi) – and any attempt at an answer that could be given within the limited scope of this introduction cannot be anything but superficial. This is why we will simply refrain from trying to

---

1 More recently, Ihab Hassan has opened an essay as follows: "*What Was Postmodernism?* What was postmodernism, and what is it still? […] Like a ghost, it eludes definition. Certainly, I know less about postmodernism today than I did thirty years ago, when I began to write about it. This may be because postmodernism has change, I have changed, the world has changed" (1).

2 According to Ihab Hassan, "[i]t seems that an English salon painter, John Watkins Chapman, used the term, back in the 1870s, in the sense that we now speak of Post-Impressionism" (6). Reverend J. M. Thompson also had a very different kind of postmodernism in mind when he argued in 1914 that "[t]he *raison d'être* of Post-Modernism is to escape from the double-mindedness of Modernism" (744-745). In Literary Studies, the term 'postmodernismo' was first used in Frederico de Onís' *Antología de la poesía española e hispanoamericana (1882-1932)*, published in 1934, to denote a reaction against modernism.

provide any possible answers, but will rather take one of the many definitions of postmodernism as a starter. According to David Coughlan, postmodernism is

> anti-essentialist and anti-foundationalist; it sees as problematic the question of universal truths, true representation, or absolute reality; it does not hold with the autonomous, rational subject; it questions the notion of non-gendered, non-historical, non-ethnocentric reasoning; it interrogates Enlightenment ideology; it views historicism favourably; it rejects the labels of relativism or nihilism; it posits heterogeneity, difference, fragmentation, and indeterminacy as positive forces in cultural discourse (par. 6).

As anti-foundationalist as the postmodernist movements may be, their ideological roots can be clearly traced to a small number of foundational writings some of which are poststructuralist.[3] These foundational writings of postmodernism include: firstly, the fictional writings of Jorge Luis Borges and Vladimir Nabokov, both of whom wrote highly postmodernist pieces years before postmodernism became en vogue during the 1960s; secondly, Umberto Eco's *Opera aperta* (1962; *The Open Work*), which not only puts strong emphasis on the interactions between work and reader, but also insists on the polysemy inherent in any cultural text, and is in many ways introducing ideas that later cemented Eco's position as one of the major poststructuralist thinkers; thirdly, Roland Barthes' *Eléments de sémiologie* (1965; *Elements of Semiology*), in which he shows how first-order languages are described by meta-languages which, in turn, would need yet another language to be described, thus indicating how the structuralist system of language is regressive; and finally, Jacques Derrida's famous "Structure, Sign, and Play in the Human Sciences" lecture at a conference at Johns Hopkins University in 1966, which is generally regarded as a manifesto against structuralism as well as the foundational speech of a movement that came to be known as deconstruction. Especially the abovementioned names of Eco, Barthes, and Derrida again point to the close relation between poststructuralism and postmodernism as well as to the fact that, as Michael Rozendal puts it in his contribution to this volume, "[p]ostmodernism was – and may still be – an interaction between European theory and American material, […] embodied in the journeys that Jean Baudrillard and Umberto Eco took across the brash confident land of hyperreal simulations" (10). Unfortunately, there are no essays in this volume that explicitly discuss Eco's or Barthes' writings; however, Derrida is dealt with in detail in the first essay of this section and reappears throughout the collection at hand. In addition to his just mentioned speech, Derrida has mainly

[3] Postmodernism cannot be simply equated with poststructuralism, even if the cultural movement(s) of postmodernism is intricately connected with the philosophical movement(s) of poststructuralism.

become famous for his coinage of *différance*, a deliberate misspelling that plays on the fact that 'différer' means both 'to differ' and 'to defer,' indicating that meaning is theoretically endlessly (temporally and spatially) deferred in a *chaîne signifiante* (signifying chain) in which meaning can only be constructed through difference to other signs[4], a process denied by certain groups in power (who, in postmodernity, no longer possess 'real' power but only signs of power) by assigning certain signs the value of "transcendental [...] signified[s]" (Derrida 281). In combination with the Foucauldian notion of the subject's inability to escape discursive systems, *différance* is one of the most central concepts of postmodern thought.

Following the abovementioned ideas by Barthes and Derrida, Jean-François Lyotard defines postmodernism as "incredulity towards metanarratives" (xxiv) – a phrase that appears time and again throughout the volume – arguing that scientific knowledge needs philosophical or political narratives for legitimization, thus being enmeshed in narrative systems, i. e. language, where there is "no [more] universal metalanguage" (41). Lyotard also mentions the increasing importance of technology in our age and warns that innovations in technology can no longer be 'real' innovations, since due to the fact that technology is part of the system, any innovation cannot but be a result of that very system (or at the very least will always be described using the same language and thus be embedded within the system); an idea that, in different form, found literary treatment in Thomas Pynchon's repeated use of the concept of entropy. Jean Baudrillard, who "has been hailed as the guru of postmodernity" (Poster 662), takes Lyotard's notion of the link between technology and signs a step further by claiming that postmodern capitalism is defined by a "political economy of the sign" (*Mirror* 121). According to Baudrillard, in our postmodern world, representation has been replaced by simulation. Since the postmodern reality can no longer be real "because the real is no longer possible" (*Simulacra* 19), reality has turned into a hyperreality in which "models of a real" are generated "without origin or reality" (*Simulacra* 1).

The essays in this opening section enter into a dialogue with some of the abovementioned critics and concepts. In the first contribution to this section, "Apocalypse?! Now?!," Michael Phillips demonstrates the value of deconstructionistically close-reading J. Hillis Miller's well-known apocalyptical-deconstructionist reading of Joseph Conrad's classic *Heart of Darkness*. Miller's

4 Even though Derrida's paper "Cogito et histoire de la folie" (1963) is usually credited as the origin of this idea (see e. g. Schultz and Fried 12), it is already present in Jacques Lacan's "L'instance de la lettre dans l'inconscient ou la raison depuis Freud" (1957; published in *Écrits*; see 497-498, 502-503, and, especially, 523-528).

obvious intention to read *Heart of Darkness* in an apocalyptic way – triggered by the title of Francis Ford Coppola's cinematic adaptation of the novella, *Apocalypse Now*, Mike argues, inexorably leads to a "nihilism of which the deconstructionist worldview was so often accused" (30) and rather disregards the ambiguity inherent in language that is meta-referentially and meta-linguistically evoked in the novella. Rather than following in Miller's footsteps, Mike suggests that Conrad's masterpiece operates in a system of freeplay, and even though it is part of this very system (and well aware of it), *Heart of Darkness* "is neither a celebration nor a condemnation of freeplay, but rather an observation of the destabilized worldview that can result when cultural (or other) discourses overlap in an individual" (52).

In "Writing Ahead of the Times," the second essay of this section, Simone Puff shows that Zora Neale Hurston's *Their Eyes Were Watching God*, a clearly pre-postmodern work, is filled with characteristics generally ascribed to postmodernist literature. The most apparent ones, according to Simone, "are blurred distinctions between 'high' and 'low' culture and the rejection of metanarratives combined with the creation of alternative *petits récits*" (67). Simone does also not fail to highlight the importance of the diachronicity of her own reading of Hurston's work, emphasizing that while the novel constituted a mininarrative at the time of its writing, the "canonization of Hurston's novel [...] elevated *Their Eyes Were Watching God* to a metanarrative" (ibid.).

The final contribution to this section, "A Horrific Welcome to the Desert of the Real," penned by Michael Fuchs, argues that postmodernist horror films intelligently interact with what has been referred to as the 'postmodern condition,' which is – following Baudrillard – defined by the precession of simulacra, i. e. postmodern culture is not merely articifial, but rather, there is no more distinction between 'reality' and artifice. Among others, the simulacral character of the diegetic reality of these films is exposed through the incessant use of intertextuality and meta-references. But against the popular conception that these metagames mainly serve to disrupt viewer expectations and merely lay bare the fictionality of a given film, Michael argues that by "trap[ping] the viewer in a constant oscillation between the signs of a seemingly infinite *chaîne signifiante*" (72), these movies uncover "one of the most pressing anxieties of the post-industrial age[:] [...]whether there is a – and if there is, what is the – difference between film, or, more generally, fiction, and 'reality'" (89).

WORKS CITED

Baudrillard, Jean. *The Mirror of Production*. 1973. Trans. Mark Poster. St. Louis, MO: Telos, 1975. Print.

—. *Simulacra and Simulations*. 1981. Trans. Sheila Faria Glaser. Ann Arbor, MI: U of Michigan P, 1994. Print.

Coughlan, David. "Postmodernism." *The Literary Encyclopedia*. The Literary Dictionary Company, 20 December 2005. Web. 15 March 2010.

Derrida, Jacques. "Structure, Sign, and Play in the Discourse of the Human Sciences." 1966. *Writing and Difference*. 1967. Ed. and Trans. Alan Bass. Chicago, IL: U of Chicago P, 1978. 278-294. Print.

Foster, Hal. "Postmodernism: A Preface." *The Anti-Aesthetic: Essays in Postmodern Culture*. Ed. Hal Foster. Port Townsend, WA: Bay, 1983. ix-xvi. Print.

Fried, Lewis L. B., and William R. Schultz. *Jacques Derrida: An Annotated Primary and Secondary Bibliography*. New York, NY: Garland, 1992. Print.

Hassan, Ihab. "From Postmodernism to Postmodernity: The Local/Global Context." *Philosophy and Literature* 24.1 (2001): 1-13. Print.

Hutcheon, Linda. *A Poetics of Postmodernism: History, Theory, Fiction*. London: Routledge, 1988. Print.

Jameson, Fredric. "Postmodernism and Consumer Society." *The Anti-Aesthetic: Essays in Postmodern Culture*. Ed. Hal Foster. Port Townsend, WA: Bay, 1983. 111-125. Print.

Lacan, Jacques. "L'instance de la lettre dans l'inconscient ou la raison depuis Freud." 1957. *Écrits*. Paris: Seuil, 1966. 493-528. Print.

Lyotard, Jean-François. *The Postmodern Condition: A Report on Knowledge*. 1979. Trans. Geoff Bennington and Brian Massumi. Manchester: Manchester UP, 1984. Print.

Poster, Mark. "Baudrillard, Jean." *Routledge Encyclopedia of Philosophy*. Ed. Edward Craig. New York, NY: Routledge, 1998. 662-663. Print.

Thompson, J. M. "Post-Modernism." *The Hibbert Journal* 12.4 (1914): 733-745. Print.

APOCALYPSE?! NOW?! *HEART OF DARKNESS* AS A DE(CON)STRUCTIVE SURVIVAL GUIDE FOR POSTMODERN TIMES

MICHAEL PHILLIPS

> It is precisely 'because deconstruction neither mandates nor authorizes any course of action' that Deconstructionism does its harm. Students, would-be lovers of knowledge, learn to brush aside the Socratic imperative, and accept the prejudices of the world simply because they are what is.
>
> reader response to a Stanley Fish article in the *New York Times*

The passage cited above was a reader response to one of two *New York Times* articles about deconstruction in America written by Stanley Fish in 2008. These articles, which Fish's editor thought would "elicit a small number of responses from readers interested in continental philosophy," in fact provoked about 900 responses in the ensuing weeks, leading Fish to conclude that "there's life in that old dog yet." This is not surprising, since the ideas that made deconstruction so threatening are far older than the movement itself and have long outlived the furor it originally caused. This debate was sparked by the deconstructionist practice of vigorously analyzing the systems of meaning by which human knowledge is defined. These analyses focused on the constructed nature of knowledge, thereby demonstrating that ideas and values that certain cultures accept as 'natural' are actually constructed by these cultures. This idea fed into postmodernism, in which the move away from the idea of fixed, stable meaning and towards an emphasis on the culturally constructed nature of ideas continued.

This shift was also evident in literature, where conventional narrative structure was increasingly replaced by a more disjointed narrative style. Such structural irregularities invoke a deconstructionist view of meaning by foregrounding the role of narrative structure and forcing the reader to play a more active role in the process of creating meaning. The idea of an active reader in turn carried over into the perception of the role of the literary critic. Where structuralism claimed to privilege the text, deconstruction emphasized the interactive process by which critic and text combine to create a new meaning.

In the worlds of both social and literary criticism, reaction to this idea was wide-ranging and intense. On the social level, while some celebrated a perceived liberation from the tyranny of fixed ideas, others condemned the nihilism they believed was implied by a system that denied the possibility of fixed meaning. Similarly, in literary circles, some critics celebrated the liberation from prescribed literary and critical standards, while others deplored the abandonment of long-standing literary values.

In this paper, I will explore the treatment of these issues presented in Joseph Conrad's *Heart of Darkness*. Although it pre-dates deconstruction by several decades, the text grapples with the fundamental epistemological challenge that lies at the heart of deconstruction, which was put forth in Conrad's time by Nietzsche. To begin, I will look at the seminal article "Structure, Sign, and Play in the Discourse of the Human Sciences," in which Jacques Derrida delineated the philosophical issues at stake and outlined some reactions to the deconstructionist challenge. I will then analyze J. Hillis Miller's article "*Heart of Darkness* Revisited" as a deconstructionist reading of *Heart of Darkness*. Although Miller was an early champion of deconstruction on the American literary scene, his reading finds in the text the exact nihilism of which the deconstructionist worldview was so often accused. By refining and re-applying some of Miller's critical tools, I will then offer a different interpretation, which argues that the text does not offer a definitive moral judgment on the deconstructionist worldview. Instead, it sets out to reveal the constructed nature of meaning and to explore the practical implications of a system of flexible meaning. In so doing, it presents both the potential dangers of such a system and a possible method for meaningful, responsible human existence within such a system. Furthermore, I will show how the text anticipates postmodernism by constructing a subject position that compels the reader to play an active role in the joint reader-text process of meaning creation.

THE HEART OF DECONSTRUCTION

Jacques Derrida's 1966 speech "Structure, Sign, and Play in the Discourse of the Human Sciences" is widely regarded as the foundational statement for deconstruction. In it, Derrida outlines some of the primary themes of what eventually came to be called 'deconstruction.' He begins with an analysis of structuralism, which he suggests relies on a belief in a fixed center that anchors the system of interrelated meanings. Derrida calls this center the "transcendental signified" and claims that the history of structural thought, which he also calls "logocentrism," consists of "a series of substitutions of center for center" (279). This pattern, he argues, reveals a "force of desire" for "reassuring certitude" (ibid). In other words, it is symptomatic of a human need for stability and coherence.

Citing the works of Nietzsche, Freud, and Heidegger, Derrida then identifies a rupture in this pattern of substitution. Rather than providing a stabilizing center,

Derrida suggests that these thinkers focused on the complex processes and relations through which meaning is formed. As such, their works tended to foreground both "the structurality of structure" (ibid.) and the fluid ways in which the structure is continually manipulated to create new meaning, a process which Derrida calls "freeplay." Derrida then posits two possible reactions to the removal of a transcendental signified, one negative and one positive:

> Turned towards the lost or impossible presence of the absent origin, this structuralist thematic of broken immediacy is therefore the saddened, *negative*, nostalgic, guilty, Rousseauistic side of the thinking of play whose other side would be the Nietzschean *affirmation*, that is the joyous affirmation of the play of the world and of the innocence of becoming, the affirmation of a world of signs without fault, without truth, and without origin which is offered to an active interpretation. (292)

Although this "active interpretation" would eventually become a fundamental tenet of deconstruction, Derrida also identifies a limitation to this approach. He argues that even those who would criticize a system of meaning can never completely escape the terminology and discourse of the very system they criticize. To illustrate this problem, he explores Claude Lévi-Strauss's use of the nature/culture opposition within his ethnological works. Essentially, Derrida demonstrates that Lévi-Strauss was aware of the limitations of this distinction, yet he continued to use it as an analytical tool. Derrida writes that this approach

> [...] consists in conserving all these old concepts within the domain of empirical discovery while here and there denouncing their limits, treating them as tools which can still be used. No longer is any truth value attributed to them; there is a readiness to abandon them, if necessary, should other instruments appear more useful. In the meantime, their relative efficacy is exploited, and they are employed to destroy the old machinery to which they belong and of which they themselves are pieces. (284)

The focus here on destruction would seem to justify the frequent allegations of nihilism that were leveled against deconstruction. However, in his ensuing discussion, Derrida points out the creative potential of this approach, which Lévi-Strauss called *bricolage*. *Bricolage* involves taking the available (admittedly imperfect) analytical methods and then adapting and using them to forge a new tool that in some way helps make sense out of the unfamiliar. Accordingly, Lévi-Strauss called his own work on South American mythology a "myth of mythology" that would "ensure the reciprocal translatability of several myths" (Derrida 287). Rather than an ultimate truth, he saw his work as an interpretative tool that others could take up and modify as necessary. As Lévi-Strauss wrote: "Should fresh data come to hand, they will be used to check or modify the formulation of certain grammatical laws, so that some are abandoned and replaced by new ones" (8).

Derrida then expands the idea of *bricolage* beyond the realm of social sciences through his concept of "supplementarity." He argues that the "movement of signification adds something, which results in the fact that there is always more, but this addition is a floating one because it comes to perform a vicarious function, to supplement a lack on the part of the signified" (289). Here, Derrida puts a positive spin on what would become deconstruction. The work of deconstruction is not simply the destruction of former systems, but rather an ongoing process by which one engages with disparate systems of meaning and forges meaning out of this rich chaos. This approach is particularly relevant in postmodern times, in which cultures and value systems mingle and interact to an ever increasing degree, thereby challenging previously stable cultural systems of meaning. In this context, *bricolage* (or supplementarity) can be seen as a method by which individuals can make some sense out of the complexities of the postmodern age.

DECONSTRUCTION IN LITERATURE

J. Hillis Miller was one of the leading figures in the American movement that sought to apply Derrida's principles of deconstruction to literary criticism. Echoing Derrida's ideas, Miller proclaimed that "all words are metaphors – that is, all are differentiated, differed and deferred. Each leads to something of which it is the displacement in a movement without origin or end" ("Ariadne's Thread" 58). From this perspective, the text represents a complex system of potential meanings, which is open to potentially endless acts of interpretation. The reader therefore becomes a species of *bricoleur*, since "the pattern is subject to 'free play,' is formally 'undecidable.' Meaning emerges from a reciprocal act in which interpreter and what is interpreted both contribute to the making or the finding of a pattern" (Miller, "Fiction and Repetition" 191).

Critics were quick to object that this attitude assigns a greater importance to the reader or critic than to the text itself. In his bestselling book *The Closing of the American Mind*, Allan Bloom summed up this attitude:

> The interpreter's creative activity is more important than the text; there is no text, only interpretation. Thus the one thing most necessary for us, the knowledge of what these texts have to tell us, is turned over to the subjective, creative selves of these interpreters, who say that there is both no text and no reality to which the texts refer. (379)

Although it sold lots of copies, Bloom's simplistic reduction misstates the deconstructionist position. Even in his early essay, Derrida already indicated some limitations to the game of philosophical freeplay:

> The quality and the fecundity of a discourse are perhaps measured by the critical rigor with which this relationship to the history of metaphysics and to inherited concepts is thought [...]. It is a question of putting expressly and systematically the

> problem of a discourse which borrows from a heritage the resources necessary of that heritage itself. A problem of economy and strategy. (3)

Far from denying the existence of texts, Derrida advocated a continued critical engagement with them. As he wrote: "What I want to emphasize is simply that the passage beyond philosophy does not consist in turning the page of philosophy (which usually amounts to philosophizing badly), but in continuing to read philosophers *in a certain way*" (288).

Miller adopted this ethos for his literary criticism, citing the need for a certain restraint in literary criticism:

> Deconstruction attempts to resist the totalizing and totalitarian tendencies of criticism. It attempts to resist its own tendencies to come to rest in some sense of mastery over the work. It resists these in the name of an uneasy joy of interpretation, beyond nihilism, always in movement, a going beyond which remains in place [...]. ("Stevens' Rock" 197)

While both Derrida and Miller suggest a kind of *bricolage* approach, it is worth noting at this point that Miller invokes an "uneasy joy" of interpretation. Ultimately, this uneasiness, a kind of lingering logocentric insecurity, haunts Miller and has a profound effect on his interpretation of *Heart of Darkness*. In his essay "*Heart of Darkness* Revisited," Miller argues that Conrad's novella reveals the impossibility of both meaningful human existence and interpersonal communication within a freeplay system. In essence, he assigns the text to the negative school of thought about freeplay. However, a closer examination of the text suggests that Miller's reading fails Derrida's test of "critical rigor." In his reading, the critic's supplement takes precedence over the original text, or as Miller himself writes, it is a case "covering over while claiming to illuminate" ("Revisiting" 220[1]). An examination of the generic models that Miller uses in his analysis will provide a useful example of interpretive *bricolage* and the powerful yearning for logocentric resolution that informs it, and it will also point the way towards a less logocentric interpretation of the text.

DEFINING PARABLES

Miller defines parable as "the use of a realistic story [...] to express another reality or truth not otherwise expressible" (206). This definition captures the most essential element of the parable – the audience's assumption that there are two

1 Unless indicated otherwise, all of the following quotations of J. Hillis Miller are taken from his "*Heart of Darkness* Revisited" essay.

different meanings involved in the story. This audience awareness is essential for the proper functioning of a parable, since without it there is a danger that the audience will miss the secondary meaning completely. However, Miller's definition does not adequately account for the way in which these meanings interact to accomplish the goal of the parable. To understand this process, we must break down all of the assumptions that lie behind the different terms used in Miller's definition. The first question is: What are the most important attributes of the 'realistic' story? In a parable, this realistic story must be completely naturalized so that the audience can grasp the 'literal' meaning. To use Miller's example, the Biblical parable of the sower (Matt. 13.1-9) is targeted towards an agricultural society, in which the connection between the seed, fertile soil and the subsequent plant is a part of the communal knowledge. The second criterion for the parable's realistic story is that it must evoke some value that is universally accepted. In the parable of the sower, this value is that the growth of plants is a natural and desirable thing. Because this value, which I will call the 'common-sense value,' is so completely naturalized, it is never directly stated. However, it hovers in the background and, as we will see, plays an important role in the successful operation of the parable.

Miller defines the story's second meaning as "another reality or truth not otherwise expressible." This "truth," traditionally called the 'moral of the story,' is actually the value that the parable seeks to instill in the audience. However, Miller's claim that the moral is "not otherwise expressible" is inaccurate. In the case of the parable of the sower, Jesus states the meaning of the parable in more explicit terms just a few verses later, basically explaining that those who accept his teachings will live a prosperous life and multiply (Matt. 13.18-23). This shows that the moral of the story is *not* inexpressible. In fact, a direct statement of the moral would be a *clearer* form of expression. So how does the moral differ from the common-sense value, and what is the purpose of the parable?

The difference between the two values lies in their levels of popular acceptance, or what Derrida might call their "truth values." While the common-sense value has nearly universal acceptance, the moral is not yet completely accepted as truth by the audience. While everyone would agree that seeds planted in fertile soil will grow and produce valuable crops, some might still question the value of adopting Jesus' value system. The goal of the parable is to overcome this doubt and to naturalize the values encoded in the moral. To do this, the narrator carefully constructs the realistic story such that the only interpretation that makes sense is the one that supports the desired link between the common-sense value and the moral. When this connection is made, the audience subconsciously transfers the truth value from the common-sense value to the moral, thereby naturalizing the moral.

Putting this all together, we arrive at a more specific understanding of the structure and function of a parable. A parabolic text is one that is carefully constructed to encourage the audience to form an associative link between a realistic story, which is easily comprehensible and evokes a widely accepted, common-sense value, and a second meaning (i. e. the moral). The goal of fostering this associative link is to graft the truth status already accorded to the common-sense value onto the moral of the story. The emotional satisfaction that accompanies the 'a-ha moment' (i. e. when the audience grasps the connection between the two meanings) masks the subtle discursive maneuvers that transpire at this moment, in which the moral either achieves or moves closer to the label of Truth. With this understanding of the parable in place, I can now turn to the difference between the parabolic and apocalyptic tales.

PARABLE VS. APOCALYPSE

Like the parable, the apocalyptic story also sets out to teach a lesson. However, the important distinction between the two narrative strategies lies in the manner in which the narration establishes the validity of the stated truth. In an apocalyptic tale, the source of the tale's validity is clearly stated. Miller uses the biblical Book of Revelation as his example and points out the proliferation of witnesses in the story. However, despite the many witnesses, the important thing to recognize here is that the source of the tale's authority is clearly identified at the end of the chain of witnesses (i. e. God). As such, the structure of the apocalyptic story is inherently logocentric. Unlike the parable, which deemphasizes the cultural value code that sanctions the parable's message, the apocalyptic story explicitly identifies the transcendental signified at the heart of the story's system of meaning. This also points to the different subject positions constructed by the two forms of narrative. While the reader of an apocalyptic story passively receives the pre-determined meaning, the parable reader must play an active role in constructing the meaning. Although there is usually only one carefully predetermined interpretation of the parable, the audience is still 'allowed' to make the final connection that leads to this interpretation.

Before proceeding, it is important to emphasize the different impacts these two models have on the interpretive process when literary critics employ them as analytical tools. Whereas the parabolic model, with its emphasis on the complex processes by which meaning is *produced*, channels the interpretive effort towards an analysis of these operations, the apocalyptic model, with its focus on the original source of the *revealed* meaning, places the interpretative emphasis on the search for or analysis of an 'essential' meaning. As will become evident, the nihilistic overtone that characterizes Miller's interpretation is ultimately a function of his focus on the apocalyptic model in his analysis.

J. HILLIS MILLER IN THE *HEART OF DARKNESS*

Within the first few pages of the text, the narrator of *Heart of Darkness* uses a dual image to express the difference between Marlow's stories and those of other sailors:

> The yarns of seamen have a direct simplicity, the whole meaning of which lies within the shell of a cracked nut. But Marlow was not typical (if his propensity to spin yarns be excepted), and to him the meaning of an episode was not inside like a kernel but outside, enveloping the tale which brought it out only as a glow brings out a haze, in the likeness of one of these misty halos that sometimes are made visible by the spectral illumination of moonshine. (30)

Although Miller argues that the moon figure represents the parabolic structure of Marlow's stories, his analysis actually conforms to the apocalyptic model. Due to his own apocalyptic fixation on the central signified of the text, Miller ignores the complex parabolic operations of the text. This tendency is first noticeable when Miller links the darkness in the moon figure with the literal and ominous darkness of the African jungle. To support this link, he cites Marlow's description of a feeling in the jungle "like evil or truth, waiting patiently for the passing away of this fantastic invasion" (38), as well as his assertion that the wilderness had taken "a terrible vengeance" (99) on Kurtz. By linking the darkness in the moon image (i. e. the story's meaning) and the darkness in the African wilderness, Miller essentially conjures up a fixed eternal signified to anchor the meaning of his own logocentric interpretation. This leads to the following conclusion:

> The direction of the flow of language reverses. It flows from the darkness instead of toward it [...] the wilderness can speak through [Kurtz], use him so to speak as a ventriloquist's dummy through which its terrible messages may be broadcast to the world: 'Exterminate all the brutes!' 'The horror!' (216)

In this passage, it is evident that Miller is no longer describing a system of freeplay. Instead, he has converted the *absence* of a transcendental signified, on which the system of freeplay is based, into a powerful *presence*. The darkness becomes a central anchor that controls the meaning of the text and eliminates the possibility of freeplay, thereby making Miller's interpretation a logocentric model of a system that precludes free will (i. e. the control of meaning by the individual). But does the *text* support this reading? In effect, Miller's entire interpretation hinges on his questionable assignment of a moral value to the African wilderness. Miller removes the inherent uncertainty in Marlow's statement about "an evil *or* truth" (my emphasis) and conjures into existence an "evil truth." In the end, Miller's nihilistic conclusions are not in fact supported by the text but are rather a product of the apocalyptic model that Miller brings to the text. Miller himself indicates his awareness of this fact when he writes: "I have attempted to perform an act of generic classification, with all the covert violence and unreason of that act, since no work is wholly commensurate with the boundaries of any genre" (220).

If one removes the biases of the apocalyptic model, it becomes apparent that the parabolic model is much more useful for understanding the way the text operates. However, the model must be further adapted in this case, for the novella does not operate like a conventional parable, but rather as a collection of overlapping, distinctly deconstructionist, or postmodern, parables. To understand the difference between conventional and deconstructionist parables, we return to the narrator's nut/moon image.

OF MOONS AND NUTS – TWO FORMS OF PARABLE

In Miller's reading, the nut represents "typical stories," which he defines as stories whose meanings "are easily expressed, detachable from the stories and open to paraphrase in other terms, as when one draws an obvious moral: 'Crime doesn't pay'" (208). He then comments on the way in which such stories function, suggesting that "the story itself, its characters and narrative details, are the inedible shell which must be removed and discarded so the meaning of the story may be assimilated" (ibid.). For Miller then, the "typical story" contains a clear meaning that does not challenge the audience's fundamental value system.

While both of these observations are valid, these characteristics apply directly to a typical *parable*, which normally contains exactly the kind of obvious moral that Miller cites. The problem with his analysis is the shell, which represents the narrative details of the story. Miller's use of the word "inedible" implies that the audience cannot understand or assimilate the meaning contained in the realistic story. However, in the case of the traditional parable, this is not the case. On the contrary, the meaning of the realistic story and the social code on which it is based are so completely naturalized that the audience barely notices them. They are the shell that is easily cracked to get to the moral inside. Thus the nut image is actually a good figure for the *typical parable*.

The moon, on the other hand, represents Marlow's *deconstructionist* parables. To understand this image, we can begin with Miller's interpretation:

> The atmospheric phenomenon that Conrad uses as a vehicle of his parabolic metaphor is a perfectly real one, universally experienced [...] Conrad uses realistic and almost universally known facts as the means of expressing indirectly another truth less visible and less widely known. (210)

One must ask, is "night mist" really a "*universally* experienced" atmospheric phenomenon? Like all signifiers, the visible ring of light is open to an infinite number of interpretations (e. g. a different culture might interpret the ring of light as evidence of the moon god's anger). The ring of light around the moon only means 'haze' for those who have learned that there are sometimes particles of water in the air that reflect light from the moon, and that the culture has agreed to call these particles 'haze.' This information is part of a particular culture's code of shared knowledge, or 'common sense.' Thus, in the moon image, the dark haze actually represents the audience's code of naturalized values, which in a normal parable remains in the background (i. e. like the discarded shell of the nut). In *Heart of Darkness*, on the other hand, each parable contains "rings of light" that foreground the ambiguous nature of this social code on which all meaning is based. In order to understand the inherently postmodern aspect of the text, it is necessary to identify these rings of light and analyze the roles they play in each of the interrelated parables found in the text.

CULTURE CLASH

In the first parable, which I will call the culture clash parable, the European and African characters of the realistic story represent their respective cultures.[2] Miller's apocalyptic reading yields a questionable interpretation of the moral of this parable. By granting the "evil" African wilderness omnipotent power, Miller effectively absolves Kurtz (and by extension his European culture) of responsibility for the acts that he perpetrates in the jungle. By this reading, Kurtz remains the noble European struggling to bring civilization to the corrupt Africans. Miller's reading thereby transforms the text into a traditional parable (i. e. one that conforms to the 'nut model'), with a clear meaning and no challenge to the audience's fundamental value system. There are certainly elements in the story that support this interpretation, such as Marlow's often ominous depiction of the natives and his repeated expressions of admiration for Kurtz. However, this reading ignores the many passages in which Marlow casts doubt on the preconceived sense of European cultural superiority. These passages are in fact the key elements that make Marlow's story different from typical parables.

---

[2] It is perhaps more accurate to say that the European characters represent the European culture and the African characters represent an unfamiliar culture. A discussion of the implications of Conrad's exclusive focus on the European perspective is beyond the scope of the paper. The interested reader can find more about this topic in Chinua Achebe's *An Image of Africa: Racism in Conrad's "Heart of Darkness"* and the various critical responses that it provoked.

Typical parables tap into the audience's established value code and use it to accomplish their goals, but leave the code itself in the background. Marlow's parable, on the other hand, draws attention to its code. Although the culturally acceptable meaning is given, the text contains disturbing elements that foreground the binary value assumptions upon which this interpretation is based and questions their validity. In Derrida's terms, these disturbing elements reveal the "structurality of structure." Or, to use the terms of the moon image, the comfortable interpretation (i. e. Miller's reading) is actually the bright moon, and the disturbing elements are the rings of light that foreground the nebulous, shifting nature of meaning (i. e. the dark mist). The following example of one such disturbing element will help to clarify this concept.

In the text, Marlow engages a group of cannibalistic Africans to work on the steamboat. Europeans, for whom cannibalism is one of the ultimate taboos, would automatically label any culture that engages in this activity 'uncivilized.' In other words, the practice of cannibalism allows Europeans to place Africans on the other side of a comfortable binary opposition, thereby reaffirming their European sense of identity (and superiority). However, Marlow challenges this assumption by emphasizing that the cannibals on the steamboat did *not* eat the white people, despite the fact that they were starving and had a clear numerical superiority. Marlow says of them:

> "What possible restraint? Was it superstition, disgust, patience, fear – or some kind of primitive honour? No fear can stand up to hunger, no patience can wear it out, disgust simply does not exist where hunger is; and as to superstition, beliefs, and what you may call principles, they are less than chaff in a breeze." (77)

The only explanation that Marlow does not dismiss is "some kind of primitive honour." By attributing a moral code to the cannibals, the text foregrounds the European/African binary on which European identity is based and forces the audience to re-evaluate the cultural assumptions that support their division of humanity into 'civilized' and 'savage.'

It is important to note that the text offers no clear judgment of the relative merits of African vs. European culture. Instead, the text simply calls into question the European assumption of cultural superiority. This highlights the inherently deconstructionist nature of Marlow's parable. The text essentially thrusts the reader into the realm of freeplay. Through their encounter with the text, readers have the same disconcerting intercultural experience that Marlow had in Africa, but without leaving the comfort of their reading chair, so to speak. By maintaining an inherent ambiguity, the text constructs an active subject position for the readers, who are compelled to form conclusions about the validity or potential meaning of an African/European binary opposition based on inconclusive information. In essence, the readers join both Marlow and the narrator in the effort to make sense out of a logocentric worldview that has been destabilized by leaving the confines of the cultural system on which it is based.

LOGOCENTRISM VS. DECONSTRUCTIONISM

This leads us to the second parable found in the text – the philosophical parable. The culture clash parable essentially sets the stage for this parable by destabilizing the logocentric view of fixed meaning. In the philosophical parable, the logocentric and deconstructionist discourses meet on the battlefield of Marlow's body. Early in the text, Marlow reveals his fundamental dedication to a logocentric view of 'Truth' in a particularly revealing narrative aside to his audience:

> "You know I hate, detest, and can't bear a lie, not because I am straighter than the rest of us, but simply because it appalls me. There is a taint of death, a flavour of mortality in lies—which is exactly what I hate and detest in the world—what I want to forget. It makes me miserable and sick, like biting something rotten would do. Temperament, I suppose." (54)

Despite his frequent criticism of his fellow Europeans, Marlow remains deeply invested in the (alleged) fundamental values of European civilization – honor and honesty. While his experiences in Africa undermine his faith in these values, Marlow is reluctant to abandon his view of a world with a right and wrong that can be distinguished by a strong, moralistic individual. In Kurtz, Marlow hopes to find the perfect role model of such a man, and even when he is confronted by evidence that undermines this image, he is reluctant to give it up. In this case, Marlow's logocentric longing for "reassuring certitude" compromises his ability to interpret the meaning of Kurtz's story. Marlow says:

> "He had summed up – he had judged. 'The horror!' He was a remarkable man. This was the expression of some sort of belief; it had candour, it had conviction, it had a vibrating note of revolt in its whisper, it had the appalling face of a glimpsed truth – the strange commingling of desire and hate." (116)

Note the ambiguity of this key passage, which does not explicitly define Kurtz's judgment or the "glimpsed truth." This is where Miller steps in to offer his apocalyptic reading: "The truth behind the last witness [...] is, no one can doubt it, death, 'the horror'; or, to put it another way, 'death' is another name for what Kurtz names 'the horror.' No man can confront that truth face to face and survive" (214-215). This passage is a near perfect expression of the negative school of thought about freeplay, which argues that the human mind cannot survive the loss of a transcendental signified. By this reading, Kurtz remains the brave hero, while Marlow is simply a failed witness who has "nothing to bear witness to, nothing to reveal by the process of unveiling that makes up the whole of the narration of *Heart of Darkness*" (215).

However, Miller's reading ends when Kurtz dies. As Miller says: "All the reader gets is Marlow's report of Kurtz's last words, that and the description of the look upon his face" (ibid.). Of course, this is *not* all the reader gets, and if we are to understand the meaning of the philosophical parable, we must look closer at the structure of the text and in particular at the events that transpire after Kurtz's death. The philosophical parable also has its "rings of light" – disturbing elements that undermine Miller's logocentric interpretation. A closer look at these elements suggests that the real goal of the story is not to condemn freeplay, but simply to raise audience awareness of the existence of the dark haze out of which meaning is formed.

IN WHICH THE TEXT DECONSTRUCTS ITSELF

In the philosophical parable, the dark haze represents the fundamental processes by which one human being is able to communicate meaning to another human being. In a stable, logocentric system, a direct, reliable line of communication between speaker and hearer is assumed. However, the postmodern or deconstructionist worldview, which posits a constantly mutating and evolving system of meaning, presents a dilemma. Even assuming that the intention is to communicate a meaning directly to another individual, how can one ever be certain that this other individual will interpret this meaning correctly? This discomforting idea, which challenges the assumed faith in the communicative process, is an inescapable aspect of the deconstructionist worldview, and it is the aspect that the text seeks to communicate to the reader. It does this by using narrative techniques that constantly undermine the possibility of any comfortable sense of resolution. These techniques are the rings of light that give the philosophical parable its distinctive postmodern flavor.

Perhaps the most important aspect of the book that works against comfortable interpretation is the narrative structure itself. Miller's apocalyptic reading focuses on the abundance of storytellers and stories found in the text. He likens this to the biblical Book of Revelation, which contains a "proliferation of witnesses, one behind another" (214), and suggests that this structure draws attention to the narrative process itself. In Miller's words, "the unveiling unveils unveiling" (ibid.). Since each witness describes the narration of the previous witness, the narrative process by which the speaker constructs meaning is continually foregrounded.

While this is also true of *Heart of Darkness*, the focus of attention on the narrative process plays a different role than in the biblical story, due to a key structural difference. The biblical story features an orderly transmission of stable meaning from witness to witness, all of whom share a faith in both the intentions of the messengers and the source from which the message originates. This creates a sequential, narrative progression from past into present (i. e. God told Jesus, who then told the angel, who then told John, who is now telling the seven churches). *Heart of Darkness*, on the other hand, features an uneven structure of overlapping narratives. Marlow constantly interrupts his narration to relate other characters' stories about Kurtz. He also pauses frequently to interpret information for the audience or even to comment on his own narrative ability. Each of these interruptions represents a disturbance in both the time and place of the narrative structure. At times, the reader is on board the steamboat, witnessing events from Marlow's perspective. At other times, the reader travels back in time to see Kurtz through the eyes of other characters (e. g. the accountant, the Russian, the Intended, etc.). At still other times, the reader travels forward in time and becomes a member of Marlow's audience on board the *Nellie*, watching Marlow tell his story through the eyes of the unnamed narrator. This structure anticipates the temporal and spatial discontinuities that would become so prevalent in postmodernist works and provides the text with its distinctive, postmodernist element of indetermination. Rather than a logical transmission of a fixed meaning (i. e. as found in the apocalypse), there is a constant re-evaluation and redefinition of meaning based on new information, all of which heightens the reader's awareness of the inherently constructed nature of meaning.

In addition to these fundamental structural irregularities, the text lacks the reliable witnesses and clear source of authenticity found in the typical apocalyptic story. Instead, the information sources found in the text are all questionable, either due to the manner in which the message was received (e. g. partially overheard conversations or notes written in an unknown language) or the possible motivations of the speaker (e. g. the brickmaker, the manager, etc.). It is important to emphasize that the two main narrators are also unreliable sources of information. This is clear from the beginning of the text, when the unnamed narrator employs his ambiguous moon/nut image, and Marlow says of his own tale:

> "[...] It was the farthest point of navigation and the culminating point in my experience. It seemed somehow to throw a light on everything about me – and into my thoughts [...] not very clear either. No, not very clear. And yet it seemed to throw a kind of light". (32)

The unreliability of information sources is underscored throughout the text. Thus, Marlow says that the Russian's existence "was improbable, inexplicable and altogether bewildering. He was an insoluble problem" (82), and he describes the Manager's enigmatic smile that could "make the meaning of the commonest phrase appear absolutely inscrutable" (49). In the first encounter with the manager, Marlow even provides an example of one of his own interpretive missteps. When the Manager, after just a few vague questions, determines that the steamboat repairs will take three months, Marlow concludes that the man is a "chattering idiot." However, he quickly confesses the error of this conclusion, which he only realized when he saw how precisely the manager had estimated the time required for the repairs (50).

All of these subversive elements give the text its distinctively postmodernist, deconstructionist aspect of uncertainty. To use the terms of the moon image, these subversive elements are the rings of light that draw the reader's attention to the dark, shifting nature of meaning in a system of freeplay. They also construct an active subject position for the reader, basically compelling the reader to engage with the text and create an interpretation out of often contradictory or incomplete information. If we embrace this subject position and look beyond Marlow's frequent professions of admiration for Kurtz, another interpretation of Kurtz emerges. The key to this interpretation is in Marlow's description of the human heads that Kurtz had placed on stakes in the jungle. Here, Marlow pauses in his narration to explain this symbol for the audience:

> "[...] I want you clearly to understand that there was nothing exactly profitable in these heads being there. They only showed that Mr. Kurtz lacked restraint in the gratification of his various lusts, that there was something wanting in him – some small matter which, when the pressing need arose, could not be found under his magnificent eloquence. Whether he knew of this deficiency himself I can't say. I think this knowledge came to him at last – only at the very last." (99)

In the context of this passage, Kurtz's final words take on a completely different meaning than what Miller suggests. The "horror" that Kurtz invokes on his deathbed is not the evil of the African wilderness, but rather his horrible realization of his own corrupt desire for wealth and power.[3] Although the explanation reveals Marlow's reluctance to give up his idealized image of Kurtz, it also demonstrates that he has understood the source of Kurtz's universally proclaimed greatness. It is not his high moral character, but rather his substantial rhetorical talent, or his ability to manipulate meaning. As the journalist tells Marlow, Kurtz "could get himself to believe anything – anything. He would have been a splendid leader of an extreme party" (100). Ultimately, Kurtz's story depicts the potential misuse to which the system of freeplay can be put, but it does not condemn the system itself as inherently evil.

---

[3] Since Kurtz represents European imperialism, this flaw also reflects the text's judgment of European imperialism. Conrad in effect unmasks the hypocrisy of the 'spreading civilization' rhetoric that was used to mask the economic motives of European imperialism. A more detailed discussion of this aspect of the text can be found in Adam Hochschild's book *King Leopold's Ghost*.

THE BIG LIE

The logocentric dilemma deepens in Marlow's encounter with the Intended, in which two core logocentric values come into conflict. On one side is Marlow's personal commitment to truthfulness, and on the other side is his lingering commitment to his idealized image of European society, which shows his logocentric longing for a comfortable, stable identity and worldview. The Intended is a symbol for this society. As a noblewoman, she has lived a sheltered life, her only source of information being the doctrine forced upon her by male-dominated society. Thus, she is the embodiment of the carefully constructed, logocentric European value system, which is threatened by the deconstructionist concept of freeplay. In his struggle to preserve the Intended's beliefs (i. e. the European value system), Marlow grows angry and tells his first 'half-truth' about Kurtz's death: "His end [...] was in every way worthy of his life" (123). However, when he sees the Intended's pain, he says, "My anger subsided before a feeling of infinite pity" (124). Marlow forsakes his commitment to absolute, logocentric Truth and chooses instead to spare the Intended by lying. With his final words, Marlow delivers the moral of the philosophical parable:

> "It seemed to me that the house would collapse before I could escape, that the heavens would fall upon my head. But nothing happened. The heavens do not fall for such a trifle. Would they have fallen, I wonder, if I had rendered Kurtz that justice that was his due? Hadn't he said he wanted only justice? But I couldn't. I could not tell her. It would have been too dark—too dark altogether." (124)

When framed in this way, the reader can't help but sanction or even praise Marlow's lie, since the professed motivation is to protect the Intended's feelings. In so doing, the reader falls into Marlow's carefully constructed rhetorical trap. The positive connotation of the common-sense value (i. e. Marlow's chivalric action to spare the feelings of a pure and selfless woman) is transferred to the unstated value – namely the superiority of deconstruction's view of mutable truth. Deconstruction, with its flexible concept of truth, is 'proven' to have a greater capacity for humanity and compassion than is possible under an absolute faithfulness to logocentric Truth. Deconstruction wins.

Of course, such an interpretation undermines the main goal of the text by providing a comforting resolution for the audience. Where Miller's interpretation falls comfortably on the side of logocentrism, this interpretation cedes the moral advantage to deconstruction. However, the text can hardly be read as a ringing endorsement of the "Nietzschean joy" of freeplay. As mentioned earlier, the reader by this time knows to approach Marlow's judgments with skepticism. In case the reader has forgotten, the final images of the Intended's bitter reaction and the "somber river" flowing out into an "immense heart of darkness" (125) effectively undermine any sense of comfortable resolution. Read in the context of these images and the established sense of unreliability of the narrators, the reader can't help but deconstruct Marlow's professed motivation for lying. Is Marlow really lying to protect the woman, or is there another reason?

In fact, there is a strong implication in the text that the main motivation behind Marlow's fateful lie is to protect the social order that the Intended represents and upon which Marlow's own sense of identity relies. This highlights two important issues related to the conflict between logocentrism and freeplay. First, it shows that the professed logocentric values of truth and honesty are a mask for the real practice of *bricolage* (i. e. manipulation), which is happening all the time. Just as the rhetoric of 'spreading civilization' is used to mask the economic motivations behind the colonization of Africa, so too is the rhetoric of 'honor and honesty' used to mask the continual manipulations of meaning by which society operates. And second, there is an implication that this manipulation is necessary to maintain the social order. Early in the text, Marlow talks about the world of women, which is "out of touch with truth." He suggests that if this world actually existed, "[s]ome confounded fact we men have been living contentedly with ever since the day of creation would start up and knock the whole thing over" (40). However, the end of the story reveals that the *male*-constructed society is essentially the same, and the 'truth' of deconstruction could serve as the fatal fact that could mean the end of the social order.

Marlow spells this out more clearly in one of his narrative asides. Describing his efforts to navigate the treacherous river – a clear metaphor for one's efforts to live and survive in the world – he says:

> "When you have to attend to things of that sort, to the mere incidents of the surface, the reality—the reality, I tell you—fades. The inner truth is hidden—luckily, luckily. But I felt it all the same; I felt often its mysterious stillness watching me at my monkey tricks, just as it watches you fellows performing on your respective tightropes for—what was it? half-a-crown a tumble—" (62)

The "hidden truth" here is that there is no "hidden truth." In other words, there is no transcendental force giving meaning to one's efforts in life. At this point, the narrator describes an interruption by one of the other listeners, "'Try to be civil, Marlow,' growled a voice, and I knew there was at least one other listener awake besides myself" (ibid.). The admonition to "be civil" is another way of telling Marlow to show some respect for society's values. Here, Conrad echoes the moment in the Bible when Jesus returns to Nazareth and tries to preach his parables. The people there reject him, and Jesus says, "A prophet is not without honor, save in his own country, and in his own house" (*American Standard Version*, Matt. 13.57). The same is true for Marlow. Those who have prospered within the European value system are not interested in Marlow's deconstructionist worldview.

However, Marlow's reaction reveals his attitude towards the inherent conflict between the logocentric and deconstructionist value systems: "I beg your pardon. I forgot the heartache which makes up the rest of the price. And indeed what does the price matter, if the trick be well done? You do your tricks very well. And I didn't do badly either, since I managed not to sink that steamboat on my first trip" (62). Marlow is not an apocalyptic preacher or a deconstructionist Jeremiah. He recognizes that the time for implementing this worldview has not yet come, and chooses instead to live in exile. However, he does not succumb to a dark nihilism or retreat into seclusion. Rather he chooses to live among seamen. Although many seamen may still be deaf to his message (as the growl from the darkness reveals), he is more likely to find a receptive ear there, among people who are somewhat removed from the regulating influence of society. Like Jesus, Marlow follows the advice found in the biblical parable of the sower and seeks out the fertile soil where he can plant his philosophical seeds.

Ultimately, the goal of the text is not to pass moral judgment on the concept of freeplay, but rather to make the reader see and accept this view of the constructed nature of meaning. It is neither good nor bad, but rather the likely outcome of a world in which cultures and value systems overlap. However, although the text does not glorify life in a freeplay system, it also does not descend into the kind of apathy suggested by the *New York Times* reader in the opening quote, in which one simply accepts the prejudices of the world. Rather, it offers a continuous process by which one can survive in a freeplay system and perhaps lead a socially responsible and personally meaningful existence. To understand this vision, we must look at a third parable in the text, the identity parable.

DECONSTRUCTION, *BRICOLAGE*, AND HARD WORK

In the identity parable, the events in Africa represent a confrontation with the Other, which plays a crucial role in the definition of one's own identity and 'reality.' Marlow's struggle, in turn, depicts the individual identity crisis precipitated by this confrontation. It is important to acknowledge that the text does *not* suggest that this identity crisis occurs for every individual who encounters a foreign value system. This is evident in the narrator's initial description of the "typical" sailor, for whom "a casual stroll or a casual spree on shore suffices to unfold for him the secret of the whole continent, and generally he finds the secret not worth knowing" (29-30). Such sailors represent individuals who simply reject all information that goes against their own cultural programming. By labeling them "typical," the narrator implies the predominance of this form of existence. Marlow, on the other hand, experiences what could be termed a postmodern awakening – a realization of the constructed nature of those values that he had previously seen as natural. His experiences in Africa unsettle his preconceived European ideas and force him into the world of freeplay. When Marlow returns to his native culture, he is challenged to construct some sort of identity and value system that will relieve the tension between his earlier, logocentric worldview and his newfound deconstructionist knowledge. The identity parable depicts this struggle.

In terms of the parabolic model, the realistic story of the identity parable takes place on board the deck of the *Nellie*. It is essentially the narrator's depiction of Marlow's struggle to construct a meaningful narrative and deliver this narrative to his audience. On the secondary level, the narrative process represents the individual's struggle to construct and maintain a coherent identity and worldview within a freeplay system. On this level, the narrator's tale presents a means of survival in a freeplay world. The individual's survival is founded on an ongoing process that is essentially the equivalent of deconstructionist *bricolage*.

The first step in this process is the intake and processing of new experiences and information. This analytical step is foregrounded in Marlow's frequent narrative asides. In fact, each time Marlow reports on information received from another source, he uses a narrative aside to analyze the information. Thus, Marlow *deconstructs* each message, carefully contemplating such factors as the means of communication and the possible motivations of the source. Marlow emphasizes the importance of this critical function when he points out the Russian's failure to perform it:

> "[…] I did not envy him his devotion to Kurtz, though. He had not meditated over it. It came to him, and he accepted it with a sort of eager fatalism. I must say that to me it appeared about the most dangerous thing in every way he had come upon so far. (83)

Of course, the irony here is that the story actually represents Marlow's own ongoing efforts to deconstruct the meaning of Kurtz, which leads to the next step in the process.

Marlow's deconstruction is not an exercise in destruction, but rather feeds into *bricolage*, a concerted effort to construct some kind of meaning out of the materials of the analysis. In terms of the identity parable, Marlow's struggle to integrate information from disparate sources into a coherent narrative represents the individual's ongoing efforts to incorporate meaning from new experiences into his/her own identity construct. The steamboat image adds another level of representation to this process. Marlow says of his still crippled craft:

> "[…] she was nothing so solid in make, and rather less pretty in shape, but I had expended enough hard work on her to make me love her. No influential friend

> would have served me better. She had given me a chance to come out a bit—to find out what I could do. No, I don't like work. I had rather laze about and think of all the fine things that can be done. I don't like work—no man does—but I like what is in the work,—the chance to find yourself. Your own reality—for yourself, not for others—what no man can ever know. They can only see the mere show, and never can tell what it really means." (56-57)

Here, the physical exercise of constructing the ship represents two parallel tasks – the narrative effort to construct a story and the human effort to maintain a viable identity. In terms of meaning formation, this image shifts the focus from the final goal to the process. In other words, fulfillment comes not from the end product (a fixed meaning), but rather from the act of creation itself. Although it may be hard work, failure to engage in this task leads to a hollow existence. This meaningless existence is symbolized in the text by the brickmaker who never makes bricks, of whom Marlow says, "it seemed to me that if I tried I could poke my finger through him, and would find nothing inside but a little loose dirt, maybe" (54).

Beyond self-fulfillment, the text also suggests the potential for a communal benefit that can come out of the *bricoleur* mode of existence. In his description of the events in Africa, Marlow encodes a positive value for this creative exercise by establishing another binary opposition. The negative side of the binary opposition is inhabited by the chattering pilgrims, who never even lift a "little finger" (52), and the members of the El Dorado Exploring Expedition, of whom Marlow says, "there was not an atom of foresight of serious intention in the whole batch of them, and they did not seem aware that these things are wanted for the work of the world" (58). These people are not socially responsible creators, but rather selfish consumers. Thus Marlow says of the Pilgrims' scheming, "nothing ever came of it, of course. It was as unreal as everything else – as the philanthropic pretense of the whole concern, as their talk, as their government, as their show of work" (53). On the positive side of the binary opposition, Marlow places such characters as the boilermaker and the African helmsman, each of whom is dedicated to his job. Their tasks may be small and inglorious, but they nevertheless contribute to the greater good. Marlow himself also falls on this side of the binary opposition, since he continues to tell his story in the hope that he can make his audience understand the freeplay nature of the world.

COMMUNICATION BREAKDOWN

But what of the abovementioned communication insecurity that is an inherent part of every deconstructionist system? Even with the best of intentions, how can one be sure that one's meaning is properly interpreted by other people? Marlow addresses this issue directly in his most explicit meta-referential aside, when he says to his audience on board the *Nellie*:

> "[…] Do you see the story? Do you see anything? It seems to me I am trying to tell you a dream – making a vain attempt, because no relation of a dream can convey the dream-sensation, that commingling of absurdity, surprise, and bewilderment in a tremor of struggling revolt, that notion of being captured by the incredible which is of the very essence of dreams. …"
> He was silent for a while.
> "… No, it is impossible; it is impossible to convey the life-sensation of any given epoch of one's existence – that which makes its truth, its meaning – its subtle and penetrating essence. It is impossible. We live, as we dream – alone. …"
> He paused again as if reflecting, then added:
> "Of course in this you fellows see more than I could then. You see me, whom you know. …"
> It had become so pitch dark that we listeners could hardly see one another. For a long time already he, sitting apart, had been no more to us than a voice. There was not a word from anybody. The others might have been asleep, but I was awake. I listened, I listened on the watch for the sentence, for the word, that would give me the clue to the faint uneasiness inspired by this narrative that seemed to shape itself without human lips in the heavy night air of the river. (55)

Miller interprets Marlow's words about "living and dreaming alone" as the "extra twist" of Conrad's work, which is that meaning cannot be exchanged between individuals in a freeplay system: "The darkness enters into every gesture of enlightenment to enfeeble it, to hollow it out, to corrupt it and thereby to turn its reason into unreason, its pretence of shedding light into more darkness" (218). However, the attentive reader will know better than to take the words of the unreliable Marlow at face value. In particular, the narrator's interjection to describe Marlow's pause to "reflect" alerts the reader that they should also be reflecting on the meaning of Marlow's words. And significantly, after uttering his line about living and dreaming, Marlow does not throw himself into the river in despair, but rather *continues his story*. Despite his realization of the inherent challenges imposed by a system of freeplay, he persists in his efforts to construct a meaningful narrative.

Furthermore, the narrator, who is "on the watch," is a perfect symbol for the active audience. His longing to find the key to unlock the mystery is emblematic of what Derrida described as the human longing for "re-assuring certitude." Of course, the irony here is that, by the deconstructionist reading, the "faint uneasiness" *is the message of the story*. The "subtle and penetrating essence" of that "epoch" in Marlow's life was precisely the feeling of uneasiness that results when one's worldview and value system is disrupted. The narrator's professed uneasiness is thus a testament to the success of Marlow's narrative endeavor to share his meaning (with at least one member of the audience). Using his narrative, Marlow has invoked in the narrator the same feelings that he himself felt in response to his experiences in Africa. Both characters have begun to understand the freeplay of meaning, and they are now adapting the personal narratives by which they define their identities to incorporate this idea – Marlow by telling the story to the sailors on the *Nellie*, and the narrator by telling the story to the readers.

This is where the text provides a vivid example of supplementarity. Here, the readers sees the message, which is an understanding of the nature of freeplay and its ramifications on human existence, gradually evolving as it is passed from one witness to the next. We go from Kurtz's ambiguous final words, to Marlow's interpretation of the meaning of those words (i. e. the revelation of Kurtz's tragic flaw), to the narrator's account of Marlow's story, which further foregrounds the role of the narrative process in negotiating meaning and existence in a world of freeplay. Each witness adds his own supplement, and by depicting their own struggles, Marlow and Kurtz also draw the readers into the deconstructionist worldview and start them on the path to negotiating the resultant dilemma. This undermines Marlow's argument about "living and dreaming alone," since here we see a connection being made through the interactive narrative process. The possibility for this connection is reinforced symbolically by Marlow's relationship with his helmsman, which Marlow explains to his audience in the following aside:

> "Well, don't you see, he had done something, he had steered; for months I had him at my back—a help—an instrument. It was a kind of partnership. He steered for me—I had to look after him, I worried about his deficiencies, and thus a subtle bond had been created, of which I only became aware when it was suddenly broken. And the intimate profundity of that look he gave me when he received his hurt remains to this day in my memory—like a claim of distant kinship affirmed in a supreme moment." (78-79)

If we read this passage as a symbol of the narrative process, it shows that this process can form a bond between speaker and hearer, who are engaged in a mutual, interactive effort to construct meaning.[4]

[4] Here the text even goes so far as to suggest that individuals from different cultures can form a meaningful bond out of the shared task of creation. Marlow's lingering prejudice, evident in his assumption of his helmsman's "deficiencies," indicates the obstacles to this connection. However, it is not a picture devoid of hope.

THE ROLE OF LITERATURE

But how does literature fit into this equation? Here we have to recall the narrator's statement that the story "seemed to shape itself without human lips" (55). If we accept that the story has successfully revealed the process of freeplay and evoked the uneasiness experienced when the logocentric mind first encounters this worldview, we see that the narrator's description supports the ability of literature to transfer meaning. By this reading, Marlow's invisibility symbolically suggests that direct human contact is not the only way to transfer meaning. In other words, this scene undermines what Derrida called the logocentric "determination of Being as presence" (291), or the privileging of oral over textual communication. Although the text does not deny the uncertain nature of communication in a freeplay system, it still suggests that literature can play an important role in the construction of meaning.

This is also evident in the description of the one book that actually appears in the story – the book of seamanship by Towson or Towser (in a subtle gesture of self-deprecating humor, Conrad makes Marlow unable to remember the author's name):

> Not a very enthralling book; but at the first glance you could see there a singleness of intention, an honest concern for the right way of going to work, which made these humble pages, thought out so many years ago, luminous with another than a professional light. The simple old sailor, with his talk of chains and purchases, made me forget the jungle and the pilgrims in a delicious sensation of having come upon something unmistakably real. Such a book being there was wonderful enough; but still more astounding were the notes penciled in the margin, and plainly referring to the text. I couldn't believe my eyes! They were in cipher! (65-66)

This book of seamanship, although seemingly irrelevant in the middle of a jungle, still provides an inspiration due to the honest effort that its author put into it. However, as with all communication, this is only one side of the process of meaning making. Readers bring their own context and add their own supplements to the text to create a new meaning. The notes in the margin of Towson's book, written in an incomprehensible language, are a graphic representation of the process of *bricolage* or supplementarity in action. They are the thoughts and ideas that one reader brings to the book, which other readers can never exactly understand. They embody the limitless potential for interpretation contained in every text and the necessity, or in fact the inevitability of interpretation.

Kurtz's Report is another example of a text within the text. This powerful work even inspires Marlow to take on the temporary role of literary critic when he says, "It was eloquent, vibrating with eloquence, but too highly strung, I think. [...] But it was a beautiful piece of writing. The opening paragraph, however, in the light of later information, strikes me now as ominous" (77-78). Of course, it is not the opening paragraph but rather the ominous final postscript that Conrad, as editor, eventually removes. In so doing, he provides a perfect illustration of the manipulation to which all texts are inevitably vulnerable. Just as Miller's interpretation of *Heart of Darkness* modifies the text to suit his own logocentric, apocalyptic ends, Marlow edits Kurtz's text so it will fit into the logocentric worldview that he is not yet ready to abandon.

CONCLUSION

I have suggested that *Heart of Darkness* is a collection of inherently postmodern or deconstructionist parables. The meaning system presented in the text anticipates the postmodern world, in which cultures overlap and the roots of cultural value systems are revealed and challenged. Within this context, the text suggests a kind of *bricolage* mode of existence for the individual in a freeplay system. This mode of conduct involves the careful deconstruction of systems of meaning, which yields the raw materials for a constant process of building and maintaining an evolving personal identity. Although the text argues for the potential personal fulfillment to be gained from this approach, it is important to recognize that the text makes no effort to mask the difficulty of this process of identity maintenance, which Marlow at one point calls "an obscure, back-breaking business" (77).

On the communal level as well, the text refuses to pass a moral judgment on the freeplay system. On the one hand, it highlights the potential communal benefit of this *bricolage* approach by establishing a value-infused binary opposition. This opposition places creative, compassionate *bricoleurs* (e. g. Marlow) opposite greedy, selfish, logocentric individuals (e. g. the pilgrims and various Company men). On the other hand, the story of Kurtz testifies to the damage that can be done by a master *bricoleur* who manipulates the freeplay system to satisfy his own corrupt desires. Furthermore, the text is explicit about the challenges facing even the most well-intentioned individual who tries to share his world-vision with his fellow man, a process which is always complicated by the ambiguous nature of meaning and the important role of interpretation.

Thus it becomes apparent that Conrad's work is neither a celebration nor a condemnation of freeplay, but rather an observation of the destabilized worldview that can result when cultural (or other) discourses overlap in an individual. Conrad was no doubt keenly aware of the inevitable tension that must result when this deconstructionist worldview comes into contact with the established, logocentric cultural order. Perhaps Marlow's decision *not* to share his new deconstructionist insight with Kurtz's Intended also reflects Conrad's intuition that the logocentric world was not ready for the direct attack that Derrida would mount seventy years later. Nevertheless, in its own way, the novella has helped further the cause of challenging logocentrism. The text not only depicts freeplay and *bricolage* in action, but through its parabolic structure constructs a subject position that forces the reader to become a deconstructionist *bricoleur*. Thanks to its structural irregularities and its unreliable sources of information, the text thrusts readers into the world of freeplay and compels them to form their own interpretations. The quantity and variety of the criticism that has been written about this small novella are proof of the text's powerful ability to destabilize the readers' comfortable, logocentric worldviews and transform them into deconstructionist readers and active *bricoleurs*. On the other hand, the passion with which these readers and critics have defended their interpretations testifies to the enduring lure of logocentrism. Although the postmodern world has seen a rise in the deconstructionist perspective, there is little to suggest that the human longing for a "reassuring certitude" will disappear any time soon. Indeed, the continued passion of such literary debates is powerful evidence of the continued relevance of Derrida's definition of man as "that being who [...] throughout his entire history [...] has dreamed of full presence, the reassuring foundation, the origin and the end of play" (292).

WORKS CITED

Bloom, Allan. *The Closing of the American Mind*. New York, NY: Simon & Schuster. Print.

Conrad, Joseph. *Heart of Darkness*. 1899. "Heart of Darkness." *Heart of Darkness & Other Stories*. London: Wordsworth, 1999. 29-105. Print.

Derrida, Jacques. "Structure, Sign, and Play in the Discourse of the Human Sciences." 1966. *Writing and Difference*. 1967. Ed. and Trans. Alan Bass. Chicago, IL: U of Chicago P, 1978. 278-294. Print.

Fish, Stanley. "French Theory in America, Part Two." *New York Times*. The New York Times Company, 20 April 2008. Web. 12 October 2009.

Lévi-Strauss, Claude. *The Raw and the Cooked*. 1969. Transl. John and Doreen Weightman. Chicago, IL: U of Chicago P, 1983. Print.

Miller, J. Hillis. "Fiction and Repetition: *Tess of the d'Urbervilles*." *Forms of Modern British Fiction*. Ed.Allan Warren Friedman. Austin, TX: U of Texas P, 1975. 43-71. Print.

—. "Stevens' Rock and Criticism As Cure, II." *Georgia Review* 30 (1976): 345. Print.

—. "Ariadne's Thread: Repetition and the Narrative Line." *Critical Inquiry* 3 (1976): 57-77. Print.

—. "*Heart of Darkness* Revisited." 1985. *Heart of Darkness*. 2nd Edition. Ed. Ross C. Murfin. Boston, MA, and New York, NY: Bedford-St. Martin's, 1996. 206-220. Print.

WRITING AHEAD OF THE TIMES? A POSTMODERN READING OF ZORA NEALE HURSTON'S *THEIR EYES WERE WATCHING GOD*

SIMONE PUFF

While cultural critic bell hooks rightly maintains in "Postmodern Blackness" that postmodernism as a "discursive practice" is "dominated primarily by the voices of white male intellectuals and/or academic elites" (24) rather than people of color[1], on a more practical level, quite a few literary works by people of color – in particular by black women writers – have been analyzed from a postmodernist point of view.[2] Here, the fiction of Nobel Prize Laureate Toni Morrison, or the works by Octavia Butler and Gloria Naylor serve as contemporary examples.[3] Even though postmodernism as a form of literary criticism only emerged in the second half of the twentieth century, with Jean-François Lyotard's *The Postmodern Condition: A Report on Knowledge* (1979, trans. 1984) becoming one of its seminal works[4], it is rewarding to examine pre-postmodern texts and look for early indications foreshadowing a postmodern literary aesthetic. By doing so, Harlem Renaissance writer Zora Neale Hurston can be considered a precursor to an era that has "come to be accepted as a general post-1960s period label attached to cultural forms that display certain characteristics such as reflexivity, irony, parody, and often a mixing of the conventions of popular and 'high art'" (Natoli and Hutcheon vii). So far, hardly any attempts have been made to conceptualize the ways in which her masterpiece *Their Eyes Were Watching God* (1937) can be related to postmodern theory; yet there is a lot to shed new light on the novel. Borrowing from Peter Barry's list "What postmodernist critics do," I

---

1 As a prominent exception, hooks lists Black scholar Cornel West with, for example, his 1988 essay on "Postmodernism and Black America."

2 Yet this has not always been the case: In her 1987 essay "Beginning to Theorize Postmodernism," Linda Hutcheon refers to an account by Susan Suleiman and claims that "literary discussions of postmodernism often appear to exclude the work of women (and, one might add, often of blacks as well), even though female (and black) explorations of narrative and linguistic form have been among the most contesting and radical" (257).

3 In *Signs and Cities* Madhu Dubey provides a comprehensive analysis of some of the most well-known novels written by women of color in the realm of postmodernism.

4 Despite the fact that – as Gary Browning claims – "Lyotard was a French theorist" whose "development of [...] thinking reflects political and philosophical currents shaping post-Second World War France" (42), his thoughts reached an audience worldwide and were influential in shaping postmodernist thought after *La Condition postmoderne* was translated into English in 1984 (Bertens 123).

will try to "discover postmodernist themes, tendencies, and attitudes" in *Their Eyes*, while at the same time looking at the blurred distinctions between 'high' and 'low' culture and highlighting how Hurston's text signifies "hybrid blends of the two" (91). This will be done in an attempt to relate Hurston's pre-postmodern work to Lyotard's concept of metanarratives and to expose what I read as a break with it.

Some scholars argue that a long time prior to the formation of postmodernist thought black cultures experienced some of the characteristics described as postmodern today. As Russell A. Potter notes in *Spectacular Vernaculars*, due to the "bulwarks of slavery and colonialism" (6), African American culture is shaped by subjective acts of resistance, which is why "black cultures conceived *postmodernism* long before its 'time'" (ibid.). Black cultures, as he continues quite graphically, "have inhabited the contradictory space of what Gilroy calls the 'slave sublime,' have glimpsed the fundamental rottenness of European modernism from its very intestines long before Europe noticed any trace of indigestion" (ibid.). Madhu Dubey follows this argument and also refers to Doreen Massey claiming that due to slavery and colonialism, people – clearly, people of color – conceived of their reality and subjectivity as highly fragmented (20-21). Massey thus also echoes W.E.B. Du Bois' famous conception of a "double-consciousness," a "sense of always looking at one's self through the eyes of others" (364), long before postmodernism came into being. As a consequence, Dubey argues, "what is being proclaimed as a novel feature of postmodernism has in fact been long familiar to the West's 'others'" (21). Of course, one needs to qualify Dubey's comment here, as fragmentation was already a common feature in modernism, but in contrast to postmodernism, modernists felt threatened by social and existential fragmentation and were often "yearning […] to escape from this situation" (Hawthorn 121).[5] This, however, is not the case with postmodernists, who – despite their focus on a "fragmented and unstable subjectivity" (Dubey 17) – reject "the tragic and pessimistic elements in modernism in the conclusion that if one cannot prevent Rome burning then one might as well enjoy the fiddling that is left open to one" (Hawthorn 123).

Hurston can certainly not be considered a postmodernist writer per se; only some of her writings seem to anticipate postmodernism. Yet, when looking back at her famous essay "How it Feels to Be Colored Me" (1928), it becomes clear that she rejected any pessimism about, or fear of, this fragmentation:

---

5 This example once again illustrates that there is only a fine line of distinction between modernism and postmodernism, which – as Andreas Huyssen argues – makes "the definition of its boundaries exceedingly difficult, if not per se impossible" (59).

> [...] I am not tragically colored. There is no great sorrow damned up in my soul, nor lurking behind my eyes. I do not mind at all. I do not belong to the sobbing school of Negrohood who hold that nature somehow has given them a lowdown dirty deal and whose feelings are all hurt about it. Even in the helter-skelter skirmish that is my life, I have seen that the world is to the strong regardless of a little pigmentation more or less. No, I do not weep at the world – I am too busy sharpening my oyster knife. (153)

Given this attitude, it seems not surprising that Hurston's controversial autobiography *Dust Tracks on a Road* (1942) was analyzed from a postmodern angle on several occasions (see, for example, P. Walker) and that her play *Mule Bone* (1930)[6] received critical attention through the lens of postmodernist discourse (see Staple). Moreover, in a foreword to the 1990 edition of *Tell My Horse* (1938), Ishmael Reed calls this collection of voodoo/hoodoo traditions in Haiti and Jamaica "postmodernist." He attributes his evaluation to Hurston's use of different techniques and genre-mixing: "The Zora Neale Hurston of *Tell My Horse* is skeptical, cynical, funny, ironic, brilliant, and innovative. With its mixture of techniques and genres, this book [...] is bound to be the postmodernist book of the nineties" (Reed xv). Even though this has "proven to be something of an overstatement," as Lovalerie King argues in *The Cambridge Introduction to Zora Neale Hurston* (115), there are several scholars who have looked at *Tell My Horse* through a postmodernist lens (115-116).

At first glance, there is nothing postmodernist about *Their Eyes Were Watching God* and the story of Janie Crawford Killicks Starks Woods, a southern black female character who has been searching for consciousness, independence, and – ultimately – self-fulfillment all her life, has been "tuh de horizon and back" (Hurston 284) and, now being in her early forties, has finally come home to the all-black town of Eatonville, Florida, to tell her life story to her friend Pheoby Watson. Indeed, authors like Madhu Dubey put southern folk texts with a "literary tendency to feminize and locate authentic black culture in the rural South" (146) in contrast to urban, postmodernist texts. According to Dubey, these southern folk texts are "saturated with all the signs of racial authenticity – vernacular idioms, rootedness in nature, and a strong sense of place, family, cultural tradition, and community" (ibid.), all characteristics that can also be applied to Hurston's novel. Yet Dubey observes a growing interest from the 1970s onward to revive forms of southern folk aesthetic in postmodernist discourse, especially in contrast to postmodern urban cities. This leads to her assertion that the "southern

---

6 The play was co-authored with Langston Hughes in 1930 and posthumously published in 1991.

folk aesthetic has gained momentum in the postmodern era" (147).[7] That this southern folk aesthetic in Hurston's novel contains realist as well as modernist elements is beyond question. Black southern lifestyle and folk culture elements certainly lend themselves to a realist interpretation, yet scenes like the one with the talking buzzards (Hurston 96-97) – a veritable parody of the mocking funeral ceremony for Matt Bonner's dead mule – rather resemble an account of 'magical realism' and counter a realist interpretation of the story. As Henry Louis Gates, Jr. observes: "This allegory […] shatters completely any illusion the reader might have had that this was meant to be a realistic fiction" (201). As far as modernist elements in the novel are concerned, we can safely agree with Gates' superb analysis of the novel in his essay "Zora Neale Hurston and the Speakerly Text," which relates the overall theme of the protagonist's search for consciousness in combination with the "dialogical rhetoric of the text" (208) to modernism. Yet, when one looks closely at what Gates terms the "speakerly" elements of the text, that is, the "dramatic shifts in the idiom in which the voice of the narrator appears" (214), I argue that this might be more readily understood as a postmodernist element, not least because it blurs the distinction between what was generally termed 'high' and 'low' culture. Hurston's rhetorical strategy does not only privilege the diction of vernacular oral speech, as Gates argues, but also uses a "dialect-informed free indirect discourse" (192) in which the narrator's voice often blends with the idiomatic voice of Janie or, for that matter, with that of the black community.

Upon close analysis, *Their Eyes Were Watching God* also shows a clear rejection of what Lyotard termed "metanarratives" (xxiv)[8], with no obvious sign of "nostalgia for the lost narrative" (41). A metanarrative is – to sum it up with Readings' interpretation in *Introducing Lyotard* – a "story that can reveal the meaning of all stories, be it the weakness or the progress of mankind. Its metanarrative status comes from the fact that it talks about the many narratives of culture so as to reveal the singular truth inherent in them" (63). In literature, one could argue, such metanarratives are often found in canonized works that serve as model narratives and ideological frameworks for others. Lyotard refers to Hegel and Marx in particular, even though it was the dismissal of their works

---

[7] See Dubey's comparative analysis of Toni Morrison's *Song of Solomon* and Gloria Naylor's *Mama Day* in *Signs and Cities*.

[8] The terms *metanarrative*, *grand narrative*, and *master narrative* are used synonymously in scholarly treatments of Lyotard's concept, just as the term *mininarrative* is analogous with *little narrative*.

that his critics found most faults with (see, for example, Browning[9]). This paper does not aim at critiquing Lyotard's concepts, though, not only because this was done elsewhere but also because the French thinker later admitted that his analysis of the postmodern condition was what Browning called a "sketchy review" (30). Nevertheless, and despite possible flaws in argumentation, Lyotard's "incredulity towards metanarratives" (xxiv) serves as an important reference here because it came to explain postmodernism on a large scale. Very broadly speaking, anything 'deviant' from or in opposition to a meta- or grand narrative would fall into Lyotard's category of a mini- or little narrative – *petit récit* in the French original – thereby "resist[ing] incorporation into such totalizing histories of cultural representation or projects for culture" (Readings 63). Culture is then no longer seen as one entity, but "as a patchwork of little narratives" (65), as Readings continues:

> For Lyotard, a skepticism has led us to understand culture as discontinuous and fragmentary; cultural representations are too disparate to permit a universal point of view. Culture is not one field but a series of local or minoritarian representations organized by narratives. (65)

While this is Lyotard's basic argument, a common misinterpretation of the mininarrative should be kept in mind. As stated by Beatrice Skordili in the *Encyclopedia of Postmodernism*, "postmodernism is not the replacement of grand narratives by little narratives, but rather the conditions by which little narratives become viable political strategies" (231). Hence, I argue that Hurston's *Their Eyes Were Watching God*, which clearly rejects the paradigm of the African American protest novel so common at the time of its publication, is more than aesthetic deviation (art for art's sake). Writing a story almost devoid of racial tensions at that time can be interpreted as a political strategy, thereby becoming one of the mininarratives Lyotard proposed. Hurston, thus, goes against the grain by not only breaking with traditional images of black women in literature, who were mostly doomed to the fate of a tragic mulatta[10], but also by offering a counterimage of how life can be led almost free from White people's influence. When political intervention is not possible on a large scale, as Skordili argues, "local intervention appears like a viable solution" (230). It was precisely the notion of local intervention that Hurston wove into her narrative by dealing with a black

---

9 Browning has particularly harsh words for Lyotard, referring to his dismissal of general theories as "too sweeping" (106), even calling it "perverse" a few pages later (149).

10 The term *tragic mulatto/a* describes a widely used stereotypical literary character that originated in abolitionist literature. Characteristically, these characters are, as Werner Sollors maintains in a chapter of his book *Neither Black Nor White Yet Both*, "exceptionally beautiful but often doomed" (224).

female heroine in an all-black town in rural Florida between the 1920s and 1930s. Contrary to common practice, however, this heroine does not end as a tragic mulatta figure but rather speaks herself into being in a coming-of-age narrative.

Clearly, Hurston, as a black woman growing up in the American South of the early twentieth century, experienced fragmentary cultures first hand; something she subsequently incorporated in her work. It comes as no surprise that she rejected or simply dismissed metanarratives of her time. Instead, she seemed to have created several mininarratives, which – according to Peter Barry – are "provisional, contingent, temporary, and relative and which provide a basis for the actions of specific groups in particular local circumstances" (87). Thus, what Gary K. Browning terms "Lyotard's obituary for grand narratives" (1) can be found in Hurston's novel on various occasions, suggesting that Hurston was – as in so many other instances – ahead of the times[11]. Perhaps because she always seemed to be one step ahead, the novel – nowadays regarded a masterpiece in African American Literature and heralded by many feminists of any color[12] – was poorly received by most critics of her time. Particularly many of her more famous black male contemporaries criticized her for what they perceived to be ridiculing black life and oversimplifying it (Locke in Gates and Appiah 18), with Richard Wright probably being her fiercest opponent. In a review that appeared in the year of the novel's publication, Wright goes so far as to deem her novel to contain neither theme nor message and to accuse Hurston of continuing the tradition of the minstrel show (in Gates and Appiah 16-17), the latter statement being interpreted by Lovalerie King as "[having] stopped just short of referring to Hurston as an *Uncle Tom*" (113). A major reason for Wright's strong criticism was Hurston's extensive use of African American vernacular, or black dialect, which, as Gates notes in his essay, signified mental inferiority among other negative aspects (176). King argues that it is precisely this style that appalled Hurston's contemporaneous critics that she is now praised for (112). As Michael Awkward maintains in his introduction to *New Essays on Their Eyes Were Watching God*, for a very long time "the black artist's primary responsibility was to create protest fiction that explored America's historical mistreatment of blacks, boosting black self-esteem and changing racist white attitudes about

[11] Helen A. Robbins even calls Hurston "A Postmodern Writer Before Her Time."

[12] As M. Genevieve West points out, there is an ongoing debate among feminists as to whether Hurston had a feminist consciousness and whether or not her novel can be considered expressing a form of early feminism (5), and Valerie Boyd, for example, believes that "in its critique of black male-female relationships [...] [it] is also protest literature," thereby drawing attention to feminist thought (304).

Afro-Americans in the process" (3). Yet, this is far from what Hurston did in her work (Awkward 2-3). Awkward's comment, however, already leads to one element that can retrospectively be considered postmodernist in *Their Eyes Were Watching God*, namely Hurston's choice to focus on an all-black community in Eatonville, Florida. Her decision to set a large part of the story in a rural, southern town during the Jim Crow era creates what bell hooks termed "a space of resistance" ("Choosing" 149). By giving the illusion that the characters choose these margins voluntarily and not because of racial segregation, which would have made life far worse in other places, Hurston gives the characters of Eatonville the possibility to turn their backs on white America, thereby weaving a subtle political message into the narrative. The fictional Eatonville, almost completely free from any influence of white society, was modeled on Hurston's hometown with the same name and was considered a "rare haven," as Holly Eley claimed in her introduction to the 1986 Virago edition of *Their Eyes Were Watching God* (viii). Instead of focusing on the race problem, Hurston wrote about black 'wholeness' making her characters focus solely on themselves: "They are free because they have eschewed white cultural institutions and have built on those of their own community and on their African past" (Eley x). Indeed, except for a brief time after the hurricane when two white officials with guns force Tea Cake to help bury dead bodies and ignorantly call him "Jim" (251), the novel is more or less free from references to white oppression. Yet, in this scene it becomes clear that Hurston is certainly not in denial of segregation or racism, making references to segregated white and black cemeteries (253) and Jim Crow laws (254). Nevertheless, for the most part of the novel she feels no necessity to broach the issue of racial segregation that reduced African Americans to a 'separate but *un*equal' status in society. And even when she writes about racism and white supremacist attitudes, she defies the common anger in black society and lets her characters comment light-heartedly on the uneasy relationship between blacks and whites, as seen in a conversation between Tea Cake and Janie:

> "It's bad bein' strange niggers wid white folks. Everybody is aginst yuh."
> "Dat sho is de truth. De ones de white man know is nice colored folks. De ones he don't know is bad niggers." Janie said this and laughed and Tea Cake laughed with her. (255)

In other words, as Sherley Anne Williams contends in the afterword to *Their Eyes Were Watching God*, "[i]t isn't the white man's burden that Janie carries; it is the gift of her own love" (297). Or, to say it with Valerie Boyd, Hurston "was interested in what black people felt and said and did after they'd banished the white man from their minds and turned their thoughts to more interesting things" (305). Hurston's decision to neglect the tensions between blacks and whites and instead focus on the depiction of a black woman and her life in an all-black community can be considered a counter-element to the discourses of a white patriarchal society. Simultaneously, her novel serves as a counter narrative to the black protest novel that was common at the time of the novel's publication. This type of protest fiction focused on the black man's anger and hurt while he was suffering from white oppression, and culminated in the publication of Richard Wright's *Native Son* (1940). Of course, this is what caused Hurston problems in her career, for – as Hurston's biographer Robert E. Hemenway recalls – black authors whose books "were not about the 'race problem' […] seldom sold well" (5). Eley goes so far as to claim that "Hurston was incapable of portraying black people as humiliated victims, warped by racial oppression" (xiii). This, in turn, left her with little money and dying in obscurity as a "literary has-been, a marginalized, out-of-print outsider" (West 1). Still, one can safely argue, as Boyd does, that by writing about a black woman's quest for freedom without white society's influence and by celebrating the black oral traditions in the South the way Hurston does, the novel "becomes protest literature on yet another level: It protests white oppression by stripping it of its potency, by denying its all-powerfulness in black people's lives" (305). Bringing in Lyotard again, this can be interpreted as just one out of many mininarratives surfacing in the story, especially considering the fact that it was mostly whites who were reading Harlem Renaissance fiction at the time of the novel's publication.

The text not only opposes the metanarrative of white oppression, it also protests traditional patriarchal (black) male-female relationships, which were often characterized by male dominance, female subjugation, and the notion that women were not able to live independently, as Janie was told in many accounts like the following:

> "Uh woman by herself is uh pitiful thing[.]" […] "Dey needs aid and assistance. God never meant 'em tuh try tuh stand by theirselves. You ain't been used tuh knockin' round and doin' fuh yo'self, Mis' Starks. You been well taken keer of, you needs uh man." (139)

Obviously, Janie does not heed this advice from town members, however well-intentioned but still influenced by patriarchal attitudes. Instead, she runs off with Tea Cake, who, being twelve years her junior, of working-class status, and of dark skin color, is clearly not the future husband the community has in mind for her. In fact, he is considered completely unfit company for someone like Mrs. Mayor Starks. Still, it is Janie's wish to stop living the way her grandmother wanted her to (Hurston 171), which was "sittin' on high" (32) without clear instructions as to what to do up there, and finally live with the man that "could be a bee to a blossom – a pear tree blossom in the spring" (161). Again, this part of the plot is meant to reject a prevalent metanarrative in early twentieth century society, which was for a woman to stay "in place" and always put aside her own needs for the sake of her husband's. Hurston, however, who sends Janie on a journey in search for self-fulfillment "tuh de horizon and back" (284), provides a counter-image to the traditional picture of black femininity, which is one reason that makes the story susceptible to interpretation from a postmodernist perspective. A few decades later, Lyotard recounts:

> We no longer have recourse to the grand narratives – we can resort neither to the dialectic of Spirit nor even to the emancipation of humanity as a validation for postmodern scientific discourse. But [...] the little narrative [*petit récit*] remains the quintessential form of imaginative invention [...]. (60)

In Hurston's novel this "imaginative invention" can be found in Janie's journey to the horizon and her resistance to submit to what her first two husbands wanted to make of her. First, she runs away from her husband Logan Killicks, who wanted to buy a second mule for her to work with, an undertaking that foreshadows what he thought she should become (a mule that is[13]). After many unhappy years in her second marriage with Jody "Joe" Starks, who regards her as little more than his trophy and an object to be adorned with, she finally speaks up to him. Yet, Jody Starks conceives of himself only as "a big voice" (48), and, when becoming older and weaker, ridicules Janie in order to bolster his insecure self. In this regard, Diana Coole's explanation of what she calls a master narrative is appropriate: While such a master narrative always has to do with the subject adopting "a position of mastery in relation to its objects" (110), it also "suggests a specifically gendered position, in which the subject adopts a masculine stance and where that which is to be mastered is in some sense feminine" (110-111). Thereby, Hurston not only rejects the master narrative on the outside, but also shows her rejection from the inside: With Janie as the protagonist, she seems to reject both the position of mastery as well as traditional gender roles. When Janie is finally free to marry Tea Cake and leaves Eatonville with him, she puts all her inheritance money into a bank and starts working in the swamps of Florida by Tea Cake's side; not because she is dependent on him, but because she wants to be by his side. This rejection of the patriarchal metanarrative also goes along with an interpretation by Craig Owens who maintains, according to Barbara Creed, "that not only is the status of narrative in question but also that of representation, specifically man's androcentric representation of the world in which he has constructed himself as 'subject'" (Creed 403). Hurston no longer leaves the territory to men, so to speak, but engages in questioning this androcentric

[13] See also Hurston's phrase of "de mule uh de world" (29).

representation by putting herself and her black female protagonist out there to counter both the existing dominant narratives and their representations.

Janie's character can be considered a rejection of metanarratives not only because of her drive for independence and love but also because of her physical appearance. As Dubey recalls, "for Houston Baker, the Old South is home to a racially pure cultural tradition that is 'mulattoized' as it migrates to the urban North" (157). Even though this notion of racial purity in the South may be debated, considering the large number of biracial slaves that were fathered by white slave masters, if we follow Dubey's conception, Hurston again breaks with the conventional. Incorporating a light-skinned black woman with a "coffee-and-cream complexion and [...] luxurious hair" (Hurston 208) in her story set in the Deep South was by itself not that groundbreaking; nevertheless she succeeds in being revolutionary precisely because of how the story ends. Hurston's light-skinned black woman protagonist is not destined to die as a tragic mulatta, that is, according to Williams, one who is "too refined and sensitive to live under the repressive conditions endured by ordinary blacks and too colored to enter the white world" (289). Rather, she portrays Janie as a woman who manages to live a life more or less free from racial oppression and completes a journey of self-fulfillment despite two oppressive husbands and an equally oppressive grandmother, all elements that can be considered revolutionary after all. Or, to say it with Gates, "Janie develops from a nameless child, known only as 'Alphabet,' who cannot even recognize her own likeness as a 'colored' person in a photograph, to the implied narrator of her own tale of self-consciousness" (185).

Another postmodernist element is Hurston's unique way of mixing prose fiction and oral storytelling, the latter of which must have been very familiar to her after having grown up in a black community in the South. The use of African American southern vernacular is, of course, commonly regarded as an element of naturalism and realism, yet here it foregrounds postmodernist narrative strategies precisely because the vernacular not only appears in dialogue but also enters the free indirect discourse of the narrative. Gates compellingly analyzes Hurston's writing technique as follows:

> Hurston uses free indirect discourse not only to represent an individual character's speech and thought but also to represent the collective black community's speech and thoughts, as in the hurricane passage. This sort of anonymous, collective, free indirect discourse is not only unusual but quite possibly was Hurston's innovation, as if to emphasize both the immense potential of this literary diction, one dialect-informed as it were, for the tradition, as well as the text's apparent aspiration to imitate oral narration. (214)

Even if this might be putting Gates' analysis to unintended use, from the basis of his argument it is easy to claim that by blurring boundaries between what typically is dialect-free narration in free indirect discourse and black diction in dialogue, that is, in direct discourse, Hurston transgresses boundaries that usually separate 'high' and 'low' culture. Whereas standard forms of third person narration can be considered more of a 'high' culture element, the oral forms of storytelling – even in written form – are typically read as expressions of 'low' culture; something to be found in the vernacular and in the realm of folk traditions. By mixing these two elements in free indirect discourse, Hurston mocks the artificial distinction, thus creating a mininarrative that does not only serve the purpose of aesthetic deviation but also sends out a political message, though very subtly. One could therefore argue that the combination of Standard English and vernacular becomes "dialect-informed free indirect discourse" (Gates 192) and rejects the boundaries between so-called 'high' and 'low' culture, another feature regularly attributed to postmodernist texts. Likewise, incorporating oral vernacular elements into a narrative is a form of both pastiche and parody. Hurston's blurring of the forms of 'high' and 'low' culture starts with Janie's first encounter with Joe Starks.[14] There, Hurston juxtaposes the narratorial voice in Standard English – which many critics consider beautiful, highly figurative prose – with narrative elements in African American vernacular. Within only a few paragraphs we find all three rhetorical styles Hurston uses: direct discourse, free indirect discourse – at times influenced by Joe's diction – and, last but not least, indirect discourse:

> The noon sun filtered through the leaves of the fine oak tree where she sat and made lacy patterns on the ground. She had been there a long time when she heard whistling coming down the road. It was a citified, stylish dressed man with his hat set at an angle that didn't belong in these parts. (47)

After a more detailed description of Joe Starks' appearance from the perspective of an omniscient voice relating the story in indirect discourse, the narrator slips into Joe Starks' consciousness and reflects what he has told Janie, even though the narrator certainly influences the account:

> Joe Starks was the name, yeah Joe Starks from in and through Georgy. Been workin' for white folks all his life. Saved up some money – round three hundred dollars, yes indeed, right here in his pocket. Kept hearin' 'bout them buildin' a new state down heah in Floridy and sort of wanted to come. But he was makin' money where he was. But when he heard all about 'em makin' a town all outa colored folks, he knowed dat was de place he wanted to be. (47-48)

This passage in free indirect discourse could have well been written in quotation marks, were it not for the third person account that indicates it is no longer told

---

14 Gates uses the aforementioned 'hurricane passage,' which, of course, is another convincing example of black diction permeating free indirect discourse (see Hurston 232).

from Joe's perspective. Apart from that, when reading the whole novel and paying special attention to the black diction in direct speech, it becomes evident that there is a subtle distinction between the vernacular in free indirect discourse and the one in direct discourse, the latter being more explicit in writing, as can be seen in the passage when Joe asks Janie about the whereabouts of her parents, and she readily replies in strong vernacular: "'Dey dead, Ah reckon. Ah wouldn't know 'bout 'em 'cause mah Grandma raised me. She dead too'" (48). It is interesting but unusual to observe that other white characters, like, for example, the white doctor Janie sends for after Tea Cake caught rabies, speak southern rural vernacular too: "'Janie, I'm pretty sure that was a mad dawg bit yo' husband. It's too late to get hold of de dawg's head. But de symptoms is all there'" (262). Only Janie's defense lawyer in court talks Standard English, which is, of course, the result of institutional conventions.

Since the majority of the text is made up of conversations in southern rural dialect, Hurston favors black diction over Standard English. As Gates observes, these "long exchanges of direct discourse [...] seem to be present in the text more for their own sake than to develop the plot[,] [...] as if to display the capacity of black language itself to convey an extraordinarily wide variety of ideas and feelings" (199). In contrast to novels such as Jean Toomer's *Cane* (1923), which also incorporates black dialect, Hurston's novel does not seem to create binary oppositions between the narrating voice in Standard English and the elements in vernacular speech (Gates 178). Rather, as Gates continues, by drawing on *skaz*[15], a concept developed by Russian Formalism, the "speakerly" elements serve the purpose of representing oral traditions "to emulate the phonetic, grammatical, and lexical patterns of actual speech and produce the 'illusion of oral narration'" (Erlich qtd. in Gates 181). This "speakerly" text, which – as Gates admits – derives from what Roland Barthes called "readerly" and "writerly" texts[16], "seems designed to mediate between [...] a profoundly lyrical, densely metaphorical, quasi-musical, privileged black oral tradition on the one hand, and a received but not yet fully appropriated standard English literary tradition on the other hand" (174). Gates provides an in-depth analysis of Hurston's narrative technique,

15 *Skaz*, as Gates explains, is a form of text that "seems to be aspiring to the status of oral narration" (xxvi). In *The Signifying Monkey* he calls this form the one that most closely resembles Hurston's rhetorical strategy.

16 In *S/Z*, Barthes mentions and explains these two neologisms, which appeared in the French original as *lisible* and *scriptible*, and which are used to differentiate between what Barthes calls "classic texts," giving the reader already a meaning, and texts lacking this final meaning, thus making the reader "no longer a consumer, but a producer of the text" (4).

which is why one more quotation shall exemplify how he interprets what I call mixing of 'high' and 'low' culture:

> Hurston's narrative strategy depends on the blending of the text's two most extreme and seemingly opposed modes of narration – that is, narrative commentary, which begins at least in the diction of standard English, and characters' discourse, which is always foregrounded by quotation marks and by its black diction. (191)

It is this position of a text on two opposite ends, one clearly in the realm of 'high' culture and the other one in the realm of folk culture, which can be viewed as a further trace of postmodernism in *Their Eyes Were Watching God.*

All in all, Hurston's text easily lends itself to a 'pre-postmodern' reading. Among such pre-postmodernist elements are, as stated above, blurred distinctions between 'high' and 'low' culture and the rejection of metanarratives combined with the creation of alternative *petits récits.* Matters become more complex, however, if one takes into account the abovementioned status of Hurston's novel today. At the time of its publication, her novel was groundbreaking, focusing on a black female protagonist who is not doomed to end her life as a tragic mulatta but strives for self-awareness and self-fulfillment. Janie's story is told in both African American vernacular and by means of an omniscient narrator figure using a mixture of Standard English and black diction. During Hurston's writing career, it was the protest novel that served as a template among black American writers. By focusing on notions of black feminine 'wholeness,' however, Hurston finds a way to bypass this metanarrative of protesting racial discrimination and white oppression. All these characteristics allow for arguing for Hurston's text as a set of mininarratives which emphatically reject their 'bigger brothers.'

Today, however, the reading of the novel can also be contextualized differently. I propose that when novelist Alice Walker reclaimed Zora Neale Hurston's writings in the 1970s, she set in motion the formation of yet another metanarrative. In her essay "Looking for Zora" (1975), for example, Walker claims to honor her literary ancestress by discovering and reclaiming her grave as well as her work (93-116). When in the foreword to Hemenway's well-known biography on Hurston, Alice Walker asserts that "[*t*]*here is no book more important to me than this one*" (xiii), she clearly marks the novel's importance for establishing a new metanarrative, which can "reveal the meaning of all stories" (Readings 63). Walker's resurrection of Hurston's work went in line with the claim of what she would call early "womanist"[17] writings. This then led to the canonization of Hurston's novel, and elevated *Their Eyes Were Watching God* to a metanarrative

---

[17] For definitions of what Walker terms "womanist," see her collection of essays *In Search of Our Mothers' Gardens* (1983: xi-xii).

by heralding Hurston as the prime black southern folklorist. The fact that Hurston has become a "contemporary academic celebrity" (Dubey 144), with her work now assuming a steady position in the African American canon, the feminist canon, as well as the general canon of American fiction (Gates 180), is but one reason that indicates this change in development. Today, as Awkward points out, both black and white feminist scholars are interested in *Their Eyes Were Watching God*, and especially black women writers are said to engage in "repeating, imitating, or revising her narrative strategies" (Gates qtd. in Awkward 4). In *Zora Neale Hurston and American Literary Culture*, M. Genevieve West cites several critics who maintain that "Hurston's once-dismissed love story becomes 'an often overlooked classic of Afro-American literature' [and] *Their Eyes* 'belongs in the same category – with that of William Faulkner, F. Scott Fitzgerald, and Ernest Hemingway – of enduring American literature'" (238).

From what could be called a pre-postmodern perspective, which is simultaneously a period during which Hurston's text was not yet as widely recognized as today, her novel can be interpreted as postmodernist and analyzed with Lyotard's concept of "incredulity towards metanarratives" (xxiv). Nowadays, however, this statement is only partially correct because one can assume that the canonization – almost to a state of glorification – of Hurston's text has led to the formation of yet another metanarrative. There is an analogy to what happened to Lyotard, who was criticized for exactly that: "Lyotard's sociological reading of the present and his projection of an ominous future, [...] has been characterized perceptively [...] as assuming the style of [a] grand narrative generally deprecated by Lyotard" (Browning 84). Hence, if we consider Hurston's work today it might be difficult to recognize this rejection of grand narratives precisely because on the level of its reception the novel received such a wide acclaim from the 1970s onward. In effect, Hurston was elevated to a writer of metanarrative status, just like Lyotard, who – as Hawthorn maintains – created "a definition which is itself, paradoxically, something of a metanarrative" (121). As a consequence, a striking similarity can be identified between the French philosopher Lyotard and the Harlem Renaissance writer Hurston: Both seem to have unwittingly initiated yet more metanarratives with their writing, all despite the fact that both despised them so much.

WORKS CITED

Awkward, Michael. "Introduction." *New Essays on Their Eyes Were Watching God*. Ed. Michael Awkward. Cambridge, MA: Cambridge UP, 1990. 1-27. Print.

Barthes, Roland. *S/Z*. 1970. Trans. Richard Miller. London: Jonathan Cape, 1974. Print.

Barry, Peter. *Beginning Theory: An Introduction to Literary and Cultural Theory*. Manchester: Manchester UP, 1995. Print.

Bertens, Hans. *The Idea of the Postmodern: A History*. London: Routledge, 1995. Print.

Boyd, Valerie. *Wrapped in Rainbows: The Life of Zora Neale Hurston*. New York, NY: Scribner, 2003. Print.

Browning, Gary K. *Lyotard and the End of Grand Narratives*. Cardiff: U of Wales P, 2000. Print.

Coole, Diana. "Master Narratives and Feminist Subversions." *The Politics of Postmodernity*. Eds. James Good and Irving Velody. Cambridge, MA: Cambridge UP, 1998. 107-125. Print.

Creed, Barbara. "From Here to Modernity: Feminism and Postmodernism." 1987. *A Postmodern Reader*. Eds. Joseph Natoli and Linda Hutcheon. Albany, NY: SUNY P, 1993. 398-418. Print.

Dubey, Madhu. *Signs and Cities: Black Literary Postmodernism*. Chicago, IL: U of Chicago P, 2003. Print.

Du Bois, W.E.B. *The Souls of Black Folk*. 1903. *Writings: The Suppression of the African Slave-Trade / The Souls of Black Folk / Dusk of Dawn / Essays and Articles*. New York, NY: Library of America, 1986. 357-547. Print.

Eley, Holly. "Introduction." *Their Eyes Were Watching God*. Zora Neale Hurston. New York, NY: Virago, 1986. vii-xv. Print.

Gates, Henry Louis, Jr. "Zora Neale Hurston and the Speakerly Text." *The Signifying Monkey: A Theory of African-American Literary Criticism*. New York, NY: Oxford UP, 1988. 170-216. Print.

Gates, Henry Louis, Jr., and K. A. Appiah, eds. *Zora Neale Hurston: Critical Perspectives Past and Present*. New York, NY: Amistad, 1993. Print.

Hawthorn, Jeremy. *A Concise Glossary of Contemporary Literary Theory*. 2nd Edition. London: Arnold, 1994. Print.

Hemenway, Robert E. *Zora Neale Hurston: A Literary Biography*. Urbana, IL: U of Illinois P, 1977. Print.

hooks, bell. "Choosing the Margin as a Space of Radical Openness." *Yearning: Race, Gender, and Cultural Politics*. Boston, MA: South End, 1990. 145-154. Print.

—. "Postmodern Blackness." *Yearning: Race, Gender, and Cultural Politics*. Boston, MA: South End, 1990. 23-31. Print.

Hurston, Zora Neale. "How it Feels to Be Colored Me." 1928. *I Love Myself When I am Laughing … and Then Again When I Am Looking Mean and Impressive: A Zora Neale Hurston Reader*. Ed. Alice Walker. Old Westbury, NY: Feminist P, 1971. 152-155. Print.

—. *Their Eyes Were Watching God*. 1937. New York, NY: Virago. 1986. Print.

Hutcheon, Linda. "Beginning to Theorize Postmodernism." *A Postmodern Reader*. Eds. Joseph Natoli and Linda Hutcheon. Albany, NY: SUNY P, 1993. 243-272. Print.

Huyssen, Andreas. *After the Great Divide: Modernism, Mass Culture, Postmodernism*. Bloomington, IN: Indiana UP, 1986. Print.

Lyotard, Jean-François. *The Postmodern Condition: A Report on Knowledge*. 1979. Trans. Geoff Bennington and Brian Massumi. Minneapolis, MN: U of Minnesota P, 1984. Print.

King, Lovalerie. *The Cambridge Introduction to Zora Neale Hurston*. Cambridge, MA: Cambridge UP, 2008. Print.

Natoli, Joseph, and Linda Hutcheon. "Introduction." *A Postmodern Reader*. Eds. Joseph Natoli and Linda Hutcheon. Albany, NY: SUNY P, 1993. vii-xiv. Print.

Potter, Russell A. *Spectacular Vernaculars: Hip-Hop and the Politics of Postmodernism*. Albany, NY: SUNY P, 1995. Print.

Readings, Bill. *Introducing Lyotard: Art and Politics*. London: Routledge, 1991. Print.

Reed, Ishmael. "Foreword." *Tell My Horse: Voodoo and Life in Haiti and Jamaica*. Zora Neale Hurston. Ed. Henry Louis Gates, Jr. New York, NY: Harper & Row, 1990. xi-xv. Print.

Robbins, Helen A. "The Ethnography of Zora Neale Hurston: A Postmodern Writer Before Her Time." *Arizona Anthropologist* 7 (1991): 1-11. Print.

Sollors, Werner. *Neither Black Nor White Yet Both: Thematic Explorations of Interracial Literature*. Oxford: Oxford UP, 1997.

Skordili, Beatrice. "little narrative." *Encyclopedia of Postmodernism*. Eds. Victor E. Taylor and Charles E. Winquist. London: Routledge, 2001. 230-232. Print.

Staple, Jennifer. "Zora Neale Hurston's Construction of Authenticity through Ethnographic Innovation." *Western Journal of Black Studies* 30.1 (2006): 62-68. Print.

Walker, Alice. "Foreword: Zora Neale Hurston – A Cautionary Tale and a Partisan View." 1976. *Zora Neale Hurston: A Literary Biography*. Robert E. Hemenway. Urbana, IL: U of Illinois P, 1977. xi-xviii. Print.

—. "Looking for Zora." 1979. *In Search of Our Mothers' Gardens: Womanist Prose*. San Diego, CA: Harcourt, 1983. 93-116. Print.

Walker, Pierre A. "Zora Neale Hurston and the Post-Modern Self in *Dust Tracks On a Road*." *African American Review* 32.3 (1998): 387-399. Print.

West, M. Genevieve. *Zora Neale Hurston and American Literary Culture*. Gainesville, FL: UP of Florida, 2005. Print.

Williams, Sherley Anne. "Afterword." *Their Eyes Were Watching God*. Zora Neale Hurston. New York, NY: Virago, 1986. 287-297. Print

A Horrific Welcome to the Desert of the Real: Simulacra, Simulations, and Postmodern Horror

Michael Fuchs

Night has fallen over the small Californian town of Woodsboro. Blond high school darling Casey[1] is home alone waiting for her boyfriend. In order to kill time, she is watching a movie and preparing some popcorn. A stranger calls; not once, not twice, but three times. While the first two calls come to a rather quick end when Casey hangs up, the stranger succeeds in catching Casey's interest in talking to him the third time around. After discussing their favorite scary movies[2] in an often-parodied scene, the caller discloses that he is actually watching Casey while they are talking. Casey hangs up again, checks whether she can see someone outside and locks the doors. She is unsure whether the caller was serious, but the viewer knows, or at least thinks to know, better, since the caller's presence is implied by a number of shots. Suddenly the doorbell of the front door rings, indicating a nightly visitor watching her and verifying the viewer's assumption that indeed, Casey is in danger.

> Casey: Who's there? [pause] Who's there? [pause] I'm calling the police. [phone rings and she picks it up]
>
> Stranger: You should never say, "Who's there?" Don't you watch scary movies? It's a death wish. You might as well just come out here and investigate a strange noise or something.

The fact that the caller has captured Casey's boyfriend and will kill him if she cannot pass a horror film trivia is part of the convoluted meta-referential game that *Scream* (1996) plays. Though also a part of the aforementioned game, the fact that Casey is killed just minutes after being told that she should not have asked "Who's there?" is the most interesting one in the context of the interrelation between postmodernist horror and postmodern theory, especially Jean Bau-

---

1 The naming is significant, since it is usually the *final girl*, i. e. the one that in the end confronts and defeats the killer (only for him to reappear in the sequel) that has boyish characteristics, among them a boyish name.

2 The original title of *Scream*'s script was *Scary Movie*; needless to say that a film franchise that spoofs *Scream* (especially in the first film of the series) and other horror (and in later incarnations also science fiction and fantasy films) movies took over that name. *Scream*'s title, of course, refers to Edvard Munch's famous expressionist painting, a reference that is highlighted by the killer's mask (actually, it should be 'killers' masks'). The title also references the relatively early postmodernist horror film *The Last Horror Film* (1982), in which a diegetically produced horror movie is also entitled *Scream*.

drillard's theories. Under the assumption that the diegetic reality of *Scream* is exactly that – a reality, this scene suggests that reality follows fiction. In the case at hand, the mise-en-scène of a 'real' murder follows the rules of a conventional slasher[3] killing. However, this is not simply a reworking of the age-old question of who holds the upper hand in the imitation game between life and art. Rather, this scene is a reflection of and on postmodern[4] 'reality,'[5] in which signs not only influence the way we perceive the world we live in, but rather replace any fixed conceptions of reality altogether. This so-called postmodern condition, where 'reality' is constructed by representations, is also depicted in a number of postmodernist[6] horror films in a way that is typical of the horror genre. The meta-games found in these films accomplish much more than the mere disruption of viewer expectations. In fact, these meta-games, which trap the viewer in a constant oscillation between the signs of a seemingly infinite *chaîne signifiante*, rather than "shunning [...] important issues" (Wolf 69), are the very mechanism by which postmodern horror films perform a function that has defined the genre since its inception: tapping into the most fundamental fears of society.

But before venturing to discuss this postmodernist twist that defines a number of horror films which have been released since the early 1980s, let me first introduce some major milestones in the development of the conceptualization of the simulacrum, ending with Jean Baudrillard's concepts of the precession of simulacra as well as simulation. I would also like to briefly discuss how the epistemological as well as ontological questions that have been put into a different light by much of postmodern theory have already been touched upon by pre-postmodern horror films.

---

3 According to Carol J. Clover, the conventions of the slasher movie are the following: a killer whose childhood is in some way at stake, suffers from gender confusion, or is in other ways sexually disturbed; the events occur at a secluded place; the killer uses a phallic weapon; sexual transgression is punished; and the surviving final girl (28-35).

4 In the vein of Linda Hutcheon and others, I want to clearly differentiate between postmodern/postmodernity and postmodernist/postmodernism. The first pair of terms connotes the era of the "post-industrial society," to use Daniel Bell's term, and the latter stands for a cultural movement, "the dominant of [which] is *ontological*" (McHale 9).

5 According to Vladimir Nabokov "reality [is] one of the few words which mean nothing without quotes" (*Lolita*. 1955. New York, NY: Random House, 1997. 306).

6 Without going into detail, according to my definition, postmodern*ist* horror is a kind of postmodern horror, a sub-genre even. Its central feature is a high level (and specific kind) of meta-referentiality, i. e., the film shows an awareness of its own artificiality. 'Postmodern,' on the other hand is used as a primarily temporal marker, even if there is enormous connotative academic ballast attached to the term. I suggest that the era of postmodern horror started in 1978, when *Halloween* and *Dawn of the Dead* were released.

SIMULACRA AND SIMULATIONS

What do you associate with Jean Baudrillard? Simulacra. What does that concept mean? Signs determine the way we perceive the world around us. Sounds familiar? I suppose it does. Cultural Theory 101. But this is not the whole story. Fact of the matter is that the concept of simulacra is not something that Jean Baudrillard invented. The concept can be traced to one of the great Western thinkers, Plato, who first discussed the idea of the simulacrum in his works *Sophist* and *Republic*.[7]

It is well known that according to Plato the universe is split; there is the sphere of Ideas (*eidos*), in which things exist in their true, real form and there is the world surrounding us in which all that we can find are copies (*simulacra*) of those Ideas. Plato makes clear that he fears representers who pretend to be (in contact with the) real, and not just earthly copies thereof. The potential danger Plato sees in this context is that the pretention of not being merely a representation or of telling the Truth may be misused in order to manipulate people (*Republic* 600e-602b).[8] In *Sophist*, a distinction is made between the creation of likenesses (*eikones*) and of semblances (*phantasmata*). The first is the creation of a copy that is somewhat different from the original (e. g. taking perspective into account when creating a statue or painting) while the latter merely seems to look like the thing it simulates (cf. 236a-d).[9] Plato's primary objective in this section, however, is the distinction "between good and bad copies, or rather copies (always well founded) and simulacra (always engulfed in dissimilarity)" (Deleuze 257). Shortly after, the sophist alludes to the fact that "all the world's a stage," or, in other words, reality is nothing but a simulation (cf. 239d-254b).

---

7 To my knowledge, it is only in the Latin translations of *Politeia* (*Republic*) that the term 'simulacra' is explicitly used: "Atque ita demum solem ipsum suspiciet neque iam in aquis et aliena in regione simulacra ipsius spectabit, sed ipsum secundum se ipsum in sede propria speculabitur et, qualis sit, cognoscere poterit" (516b; *Platonis de re publica*, Tralatione Marsilii Ficini, ca. 1475). In Ovid's *Metamorphosis*, the mirror image of Narcissus is once referred to as "simulacra" (line 431), which opens up an extremely interesting line of thought in terms of identity construction from a Lacanian perspective. Unfortunately, following this idea is entirely beyond the scope of this paper.

8 This is the reason why Plato wanted to banish artists from his republic.

9 Jacques Lacan tries to show "why Plato protests against the illusion of painting [i. e. something that looks like the thing it simulates]. The point is not that painting gives an illusory equivalence to the object, even if Plato seems to be saying this. The point is that the *trompe l'œil* of painting pretends to be something other than what it is [...]. The picture does not compete with appearance, it competes with what Plato designates for us beyond appearance as being the Idea. It is because the picture is the appearance that says it is that which gives the appearance that Plato attacks painting, as if it were an activity competing with its own" (112).

The Allegory of the Cave (*Republic* 514a-520a) complicates the issue. In it, Plato describes a world in which what is perceived to be real is, in fact, illusion. He pictures a cave inhabited by prisoners who have been chained and immobilized since their childhood. Behind the prisoners is an enormous fire, which they cannot see, since even their heads are fixed. Some people put on a shadow play for the prisoners, and the prisoners furthermore can hear the echoes from the noises produced by those people. Plato suggests that to the prisoners "the shadows of artefacts [...] constitute the only reality" (515c). If one of the prisoners were set free, "he'd [...] think that there was more reality in what he'd been seeing before than in what he was being shown now" (515d), indicating that reality is what one expects reality to be. Gradually, the prisoner would get to know the real world, but if he then were imprisoned again and tried to tell the other prisoners of the real world, he would be considered a madman.[10] To summarize very briefly, according to Plato, mankind is neither able to understand truth nor to perceive reality; it is caught in a mode of existence in which it takes replicas (simulacra) for originals (the real).

There have been countless critiques, interpretations, and reconceptualizations of Plato's ideas[11], but for the purposes of this paper, I may propose to take a gigantic leap in time to Gilles Deleuze's critique of Plato's conception of simulacra. According to Deleuze, "Plato discovers in the flash of an instant that the simulacrum is not simply a false copy, but that it places in question the very notations [*sic*] of copy and model" (256). "It harbors a positive power which denies *the original and the copy, the model and the reproduction*" (262). While Fredric Jameson claims that the simulacrum is a copy twice removed from reality (*Postmodernism* 30), Deleuze suggests that it is of another nature altogether. In contrast to a copy, which is defined by some sort of internal and essential resemblance to the original or model, the simulacrum shows an external and deceptive resemblance to a presumed model. This external resemblance is, however, only a surface effect, an illusion. Furthermore, it is a means and not an end[12]: mimicry is

[10] Note the mythic structure at work here: hero undergoes a life-changing experience, but is unable to communicate the path to enlightenment (cf. Joseph Campbell's *Hero with a Thousand Faces*).

[11] For example, Johann Heinrich Lambert wrote in a letter in response to Immanuel Kant's idea of space as an a priori category: "[...] das Simulacrum spatii et temporis [...] ist eine Nachbildung des wirklichen Raums und der wirklichen Zeit, und läßt sich davon ganz wohl unterscheiden" ["the spatial and temporal simulacrum [...] is a replica of real space and real time, and can be differentiated from real space and time" – my translation] ("Brief vom 13. Oktober 1770 von Johann Heinrich Lambert." *Kant's Briefwechsel*. Vol I. Berlin: de Gruyter, 1922. 109).

[12] In hyperreality, "the whole traditional world of causality [...] [comes] in question: the perspectival, determinist mode, the 'active,' critical mode, the analytical mode – the distinction between

camouflage, as Jacques Lacan suggests (99). Keeping with the war metaphor, simulacra rage war against reality. This is where Jean Baudrillard comes into play.

According to Baudrillard, simulacra have successively taken over territory from reality. He sketches stages of this process partly in his works *Symbolic Exchange and Death*, originally published as *L'Echange symbolique et la mort* in 1976 (reprinted in *Selected Writings*), and *Simulacra and Simulations* (*Simulacres et Simulation*, 1981). The first stage of the process is a pre-simulacran one, the symbolic order, which is marked by a fixed system of signs and the central idea of mimesis, a realistic representation of reality. In this stage, a basic reality is thus reflected (*Simulacra* 6).

The following stage is the first order of simulacra (era of the counterfeit). It is marked by competition for meaning as the simulacrum tries to restore an ideal image of nature ("Symbolic Exchange" 136) and thereby "masks and denatures a profound reality" (*Simulacra* 6). At this stage, there is still an easily detectable difference between the simulacrum and reality ("Symbolic Exchange" 136-137). At first glimpse[13], the Frankenstein Monster is a prime example of a first order simulacrum. It may be constructed of human parts, but it is not what would generally be termed 'human.' This notion is even alluded to in the movie *Bride of Frankenstein* (1935), when Henry Frankenstein[14] (Colin Clive) and Dr. Praetorius (Ernest Thesiger) are about to reanimate a dead heart in order to create a mate for the Monster:

> Dr. Praetorius: Is there any life yet?
> Frankenstein: No. Not life itself yet. [pause] This is only the simulacrum of life.

The second order of simulacra (era of production) is characterized by mass production of copies originating from a single prototype. Due to technological advancement – though not creating a technologically determinist model[15] – the differences between the copy and the original blur to the point where they can no longer be perceived ("Symbolic Exchange" 136-137), thereby masking "the

---

cause and effect, between active and passive, between subject and object, between the end and the means" (Baudrillard, *Simulacra* 30).

13 "At first glimpse" because a poststructuralist reading of the Monster (e. g. following Donna Haraway's "Cyborg Manifesto") would actually allow the deconstruction of the category human.

14 As is probably known, in Mary Shelley's novel, the mad scientist is called Victor Frankenstein while his best friend is named Henry Clerval.

15 According to Steven Best and Douglas Kellner, Baudrillard "advances a sort of technological determinism whereby models and codes become the primary determinants of social experience" (119) because he "never specifies the economic or social forces" (ibid.) behind the primacy of the sign.

absence of a profound reality" (*Simulacra* 6). An example of this lack of a difference is presented in *Blade Runner* (1982). As is probably known, the plot of this dystopian science fiction movie, set in the Los Angeles of the year 2019, revolves around an android hunter (the titular Blade Runner) named Deckard, played by Harrison Ford. In order to differentiate between androids and human beings, Blade Runners use an emotional response test. On his journey, Deckard meets Rachel (Sean Young), the prototype of a new android generation that believes to be human (while the earlier generations were aware of their artificiality) and which just barely fails the test. The longer Deckard is with the prototype, the more he (as well as the viewer) becomes unsure about the borders between man and machine. At the end of the film, doubts arise as to whether Deckard – the man hunting replicants – is not a replicant himself.[16]

While Baudrillard draws up this development, "the passage from a metallurgic into a semiurgic society" (*Political Economy* 185), in successive stages, what he is really interested in is the final phase of his model, the third order of simulacra, the era of simulation, in which the machine has been replaced by information as mode of production. In the postmodern age, there is no more "relation to any reality" (*Simulacra* 6), thereby also agreeing to Deleuze's abovementioned claim that the (postmodern) simulacrum has no link to reality anymore: "[I]t is always a false problem to wish to restore the truth beneath the simulacrum" (*Simulacra* 27).[17] In the postmodern world, there are no more distinctions between the real and the unreal. Instead, postmodernity is characterized by a hyperreality in which the real is constructed on the basis of models. The real of hyperreality, therefore, is no longer simply given, but is artificially produced as real, turning into "*reality for its own sake*, the fetishism of the lost object: no longer the object of representation, but the ecstasy of denial and of its own ritual extermination" ("Symbolic Exchange" 145). Thus, "unreality no longer resides in the dream or fantasy, or in the beyond, but in the *real's hallucinatory resemblance to itself*" (ibid.). Models come to determine our realities, and the boundaries between the hyperreal and the real are eliminated. Moreover, not only do these boundaries disappear, but the simulated reality becomes the determinant of

---

16 While there are hints at the possibility of Deckard being a replicant in the original theatrical cut, the likeness is increased in the director's cut (as well as the 2007 final cut, which is largely based on the director's cut).

17 There is, however, one central difference between their ideas in this context: in contrast to Gilles Deleuze and Félix Guattari, who in *Anti-Oedipus* claim that "the real is not impossible; it is simply more and more artificial" (34), Jean Baudrillard sees reality vanishing altogether in the postmodern reality (cf. "Symbolic Exchange" 143-146). Similar to Deleuze and Guattari, Fredric Jameson has famously exclaimed the "transformation of reality into images" (*Cultural Turn* 14) in postmodernity.

the real. In this way, Baudrillard takes the poststructuralist critique of the impossibility of referentiality to the extreme, claiming not merely that mankind has neither direct nor indirect access to reality, but rather that constructed, mediated realities precede the postmodern reality altogether.

HORROR FILMS AND PERCEPTION

One of the central issues of Baudrillard's (as well as much of poststructuralist) theory is challenging old answers to questions about our perception and making sense of the world we are part of: How can I know the world I am part of? With what degree of certainty can I know it? Are there limits to the knowable? In poststructuralist theory, these epistemological matters are intricately linked to ontological ones: How is reality constructed? Is there only one reality? How do I act in 'my' reality? Is 'I' a fixed category?

An investigation of the visual construction of horror films, even pre-postmodern ones, shows that the horror genre in general is concerned with epistemological matters in a similar way as poststructuralist theory is. Horror writer H. P. Lovecraft once rephrased Sigmund Freud's claim that things paradoxically known yet at the same time unknown are perceived as *unheimlich*[18] by human beings as follows: "The oldest and strongest emotion of mankind is fear, and the oldest and strongest kind of fear is fear of the unknown" (qtd. in Barker 49). This threat resulting from the interrelation between the known and the unknown is one of the central characterizing features of the horror genre, which is also emphasized by Robin Wood's (77-80) definition of horror cinema, which can very briefly be summarized as 'normality is threatened by the monster.' Even though Wood is primarily concerned with the interrelation between psychoanalytical and ideological questions, this statement can easily be rephrased into 'the known world is threatened by the monster symbolizing the unknown world.' According to Charlene Bunnell, this opposition between the known and the unknown world is embedded in the age-old motif of light/day versus darkness/night:

> One world is the external one – cultural and institutional; it is "light" because it is familiar and common. The other world is the internal one – primitive and intuitive; it is dark, not because it necessarily signifies evil (although it may), but because it is unfamiliar and unknown. (81)

---

[18] For a more detailed account on the postmodern uncanny, see Petra Eckhard's contribution to this volume.

It is noteworthy that this opposition of dark vs. light is linked to perception, more specifically vision. In darkness, we cannot see (clearly) and this perceptive problem turns into an epistemological one as darkness equals the unknown. Horror films use the light vs. dark motif in order to make the viewer question the reliability of his senses and, by extension, his construction of reality, thereby underlining that the viewer's reality is just one of many versions of reality.

A prime example for very explicit usage of darkness to symbolize the unknown can be found in the 1940s' productions of RKO. "'We tossed away the horror formula right from the beginning,' Lewton[19] said. 'No grisly stuff for us. No masklike faces, hardly human, with gnashing teeth and hair standing on end. No creaking physical manifestations. No horror piled upon horror'" (Siegel 31). The decision not to show the monster in (for the times) horrifying makeup and well lit, as was the case with Universal's monsters, was influenced by economic issues, since RKO simply did not have the financial resources to pay for the extravagant makeup. However, this characteristic of hardly ever (if at all) showing the monster also had deep psychological implications: "The stories [Val Lewton] produced are dramatizations of the psychology of fear. Man fears the unknown – the dark, that which may lurk in the shadows. [...] That which he cannot see fills him with basic and understandable terror" (Bodeen 215), a notion with which also Slavoj Žižek agrees when he notes that "[i]nstead of showing the terrifying monster (vampire, murderous beast), its presence is indicated only by means of off-screen sounds, by shadows, and so on, and thus rendered all the more horrible" (144). In *I Walked with a Zombie* (1943), for example, a walk through the Haitian jungle in the middle of the night is probably the most terrifying scene of the film, although it is only the mere possibility of a threat, the unknown lurking in the darkness that surrounds the characters (as well as the extremely effective use of music), which makes the scene thrilling. As Val Lewton once said: "The horror addicts will populate the darkness with more horrors than all the horror writers in Hollywood could think of" (qtd. in Siegel 32).

Horror films have acknowledged the existence of the unknown in our world already since pre-postmodern times, because they have always made viewers

---

19 Val Lewton produced the majority of RKO's horror pictures in the 1940s. Together with Jacques Tourneur, who usually directed Lewton's horror films, he had an enormous influence on horror movies in the 1940s. They were so influential that numerous horror film histories call the 1940s either the Lewton or Tourneur Era. It should, however, be added that these histories usually underestimate the impact that Universal, which is usually taken as the benchmark for 1930s' horror, still had, releasing not only numerous sequels to their classic horror series (4 *Invisible Man* sequels, 4 *Mummy*, 2 *Frankenstein*, 1 *Dracula* as well as 2 films that united monsters from different franchises) but also introducing new monsters in films like *The Wolf Man* (1941), not to mention the *Abbott and Costello* horror comedies.

question their knowledge of the world as well as what is perceived as reality. As such, already pre-postmodern horror films expressed ideas popularized by postmodern theory.[20] Can we know the world merely by observing it? Do we not, in order to know the world, construct a certain version of it? Are there not aspects we (consciously or unconsciously) do not integrate into our version of it? Even classic horror films suggest that we lack the means to (fully) understand and know the world surrounding us.

POSTMODERN HORROR AND THE DESERT OF THE REAL

After the outline of a more general relation between the horror film and postmodern ideas, it is now time to turn to more explicit incarnations of Baudrillardean ideas in postmodern horror. *The Thing* (1982) may serve as a first example to demonstrate how horror films can express concepts found in Baudrillard's theories:

The story of John Carpenter's 1982 remake of the 1951 movie *The Thing from Another World* centers on an American research team in the Antarctic. At the beginning of the movie, a husky is chased by a helicopter manning two Norwegians from their nearby research facility. Not understanding the Norwegians' motivations for trying to kill a (seemingly) harmless animal, the Americans give shelter to the dog. After one of the Norwegians has gotten off the helicopter, the Americans think that he is attacking them, but as a result of some rather unforeseeable events, both of the supposedly insane Norwegians die. Wanting to investigate the situation, the Americans go to the Norwegian facility and find it incinerated. They recover a carcass and discover that it is some alien life form. Soon after, it becomes clear that the dog is the alien[21]. The alien then takes various shapes over the course of the film, but the deciding factor is that it remains entirely unclear as to whether the alien actually has an original – or 'real' – form. This is in stark contrast to the 1951 adaptation of the same material[22], in which the alien does not only have a specific form, but is also clearly different to human beings. This distinction between human and alien is deconstructed in Carpenter's film, since the alien also takes the shape of some of the American scien-

---

[20] As Roger Salomon states: "Horror narrative exploits the assumptions of postmodernism before postmodernism" (139).

[21] One cannot say with absolute certainty whether the alien is merely a parasite or is able to take the shape of any living being. In either case, one can never tell its 'true' form.

[22] In Don A. Stuart's novella *Who Goes There?* (1938), on which both films are based, the alien can assume the shape and personality of any creature it devours.

tists, thereby not only questioning the distinctions between human and alien as well as reality and appearance, but also contrasting the 'normality' of the crew with the knowledge that one or some of them are no longer human. Furthermore, the alien "constantly generat[es] copies without originals" (Piñedo 104) and thus represents the third order simulacrum par excellence.[23] A similar claim can be made about a scene in *Scream 3*. During the shooting of the third part of the fictional film franchise *Stab*[24], a serial killer appears and starts killing the movie's actors. After he finds Sidney (Neve Campbell), the secludedly living heroine of the first two *Scream* films, she decides to go to the studio in which *Stab 3* is produced and meets characters known from the first two films of the trilogy. For the momentary purposes, it becomes really interesting when Sidney gets onto the set of *Stab 3*, which is a replica of Woodsboro, the town in which the events of the first *Scream* movie took place. Sidney enters 'her' house and goes up to 'her' room (see Illustration 1). A dialogue from *Scream* that is supposed to be a manifestation of Sidney's instable mind is heard; Sidney still knows her lines. Suddenly, a masked man appears in similar fashion as Billy (one of the killers) did in the first film and attacks Sidney. Much like in *Scream*, Sidney falls off the roof to be saved.[25] When she then describes the assault to detective Kincaid (Patrick Dempsey), Sidney underlines the equation of the set and Woodsboro even more: "I know he was there. [...] He was there in Woodsboro." Sidney, however, was not in Woodsboro. She was on a set representing Woodsboro, which, however, is merely a fictional town constructed as setting for the first part of the *Scream* trilogy. Thus, the Woodsboro where Sidney was just attacked is nothing more than a copy of a copy without original in the truest sense of the word.

---

23 From another perspective, the alien may well serve as a prime example for the fluidity of postmodern identity.

24 It is interesting to note that while the first part of the *Stab* franchise (parts of which are depicted and discussed in *Scream 2*) is based on the 'real-life' events presented in *Scream*, thus being a case of art imitating life (the stress should be on *imitating*, since *Stab* is not a 'realistic' representation of these events, which is underlined by using several horror clichés that *Scream* deftly avoids) while in *Scream 3*, it is rather the case of simulacra preceding 'reality,' since the events in *Scream 3* take place as laid out in the script for *Stab 3*. In *Scream 2*, there is even a discussion in a film class at Windsor College about the question of whether art imitates life or life imitates art.

25 We thus also witness a strange conflation of past and present (for a more detailed account on temporality in contemporary film, see Cornelia Klecker's contribution to this volume) as well as a spatialization of temporality (the past is represented as a space, in this case, a house) in this scene.

Illustration 1: Sidney Prescott (Neve Campbell) meets her ([re-]constructed) past in *Scream 3* © Dimension Films, 2000

It would be no difficult task to list more examples of third order simulacra in postmodern horror. However, it is even more interesting to note how often the reality of postmodern horror films not merely replicates the reality of previous horror films, or of preceding signs in another way, but is recognized as such by character within the diegesis. In the 2003 horror flick *Bloody Murder 2*, for example, two characters become aware that the events they are experiencing mirror a traditional slasher movie plot:

Sofie:	Don't tell me you actually believe that stuff about Trevor Moorehouse[26].
Elvis:	Na, I'm just messin' with you. I mean even if I did, would a guy like me be hangin' 'round much longer?
Sofie:	What do you mean "a guy like you"?
Elvis:	A black man! Ev'rybody knows black guys get it first in horror movies. It's like Horror Films 101.[27]
Sofie:	Black guys? What about women? Girls always bite early in those movies, usually after they show their boobs.
Elvis:	Yeah, but even so, I still have it worse.
Sofie:	How do you figure?
Elvis:	You have some degree of choice whether to show your boobs or not and to whom. Me? I'm black no matter what I do.

[26] In the fictional universe of the *Bloody Murder* films, there is the legend of a certain Trevor Moorehouse who lives in the woods surrounding the camp and stalks and kills campers and camp counselors – shades of Jason Voorhees of the *Friday the 13th* franchise.

[27] This is plain wrong, even if this statement is made in a number of meta-referential horror films. African American characters are definitely not in the best position to survive a horror film, but they (that is, if the film features any African-Americans at all) are usually not killed before the 45-minute-mark.

Unsurprisingly, the African American character (Raymond Novarro Smith) is killed; not instantly, but some twenty minutes after this dialogue. Sofie (Amanda Magarian), who decides not to show her boobs, survives, whereas Angela (Tiffany Shepis), the only character in the film who does, is also the only female victim of the killer. Another example of this phenomenon can be found in the most playful of the *Friday the 13th* films, *Jason Lives* (1986), when a young couple crosses Jason's (C. J. Graham) path in the midst of the nightly woods and Lizabeth (Nancy McLoughlin) tells her boyfriend (Tony Goldwyn), "Darren, we better turn around [...] [b]ecause I've seen enough horror movies to know any weirdo wearing a mask is never friendly." In most cases, these films, even while underlining their fictionality by way of comparison to horror conventions the audience supposedly knows, keep their "reflexivity and self-consciousness firmly within the confines of the diagesis [*sic*]" (Tudor 110). On first sight, one may thus easily claim that these films do not question the existence of any extra-compositional reality. However, the fact that these films explicitly question their own (diegetic) realities while taking the outside reality for granted has another function. The films are "presented as imaginary in order to make us believe that the rest is real" (Baudrillard, *Simulacra* 12).

Somewhat more interesting are two films which initiated the mid-1990s heyday of meta-horror, *New Nightmare* and *In the Mouth of Madness*. Unfortunately, both flopped at the box office[28] whereas *Scream* cashed in big time in their footsteps, using a less complicated[29] version of the concepts presented in the two abovementioned films[30].

New Nightmare (1994) rather explicitly tells the audience early on that the borders between realities are more than just flexible: Heather Langenkamp, who played Nancy in two earlier parts of the *Elm Street* franchise, plays Heather Langenkamp, who is about to star in a new *Elm Street* picture; Wes Craven, the writer and director of both the initial *Nightmare* and the very film we are watch-

---

[28] *New Nightmare* did not perform that poorly on its opening weekend, when it was third at the U. S. box office behind *Pulp Fiction* (which opened on the same day as *New Nightmare*) and *The Specialist* (which was in its second week), but it already closed after four weeks, grossing less than 20M – in a year that saw two horror movies in the top 20 of the annual U. S. box office numbers: *Interview with the Vampire* and *Wolf*. *In the Mouth of Madness* was forth at the U. S. box office on its opening weekend, which, however, was a poor weekend in general. In total, *Mouth* could not even surpass 10M.

[29] Horror film geek Jamie suggests in *Scream* that "if it gets too complicated, you lose your target audience," which was probably Wes Craven's conclusion after writing and directing *New Nightmare* and before directing *Scream*, which was written by Kevin Williamson.

[30] Another horror film that may be added to this 'too intelligent for its own good' list is *The Return of the Texas Chainsaw Massacre* (1994).

ing, plays Wes Craven, who is on the diegetic level working on the script of a new Freddy movie; Robert Englund, the actor breathing life into the notorious child murderer Freddy Krueger, plays Robert Englund; Freddy Krueger – according to the credits – plays "himself" and so on. All in all, the film plays a highly convoluted meta-referential game. At one point in the movie Wes Craven (the fictional character? the director and screenwriter of the movie we are watching?) outs Freddy Krueger as rhetorical construct that symbolizes primal fears; a rhetorical construct that tries to invade reality. However, that is not all-too terrifying for Wes, since he still wants to base his latest script on his nightmares about Freddy's very attempt to transgress the border between fiction and reality:

Wes:	I can tell you what the nightmare's about so far. It's about this entity – whatever you want to call it. It's old. It's very old. It's existed in different forms in different times. The only thing that stays the same is what it lives for. […]
Heather:	Captured? How?
Wes:	By storytellers, of all things. Every so often, they imagine a story good enough to sort of catch its essence. And then, for a while, it's held prisoner in the story. […] When the story dies, the evil is set free.
Heather:	You're saying that Freddy is this ancient thing?
Wes:	Right. The current version. And for ten years he's been pretty much held captive as Freddy in the Nightmare on Elm Street series, but now that the films have ended, the genie's out of the bottle. [...] He's sort of used to being Freddy now and he likes our time and space so he's decided to cross over out of films into our reality.

Up to this point, all of the events may have been strange, but in some way still explainable rationally. This scene, however, ends with a close-up of Wes' computer screen. He has obviously been working on his script and we see that Wes had written the very same dialogue we just witnessed. Having thereby already evoked the ghost of Baudrillard, the on-screen events take it a step further when the computer screen announces a fade to black and our screen willfully follows these preceding signs and turns black.

During her final encounter with Freddy, Nancy finds a script: "The more she read, the more she realized what she had in her hands was nothing more or less than her life itself; that everything she had experienced and thought was bound within these pages." After disposing of Freddy, the script lies on her son Dylan's bed. Heather turns to the final page:

Illustration 2: *New Nightmare*'s ending (see quotation on next page) is its beginning (see illustration; illustration composed of tilting shots of the workbench); *New Nightmare* © New Line Cinema, 1994

Dylan:	Is it a story?
Heather:	Yeah. It's a story.
Dylan:	Read me some.
Heather:	[turns to beginning] We open on an old wooden bench. There's fire and tools and a man's grimy hands building what soon is revealed as a gleaming set of claws. And the claws are moving now as if awakening from a long and unwanted sleep. Then a man lays one trembling hand flat upon the table and with his other picks up a thick, sharp blade. Behind the lights, faces watch from the darkness ready to laugh or scream in terror.

In this way, the film closes in on itself, ending with its beginning. The film resembles a Möbius strip and suggests that what happens in reality is as fictional as the action contained in a movie script while cinematic events are as real as reality. What is also interesting to note is that once all the dust has settled and all the smoke has cleared after reality and fiction have faced off, what still stands tall is the assumedly long-dead author and his script.[31]

In the Mouth of Madness (1994) is a similar case. The film opens when John Trent (Sam Neill), a private investigator specializing in insurance fraud, is imprisoned in a mental institution. Layer after layer it is then revealed how he came into this situation. After some rather weird occurrences connected to the name Sutter Cane, a name that John had not known at that point in time, a publishing house asks John to investigate the disappearance of the popular horror author of the very name Sutter Cane (Jürgen Prochnow). Even though John thinks that this is some marketing stunt, he accepts the case. After getting to know Sutter Cane by way of his novels, John comes to believe that the fictional town that provides the setting for many of Cane's novels, Hobb's End, is real. John and Linda Styles (Julie Carmen; a representative of the publishing house) find the town and everything is as described in Sutter's novels. The inhabitants of the small town behave strangely; in many respects, their actions mirror the actions in Cane's novels. When John is about to leave the strange town (which he, however, cannot do), Linda suggests that Cane's books have turned into reality for whatever reason. The two then meet Sutter Cane in the town's church, where John is exposed to Sutter Cane's latest – and yet unfinished – novel *In the Mouth of Madness*. When some time later Sutter tells John that he (Sutter) is nothing but a character in one of his novels and the character Sutter (and thus the 'real' Sutter as well) will destroy humanity in order to free a race of ancient beings, John is at the edge of going bonkers. He repeatedly destroys the manuscript of *Mouth of Madness*,

---

[31] Similarly, Terrance R. Lindvall and J. Matthew Melton note with reference to the ending of *Duck Amuck*: "In the chaotic world of the simulacra one finds not a referent, but an author" (211).

which he continually receives over the next couple of weeks. However, when he returns to the publishing house one day, he discovers that he actually delivered the manuscript several months ago and also finds out that *In the Mouth of Madness* has been a bestseller and that a movie adaptation is about to hit theaters. John snaps, kills a number of people and is arrested. At that point, the story returns to its beginning as John finds himself in the cell of a mental institution. The next morning, he finds the door of his cell open and outside a bloody mess. A radio announcer is heard speaking of people going on psychotic killing sprees after reading Sutter Cane's novels. When passing a movie theater, John sees that *In the Mouth of Madness* is showing (see Illustration 3). It is directed by John Carpenter (as is the film we are watching), produced by New Line Cinema (as is the film we are watching) and stars – among others – John Trent and Linda Styles. The moving images of the diegetic screen mirror earlier scenes from 'our' film. John begins to laugh in an insane way, but after some moments his laughter turns into desperate sobbing. John has realized that his reality was nothing but a mediated reality. And so is ours. In the same way that John starts to cry in the moment of realizing the unreality of his existence, his lack of getting in contact with the real, so may we, as all of our existence is nothing but constructed.[32]

Illustration 3: John Trent comes to realize that his live is a movie; *In the Mouth of Madness* © New Line Cinema, 1994

Untangling the convoluted filmic incest, as Thomas Pynchon may call it, in movies like *New Nightmare* and *Mouth of Madness* resembles fighting a losing battle. Indeed, these films not only suggest that there is no distinction between the

[32] Both *New Nightmare* and *In the Mouth of Madness* end with their respective beginnings. I may again refer to Cornelia Klecker's contribution to this volume for an account of how this notion is related to postmodern cinema and postmodern conceptions of temporality.

known and unknown, but also that we simply cannot know the world around us. George A. Romero's fifth *Living Dead* film, *Diary of the Dead* (2007), makes the issue at stake more explicit: the diegetic creators of the film claim that they edited the supposedly documentary footage we are seeing in order to both make it more appealing and elicit two kinds of responses – an aesthetic one (being scared) as well as an intellectual one (not believing what television tells you), maybe even a third, political (fighting against media conglomerates), response:

> We made a film - the one I'm going to show you now. [...] Like that cameraman from Channel 10, [Jason] wanted to upload it so that people, you, could be told the truth. [...] I did the final cut on Jason's laptop. I've added music occasionally for effect, hoping to scare you. You see, in addition to trying to tell you the truth, I am hoping to scare you so that maybe you'll wake up. Maybe you won't make any of the same mistakes that we made.

The suggestion that the effects were added so that "you'll wake up" not only emphasizes the abovementioned intellectual response expected, but also asks the viewers to realize that movies are not reality, and by mentioning the news alongside movies extends this claim to news as well. There is a rather paradoxical statement embedded in the voiceover quoted above, since the film suggests that one cannot trust news shows, since they do not show 'reality.' However, the truth of the film that is exposed as being constructed (that is, the pseudo-documentary one is watching) is beyond question. To rephrase, when I (re)construct reality and lay bare the constructedness of my version of truth, it is acceptable and possibly even 'real,' but when others construct reality and mask the constructedness, it turns into unreality. This line of thought may seem strange at first, but it is in accordance with postmodern theory, because what one can witness here is that "it is no longer a question of false representation of reality [...] but of concealing the fact that the real is no longer real, and thus saving the reality principle" (Baudrillard, *Simulacra* 12-13).

CONCLUSION

In postmodernist horror, 'natural' laws have been replaced by mediated ones, be that rules of the horror genre, conventions of a certain horror franchise, rules of filmmaking, rules of the construction of the news, etc. and are thereby reflective of the "broadcast yourself" kind of mediated culture which we are all part of. It is probably no exaggeration to claim that the majority of the knowledge of the world we live in is gained through the media's representation of the world. How we make sense of the world is largely controlled by the media, eradicating the idea of the media as mediator between those producing the mediated messages and those receiving, or consuming, them. Thus,

> the 'traditional' status of the media themselves, characteristic of modernity, is put in question. […] The medium is the message not only signifies the end of the message, but also the end of the medium. There are no more media in the literal sense of the word […] – that is, of a mediating power between one reality and another, between one state of the real and another. (Baudrillard, *Simulacra* 82)

Postmodernist horror expresses the idea, or rather the fear, that the world surrounding us is actually very different from the way it is represented, maybe even "stranger than fiction," as the title of a recent movie suggests. This notion is furthermore used as one of the primary sources of fear in postmodernist horror. No longer is there a need for the classic horror monsters of the past; they may even be deconstructed by laying bare their rhetorical symbolism as representations of age-old fears, as is the case in *New Nightmare*.

The horror film centers on our rationalistically dogmatized fear of losing control. While earlier horror films, but also many contemporary ones that rather strictly follow the classic conventions of the genre, expressed this fear through the possible loss of (trust in) sensory perception or loss of control over the laws of nature, the postmodernist horror film directly links this fear to how the media control us by producing a certain version of reality. There is a rather easy conclusion to be drawn from the issues presented in postmodernist horror: control over the media equals control over the world.

In 1972, Wes Craven's first feature horror film *The Last House on the Left* was framed by a promotional campaign in order to distance the viewer from the violent on-screen events, since the depicted violence was supposed to be too extreme for audiences. In contrast to the film's opening disclaimer that "the events you are about to witness are true," the promotional tag line – "To avoid fainting, keep repeating: 'It's only a movie,' 'It's only a movie!'" – implied that emphasizing the fictional, or mediated, or constructed, nature of the on-screen violence was reassuring. In *Scream 2*, however, a dialogue between two women during a sneak preview of the fictional film *Stab* questions this notion:

Woman A:	That's it! I am not going back in there.
Woman B:	Come on, you chickenshit. It's just a movie.
Woman A:	No, it's not just a movie. It's a true story.

While there is a diegetic reasoning for the final statement of this exchange[33], the viewer knows better: s/he watches a movie and the diegetic reality may be just that – diegetic, a fiction – but since the characters of the film define their reality in relation to the fictitiousness of the film-within-the-film *Stab*, based on which also the viewer constructs her/his reality in difference to artificiality, does that by

[33] See no. 24, p. 80.

analogy not also make the outside, extra-compositional, world a fiction? Horror films have always uncovered hidden social anxieties and the question whether there is a – and if there is, what is the – difference between film, or, more generally, fiction, and 'reality' is one of the most pressing anxieties of the post-industrial age. The possible lack of a difference between 'reality' and fiction is "our collective nightmare" (Wood 78).

WORKS CITED

Barker, Clive. *Clive Barker's A-Z of Horror*. Ed. Stephen Jones. New York, NY: HarperPrism, 1997. Print.

Baudrillard, Jean. *For a Critique of the Political Economy of the Sign*. 1972. Trans. Charles Levin. St. Louis, MO: Telos, 1981. Print.

—. "Symbolic Exchange and Death." 1976. *Jean Baudrillard: Selected Writings*. 2nd Edition. Ed. Mark Poster. Trans. Charles Levin. Palo Alto, CA: Stanford UP, 2002. 119-148. Print.

—. *Simulacra and Simulations*. 1981. Trans. Sheila Faria Glaser. Ann Arbor, MI: U of Michigan P, 1994. Print.

Best, Steven, and Douglas Kellner. *Postmodern Theory: Critical Interrogations*. New York, NY: Guilford, 1991. Print.

Blade Runner. Dir. Ridley Scott. Perf. Harrison Ford, Sean Young, Rutger Hauer, Daryl Hannah, et al. 1982. Warner, 2007. HD DVD.

Bloody Murder 2: Closing Camp. Dir. Rob Spera. Perf. Katy Woodruff, Kelly Gunning, Amanda Magarian, Tiffany Shepis, Tom Mullin, et al. 2003. Planet Media, 2006. DVD.

Bodeen, DeWitt. "Val Lewton." *Films in Review* 14.4 (1963): 210-225. Print.

Bride of Frankenstein. Dir. James Whale. Perf. Boris Karloff, Colin Clive, Valerie Hobson, Ernest Thesiger, O.P. Heggie, et al. 1935. Universal, 2004. DVD.

Bunnell, Charlene. "The Gothic: A Literary Genre's Transition to Film." *Planks of Reason: Essays on the Horror Film*. Ed. Barry Keith Grant. Metuchen, NJ: Scarecrow, 1984. 79-100. Print.

Clover, Carol J. *Men, Women, and Chain Saws: Gender in the Modern Horror Film*. Princeton, NJ: Princeton UP, 1992. Print.

Deleuze, Gilles. "Plato and the Simulacrum." 1969. *The Logic of Sense*. Trans. Mark Lester and Charles Stivale. New York, NY: Columbia UP, 1990. 253-265. Print.

Deleuze, Gilles, and Félix Guattari. *Anti-Oedipus: Capitalism and Schizophrenia*. 1972. Trans. Robert Hurley, Mark Seem and Helen R. Lane. Minneapolis, MN: U of Minnesota P, 1983. Print.

Diary of the Dead. Dir. George A. Romero. Perf. Michelle Moynihan, Josh Close, Shawn Roberts, Amy Lalonde, et al. 2007. Optimum, 2008. Blu-Ray.

Freud, Sigmund. "Das Unheimliche." 1919. *Gesammelte Werke*. Volume 12. Frankfurt/Main: Fischer, 1999. 227-278. Print.

Hutcheon, Linda. *The Politics of Postmodernism*. 2nd Edition. New York, NY: Routledge, 2002. Print.

I Walked with a Zombie. Dir. Jacques Tourneur. Perf. James Ellison, Frances Dee, Tom Conway, Edith Barrett, et al. 1943. Warner, 2002. DVD.

In the Mouth of Madness. Dir. John Carpenter. Perf. Sam Neill, Julie Carmen, Jürgen Prochnow, David Warner, Charlton Heston, et al. 1994. New Line, 2000. DVD.

Jameson, Fredric. *The Cultural Turn*. London: Verso, 1988. Print.

—. *Postmodernism, Or, The Cultural Logic of Late Capitalism*. Durham, NC: Duke UP, 1991. Print.

Lacan, Jacques. *The Four Fundamental Concepts of Psycho-Analysis*. 1973. Trans. Alan Sheridan. New York, NY: Norton, 1981. Print.

Last House on the Left, The. Dir. Wes Craven. Perf. Sandra Peabody, Lucy Grantham, David Hess, Fred J. Lincoln, Jeramie Rain, et al. 1972. MGM, 2002. DVD.

Lindvall, Terrance R., and J. Matthew Melton. "Towards a Post-Modern Animated Discourse: Bakhtin, Intertextuality and the Cartoon Revival." *A Reader in Animation Studies*. Ed. Jayne Pilling. London: John Libbey, 1997. 203-220. Print.

McHale, Brian. *Postmodernist Fiction*. London: Methuen, 1987. Print.

New Nightmare. Dir. Wes Craven. Perf. Heather Langenkamp, Robert Englund, Wes Craven, Traci Mittendorf, et al. 1994. Entertainment in Video, 2004. DVD.

Nightmare on Elm Street, A. Dir. Wes Craven. Perf. Heather Langenkamp, Robert Englund, Johnny Depp, John Saxon, et al. 1984. Alliance, 2008. Blu-Ray.

Piñedo, Isabel Cristina. "Postmodern Elements of the Contemporary Horror Film." *The Horror Film*. Ed. Stephen Prince. New Brunswick, NJ: Rutgers UP, 2004. 85-117. Print.

Plato. *Republic*. ca. 380 B.C. Trans. Robin Waterfield. New York, NY: Oxford UP, 1994. Print.

Plato. *Sophist*. ca. 360 B.C. Trans. Benjamin Jowett. Whitefish, MT: Kessinger, 2004. Print.

Salomon, Roger. *Mazes of the Serpent: An Anatomy of Horror Narrative*. Ithaca, NY: Cornell UP, 2002. Print.

Scream. Dir. Wes Craven. Perf. Neve Campbell, Courteney Cox, David Arquette, Skeet Ulrich, Matthew Lillard, Jamie Kennedy, et al. 1996. Kinowelt, 2009. Blu-Ray.

Scream 2. Dir. Wes Craven. Perf. Neve Campbell, Courteney Cox, David Arquette, Jamie Kennedy, Laurie Metcalf, Liev Schreiber, et al. 1997. Kinowelt, 2009. Blu-Ray.

Scream 3. Dir. Wes Craven. Perf. Neve Campbell, Courteney Cox-Arquette, David Arquette, Patrick Dempsey, et al. 2000. Kinowelt, 2009. Blu-Ray.

Siegel, Joel. *The Reality of Terror*. New York, NY: Viking, 1973. Print.

Thing, The. Dir. John Carpenter. Perf. Kurt Russell, A. Wilford Brimley, T.K. Carter, David Clennon, Keith David, et al. 1982. Universal, 2006. HD DVD.

Tudor, Andrew. "From Paranoia to Postmodernism? The Horror Movie in Late Modern Society." *Genre and Contemporary Hollywood*. Ed. Stephen Neale. London: BFI, 2002. 105-116. Print.

Wolf, Werner. "Metareference across Media: The Concepts, its Transmedial Potentials and Problems, Main Forms and Functions." *Metareference across Media: Theory and Case Studies*. Ed. Werner Wolf. Amsterdam: Rodopi, 2009. 1-85. Print.

Wood, Robin. *Hollywood from Vietnam to Reagan*. New York, NY: Columbia UP, 1986. Print.

Žižek, Slavoj. *Looking Awry: An Introduction to Jacques Lacan through Popular Culture*. Cambridge, MA: MIT P, 1991. Print.

Part II

Postmodern Chronotopoetics

POSTMODERN CHRONOTOPOETICS: AN INTRODUCTION

WALTER W. HÖLBLING & PETRA ECKHARD

The title of this section fuses the categories of time (*chrono*), space (*topos*), and aesthetic discourse (*poetics*), signaling not only an interrelationship between the three following essays but also the collapse of semantic boundaries and divisions once established by structuralist discourses. The loss of differentiation, as we have seen in the previous section, is one of the crucial features that help us to distinguish the aesthetics of modernism from those of postmodernism. This "de-differentiation" (Smethurst 72), or dissolving of boundaries, as apparent in the intermingling of genres, cultures, disciplines, agencies, and art forms, has also tremendously affected the way we conceive of time and space today. In *The Poetics of Space* (originally published in 1958), Gaston Bachelard, for example, argues that inside and outside "form a dialectic of division, the obvious geometry of which blinds us as soon as we bring it into play in metaphorical domains" (211). Especially when we imagine landscapes of postmodernity, boundaries are restrictive and limit the possibilities of interpretation along the lines of race, class, and gender.

The fact that space needs to be conceived as non-univocal is reflected in much of postmodern(ist) theoretical discourse. For example, in "Of Other Spaces," Michel Foucault remarks that "our epoch is one in which space takes for us the form of relations among sites" (par. 6). These sites, Foucault continues, "are irreducible to one another and absolutely not superimposable on one another" (par. 10). Foucault compares these sites, which he terms "heterotopias," to a mirror which, through the process of reflection, makes it possible for the subject to locate him/herself in a place where s/he is not. Thus, heterotopic spaces, such as the museum or the cemetery, are material spaces that simulate a reality and are both real and unreal at the same time. In *Thirdspace* (1996), Edward Soja argues along similar lines when he proposes that in the age of post-Fordism we need to formulate an alternative way of spatial thinking that allows for openness and ambiguity. More specifically, Soja believes that the rigid dualism of *firstspace* (i. e., materialized, social space) and *secondspace* (i. e., the imagined, cognitive space) has to be complemented by a third category, *thirdspace* – a composite of spaces or rather micro-spatialities, that is "filled with the products of the imagination, with political projects and utopian dreams, with both sensory and symbolic realities" (62). Accordingly, postmodern space is limitless, free of fences or bounds, which permits an intermingling of binarisms, such as mind and body, abstract and empirical, centre and periphery, or conscious and unconscious.

Marc Augé rightly ascribes this urge for a radical reconceptualization of space to our age of supermodernity, a late-capitalist world in which "people are always, and never, at home" (109) and in which "the experience [of] cultural contact has become a general phenomenon" (ibid.). In his "anthropology of supermodernity," *Non-Places* (1992; English translation 1995), he states that our everyday activities are more and more carried out in non-places, i. e., ahistorical spaces of transit such as motorways, supermarkets, airport lounges, etc., which results in the diminishing of organic social relations, as well as of the anthropological places in which they are acted out.

Although postmodernity is often associated with the privileging of space over time – this being the result of the 'spatial turn' in the humanities that took place in the 1990s – one must not ignore that the transition from modernism to postmodernism also marked far-reaching modifications concerning the perception and conception of time. In the postmodern aesthetic, temporality is no longer historical, i. e. oriented towards a utopian future, but rather redirected to the present. Future and past form a covalent bond with the present so that temporality as such becomes non-directional, non-linear, and non-singular. Fredric Jameson attributes this conception of time as "perpetual presents" (*Postmodernism* 293-294) to the loss of a sense of history that we experience in late capitalism, an era in which "our entire contemporary social system has little by little begun to lose its capacity to retain its own past" (293). Therefore, and as Walter Benjamin has already argued in the late 1930s, traditional historiography, i. e., to conceive of the past as something finished or static, must be challenged. Benjamin proposes a more dynamic model of history in which the past constantly interacts with the present: "The true picture of the past *whizzes* by. Only as a picture, which flashes its final farewell in the moment of its recognizability, is the past to be held fast" (695)[1]. Conceiving of history as a *caesura*, a sudden moment of standstill in which the 'then' merges with the 'now,' Benjamin foreshadows the temporal logic of today's augmented realities.

In recent studies of postmodernity, one can observe the trend that time and space are no longer treated as separate entities. Especially discourses on media, perception, and memory have generated the need to think of time and space as an entity. In *The Condition of Postmodernity* (1989), for example, David Harvey introduces the term "time-space compression" to denote the processes evoked by

---

[1] "Das wahre Bild der Vergangenheit huscht vorbei. Nur als Bild, das auf Nimmerwiedersehen im Augenblick seiner Erkennbarkeit eben aufblitzt, ist die Vergangenheit festzuhalten." English translation taken from: "On the Concept of History." *Marxists Internet Archive*. n.p. n.d. Web. 2 March 2010.

communication technology and global economy that cause spatial and temporal distances to shrink. Pierre Nora, to name another example, states that mass culture and globalization erased "real environments of memory" (7), which necessitates the extraction of the temporality that has taken root in the spatial. *Lieux de mémoire*, writes Nora, are places that have the power "to stop time, to block the work of forgetting [...] to immortalize death, to materialize the immaterial" (19). According to Paul Smethurst, the postmodern condition fosters a chronotopic, i. e. spatio-temporal way of thinking not only because postmodernity is always a "rewriting of modernity" (9), but also because in our contemporary world as well as in its cultural production, the loss of historicity is coupled with the loss of place, as evident, for example, in many works of historiographic metafiction.

The following three essays are, in different ways, engaged with chronotopoetics. In "Allegories of Playing," Michael Fuchs opens up the complexity of game space and explores the role of computer games as a spatial practice characteristic of the postmodern period. Drawing on Henry Lefebvre's triadic conception of space, Michael argues that game space is not only diegetic, i.e. "conceived," but also "lived" and "perceived," as the player actively engages in a virtual (social) network that communicates ideological content via an audiovisual channel. The poetics of game space, therefore, result from a constant interplay between the real and the imagined. Michael explains the heterotopic quality of game space as follows: "Using real-world experience, gaming experience, and knowledge gained (via bodily interaction) from the game in question, the player tries to decode these rules, create a mental model and then use that model to again interact with the game. Thus, the player experiences constant mediation between representational spaces and representations of space" (107). This constant mediation, Michael argues, has also become prevalent in our everyday lives in which, for example, smartphones have created 'user spaces' that no longer distinguish business from leisure, private from public, or the artificial from the real.

In "Fascination for Confusion: Discontinuous Narrative in Tarantino's *Pulp Fiction*," Cornelia Klecker reasons that with Tarantino's *œuvre* the technique of non-linear storytelling has entered contemporary Hollywood film. Expressing a postmodern temporality that deliberately subverts a chronology of events, a large number of today's mainstream films, Cornelia argues, relies on fragmentary narratives that confuse the temporal categories of present, past, and future. She aligns her hypothesis with Gianni Vattimo's argument that the era of postmodernity is marked by a devaluation of the 'new,' which entails the loss of a future-oriented temporality. In addition, she refers to Fredric Jameson, who declares the loss of historicity in the age of late capitalism that has brought forth a conception of time that only consists of "perpetual presents." Taking *Pulp Fiction* as an example, Cornelia shows how Tarantino translates these theoretical investigations onto the screen. *Pulp Fiction*'s narrative organization confuses narrative time with real time, enabling Tarantino "to kill a character without actually having him die" (125). Cornelia also detects non-linearity in the story's set of existents, e. g. in the spatial setting of Jack Rabbit Slim's, a fifties theme restaurant that makes the past revisit the present, and in the characters' obsession with time: "They try to control it by stopping time, going back and forth, expanding and shortening time, they try to predict the future, seize the present, and escape the past" (ibid.).

In the third essay of this section, "Uncanny Archi*text*ures: Reading Time, Space, and Representation in Paul Auster's *City of Glass*," Petra Eckhard applies Paul Smethurst's concept of the postmodern chronotope (literally timespace) as a tool to investigate Paul Auster's classic *City of Glass*. In particular, Petra's contribution looks at the spatio-temporal motif of the urban labyrinth, which Auster uses in order to evoke an uncanny state of mind in both protagonist and reader. Taking Sigmund Freud's influential 1919 essay "The Uncanny" as a point of departure, she argues that the uncanny has turned into a major trope of postmodernism as it structurally disrupts both the homogeneity of space and the linearity of time. In Auster's novel, New York City is conceived of as a space of psychological intraspection that allows for the protagonist's traumatic past to resurface. This constant "return of the repressed," to use the Freudian idiom, is also inscribed into the city's built structure that manifests itself, first and foremost, in an architecture of disorientation, luring the characters onto confusing paths that only lead to dead ends. Quinn, the detective-protagonist, is unable to solve his case as he loses himself in a complex web of dissociations. Stillman Sr., the man Quinn is asked to investigate, loses himself in his linguistic utopia to rebuild the biblical Tower of Babel in order to return to a pure and unified language. As time and space lose their fixed points of reference, also the ground of language and representation becomes more and more unstable, hence making impossible the arrival at a final truth or knowledge.

WORKS CITED

Augé, Marc. *Non-Places: Introduction to an Anthropology of Supermodernity*. 1992. Trans. John Howe. London: Verso, 1995. Print.

Bachelard, Gaston. *The Poetics of Space*. 1958. Boston, MA: Beacon, 1969. Print.

Benjamin, Walter. "Über den Begriff der Geschichte." 1939. *Gesammelte Schriften I*. Vol. 2. Frankfurt/Main: Suhrkamp, 1974. 691-704. Print.

Foucault, Michel. "Of Other Spaces." *Foucault, Info*. n.p. 2 Oct. 2009. Web. 5 March 2010.

Freud, Sigmund. "The Uncanny." 1919. *The Uncanny*. New York, NY: Penguin, 2003. 123-162. Print.

Harvey, David. *The Condition of Postmodernity*. 1989. Malden, MA: Blackwell, 1990. Print.

Nora, Pierre. "Between Memory and History: Les Lieux de Mémoire." *Represenations* 26 (1989): 7-25. Print.

Smethurst, Paul. *The Postmodern Chronotope: Reading Space and Time in Contemporary Fiction*. Amsterdam: Rodopi, 2000. Print.

Soja, Edward. *Thirdspace: Journeys to Los Angeles and Other Real-And-Imagined Places*. Cambridge, MA: Blackwell, 1996. Print.

Allegories of Playing: Spatial Practice in Computer Games

Michael Fuchs

Computer games[1] have been around for more than five decades and have successively been absorbed into mainstream culture since the 1980s, when arcade halls became widespread. Serious academic interest only arose during the latter part of the 1990s, but has been steadily increasing ever since. An inherently interdisciplinary field, game research is approached from various positions, among them narratology, frameworks derived from Film Studies, Cultural Studies, Computer Science, and Economics. This sheer mass of approaches has prompted Espen Aarseth to suggest that "a total of over 200 subfields and disciplines" ("Playing Research" 2) are involved in the study of computer games.

While there may not be 200 different approaches to analyze game space, a number of ways to discuss virtual space have emerged in the course of the last few years. A narratological perspective may, for example, suggest that while "[l]inear media, such as books and films can portray space either by verbal description or image, [...] only digital environments can present space that we can move through" (Murray 79). Even if this is an important observation, Janet Murray fails to explain how game spaces are actually produced and understood. Though also very much enmeshed in narratological frameworks, Marie-Laure Ryan's work uses spatial metaphors throughout in her classifications of digital narratives, thus indicating the importance of the spatial dimension in computer games.[2] Similarly, Lev Manovich links virtual space and narrative by suggesting that "movement through the game world is one of the main narrative actions" (247).[3] Ludological[4] approaches, on the other hand, tend to emphasize the aspect of simulation. However, this often goes so far that "the actual physical reality is disregarded, dismissed, abandoned" (Manovich 113), thereby making digital games perfect examples of "the generation by models of a real without origin or

---

1 I will use the term 'computer game' to denote both computer games in a traditional sense (played on a PC or Mac) as well as video games (console), arcade games, and games on mobile devices (cell phones, PDAs, etc.).

2 However, she also argues that all games are potential narratives; what about games like *Tetris* or sports games?

3 See also Jesper Juul: "Computer games are almost exclusively set in a space. This space is almost exclusively in two or three dimensions. Games are usually about navigation in this space" (46).

4 The term was suggested by Gonzalo Frasca in 1999 "to refer to the yet non-existent 'discipline that studies game and play activities'" (par. 12) (*ludus* [lat.] = game).

reality: a hyperreal" (Baudrillard 1). Using a framework indebted to Film Studies, Mark J. P. Wolf, for example, reduces spatial practice to merely formal aspects without considering the socio-cultural implications, providing a list of eleven different spatial modes in video games while completely disregarding the importance of sound design in terms of the construction of space.[5]

Already in 2001, Espen Aarseth's paper "Allegories of Space" prominently advanced the idea to apply concepts articulated in Henri Lefebvre's *The Production of Space* to digital games. As will become clear in the following, Aarseth ignores the central element of Lefebvre's framework – the social component – when he argues that "computer games are both representations of space (a formal system of relations) and representational spaces (symbolic imagery with a primarily aesthetic purpose)" (163). The application of Lefebvrian concepts to game space is not to be understood as the *ultima ratio* to approach the study of game space. Rather, it is a call for the multi-dimensionality of game space; a multi-dimensionality that should be taken into consideration when approaching the study of game space holistically.

THE PRODUCTION OF SPACE

In his seminal work *The Production of Space* (1991; originally published as *La production de l'espace* in 1974), Henri Lefebvre develops a triadic model of space that considers seemingly antithetic conceptions of spatiality in order to "discover or construct a theoretical unity between fields which are apprehended separately, just as molecular, electromagnetic and gravitational forces are in physics" (11). Lefebvre suggests that the "fields we are concerned with are, first, the *physical* – nature, the Cosmos; secondly, the *mental*, including logical and formal abstractions; and, thirdly, the *social*" (ibid.). In terms of game space, these three fields are rather clearly present: firstly, there is the physical space from which the user interacts with the fictional reality; secondly, the rules of the game, its narrative and its spatial configuration help in constructing a mental space; and thirdly, social interaction between players can be observed not only in various forms of multiplayer games – be they on- or offline – but also in social networks surrounding games (e. g. internet forums) as well as on gaming con-

5 Spatial modes according to Wolf (2002): text based; one screen contained; one screen contained (wraparound); scrolling (1 axis); scrolling (2 axes); adjacent spaces displayed one at a time; layers of independently moving planes; z-axis movement; multiple, nonadjacent spaces, displayed simultaneously; interactive 3D environment; represented or mapped spaces (what in narratology is referred to as *mise en abyme*).

ventions. While a number of approaches dealing with game space only focus on the spatial construction of the fictional space in visual terms, tackling such issues as point of view, identification, and immersion, it is all of these diverse spheres that have to be considered when discussing game space.

OF IDEAL AND REAL SPACES

In the introduction to *The Production of Space*, Lefebvre proposes that as a result of the detachment of mathematics from philosophy and metaphysics, space can only be regarded as an abstract and purely mental form. The starting points for this development are on the one hand Cartesian logic and the subjective space of mind on the other hand. Lefebvre suggests that the gap between "'ideal' space, which has to do with mental (logico-mathematical) categories" (14) and "'real' space, which is the space of social practice" (ibid.) has widened in the course of history, a gap that *The Production of Space* tries to bridge to a certain degree by describing the relationships between these logical conceptions of space and their relations to the body, perception, and social interaction. As indicated above, Lefebvre's ultimate goal is to "expose the actual production of space by bringing the various kinds of space and the modalities of their genesis together within a single theory" (16) by analyzing the production of space on various levels, from the linguistic code to sensory activity to social interaction.

Already at the very beginning of his work, Lefebvre takes a very skeptical stance toward "logico-mathematical" conceptions of space.[6] However, he is just as critical of a solely subjective space, which he deems not sufficient as a critical device since it does not account for lived space and philosophically belongs to spatial conceptions that in the end originate from language. What Lefebvre is most critical of in this context is what he terms the "illusion of transparency," which is the "presumption [...] that an encrypted reality be-comes readily decipherable thanks to the intervention first of speech and then of writing" (28), as well as the "illusion of opacity" (or the realistic illusion), according to which space is degraded to the objectified and measurable world of things. Deeply rooted in Marxist thought, Lefebvre emphasizes the status of space as a social product while being very critical of all language-centered philosophy, whose fetishization of the linguistic sign he equates with ideologically motivated assumptions. This ideology, which is "[c]losely bound up with Western 'culture',

---

[6] The relation between mentally constructed spatial conceptions and sensorially constructed ones has a history of its own, which I, however, cannot elaborate in this paper.

[...] stresses speech, and overemphasizes the written word, to the detriment of a social practice which it is indeed designed to conceal" (28).

The ideological implications of what Lefebvre calls "illusion of transparency" are characteristic of many western traditions of thought that give dominance to the sense of vision. Even if critical of the dominance of *logos*, Lefebvre refers to space as being coded and thus subject to historical trans-formation. He proposes that "[c]odes will be seen as part of a practical relationship, as part of an interaction between 'subjects' and their space and surroundings" (18). Lefebvre explains the relation of these codes to language as follows:

> The strategy of centering knowledge on discourse avoids the particularly scabrous topic of the relationship between knowledge and power. It is also incapable of supplying reflective thought with a satisfactory answer to a theoretical question that it raises itself: do sets of non-verbal signs and symbols, whether coded or not, systematized or not, fall into the same category as verbal sets, or are they rather irreducible to them? Among non-verbal signifying sets must be included music, painting, sculpture, architecture, and certainly theatre, which in addition to a text or pretext embraces gestures, masks, costume, a stage, a *mise-en-scène* – in short, a space. Non-verbal sets are thus characterized by a spatiality, which is in fact irreducible to the mental realm. [...] To underestimate, ignore and diminish space amounts to the overestimation of texts, written matter, and writing systems, along with the readable and the visible, to the point of assigning to these a monopoly on intelligibility. (62)

Though not explicitly mentioned in the quote above, computer games may well be together with media such as theater[7] listed as a "non-verbal signifying set." Much like a drama is meant to be performed on stage, so is a computer game supposed to be played and also similarly "characterized by a spatiality [...] irreducible to the mental realm." These non-verbal codes of spatiality, which are essential to the creation of game space, are generally ignored by narratological approaches. It may well be claimed that computer games are a spatial practice *par excellence*, since they operate through "non-verbal sets of spatial signs and symbols" and address bodies operating in space(s). Since computers entirely work on a symbolical level, the player is continuously confronted with symbolic spatial representation. These symbols are, however, partially rooted in mental constructs. If one accepts that spatiality in computer games is to a large degree constructed in non-verbal symbolic form, it becomes clear why Henri Lefebvre's anti-verbal approach is perfectly applicable in the context of spatiality in Game Studies. However, this is not to say that narrative and other rather language-centered aspects as well as sound design are not important in the construction of

---

7 For an early discussion of the similarities between theater and computer software (focusing on production), see Brenda Laurel's *Computers as Theatre* (Addison-Wesley, 1991).

game space, just that non-verbal elements should not be devalued because of our culture's lingophilia.

Lefebvre takes his critique of semiotic approaches one step further when he addresses architecture. He is positive that while there is a signifying practice involved, it cannot be reduced to "language or discourse, nor to the categories and concepts developed for the study of language," because "spatial work [...] attains a complexity fundamentally different from the complexity of a text, whether prose or poetry" (222). Spatial work is realized through social practice, and the "actions of a social practice are expressible but not explicable through discourse; they are, precisely, acted – and not read" (ibid.).[8]

This sphere of performance is a fundamental aspect of games in general, and computer games specifically. In the same way that space has to be practiced and experienced beyond the logic order of language, games have to be played; it is not sufficient to study their language without getting involved, without being immersed in the game space. This feature of gaming that surpasses language is addressed by Lefebvre when he states that language "possesses a practical function but it cannot harbour knowledge without masking it. The playful aspect of space escapes it, and it only emerges in play itself (by definition), in irony and humour" (211). However, this is not supposed to mean that knowledge production based on language is impossible (which would render Lefebvre's own work unnecessary), but rather underlines the difference between practice and detached examination. This playful aspect of space develops naturally from sensory input and its mental processing. Lefebvre opposes this playful and non-rational space to Cartesian space. He writes that

> narrow and desiccated rationality [...] overlooks the core and foundation of space, the total body, brain, gestures, and so forth. It forgets that space does not consist in the projection of an intellectual representation, does not arise from the visible-readable realm, but that it is first of all heard (listened to) and enacted (through physical gestures and movements). (200)

This is an important point raised by Lefebvre, since computer games are listened to and enacted through physical gestures and movements (via an interface). However, game space does also "arise from the visible-readable realm," unlike Lefebvre's claim suggests. But this does not invalidate his suggestions and their

[8] See Petra Eckhard's contribution to this volume on the idea that space, especially the city, can be read (cf. also Roland Barthes, "Semiology and Urbanism" [in *The Semiotic Challenge*]) as well as that the act of walking in the city resembles the act of reading (cf. also Michel de Certeau, "Walking the City" [in *The Cultural Studies Reader*, ed. Simon During]).

applicability to computer games, since the theses presented in *The Production of Space* attempt to understand and analyze these seemingly disparate ideas.

While the previous paragraphs may have suggested that Henri Lefebvre regards the mental and practical spheres of space as disparate, maybe even oppositional, concepts, this is not really the case. He introduces two categories to account for these dimensions: "Representations of Space" and "Representational Spaces." The former includes abstract, formal and rational conceptualizations of space linked to mathematics, philosophy, but also urban planning and engineering and is thus the domain of verbally constructed space, while the latter stands for direct practical experience of space in sensory ways and thus the non-verbal lived experience of space. In spatial practice, these two categories are not opposite, but rather operate in a dialectical relationship and are together responsible for the "production and reproduction and the particular locations and spatial sets characteristic of each social formation" (35).

THE PERCEIVED, THE CONCEIVED, AND THE LIVED

Since "[r]elations with two elements boil down to oppositions, contrasts or antagonisms" (39), Lefebvre suggests that spatial practice ought to be considered in a triadic way. In a first step, social spatial practice presupposes bodily performance, such as movement, gestures, and the use of one's senses. This is what he refers to as "perceived space," which is "[t]he practical basis of the perception of the outside world, to put it in psychology's terms" (40). In a second step, conceptualizations of both space and the body moving in space are influenced by scientific representations of space and the body, respectively. These scientific representations, on the other hand, are subject to ideological forces and constantly change and evolve. Lefebvre calls this sphere the "conceived space." In the final step, the "lived space" is constantly informed by the two former dimensions and is thus a product of cultural conventions.

Game space is a cultural product that is constructed on the basis of spaces created through the use of verbal signs or language (narrative spaces), but it is equally based on the user's bodily involvement (input) and non-verbal signifying practices (representational spaces). As such, all three of the dimensions listed by Lefebvre are constantly present in computer games and inform one another on a continuous basis. Firstly, diegetic game space is surrounded by various discourses on computer gaming. Within these discourses, certain expectations as to how 'reality' is to be represented in a game and how to move in a game world are interactively created. This social dimension of game space is closely connected to Lefebvre's "perceived space." The narrative space constructed via verbal, visual, and sonic elements as well as the rules pertaining to a given game make up the "conceived space" of computer gaming. Finally, the interface via which the player interacts with the game allows for bodily action, to actually 'live' the game – "lived space." What is especially interesting in the context of game space is how the relationship between these three different modalities of space can be addressed. Lefebvre defines the relationships of spatial practice as follows:

> The object of knowledge is, precisely, the fragmented and uncertain connection between elaborated representations of space on the one hand and representational spaces (along with their underpinnings) on the other; and this 'object' implies (and explains) a subject – that subject in whom lived, perceived and conceived (known) come together within a spatial practice. (230)

Thus, if only representations of space are considered when studying spatial practice, lived experience and thus the actual processes of spatial creation are excluded. In other words, it is important to consider all the cultural processes that influence the creation, maintenance, and experience of cultural artifacts. This again underscores that a holistic approach to game space must not only take formal aspects of spatial representation into account but also – and maybe even more importantly – the creation and experience of it. Since "[s]pace is not a thing but rather a set of relations between things" (83), academic inquiry has to primarily focus on the relations between the individual objects of the system rather than an individual, isolated element (such as the visual construction of the narrative space) of the system. If one accepts the production of space as a process, one cannot begin its investigation by studying the outcome.

> In Lefebvre's hand, space becomes redescribed not as a dead inert thing or object, but as organic and fluid and alive; it has a pulse, it palpitates, it flows and it collides with other spaces. And these interpenetrations – many with different temporalities get superimposed upon one another to create a present space. (Merrifield 171)

The core problem, however, is to "[g]et back from the object to the activity that produced and/or created it" (113). It is in this context that Lefebvre's roots in Marxist thought come into full force. Just as Marx, in his analysis of "commodity fetishism" in Volume One of *Capital*, strips commodities of their cultural mask, so does Lefebvre try to unmask the hidden social forces operating in the production of space in capitalist societies.

In the context of game space, this analysis is important in that it emphasizes that particular spaces generated by computer games are the result of dynamic processes which include countless elements, the most important of which are the player's interaction, auditory and visual components, and the rules of the game. On first glance, the fact that games are finite products seemingly validates an approach that solely investigates auditory and/or visual and/or linguistic elements; but according to Marxist thought, it is precisely because games *appear* as coherent and finished entities, erasing most of the references to their production, that the genesis of such a cultural product has to be critically examined. This is also the point where interdependences between socio-cultural spatial constructs and bodily perception of space come into play, because if space is assumed to be a social practice that is influenced both by sensory perception and logico-linguistic conceptions of space, there is an implicit dialectic process at work.[9] Taking this idea one step further, games – as products of spatial practice – re-enter the production cycle of spatial practice by again influencing said practice. In other words, if you play an online role playing game (the product of spatial practice) for the first time, both the actual space of the diegetic game space and the virtual social space that is shared with the other players are integrated into your conceptualization of space. Thus, computer games, as spatial products, not only serve to illustrate contemporary ideas of space, but influence these very ideas as well and thus reconfigure representational spaces.

SPATIAL PRACTICE IN POSTMODERN SOCIETY

According to Lefebvre, spatial practice in postmodern society is characterized by "a close association, within perceived space, between daily reality (daily routine) and urban reality (the routes and networks which links up the places set aside for work, 'private' life and leisure" (38). The role of computer games is thus telling of spatial practice in contemporary times. Owing to the technological advancements of the past few years, the borderlines between leisure and work have blurred. Computer games are today not only played on the same physical device as work is done – be that a(n) (HT)PC, PDA, cell, or even smartphone – but also at the same physical location. If you want to succeed in today's corporate reality, you are expected to be available 24/7/365 via cell phone or e-mail, using the same devices you use for recreational purposes. On another level, online games and the online services of next (which by now should have turned into current) generation video game consoles have brought about new ways of making money. In *Second Life*, for example, users can go on virtual shopping sprees and buy virtual items ranging from real estate over great works of literature (e. g. the Folio of Shakespeare's Complete Works) to TV sets that offer

[9] "The spatial practice of a society secretes that society's space; it propounds it, in a dialectical interaction; it produces it slowly and surely as it masters and appropriates it" (38).

Illustration 1: A MediaViewer available at XLStreet, a *Second Life* webshop, which allows the player to watch streams from *YouTube*, *DailyMotion*, *PornRabbit*, etc. in the diegetic world; price: 495 Linden-$, which amounts to ca. US-$ 2.20

YouTube clips for real money. Xbox Live, similarly, offers its users additional outfits for their avatars in exchange for Microsoft Points (1 US-$ = ca. 80 MS Points) and some game producers even allow players to unlock cheats for money (e. g. *Madden NFL 10*). Also, players often sell both high-level characters and virtual items (e. g. on eBay), thus transforming the act of playing into paid labor, as exemplified in September 2007, when a character for the online game *World of Warcraft* was purportedly sold for ca. 7,000 Euros, since the player who had created and developed the character had no job (cf. Jimenez par. 1 and 5).[10] Most prominently, however, contemporary spatial practice is highly influenced by all the non-verbal symbols that various graphical user interfaces (GUI) use; be that Windows, the GUI of a mobile phone, or – to a lesser extent – the GUI of a computer game. These interfaces are used by millions on a daily basis and deploy spatial metaphors. Thus, they are prime examples of representational spaces, spaces that are directly (or at least as close to directly as possible) accessible through images and symbols.

While representational spaces play an important role in the construction of game space, one should not forget that, from another point of view, it is representations of space that take a dominant role. It is during game design that abstract conceptualizations of space come into play. Rules that define spatial movement in the diegetic reality belong to this category. Using real-world expe-

---

[10] See e. g. Edward Castronova's *Synthetic Worlds: The Business and Culture of Online Games* (2005, Univ. of Chicago Press) for a detailed account on the economics of online gaming.

rience, gaming experience, and knowledge gained (via bodily interaction) from the game in question, the player tries to decode these rules, create a mental model and then use that model to again interact with the game. Thus, the player experiences a constant mediation between representational spaces and representations of space, which makes up the spatial practice of computer games. The interesting question, now, is how these mediations develop. According to Lefebvre, in

> theatrical space, with its interplay between fictitious and real counterparts and its interaction between gazes and mirages in which actor, audience, 'characters', text, and author all come together but never become one. By means of such theatrical interplay bodies are able to pass from a 'real', immediately experienced space (the pit, the stage) to a perceived space – a third space which is no longer scenic or public. At once fictitious and real, this third space is classical theatre space. (83)

He continues:

> [t]heatrical space certainly implies a representation of space – scenic space – corresponding to a particular conception of space [...]. The representational space, mediated yet directly experienced, which infuses the work and the moment, is established as such through the dramatic action itself. (188)

For game space, this means that the spatial practice that surrounds computer games is informed by spatial modalities of the sphere "representations of space," e. g. rules of spatial movement in the diegetic world, and "directly experienced" as well as actively constructed "representational spaces."

CONCLUSION

Henri Lefebvre's study is particularly useful for a holistic investigation of game space, since his detailed analysis of various spatial modalities and the numerous interdependencies between them, which result in a socio-historically influenced social practice, provides a new perspective on an issue that is generally approached narratologically, formally, or by tackling issues of identification and interaction (strongly influenced by Film Studies). To exemplify, the spatial practice of a contemporary first person shooter, such as *Call of Duty: World at War*, may be outlined as follows: the player is located at a certain physical space (spatial modality$_1$) from which s/he controls via an interface that interprets bodily

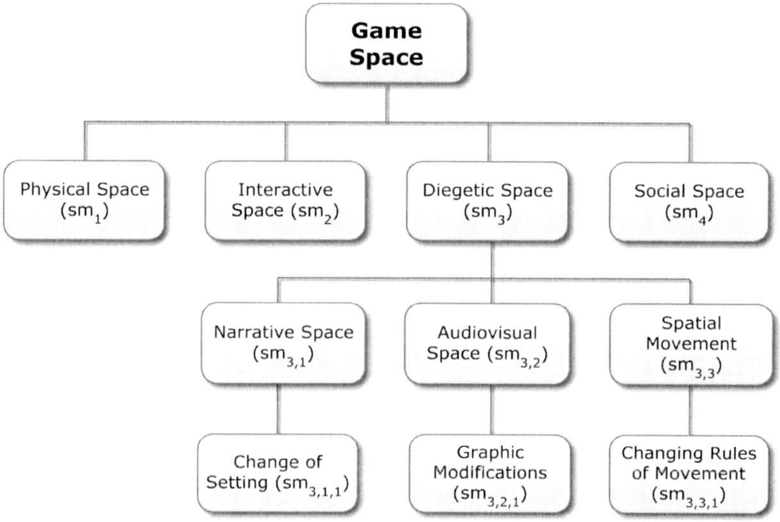

Illustration 2: Conceptualization of Game Space[11]

action (sm_2 – interactive space) a player character situated in a certain diegetic space (sm_3). This diegetic space, then, is composed of a certain narrative space ($sm_{3,1}$; in the case of *CoD: WaW*, it is the initial battles of WWII in the Pacific and Eastern Europe during which Nazi Germany and Japan have to be defeated in order to advance the plot), the audiovisual space that helps represent a 'realistic' world ($sm_{3,2}$), and rules that define spatial movement within the diegetic reality ($sm_{3,3}$). Furthermore, the game can be played online, a social space (sm_4). In some games, there are additional modifications available that e. g. change the setting of the action ($sm_{3,1,1}$) or introduce a sort of 'moon' mode that changes rules of gravity ($sm_{3,3,1}$). It is impossible to deny that it is the sum total of these interrelated elements that constructs game space, and each of the individual elements has to be accounted for in their specific way. Furthermore, it is crucial to bear in mind that computer games are not only virtual and imaginary spaces, since the digitally constructed diegetic game spaces interact with what we perceive as real spaces. After all, what we perceive as real space is the result of the "sympathetic deconstruction and heuristic reconstruction" (Soja 81) of the real-imaginary duality.

---

11 This is only a limited conceptualization, since especially the third level ($sm_{3,x,1}$) can take a myriad of forms and third-level-modifications may even be again modified, adding a fourth level.

Illustration 3: Screenshot from *Call of Duty: World at War* visualizing the narrative space

WORKS CITED

Aarseth, Espen J. "Allegories of Space: The Question of Spatiality in Computer Games." *Cybertext Yearbook 2000*. Eds. Markku Eskelinen and Raine Koskimaa. Saariharvi, Finland: Research Centre for Contemporary Culture, 2001. 152-171. Print.

—. "Playing Research: Methodological Approaches to Game Analysis." *Melbourne DAC – the 5th International Digital Arts and Culture Conference*. School of Applied Communication, Melbourne, 2003. Online. 10 March 2010.

Baudrillard, Jean. *Simulacra and Simulations*. 1981. Trans. Sheila Faria Glaser. Ann Arbor, MI: U of Michigan P, 1994. Print.

Call of Duty: World at War. v1.5. Treyarch. Activision, 2008. Windows. Computer Game.

Frasca, Gonzalo. "Ludology Meets Narratology: Similitude and Differences Between (Video)Games and Narrative." *ludology.org*, 1993. Online.

Jimenez, Cristina. "The High Cost of Playing Warcraft." *BBC News Technology*. BBC News, 24 September 2007. Online. 15 October 2009.

Juul, Jeesper. "A Clash Between Game and Narrative." *JeesperJuul.net*, 1999. Online.

Lefebvre, Henri. *The Production of Space*. 1974. Trans. Donald Nicholson-Smith. Malden, MA: Blackwell, 1991. Print.

Madden NFL 10. v1.00. EA Tiburon. EA Sports, 2009. Xbox 360. Video Game.

Manovich, Lev. *The Language of New Media*. Cambridge, MA: MIT P, 2002. Print.

Merrifield, Andy. "Henri Lefebvre: A Socialist in Space." *Thinking Space*. Eds. Mike Crang and Nigel Thrift. New York, NY: Routledge, 2000. 167-182. Print.

Murray, Janet. *Hamlet on the Holodeck: The Future of Narrative in Cyberspace*. Cambridge, MA: MIT P, 1998. Print.

Ryan, Marie-Laure. *Narrative as Virtual Reality: Immersion and Interactivity in Literature and Electronic Media*. New Edition. Baltimore, MD: Johns Hopkins UP, 2003. Print.

Second Life. v1.23.4. Linden Lab, 2003. Windows. Computer Game.

Soja, Edward. *Thirdspace: Journeys to Los Angeles and Other Real-and-Imagined Places*. Oxford, MA: Basil Blackwell, 1996. Print.

Wolf, Mark J. P. "Space in the Video Game." *The Medium of the Video Game*. Ed. Mark J. P. Wolf. Austin, TX: U of Texas P, 2002. 51-76. Print.

Fascination for Confusion: Discontinuous Narrative in Tarantino's *Pulp Fiction*

Cornelia Klecker

> Luckily, it's been well-established that time is not a fixed concept.
>
> Dr. Gregory House in *House M.D.*

In recent decades, 'postmodernism' has become an extremely dubious term which theorists have used extensively and defined in countless, often contradictory ways. One typical aspect that most scholars will, in fact, agree on is its fusion of highbrow and lowbrow art. Long gone seems the clear-cut distinction between 'proper' bourgeois art and popular culture. Some theorists, such as Theodor Adorno and Fredric Jameson, lament this development as a devaluation of art in its very essence; others, such as Walter Benjamin and Jürgen Habermas, appreciate it as democratization. Positive attitude or not, the fact remains that in the postmodern era many formerly avant-garde techniques have become mainstream and previously highly intellectual discourses have been included in popular art.

When we look at the contemporary landscape of popular film, it is remarkable how prominent non-linear plots have become. These narratives deliberately circumvent a chronological order and defy a linear structure of cause and effect. Often, it appears that stories are cut up into fragments and edited together in a seemingly arbitrary order. The decisive difference to the use of time shifts as found in classical Hollywood narrative is that the films this paper is concerned with do neither motivate these jumps in time with, for instance, distinctly marked flashbacks (e. g. by dissolves or shifts to black and white) nor clearly indicate them with, for example, voiceovers and inserts (such as 'Two Days Later,' 'Three Weeks Earlier'). All segments are presented in the narrative Now.

Since the mid-nineties, these discontinuous narratives have drawn large audiences into movie theaters. Mainstream seemed to have embraced these new techniques.[1] The prime example is Quentin Tarantino's *Pulp Fiction* (1994), which has been pinpointed the film that 'caused' the break in the movie industry.

---

[1] With 'mainstream' I mostly refer to Hollywood film, even if I have a rather broad definition of 'Hollywood,' similar to that of David Bordwell. Some of the key features, which can be freely combined, are that these films are produced and/or distributed by the major studios or their subsidiaries, have economic success, feature famous actors or directors, or are nominated by the Academy of Motion Picture Arts and Science (cf. Bordwell 17-18).

Out of nowhere came a film that defied the most basic Hollywood conventions and, nonetheless, was a huge box-office success. Many other similarly narrated films followed. Steven Soderbergh seems particularly interested in this narrative technique, as exemplified in *The Limey* (1999) and his Hollywood breakthrough *Out of Sight* (1998). Continuity but in reverse, in other words, backward narration, is a defining feature of Christopher Nolan's *Memento* (2001) and Gaspar Noé's *Irréversible* (2002). Michel Gondry's *Eternal Sunshine of the Spotless Mind* (2004) and Marc Forster's *Stay* (2006) demonstrate narrative disintegration motivated by the fact that some parts of or even the entire story takes place inside the protagonist's head. Innumerable other films with alternative plot structures could be named.

The question raised now is how non-linear narrative in popular film can be ascribed to postmodernism. Fragmented narrative structures as such are, of course, not a novelty. Variations of discontinuous narrative have been used throughout literary history. It can be traced back all the way to Homer's *Odyssey* and found as a dominant device in the modernist novel (compare at the time groundbreaking works such as James Joyce's *Ulysses* [1922] and Virginia Woolf's *Mrs. Dalloway* [1925]). Film history, too, offers many examples of alternative narrative techniques. The surrealists Luis Buñuel and Salvador Dalí, for instance, created fragmented masterpieces with *Un chien andalou* as well as *L'âge d'or* in 1929 and 1930, respectively. Similarly, the French filmmakers Alain Resnais, with films such as *Hiroshima, mon amour* (1959) and *L'année dernière à Marienbad* (1961), and Jean-Luc Godard, with movies such as *À bout de souffle* (1960), openly defied any kind of film convention. Nowadays, as mentioned above, not even Hollywood films necessarily adhere to their own rules. In other words, formerly avant-garde techniques have become mainstream.

Approaching the matter from a different angle, these films address a previously highly intellectual and 'elitist' issue on a popular and wide-ranging basis. Non-linear narrative magnificently reflects the postmodern concept of time. In order to make that argument clear, I have to elaborate on the postmodern perception of time. In 1979, the French philosopher and literary theorist Jean-François Lyotard published *The Postmodern Condition: A Report on Knowledge* in which he postulates the end of the great meta-narratives that dominated modernity. The downfall of these meta-narratives that used to be the source of all modern knowledge provided the basis for postmodern plurality. Many other theorists, even though they never labeled themselves postmodernists, such as Michel Foucault, Jacques Derrida, and Gilles Deleuze, used Lyotard's account of postmodernism as a platform for their own work. Polemically put, this downfall of the great narratives gave way to alternative ways of telling a story, to narrative structures that, as I would like to argue in this essay, are heavily influenced by this and other postmodern concepts.

POSTMODERN TEMPORALITY

Henri Bergson (with his concept of *dureé*) and Martin Heidegger (most notably with his elaborations in *Being and Time*), among others, provided the philosophical foundations for non-linear time models within which time cannot be simply divided into the three dimensions of past, present, and future. Rather, non-linearity, fragmentation, and the perpetual present have become the dominant markers of the postmodern conception of time. In *The End of Modernity*, Gianni Vattimo establishes a time model that is heavily influenced by Friedrich Nietzsche's concept of the eternal return of the Same (*ewige Wiederkehr des Gleichen*), elaborated in *Thus Spoke Zarathustra*. Vattimo uses the terms modernity and postmodernity to describe two epochs whose core distinguishing feature is the way society perceives progress. One of the main characteristics of modernity is the metaphysical paradigm of progress, i. e., being new is equated with being valid. In Vattimo's words, "modernity is that era in which being modern becomes a value, or rather, it becomes the fundamental value to which all other values refer" (*End of Modernity* 99). Secularization is the key word to describe modernity, since it explains the nature of the value that dominates this era. Religious belief is replaced by "faith in progress – which is both a secularized faith and a faith in secularization" (*End of Modernity* 100). The very notion of progress has been secularized and thus, Vattimo concludes that

> [f]or Christianity, history appears as the history of salvation; it then becomes the search for a worldly condition of perfection, before turning, little by little, into the history of progress. But the ideal of progress is finally revealed to be a hollow one, since its ultimate value is to create conditions in which further progress is possible in a guise that is always new. By depriving progress of a final destination, secularization dissolves the very notion of progress itself, as happens in nineteenth- and twentieth-century culture. (*End of Modernity* 7-8)

In other words, in the age of modernity, the 'new' becomes the central value because any kind of progressive movement lacks a final goal. Instead, progress is a development that merely leads anew to a state from which further progress is possible. In postmodernity then, the idea of progress has finally become completely obsolete; it is the period of postmetaphysics. In his essay "Die Säkularisierung des Fortschritts" ("The Secularization of Progress"), the German philosopher and sociologist Arnold Gehlen describes the experience of postmodernity as *post histoire* (or post-history). The long-standing succession of the new leads to habituation, and as a result, progress is perceived as routine. Nowadays, we need to be swamped with novelties in order to have the feeling that everything stays the same. Postmodernity is the era of the dissolution of the notion of progress. Gehlen detects a correlation in terms of ahistoricity between this dissolution and many utopian ideologies:

> Where we effectively try to make the new man, our relationship with history also changes. This happens usually by the victorious party of the advanced, which digs off the roots of the old-established powers in order to declare their own lack of history as principle for the entire society. The French revolutionaries called 1793 the year One of a new era [...]. (408; my translation)[2]

Gehlen finds a prime example in Sebastien Mercier's 1770 novel *L'an 2240*, a Rousseauian utopia in which everything is paid immediately in cash and no extinct languages are studied (408-409). As Gianni Vattimo explains, "[t]he suppression of all credit and classical languages emblematically embodies a reduction of existence to the naked present, that is, the elimination of any historical dimension" (*End of Modernity* 104). Krzystztof Pomian argues along similar lines. As Vattimo points out, Pomian characterizes modernity as a futuristic era and, parallel to Mercier's novel, explains that "the future is, literally, injected into the very texture of the present in the form of paper money [...]. The history of more than two thousand years of monetarization of the economy is also the history of a growing dependence of the present on the future" (qtd. in Vattimo, *End of Modernity* 105[3]). According to Vattimo, postmodernity is characterized by a crisis of the new and a crisis of the value of the future, two notions that are also manifested in any kind of art, from architecture to literature. Postmodern art's main aim is to rid itself of rationality, the notions of innovation and overcoming the past, and the need for progress and development (Vattimo, *End of Modernity* 105). Such a crisis of the future unavoidably alters our perception of time and history. Thus, Vattimo seems hardly surprised that many landmark works of the twentieth century, such as the already mentioned *Ulysses*, but also *Finnegans Wake* by James Joyce (1939), Robert Musil's *Der Mann ohne Eigenschaften* (*The Man Without Qualities*; 1930-1943), and Marcel Proust's *À la recherche du temps perdu* (*In Search of Lost Time*; 1913-1927), focus on the aspect of time on a contextual as well as on a structural level and defy seemingly naturalized tem-

---

[2] "Wo man nun wirklich versucht, den neuen Menschen zu schaffen, dort ändert sich das Verhältnis zur Geschichte. Dies geschieht meist so, daß die siegreiche Fortschrittsgruppe die Wurzeln der altetablierten Herrschaftsmächte abgräbt und ihre eigene Geschichtslosigkeit zum Prinzip der Gesellschaft ausruft. Die französische Revolutionäre ernannten das Jahr 1793 zum Jahr 1 eines neuen Weltalters [...]."

[3] Translated from K. Pomina, "The Crisis of the Future," published in Italian ("La crisi dell'avvenire") in *Le frontier del tempo*, ed. R. Romano. Milan: Il Saggiatore, 1981. 102.

poral linearity. In Vattimo's words, "[s]uch a crisis [of the future and the new], obviously, implies a radical change in our way of experiencing history and time, as is somewhat obscurely anticipated by Nietzsche in his 'doctrine' of the eternal return of the Same" (*End of Modernity* 106-107).

According to Gianni Vattimo, the appreciation of 'the new' is the basis for the linear and rather future-oriented perception of time during modernity. In the metaphysical concept of time, every present moment points beyond itself towards a *telos* from which this moment can be considered meaningful. In this sense, we can see modernity as the epoch during which the valuation of the new manifests the general metaphysical time structure. Postmodernity, on the other hand, is the epoch during which the new has lost its value. As a consequence, the metaphysical concept of time loses its future point of reference that used to guarantee the meaningfulness of the present. With the end of the appreciation of the new, i. e., the future, the meaning of the term 'time' changes as well. The idea that time is a movement from the past over the present towards the future, that time is always directed towards the future, was based on the implicit equation of the new, i. e., the future, with value. Due to the suspension of the metaphysical or modern valuation of the new, the whole idea of the future disappears, which, in turn, causes the metaphysical concept of time to collapse (Weiß 49-51).

Since the metaphysical conception of time ceased to be valid, the question remains what the postmetaphysical time structure, i. e., the one dominant in the postmodern epoch, looks like. As Gianni Vattimo sees postmodernity emerge with Nietzsche's work, he finds an alternative concept of time in Nietzsche's eternal return of the same events in which the three distinct segments of time, namely past, present, and future, lose their traditional connotation. Vattimo dedicates a whole chapter of his book *Il Soggetto e la Maschera* to this particular issue. In *Thus Spoke Zarathustra*, to be more precise in the chapter "On the Vision and Riddle," Nietzsche recounts how Zarathustra arrives at the gateway "This moment" ("Augenblick"), where the two never-ending paths past and future meet. Facing the gateway, the dwarf, who has been accompanying Zarathustra, asks him whether those two roads contradict each other or whether they would form a circle. Zarathustra's assumption that the latter is true finds the dwarf's agreement. He explains, "All that is straight lies [...]. All truth is crooked; time itself is a circle" (Nietzsche 136). Vattimo comments on this matter as follows:

> Not only must everything that will be have already walked along the path of the past, since its path lasts an eternity and, thus, it must have seen all that can be; but also the gateway itself that signifies the present moment has to have been there always. And if the paths of past and future are, indeed, crooked, does not the present moment drag all things behind itself? *Thus* – also itself? Past and future unite in a circle whose dizzying characteristic is that it also contains the present moment it-

> self, which, previously, seemed to be a privileged moment in this circle. The present moment itself has always been and in this 'having-been' it brings about all future things, even its own future happening. (*Il Soggetto e la Maschera* 200; my translation)[4]

The metaphysical time model becomes invalid with this belief in the eternal return of the same events. If every moment has always been there and is always going to be there, a concept of time structured into past, present, and future is not applicable any longer. Every present moment is, at the same time, its own past, i. e., its source and its own future, i. e., its own *telos* (Weiß 52).

Since modernity is the era defined by the appreciation of the new and a constant overcoming of the past, this critical overcoming cannot be a way out of modernity. Nietzsche's concept of the eternal return marks the end of this era, as it makes linear progress impossible. Being ceases to be reduced to novelty, as it was, for instance, in avant-garde movements of the first half of the twentieth century (cf. Vattimo, *The End of Modernity* 166-168). This abandonment of a linear time model results in an altered sense of history. In Vattimo's words: "It is very likely that the idea of thought's progress and emancipation through 'critical overcoming' is closely related to a linear conception of history; when critical overcoming is 'distorted' [...], history itself can no longer appear in a linear light" (*The End of Modernity* 180). The way Nietzsche suggests and Vattimo interprets it, time is not a straight line that signifies a movement from the past over the present to the future, but is a circle. This abandonment of linearity results in a breakdown of the distinct notions of past and future. Consequently, the focus inevitably lies on the present. As Joan Stambaugh explains: "Nietzsche's thought of eternal recurrence [...] transcends ordinary, everyday conceptions of space and time. [...] [P]ast and future meet in the general gateway of the present moment; all time and space come to presence in the *eternal present moment*" (Stambaugh 125; my emphasis).

This notion parallels the idea of the perpetual present that other theorists, among them Fredric Jameson, associate with postmodernity. He believes that

---

4 I have to thank my colleague Johannes Mahlknecht for aiding me in the translation from the Italian original. "Non solo tutto ciò che diviene deve aver già percorso almeno una volta la via del passato, dato che essa dura un'intera eternità e deve già aver visto realizzarsi, per questo, tutte le possibilità; ma, soprattutto, anche la porta stessa, che rappresenta l'attimo presente, deve già esser stata. E se le vie del passato e del futuro sono davvero curve, l'attimo presente non trae dietro di sè tutte le cose avvenire? Dunque – anche se stesso? –. Passato e futuro si saldano in un circolo, la cui vertiginosità estrema consiste nel fatto che anche l'attimo, che potrebbe parere un momento privilegiato in tale circolarità, vi è invece radicalmente compreso: esso è già eternamente stato e, in questo suo esser già stato, porta già con sé tutte le cose avvenire, compreso il proprio accadere 'futuro'."

one of the main features of postmodernism is the "fragmentation of time into a series of perpetual presents" ("Consumer Society" 28). According to Jameson, the chief reason for this altered perception of time during postmodernity is the "disappearance of a sense of history" (ibid.) triggered by the emergence of a late consumer or multinational capitalism. Similar to Vattimo, who declares "the end of history" (*The End of Modernity* 4) during post-modernity, Jameson believes that our contemporary society has lost its capacity to perceive its own past. Due to modern technologies, most significantly various types of media, we are exposed to a perpetual change that makes it virtually impossible for us to keep traditions of the sort that help us retain our history. Especially the media exploitation of the news seems to function as a means to wipe out immediacy, to transfer recent historical experiences as quickly as possible into the past, and thus to make us forget. In Jameson's words, the "informational function of the media would be [...] to serve as the very agents and mechanisms for our historical amnesia" ("Consumer Society" 28). Vattimo agrees when he says that contemporary history is "the history of that era in which, thanks to the use of new means of communication (especially television), everything tends to flatten out at the level of contemporaneity and simultaneity, thus producing a de-historization of experience" (*End of Modernity* 10). The postmodern perception of time is defined by a loss of a sense of history. Due to the disappearance of the historical referent, all one is left with is 'pop history,' i. e., a form of art which no longer represents and, in a sense, reconstructs the actual past that once was a real present, but merely portrays collective ideas and clichés of that past. In contemporary times, people are swamped and overwhelmed by innumerable artificially reproduced records, such as photographs and film footage, so that they find themselves "condemned to seek History by way of [their] own pop images and simulacra of that history, which itself remains out of reach" (*Postmodernism* 25). Jameson speaks of a "crisis in historicity" (ibid.) that will eventually lead or has already led anew to the question of the general organization of time and temporality within a culture that is profoundly dominated by space and spatial logic. The problem nowadays is that

> [if], indeed, the subject has lost its capacity actively to extend its pro-tensions and re-tensions across the temporal manifold and to organize its past and future into coherent experience, it becomes difficult enough to see how the cultural productions of such a subject could result in anything but 'heaps of fragments' and in a practice of the randomly heterogeneous and fragmentary and of the aleatory. These are, however, precisely some of the privileged terms in which postmodernist cultural production has been analyzed. (ibid.)

The narrative structure of the movies mentioned in the introduction is made up of exactly these "heaps of fragments" that have inevitably become the only means of expressing the sense of time in a postmodern world.

PULP FICTION

> Action is discontinuous, like every pulsation of life.
>
> Henri Bergson

> I'm curt with you because time is a factor.
>
> Winston Woolf in *Pulp Fiction*

In 1992, independent film director Quentin Tarantino released his first film, *Reservoir Dogs*. The film's plot, which rather attracted famous actors than it appealed to the audience at the time, was Tarantino's first step in completely turning around the Hollywood blockbuster scene. Already in *Reservoir Dogs* he employed an elaborate narrative structure that toys with time and consciously avoids continuity. The film is about the preparations as well as the aftermath of an attempted robbery, but the heist itself is never shown. Unlike the traditional gangster film, *Reservoir Dogs* is extremely character-driven and focuses only very little on the action. The importance that is placed on the individual characters also, at least partly, explains the plot structure. The film starts shortly before a robbery. A group of gangsters is sitting in a diner talking over some food. Next, the audience sees two of the criminals, one of them severely injured, riding in a car towards their secret meeting place, an empty warehouse, where most of the story takes place. The rest of the film is divided into several episodes, each of which is 'dedicated' to one character and marked by a black insert in which the character's name is inscribed in white letters. After these inserts, the film jumps back in time to the 'job interviews' of the respective characters. After these segments, Tarantino cuts back to the warehouse where the criminals try to figure out what went wrong and, most importantly, who had betrayed them. These conversations trigger off some flashbacks through which the viewers learn more about the robbery and the fate of some of the minor characters. Eventually, the rat is identified, and most people get killed as the film comes to an end.

Structuring the plot according to characters rather than along a linear storyline was Tarantino's first and very successful attempt at consciously avoiding chronology and thus defying traditional film grammar. Only two years later, in 1994, Tarantino's second production, *Pulp Fiction*, hit not only theaters worldwide but also the hearts of an extraordinary number of moviegoers and film critics alike. With over one hundred million dollars at the American box office and over two hundred million worldwide, as well as seven Academy Award nominations (Best Movie, Best Director, Best Actor in a Leading Role, and Best Actor in a Supporting Role among them), the Oscar for Best Original Screenplay, and the Palme D'Or at the Film Festival in Cannes, it was the surprise hit of the year. At the time, nobody would have thought that a film that overtly defied traditional Hollywood film grammar (and only cost about eight million dollars) could turn into a crowd-and-critics pleaser and a financial success. But *Pulp Fiction* was more than just a money-maker: The hype around the film has completely changed the Hollywood scene; the film and its director have turned into cults of their own. What made *Pulp Fiction* such an unusual film was its discontinuous narrative structure. Never before had a film with mainstream appeal employed a narrative technique usually only drawn on in the European avant-garde. At a first glance, *Pulp Fiction* appears to be a rather traditional episodic film. Different stories about various characters are told in fragmented sequences, and only eventually one does find out how all these people and events are interrelated. However, this movie differs from conventional films in that the timeline is cut up and rearranged seemingly arbitrarily, i. e., irrespective of a proper chronological order. Basically, the plot is divided into a prologue, an introduction, and three 'chapters' which are visually marked with black inserts and white letters saying "Vincent Vega and Marsellus's wife," "The Gold Watch," and "The Bonny Situation," respectively. Within these episodes, the stories are told chronologically; it is only the arrangement of the chapters themselves that really toys with time.

The most obvious deviation from traditional narrative is that in *Pulp Fiction* the plot is circular. The film starts in the same location and roughly at the same time as it ends and does so without using an extended flashback. *Pulp Fiction* starts 'cold,' i. e., without main titles. In the prologue, two minor characters, Honey Bunny (Amanda Plummer) and Pumpkin (Tim Roth), are introduced, but they will not appear on the screen again until the last sequence of the film. After the main titles, featuring the widely recognized *Pulp Fiction* theme, the two main characters Vincent Vega (John Travolta), who is the only one appearing in all chapters, and Jules Winnfield (Samuel L. Jackson), who appears in all but one chapter of the film, are introduced, and the audience is immediately familiarized with their very distinct personalities. The scene in the car in which Vincent and Jules keep waffling about rather irrelevant things and the next sequence in Brett's apartment that shows the first very bloody murder literally serve as introductory segments of the whole film. It foreshadows the thematic focus of the movie – senseless dialogues and violence. Next, the first proper episode of the film, "Vincent Vega and Marsellus's Wife," begins. Interestingly enough, Butch Coolidge (Bruce Willis), the third main character and protagonist of the following episode, is introduced already at the beginning of this part, even though he does not play an important role yet. The story of Vincent and Mia Wallace, Marsellus's wife (Uma Thurman), who will not be seen again during the rest of the film, starts out as an innocent dinner at a restaurant but is then overshadowed by heavy drug abuse. After that, the film cuts back to Butch, or rather a dream about his childhood. He wakes up, and only then the next episode, "The Gold Watch," starts. As mentioned above, Butch is the protagonist, and Marsellus (Ving Rhames) could be considered his antagonist, even though the real villains are the pawnshop owner and his friend Zed. In this section, Butch is established as a hero saving his enemy from sexual abuse and torture but, most importantly, he also kills the hero, or antihero, of the film, namely Vincent Vega. This fact is easily forgotten, since he disappears until the last section, "The Bonny Situation," where he suddenly reappears. The audience witnesses the murder in Brett's apartment for the second time, but this time they also find out what happened afterwards. Jules believes he has witnessed a miracle, and Vincent accidentally shoots a boy in their car. Another character, the Wolf (Harvey Keitel), helps them out of this mess, and Vincent and Jules decide to have breakfast at a diner. The viewers soon learn that it is the very same diner that Honey Bunny and Pumpkin are about to rob. Newly-converted and thus peaceful, Jules manages to talk them out of it and the film ends with him and Vincent leaving the diner. The end credits roll.

As mentioned before, the plot of *Pulp Fiction* is structured according to characters rather than chronology, which accounts for the fact that there are radical shifts in time on the one hand and, potentially more importantly, repetition and simultaneity on the other. If one wanted to sum up the story, that is, the events in chronological order, of *Pulp Fiction*, here is what happens: Vincent and Jules set out to retrieve a briefcase for their boss Marsellus in the morning. They kill three boys and take another hostage, whom Vincent accidentally shoots in a car. Another professional criminal, the Wolf, helps them out of this predicament. Afterwards Jules and Vincent have breakfast at a diner and Jules decides to quit his criminal career. Suddenly, Honey Bunny and Pumpkin draw their weapons and want to rob the place. However, Jules talks them out of it. In the evening of the following day, Vincent takes out Mia, who almost overdoses. On a Wednesday night, Butch wins a boxing fight, which he was bribed to lose, and returns to his girlfriend Fabienne (Maria de Medeiros). The next morning, Butch goes back to his apartment to retrieve his father's gold watch. He shoots Vincent and on his way back is spotted by Marsellus. Butch and Marsellus are captured by a pawnshop owner; Butch manages to break free and save Marsellus, returns to Fabienne, and Butch and Fabienne take off.

Quentin Tarantino goes to great lengths to emphasize time and location. One gimmick he uses is simply repeating a scene, or parts of it, as is the case with Jules' Bible speech in Brett's apartment, or Pumpkin's line "Garçon, coffee!" at the diner. However, he also uses much more subtle devices which will most likely only be registered during repeated viewings. In the prologue, while Pumpkin is talking about quitting robbing liquor stores, an attentively listening audience can hear Jules talking about quitting his criminal life, too. Only seconds later, during a close-up of Honey Bunny, Vincent is in the frame walking towards the restroom.

The question remains why Quentin Tarantino, apart from mere playfulness, decided to opt for this elaborate kind of discontinuity. In an interview with Charlie Rose, he explained:

> A good majority of movies that come out you pretty much know everything you're gonna see in the movie by the first ten or twenty minutes. Now, that's not a story. A story is something that constantly unfolds. [...] My story line jumps all over the place. Back and forward. (Special Feature on the *Pulp Fiction* DVD[5])

According to Tarantino, if a film is too predictable, the story is not properly told. Therefore, having a non-linear plot is one way of letting a story unfold in front of the viewers' eyes without sudden twists and surprises within the story. However, Tarantino does not hold back with his surprise at the intense and ongoing discussion of the narrative structure of *Pulp Fiction*. As he sees it, he simply followed modernist literary techniques:

> The truth of the matter is if I had written *Pulp Fiction* as a novel [...] you [Charlie Rose] would never even remotely bring up the structure. 'Coz it's, like, a novel can do that, no problem. Novelists have always had just a complete freedom to pretty much tell the story any way they thought it fit. That's kinda what I'm trying to do. The thing is, for both novels and film, seventy-five percent of the stories you're gonna tell will work better on a dramatic basis, on a dramatically engaging basis, to be told from a linear way. But there is this twenty-five percent out there that, you know, can be more resonant by telling it this way. And I think in the case of *Reservoir Dogs* and *Pulp Fiction* it gains a lot more resonance being told in this kind of wild way.

Tarantino does not at all oppose linear storytelling; he is merely of the opinion that one should use the kind of techniques most suitable for one's purpose. It is vital, though, that the audience can still follow the story. Tarantino stated that he would lose interest if he got confused, mostly because, usually, this confusion is not created on purpose but mistakenly. However, he thinks that "there is no problem being momentarily confused if you feel you're in good hands."

Momentarily confusing the audience by jumping around in time makes a film very self-conscious. But this is not the only time Tarantino calls attention to cinematic conventions. Heavily influenced by French New Wave directors, such as François Truffaut and Jean-Luc Godard, he also employs phony process shots twice (during the car rides of Butch and Vincent) and a drawing effect, when

---

5 Unless indicated otherwise, all of the following Tarantino quotes are from interviews on the DVD.

Mia non-verbally calls Vincent a 'square' (see Illustration 1). Rather unusual is also Tarantino's love for long steadicam shots during dialogue scenes. The longest, Jules and Vincent's discussion of foot massages right before they enter Brett's apartment, takes more than two and a half minutes. By refraining from any editing as in this scene and often very little editing in other scenes, Tarantino gives the audience the illusion of 'real' time; in other words, the dialogue unfolds right in front of them.

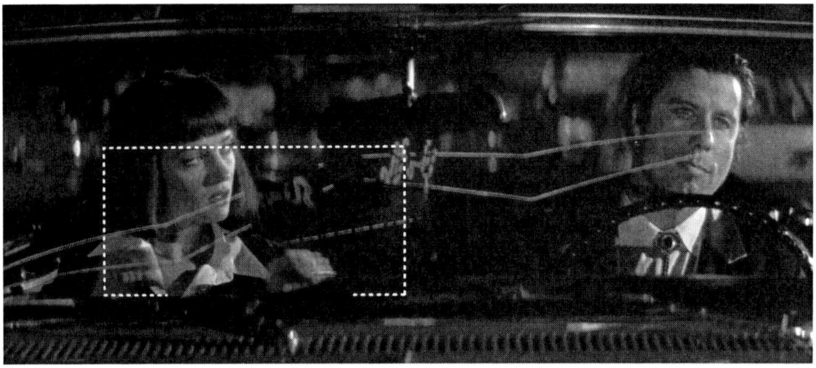

Illustration 1: Mia non-verbally calls Vincent a 'square'; *Pulp Fiction* © Miramax Films, 1994

In both *Reservoir Dogs* and *Pulp Fiction*, contrasting movie time with real time is one of Tarantino's major concerns, especially when it comes to acts of violence. In another interview he explained: "[W]hat I'm interested in is the use of violence, in stopping the 'movie' time and playing the violence out in real time. Letting nothing get in the way of it and letting it happen the way real violence does" (qtd. in McAlevey 80). In *Reservoir Dogs*, for example, the audience never actually sees the heist itself. The immediate aftermath is shown in several flashbacks, therefore in movie time, while Mr. Orange, one of the characters, seemingly bleeds to death inside a warehouse in real time, i. e., in the course of the whole movie that covers roughly two hours.

In *Pulp Fiction*, this confrontation between movie time and real time is much more complicated. In their article "A moment of clarity: Retrieval, redemption, and narrative time in *Pulp Fiction*," Cynthia Baughman and Richard Moran argue that the manipulation of narrative time generates additional enjoyment for the viewer, especially when a missing puzzle piece finally falls into place and reveals the picture (108-109). This pleasure occurs, for instance, when the viewers, at the end of the film, see Vincent and Jules changing from their bloody clothes into dorky shorts and T-shirts and thus discover why those two normally stylishly dressed characters wore them in Marsellus' bar at the beginning of the film. Another example can be found towards the end of the film, when the audience learns that Jules and Vincent happen to be in the same diner at the same time Honey Bunny and Pumpkin are about to rob it. Probably the most important structural aspect of the film is that Vincent, arguably the main character and the audience's favorite, seems to come back to life. Baughman and Moran argue that Vincent's 'resurrection' is part of the film's opposition of genre demands and real life as well as narrative time and life time. The movie fulfills generic demands; that is, it provides a happy ending with the two heroes walking off having successfully finished their latest adventure, ready to face their next. Nevertheless, this happy end is undermined by the audience's awareness of Vincent's death, and therefore the false and temporary nature of the film's happy end is emphasized (Baughman and Moran 109). I would contend, however, that by the time Vincent reappears onscreen, the viewers have already forgotten that he had, indeed, been shot. This is partly accounted for by the fact that quite some time (about twenty minutes) elapses between the killing and the re-emergence and the fact that the shooting is rather sudden, abrupt, and short. Thus, by using a discontinuous narrative Tarantino manages to kill a character without actually having him die.

Besides these aspects, the non-linear narrative has deeper motivations. According to Baughman and Moran (ibid.), the characters in *Pulp Fiction* struggle with time. They try to control it by stopping time, going back and forth, expanding and shortening time; they try to predict the future, seize the present, and escape the past. In the prologue, the conversation between Honey Bunny and Pumpkin introduces the themes of remembering and repeating:

Pumpkin:	Forget it, it's too risky. I'm through doin' that shit.
Honey Bunny:	You always say that, the same thing every time. I'm through. Never again. Too dangerous.
Pumpkin:	I know that's what I always say. I'm always right too.
Honey Bunny:	But you forget about it in a day or two.
Pumpkin:	Yeah, but the days of me forgittin' are over. The days of me rememberin' have just begun.

That Pumpkin once again forgets, and thus is still incapable of controlling his life and seizing the present, is shown by their robbery of the diner only minutes after this conversation. Noteworthy here is that, as the audience finds out at the end, Pumpkin's declaration happens at the same time and place as Jules' much more adamant decision of quitting the life of a criminal. The audience is invited to draw parallels between these two declarations and, much more importantly, to see the difference between an intervention in 'real' life and on the level of narrative. The robbery is interrupted twice. Once temporarily by the 'narrator,' that is, the director/editor, and a second time by Jules, who tries to take control over his as well as Pumpkin's and Honey Bunny's lives. These interventions on two different levels also resemble the difference in power and control between character and narrator. Jules and Vincent symbolize this difference as well. While Jules writes himself out of the story and thus survives in 'real' life, Vincent refuses to change and thus gets killed. He only survives on the level of narration (Baughman and Moran 110).

In *Pulp Fiction* the focus on temporality is highlighted by the fact that it does not only play a role in the narrative structure but is also repeatedly emphasized within the story. There are a number of overt references to time, as exemplified in a dialogue between Jules and Vincent right before murdering Brett and Roger:

Jules:	What time you got?
Vincent:	It's 7:22 in the a.m.
Jules:	No, ain't quite time yet.

Other examples are the drug dealer's wife shouting, "It's 1:30" when Vincent shows up with the almost dying Mia: "It ain't Tuesday, is it? – No, it's Thursday," Zed, one of the torturers, says to the pawnshop owner, and "every time of day is good time for pie," Fabienne explains to Butch while they are hurrying to catch the eleven o'clock train. "The clock is ticking," the Wolf points out, and it is literally, since he, Vincent, and Jules have to clean the car and get rid of the body within only one-and-a-half hours. But besides these, there are also more implicit references to time. Jack Rabbit Slim's, the diner Vincent takes Mia to, is a fifties Hollywood theme restaurant. It features outdated interior decoration, fifties music, and waiters dressed up as former icons, such as James Dean and Marilyn Monroe. This diner gives one the possibility of 'freezing' time and returning to the past. The reason for going back in time here, however, is not to alter anything or change one's course of life, but to voyeuristically indulge in a time that, in fact, never changes, that one can come home to. It is unchangeable and unthreatening, or as Vincent puts it, "a wax museum with a pulse rate."

Butch is the character most occupied with time; and, most notably, with the passing of time. His chapter is called "The Gold Watch" for a good reason. As he is introduced, Marsellus is lecturing him about the uselessness of attempting to stop the flow of time, that he is getting too old to be a boxer, and that he should better face it. In a flashback to Butch's childhood, Captain Koons narrates the story of the gold watch and how it is connected to the family history. Not only does this watch measure in minutes and hours, but in years, decades, and wars, symbolizing the history of the entire twentieth century (Baughman and Moran 111).

Jules and Vincent's story also provides two opposing stances toward lived time. By the end of the film, Jules reaches "what alcoholics call a moment of clarity," i. e., the recognition that sometimes one has to take a chance in order to redirect one's future. Vincent, on the other hand, supposes that he can leave and re-enter the flow of time at his personal will. He believes that the world will stop turning whenever he decides to take a timeout. In the film, these timeouts, three in number, are marked by his retreats into the bathroom. Unfortunately for Vince, however, time does not stop but goes on relentlessly. Therefore, whenever he returns from the bathroom, something terrible has happened. Mia has overdosed, Honey Bunny and Pumpkin have started their robbery, and Butch has returned to his apartment, finds a gun, and shoots Vincent. Vincent continually and misguidedly behaves as if he could simply freeze time while he is gone and then continue exactly where he left off. In the last sequence of the film, Vincent interrupts his argument with Jules by saying, "I've gotta take a shit. [...] To be continued." But when he returns, the situation has changed considerably. Once again, Vincent is totally unprepared for what has happened since; what he does not realize is that life goes on without him (Baughman and Moran 110-111).

CONCLUSION

Classical narrative lost its unshakably dominant position a long time ago. The traditional plot structure of exposition, crisis, climax, and dénouement are the 'remnants' of Aristotle's *Poetics*. Almost naturally, it seems rather archaic today. Consequently, new ways of telling a story have surfaced – ways that deliberately defy linearity. Many contemporary mainstream films do not explicitly indicate a shift in time or use the usual tools in order to guide the viewers (such as inserts or flashbacks). They leave the audience puzzling instead. The stories are fragmented; all segments are presented in the discourse Now and, thus, create a perpetual present of the narration. No event is placed in the past or the future, even though, chronologically speaking, it must be either the one or the other.

These kinds of films can be seen as a manifestation of the postmodern concept of time. The theories of Friedrich Nietzsche, Gianni Vattimo, and Fredric Jameson elaborated on the fact that non-linearity, fragmentation, and the perpetual present are the three foremost characteristics of the conception of time in the postmodern tradition. Along with the crisis of the value of the new and the future, our sense of history and, consequently, our experience of linear time has broken down.

Quentin Tarantino's *Pulp Fiction* has served as a prime example of postmodern narrative. It was the first American mainstream film to transpose the postmodern concept of time to the screen. Thus, *Pulp Fiction* opened the doors for many other unconventional films to come and has, not undeservedly, reached cult status. Its circular narrative structure and the use of repetition parallels Nietzsche's notion of the eternal return of the same events. By calling into question the notion of cause and effect, Tarantino's masterpiece succeeds in bringing postmodern aesthetics closer to the masses.

WORKS CITED

Baughman, Cynthia, and Richard Moran. "A Moment of Clarity: Retrieval, Redemption, and Narrative Time in *Pulp Fiction.*" *Creative Screenwriting* 1.4 (1994): 108-118. Print.

Bergson, Henri. *Materie und Gedächtnis: Eine Abhandlung über die Beziehung zwischen Körper und Geist.* 1908. Trans. Julius Frankenberger. Hamburg: Meiner, 1991. Print.

—. *Schöpferische Entwicklung.* 1921. Trans. Gertrud Kantorowicz. Zürich: Coron, 1967. Print.

Bordwell, David. *The Way Hollywood Tells It: Story and Style in Modern Movies.* Berkeley, CA: U of California P, 2006. Print.

Gehlen, Arnold. "Die Säkularisierung des Fortschritts." *Einblicke.* Frankfurt/Main: Vittorio Klostermann, 1978. Print.

Heidegger, Martin. *Sein und Zeit.* 1927. 10th Edition. Tübingen: Niemeyer, 1963. Print.

Jameson, Fredric. *Postmodernism or, the Cultural Logic of Late Capitalism.* 1991. Durham, NC: Duke UP, 1995. Print.

—. "Postmodernism and Consumer Society." 1982. *Postmodernism and Its Discontents: Theories, Practices.* Ed. E. Ann Kaplan. New York, NY: Verso, 1988. 13-29. Print.

Lyotard, Jean-François. *The Postmodern Condition: A Report on Knowledge.* 1979. Trans. Geoff Bennington. Minneapolis, MN: U of Minnesota P, 1984. Print.

McAlevey, Peter. "All's Well That Ends Gruesomely." *The New York Times Magazine* 6 December 1992: 80. Print.

Nietzsche, Friedrich. *Thus Spoke Zarathustra: A Book for Everyone and Nobody.* 1885. Trans. Graham Parkes. Oxford: Oxford UP, 2005. Print.

Pulp Fiction. Dir. and Scr. Quentin Tarantino. Perf. John Travolta, Uma Thurman, Bruce Willis, Samuel L. Jackson, et al. 1994. Miramax, 1998. DVD.

Reservoir Dogs. Dir. and Scr. Quentin Tarantino. Perf. Harvey Keitel, Tim Roth, Michael Madsen, et al. 1992. Lions Gate, 1997. DVD.

Stambaugh, Joan. *The Other Nietzsche.* New York, NY: SUNY P, 1994. Print.

Vattimo, Gianni. *The End of Modernity: Nihilism and Hermeneutics in Postmodern Culture.* 1985. Trans. Jon R. Snyder. Baltimore, MD: Johns Hopkins UP, 1988. Print.

—. *Il Soggetto e la Maschera.* 1974. Milan: Bompiani, 1994. Print.

Weiß, Martin. *Gianni Vattimo – Einführung.* Vienna: Passagen, 2003. Print.

Welsch, Wolfgang. *Unsere Postmoderne Moderne.* 6th Edition. Berlin: Akademie, 2002. Print.

UNCANNY ARCHI*TEXT*URES[1]: READING TIME, SPACE, AND REPRESENATION IN PAUL AUSTER'S *CITY OF GLASS*

PETRA ECKHARD

"What better portrait of a writer than to show a man who has been bewitched by books?" (98) asks Daniel Quinn, the protagonist of Paul Auster's *City of Glass*, at a pivotal point of the story. Even if this rhetorical question is an allusion to Cervantes and, more precisely, to his skill in toying with intertexts and authorial personae, the portrait Quinn is sketching, as every attentive reader realizes, is in fact nothing but a mirror image of Auster. Auster is indeed bewitched by books as much as he is bewitched by language. His literary practice is brimming with metafictional puns, ironic doublings and ontological uncertainties, strategies that, more often than not, make the process of reading a disquieting experience. The magic spell that is at work in Auster's oeuvre touches upon many literary and philosophical notions that are characteristic of the postmodern period. Representing a radical counter-discourse to realist fiction and the positivist attitude, Auster's writing playfully points to the virtuality and arbitrariness of language and, in a further step, to the postmodern paradigm that arriving at absolute truth or knowledge is nothing but an illusion. This shift away from epistemological issues towards ontological issues is often seen in accordance with the emergence of a postmodern aesthetic whose artistic thrill is rather attributed to the posing of questions than to finding answers. Auster's fiction excites ambiguity and intellectual uncertainty, so that, for example, we can never be sure whether a piece of writing leads us into the world of fiction or reality. Furthermore, his intertextual references suggest the phenomenological presence of earlier authors and texts and thus make the literary past an essential component of the present. Finally, his texts always highlight the strangeness that is attached to poetic diction per se, which is to render the familiar strange.

Being familiar with psychoanalytic theory, one realizes that these discursive strategies share a conceptual similarity with a notion that Freud first introduced in his 1919 essay "The Uncanny." The uncanny, for Freud, is first and foremost an intra-psychic phenomenon, a product of the unconscious mind that brings to

---

1 Derrida's *archi-écriture* (arch-writing) bears resemblance and is related to the term 'architexture' as applied in this study of the postmodern *Unheimliche*. For Derrida, *archi-écriture* denotes the process of original writing or the inscription of the trace that always brings forth *différance* and thus the endless deferral of meaning (cf. *Of Grammatology* 62).

light "everything that was intended to remain secret, hidden away, and has come into the open" (132). Belonging to "that species of the frightening that goes back to what was once well known and had long been familiar" (124), the uncanny emerges whenever the thresholds between the past and the present or/and the real and the unreal are crossed.[2] For Freud, the uncanny is therefore linked to doubles, automata, mirror-images, ghostly apparitions, or déjà vu, in other words, everything that triggers in us the notion of what Ernst Jentsch has termed "the dark feeling of uncertainty" (13).

Since the 1960s, the Freudian concept of the uncanny has experienced a major turning point in that it turned from a concept "located at the very core of psychoanalysis" (Dolar 5) into a major trope of postmodernism, delineating an aesthetic of defamiliarization, disorientation, and estrangement throughout various disciplines. The most influential re-readings of Freud's text, among them Cixous' "Fiction and its Phantoms: A Reading of Freud's 'Das Unheimliche'" or certain passages of Derrida's *Dissemination* advocate the uncanny as the aesthetic result (and tool) of deconstruction. Deconstruction, if understood as the literary and philosophical practice of bringing to light hidden meanings, always entails the ideas of rendering familiar texts strange and inciting discomfort in the reader. For example, Cixous' deconstructionist reading of Freud's "The Uncanny" regards the psychoanalyst's manifesto as "a strange theoretical novel" (525) in which Freud, in the process of getting lost in the semantic ambivalence of the concept (and term), displays several identities. In reading a psychoanalytical study as fiction, she unfolds the essay's constructedness and points to Freud's application of a "peculiar disquieting method to track down the concept das *Unheimliche*" (Cixous 525). Thus, Cixous does not only shed light onto the equivocal nature of Freud's programmatic essay (and the instability of the concept itself) but also onto the uncanny's function as a literary technique. In a talk on Animism and Animation in 2009, Anneleen Masschelein pointed out that in the 21st century, the uncanny has changed from a concept into an *un*concept due to its ever increasing fleetingness and hybridity.

This applicability of the uncanny to the postmodern age and its outcome of cultural production can, as this paper argues, mainly be attributed to fundamental changes in our perception and consciousness of time and space that are taking

[2] In this seminal essay, Freud applies his psychoanalytic approach to E.T.A. Hoffmann's romantic tale *Der Sandmann* (1816), thus also discussing the uncanny as a literary device. Freud's approach of viewing the uncanny through the lens of psycho-literary criticism already proves the concept's potential as a structural rhizome, foreshadowing the uncanny's dissemination from the 1970s onwards into other academic fields such as architecture, sociology, philosophy, and cultural studies.

place in our contemporary world. Brought forth by consumer capitalism, cultural globalization, and new information technologies, these transformations have produced what Paul Smethurst has called "the postmodern chronotope," specific spatio-temporal conditions denoting a postmodern *Weltanschauung* that is characterized by the loss of home, place, historicity, and (other) stable referents. At its very heart, the postmodern chronotope points to Lyotard's idea that the postmodern condition implies a constant rewriting or consideration of the modern, or as Smethurst argues, "a working through in the Freudian sense of the unpresentable in the past, hidden [...] not so much by the repression of memories [...] but hidden by their future-directedness" (9). Hence, the constant resurfacing of the modern that constantly disturbs both linear temporality as well as homogenous spatiality renders the unpresentable analogous to the psychological dimension of the unconscious mind, the dark point from which the uncanny originates. But how to represent the unrepresentable? How to represent the compound of ideas that has turned into an *un*concept?

Setting out from these theoretical reflections and questions, this paper uses the tool of the postmodern chronotope in order to explore the uncanny as a literary technique in Paul Auster's *City of Glass*. The novel depicts an urban world in which earlier, premodern conceptions of thought constantly come to light, thus producing a 'here' and 'now' that can no longer be described or represented in a coherent or 'conceptual' mode. Unlike most modern city novels, such as Dreiser's *Sister Carrie* or Dos Passos' *Manhattan Transfer*, that try to 'make sense' of the complexity and alienation that metropolitan life generated at the turn of the century, postmodern city novels point to the fact that making sense of the city, as Günther Lenz argues, is a hopeless undertaking: "With the emergence of postmodernism, it seemed to become increasingly difficult to 'read' the city as a 'text', to narrate the city or city life, as the concepts of 'the city' and of 'subjects' living in the city were seen as having become 'derealized'" (15). By looking at one of the most dominant chronotopic motives of the story – the urban labyrinth – this paper seeks to explore how Auster toys with time and space, thus translating this 'derealization' into an uncanny moment in both, protagonist and reader.

THE POSTMODERN CHRONOTOPE

In his 2000 book *The Postmodern Chronotope*, Paul Smethurst further develops Mikhail Bakhtin's notion of the chronotope which he introduced in a 1975 essay[3] that in the English translation is included in *The Dialogic Imagination*. Inspired by Einsteinean physics[4], Bakhtin uses the term chronotope (which translates into 'time space') to refer to "the intrinsic connectedness of temporal and spatial relationships that are artistically expressed in literature" (84). Bakhtin applies his dialogics of space and time to the generic class of the novel, a genre which since the Greek romance has developed a multiplicity of chronotopes, reflecting different ideologies and world-views.[5] For Bakhtin, the chronotope is not simply "a generic signifier" (Smethurst 67), but rather "an optic for reading texts as x-rays of the forces at work in the culture system from which they spring" (Holquist 425-426). Looking at the literary uncanny from the perspective of timespace, therefore, reveals not only how the uncanny is established in a work of narrative fiction but also, and even more importantly, provides the essential socio-cultural framework in which the uncanny, as a cultural construct, operates at a certain point in history.

Until the mid-20th century, Paul Smethurst argues, the privileging of time over space was a defining feature of Western ideology: "In modernist culture, it seems that social space was sidelined by more pressing problems of time, and place was regarded as an historical and possibly regressive construct, and therefore a hindrance to progress" (37). Indeed, modernism's goal, as apparent in the utopian architecture of Le Corbusier, was to break with the past in the sense of "replac[ing] the historical by the sleek" (Sennett 170-171). Similarly, modernist poetics were tremendously shaped by issues of historicism and linear temporality, reflecting the speed of progress and change in the mechanized age. In literature, stylistic responses to modernity's embrace of temporal flow are the stream of

---

3 The essay was first published in Bakhtin's *Вопросы литературы и эстетики* (Questions of Literature and Aesthetics). Four of the six essays of this volume are included in *The Dialogic Imagination*.

4 Bakhtin does not use the term 'chronotope' in its strict physical or mathematical sense, but rather makes use of it figuratively: "The special meaning it has in relativity theory is not important for our purposes; we are borrowing it for literary criticism almost as a metaphor (almost, but not entirely). What counts for us is the fact that it expresses the inseparability of space and time (time as the fourth dimension of space)" (84).

5 In *The Dialogic Imagination*, Bakhtin aims at a "historical poetics" (85) and thus investigates and compares the chronotopic relations as they are developed in early forms of the novel, such as the Greek Romance, the Adventure Novel of Everyday life, and the Chivalric Romance.

consciousness technique, the Bergsonian notion of *durée*[6] as a recurring theme or strategy, or the use of literary symbols that signify modern temporality.

In postmodernism, by contrast, the (literary) uncanny is no longer the product of a "temporal master-narrative" (ibid.) but rather that of spatial practice. With Foucault proclaiming that "the anxiety of our era has to do fundamentally with space, no doubt a great deal more than time" ("Of Other Spaces" par. 7) also the uncanny experiences a re- (or de-)conceptualization of its spatial and temporal features. The major reason for the favoritism of space over time that defines the so-called spatial turn in the humanities can be attributed to processes of globalization and the emergence of new media and communication systems. In particular, the shift from analogous to digital technologies of representation has not only tremendously altered our sense of perception and reality but has also transformed the notion of space into a highly variable category.

It has to be noted, however, that even if the spatial turn has prioritized space over time in postmodern theory, the temporal dimension still remains to play a crucial role. Especially the notion of spatial practice *a priori* entails the dynamics of movement and thus of temporality. Also de Certeau's definition of space heavily relies on the temporal dimension of flux, including "vectors of direction, velocities and time variables, intersections and mobile elements" ("Spatial Stories" 74). In the postmodern chronotope, however, these dynamics are neither linear, chronological, nor directional. Rather, in postmodernist and poststructuralist thought, time is highly fragmented, leaving us, as Fredric Jameson has argued, in a world of "perpetual presents" (170). More specifically, Andreas Huyssen has noted a shift away from the "present futures" of modernism to the "present pasts" of postmodernism, indicating the constant re-enacting of history and thus the constant uncanny return of the dead. Thus, both dimensions are characterized by heterogeneity and fragmentation, producing a chronotope that "admits to the unexpected, the arrival of the unfamiliar, the unhomely, all, in short, which cannot be programmed or anticipated, uncanniness itself" (Wolfreys 172).

---

6 In *Time and Free Will* (1889), Henri Bergson distinguishes between *temps* and *durée*. For him, *temps* denotes physical or objective time, time seen as a succession of events (i. e. clock time), whereas *durée* stands for subjective time, the time of the perceived present, which cannot be scientifically measured (i. e. psychological time). The stream of consciousness as a literary technique that confuses the linear chronology of time (past, present, future) was developed out of the Bergsonian concept of *durée*.

PAUL AUSTER'S *CITY OF GLASS*

Often labeled an anti-detective-story, *City of Glass*' narrative trajectories do not result in a rational explanation or a final uncovering of the mystery. Rather, all the clues that detective-protagonist Daniel Quinn collects in the city seem to point back to themselves, thus producing a complex web of dissociation. Already at the very beginning of the story does the uncanny reveal itself to the protagonist and the reader. When Daniel Quinn picks up the ringing phone in the middle of the night he hears "a voice unlike any he had ever heard [...] at once mechanical and filled with feeling, hardly more than a whisper and yet perfectly audible, and so even in tone that he was unable to tell if it belonged to a man or a woman" (7), asking for the detective Paul Auster. Whereas Quinn experiences the uncanny moment solely through the ghostliness of the unknown voice, the uncanniness the reader experiences manifests itself through the aesthetics of metafiction. As soon as the ontological author's name is mentioned on the intradiegetic plane, the reader is left in a state of alienation, as usually, echoing Foucault, "the author's name is not [...] fictional" ("What Is an Author?" 123). As stated earlier, the uncanny emerges out of the ambiguity produced by the sudden lack of boundaries between the real and the fictional world, or more specifically, from the unexpected return of the non-mimetic, i. e. all that which should have remained hidden or invisible in order to maintain the mimetic illusion.

From the very start, the narratological space of *City of Glass* is one that is constructed by fluid walls, making it a ghostly realm that lies between the categories of inside and outside and in which even a clear localization of the author has become impossible. In a similar vein, the urban fabric Quinn experiences is also one enforcing disorientation and de-differentiation. The reader is presented a city lacking a center, borderlines, and even points of reference:

> New York was an inexhaustible space, a labyrinth of endless steps, and no matter how far he walked, no matter how well he came to know its neighborhoods and streets, it always left him with the feeling of being lost. Lost, not only in the city, but within himself as well. [...] By wandering aimlessly, all places became equal and it no longer mattered where he was. (4)

Quinn's fundamental lostness, "the nowhere he has built around himself" (ibid.), is generated by the trauma that the death of his son Peter has left behind. Quinn, thus, is from the very beginning a victim of the uncanny in the traditional Freudian sense, experiencing the involuntary return of the repressed:

> Every once in a while, he would suddenly feel what it had been like to hold the three-year-old boy in his arms – but that was not exactly thinking, nor was it even remembering. It was a physical sensation, an imprint of the past that had been left in his body, and he had no control over it. (5)

In the course of the story, Quinn's distorted perception of his spatial environment, caused by "the uncanny of real experience" (Freud 154), triggers further events marked by intellectual uncertainty. These further events are, more often than not, manifestations of uncanniness that result from the interrelationship between the protagonist and his spatial surroundings. Echoing Jentsch, Freud also notes that the uncanny is a spatial phenomenon, "an area in which a person was unsure of his way around" (125). Freud continues: "[T]he better oriented he was in the world around him, the less likely he would be to find the objects and occurrences in it uncanny" (ibid.). Freud exemplifies this in recounting a personal story in which a sensation of the uncanny followed his experience of spatial disorientation:

> Strolling one hot summer afternoon through the empty and to me unfamiliar streets of a small Italian town, I found myself in a district about whose character I could not long remain in doubt. Only heavily made-up women were to be seen at the windows of the little houses, and I hastily left the narrow street at the next turning. However, after wandering about for some time without asking the way, I suddenly found myself back in the same street, where my presence began to attract attention. Once more I hurried away, only to return there again by a different route. I was now seized by a feeling that I can only describe as uncanny. (144)

Similarly, Quinn's New York is uncanny because it disturbs parameters of orientation. As a space of psychological intraspection[7], the city also becomes, as Merleau-Ponty points out, "an area of free space in which what does not naturally exist may take on a semblance of existing" (128). When Merleau-Ponty further argues that lived space[8] is always mediated through the body, he also indicates that the perception of space and the formation of identity are mutually dependent. In the following, and in consideration of the character's cognitive mappings, the focus will be placed on the chronotopic motif of the urban labyrinth that constitutes a highly relevant aspect to Auster's construction of an "architexture" of the uncanny.

---

7 'Intraspection' is a term from the field of psychology. While extraspection denotes the reflections about objects belonging to the outside world, intraspection concerns reflections about the self and the look 'within.'

8 Merleau-Ponty makes a distinction between 'lived' or 'subjective' space and 'objective' space, the latter denoting geometrical or Eucledian space, i. e. space that can be mathematically measured. 'Lived space,' on the other hand, is constructed through lived existential experiences and is thus always related to a particular subject.

Illustration 1: Labyrinth as signifier for urban complexity and protagonist's identity; taken from Paul Auster. *City of Glass*. Adapted by Paul Karasik and David Mazzucchelli. London: Faber and Faber, 2004.

"WHERE EXACTLY AM I GOING?": THE LABYRINTH

On one of the first pages of the graphic adaptation of *City of Glass* by Karasik and Mazzuchelli, first published in 1994, the close interrelation between urban space and identity is visually translated into the image of the labyrinth that comes to signify both the structural complexity of the city as well as the protagonist's fingerprint (see Illustration 1).

Bearing the name of a sacred weapon – *labyrinthos* literally meaning "the place of the double axe" – the architectural structure of the labyrinth is etymologically infused with the connotation of something threatening. Ever since ancient and medieval times, the labyrinth has represented a site of great mystery and deadly adventure. From Greek mythology we know, for example, that Daedalus' labyrinth imprisoned the monstrous Minotaur; in ancient Egypt it was the preferred architectural form used for funerary temples that, by cleverly hiding the pharaohs' bodies and treasures behind trap doors or dead ends, sometimes brought forth the death of grave robbers. In medieval Europe, cathedral labyrinths marked out on the floor of Christian churches functioned as the site of prayer rituals, symbolizing the torturous path to spiritual salvation. Regardless of the labyrinth's vast multiplicity of mythological or cultural connotations, its chronotopic function is always, as Kim Förster has argued, to indicate spatial confusion and the threat of confinement:

> In common linguistic usage, the term [labyrinth] refers to a perplexing situation in which the subject finds him- or herself trapped. At the same time, a labyrinth implicates a space which is designed only for the purpose of deliberately bewildering the labyrinth walker. In this respect, the labyrinth also entails an experience of imprisonment that precludes an unequivocal route or way out. (248; my translation)[9]

Many scholars dealing with the subject of labyrinths (among them W.H. Matthews, Herman Kern, Kim Förster or Paul Basu) further mention the necessity of distinguishing between two basic designs that also determine the way in which a subject walks through a labyrinthine space. As illustrated below, the unicursal structure, as exemplified by the Cretan type and the Chartres type, only consists of one single twisted path, leading the walker to the center and then back to the exit. In contrast, the multicursal structure is characterized by a multiplicity of

---

9 "Allein im populären Sprachgebrauch verweist der Begriff schon auf eine unübersichtliche und daher verwirrende Situation, in der das Subjekt gefangen ist. Ein Labyrinth wird aber auch mit einem Ort in Verbindung gebracht, der derart geplant und angelegt ist, dass sich das Individuum, das sich dort aufhält und fortbewegt, leicht verirrt. In dieser Hinsicht bringt das Labyrinth für den räumlich Handelnden bzw. für den Benutzer des Ortes dann häufig auch eine Gefängnisserfahrung mit sich – scheinbar gibt es keinen eindeutigen Weg und keinen Ausweg."

different paths and junctions from which the walker has to choose from. This structural difference entails that the act of moving through a unicursal labyrinth is always direct and continuous. The multicursal structure, however, does not allow continuous movement, as junctions or dead ends heavily disturb the flow of walking. As Eugenia Virginia Ellis points out: "The characteristic quality of movement through the multicursal maze is halting and episodic, with each fork or alternative requiring a pause for thought and decision, and emphasizes an individual's own responsibility for his or her own fate" (374).

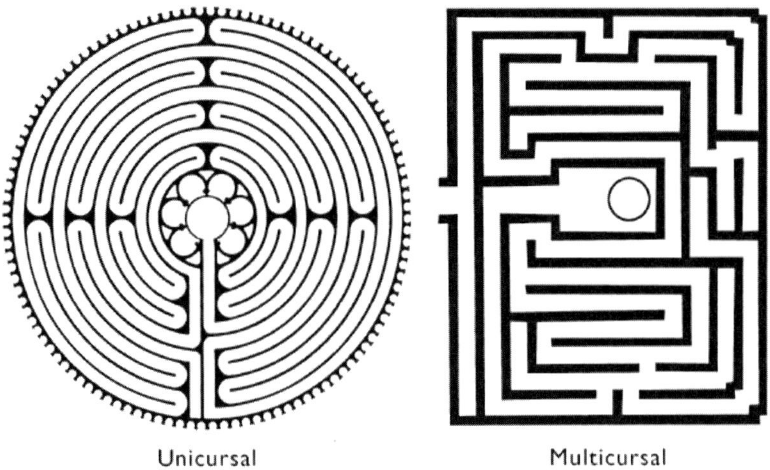

Illustration 2: Uni- vs. Multicural Labyrinth; taken from Paul Basu. "The Labyrinthine Aesthetic in Contemporary Museum Design," p. 49.

Hence, it is the multicursal form that fundamentally breaks with the linearity of time and the homogeneity of space, thus being the physical representation of a timespace that evokes the postmodern paradigms of disorientation and dedifferentiation.

Quinn's New York structurally resembles a multicursal labyrinth of untranslatable signs which lead to the fact that the character's spatial practices are all defined by aberration. As a major leitmotiv, aberration is, for example, evoked through the character of Peter Stillman Sr., the man Quinn investigates. Stillman Sr. "never seem[s] to be going anywhere" (58). He walks the streets of New York as being trapped in a multicursal labyrinth, constantly looking for clues that might guide him to the center:

> As he walked, Stillman did not look up. His eyes were permanently fixed on the pavement, as though he were searching for something. Indeed, every now and then

> he would stoop down, pick some object off the ground, and examine it closely, turning it over and over in his hand. It made Quinn think of an archaeologist inspecting a shard at some prehistoric ruin. (59)

Also Quinn is fundamentally lost or directionless, aimlessly drifting in urban space, asking himself at some point of the story: "But if I'm going out, where exactly am I going?" (12) Even his clients, Virginia and Peter Stillman Jr., simply disappear without a note, just leaving behind their empty apartment. In the process of investigation, Quinn constantly finds himself at many crossroads, intersections and dead ends, and all the things that happen to him are driven by chance alone. For example, when trying to make sense of Stillman's arbitrary wanderings through Manhattan, Quinn transcribes Stillman's daily routes in the city map and realizes that his walks form letters, an idea that is also visually represented in the novel (see Illustration 3):

> The next day gave him a lopsided 'O', a doughnut crushed on one side with three or four jagged lines sticking out the other. Then came a tidy 'F', with the customary rococo swirls to the side. After that there was a 'B' that looked like two boxes haphazardly placed on top of one another. [...] Next there was a tottering 'A' that somewhat resembled a letter [...]. And finally there was a second 'B' [...]. Quinn then copied out the letters in order: OWEROFBAB. [...] Making due allowances for the fact that he had missed the first four days and that Stillman had not finished yet, the answer seemed inescapable: THE TOWER OF BABEL. [...] But the letters continued to horrify Quinn. The whole thing was so oblique, so fiendish in its circumlocutions, that he did not want to accept it. Then doubts came [...]. He had imagined the whole thing. [...] It was all an accident, a hoax he had perpetrated on himself. (70-71)

The horror Quinn experiences is grounded in the realization that the letters bring back to mind the subject of Stillman's research project, to reconstruct the Tower of Babel. In other words, the uncanny is manifested through the unexpected return of the "'premodern' in the [post]modern" (Brooker 157). What enforces his experience of the uncanny is the intellectual insecurity of whether the letters will point to any outside reality (i. e. his detective case) or not. Of course, Stillman's transcribed walks only lead into an epistemological dead end, as in fact, the letters, or respectively the clues Quinn thinks he has gathered, only point back to themselves. Quinn, realizing that his transcriptions do not lead to a climatic discovery, finds himself stuck in the process of investigation:

> Quinn was deeply disillusioned. He had always imagined that the key to good detective work was a close observation of details. The more accurate the scrutiny the more successful the results. But after struggling these surface effects, Quinn felt no closer to Stillman than when he first started following him. (67)

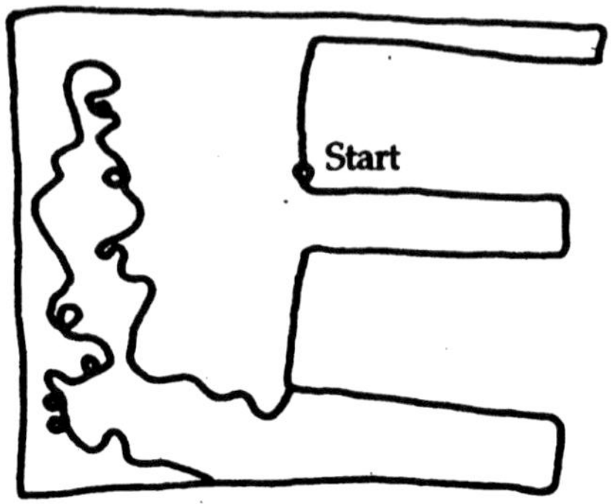

Illustration 3: Quinn comes to realize that his walks form letters; taken from Paul Auster. *City of Glass*. London: Faber and Faber, 2004.

The tower (built of letters) is not only conceived as a pars pro toto for New York's ambitious skyscraper architecture, but also hints at the linguistic confusion that is caused by the arbitrariness between signifier and signified. As Derrida writes in *Psyche: The Invention of the Other*: "The Tower of Babel does not merely figure the irreducible multiplicity of tongues; it exhibits an incompletion, the impossibility of finishing, of totalizing, of saturating, of completing something on the order of edification, architectural construction, system and architectonics" (191). Derrida, drawing on Voltaire's analysis of the entry 'Babel' in the *Dictionaire Philosophique*, also claims that 'Babel' denotes God's name (as in Oriental tongues *ba* stands for father and *bel* for God) and simultaneously "the confusion of tongues (and) the state of confusion in which the architects find themselves with the structure interrupted" (ibid. 192).

In Auster's novel the labyrinthine city is literally a text, as Roland Barthes proclaimed in "Semiology and Urbanism," or rather a hypertext, a vast assemblage of different (narratorial) paths wherein the reader and/or detective has to orientate him/herself (cf. Ellis 374). Pedestrial movement, as de Certeau suggests, becomes a space of enunciation. Hence, Stillman's walks (producing letters) can be compared to a speech act that is untranslatable, therefore leading into a blind alley. Neither Quinn nor Stillman are able to read the semiotic matrix the city lays out for them. Accordingly, they never arrive at the center of things: At the end of the novel, Quinn simply disappears into the city's nothingness, just as his clients do, and Stillman Sr., jumping off the Brooklyn Bridge, dies "in midair, before he even hit[s] the water" (123).

Also the reader gets frustrated because arriving at a neat ending, or respectively the unveiling of the mystery, is taken ad absurdum. The resolution lies in the process of walking itself and not in the arrival at a final truth, a center. Instead of finding Adriane's thread, Quinn remains trapped in New York's urban fabric as much as he remains trapped within the network of his multiple identities. The process of aimless wandering can be seen as Quinn's endless attempt to find his true self in a city that resembles a hall of mirrors. The uncanny mirrorings and reflections are expressed when Quinn identifies with his fictional detective Max Work, with Stillman's son Peter, and when he takes on the identity of the detective Paul Auster. In a further step, Quinn's confusion of the self is chronotopically translated into the multiple pathways of the labyrinth. His, or rather Stillman's, pedestrian rhetoric does not follow a logical or causal pattern but rather has an ontological relevance. When Quinn recites a line by Baudelaire, he equals spatial disorientation with the depersonalisation of the subject, the loss of self:

> Il me semble que je serais toujours bien là où je ne suis pas. In other words: It seems to me that I will always be happy in the place where I am not. Or, more bluntly: Wherever I am not is the place where I am myself. (110-111)

Baudelaire's paradoxon comes to stand for Quinn's fundamental displacement and, simultaneously, for a city that has turned into a heterotopia[10] in the Foucauldian sense, a place of the 'unhomely,' representing the spatialized 'other,' a realm that lies between the real and the unreal. But what does 'other' exactly mean for Foucault? Heterotopic spaces are 'other' in the sense that they are real but at the same time also illusionary or virtual. In *Of Other Spaces* (1967), Foucault compares the concept of heterotopia to a mirror which through the process of reflection makes it possible for the subject to locate him/herself in a place where he/she is not:

> In the mirror, I see myself there where I am not, in an unreal, virtual space that opens up behind the surface; I am over there, there where I am not, a sort of shadow that gives my own visibility to myself, that enables me to see myself there where I am absent: such is the utopia of the mirror. But it is also a heterotopia in so far as the mirror does exist in reality, where it exerts a sort of counteraction on the position that I occupy. [...] It makes this place that I occupy at the moment when I look at myself in the glass at once absolutely real, connected with all the space that surrounds it, and absolutely unreal, since in order to be perceived it has to pass through this virtual point which is over there. (par. 13)

In other words, heterotopias are real spaces that simulate reality. Just like multicursal labyrinths, with multiple pathways, halls and rooms, heterotopias confuse

---

[10] In *The Order of Things*, Foucault first applied the term heterotopia (literally 'the other space') to language: "Heterotopias are disturbing, probably because they secretly undermine language, because they make it impossible to name this and that [...] utopia permits fable and discourse: they run with the very grain of language and are part of the fundamental formulation of the fabula; heterotopias [...] desiccate speech [...] they dissolve our myths and sterilize the lyricism of our sentences" (379).

the subject's sense of orientation. Foucault's metaphor of the mirror also points to the fact that heterotopias also simulate spatially constructed identities. In *City of Glass*, these simulated identities are conceived of strategies of doubling. Quinn, for example, is confronted with two Stillman's at Grand Central Station and has to rely on chance alone to follow the 'real' man. Mirrorings, however, not only occur on the level of story, but also on the level of discourse as Auster constantly incorporates other tales (e. g. Poe's "The Man of the Crowd" and "William Wilson") that rearticulate the themes of *City of Glass*. This characteristic feature of simulation or doubling also connects the concept of heterotopia with the structure of the uncanny, the latter often described as an atmospheric value that presupposes a connection to reality but at the same time renders this reality strange.

Next to the feature of alterity, all heterotopias share the feature of structural heterogeneity and are hence characterized by a non-totalizable complexity. Foucault, therefore, refers to heterotopic spaces as sites "that have the curious property of being in relation with all the other sites, but in such a way as to suspect, neutralize or invert the set of relations that they happen to designate, mirror or reflect" ("Of Other Spaces" par. 11). Harvey helps to shed light onto Foucault's fuzzy concept when he defines it as "the coexistence in 'an impossible space' of 'a large number of fragmentary possible worlds', or more simply, incommensurable spaces that are juxtaposed or superimposed upon each other" (48). Quinn's New York is indeed a landscape of difference, "a neverland of fragments" (72), as it says in the novel. The city that is depicted resembles a chaotic space full of "broken people, [...] broken things, [...] broken thoughts" (78), a space in which a multitude of social worlds and subjectivities collide and whose institutional order has been considerably shattered. Through the simultaneous presence of spatial fragments, heterotopias are always ambiguous spaces that are constantly changing, thus making the subject more prone to experience intellectual uncertainties, or respectively the uncanny. Auster's New York is indeed a city in which, above all, uncertainty reigns. For Quinn, New York is an *ultima thule*, a place that cannot be mapped and, as such, is responsible for the fact that Quinn's attempt to unveil the detective case is a priori doomed to failure.

However, heterotopias do not only disrupt the continuity of space but also the continuity of time. For Foucault, heterotopias are heterochronic, i. e., "begin to function at full capacity when men arrive at a sort of absolute break with their traditional time" ("Of Other Spaces" par. 22). For example, in museums or cemeteries, two heterotopic spaces that Foucault mentions in his study, different time periods of the past are interconnected with the present in one single real space. In the same vein, Stillman's wanderings have the purpose to restore the ultimate past, to return to the Edenic state. It is not a coincidence that the old man's walks are limited to the area of the Manhattan Valley and the Upper West Side, the only part of Manhattan that is bordered by two parks: Riverside Park on the West and Central Park on the East. Quinn records Stillman's movements through the city as follows:

> And yet, as if by conscious design, he kept to a narrowly circumscribed area, bounded on the north by 110th Street, on the south by 72th Street, on the west by Riverside Park, and on the east by Amsterdam Avenue. No matter how haphazard his journeys seemed to be – and each day his itinerary was different – Stillman never crossed these borders. Such precision baffled Quinn, for in all other respects Stillman seemed to be aimless. (58)

The 'gardens' bordering Stillman's mobility zone are a spatialized reminder of a paradise lost and of the fact that Eden has changed its parameters of inside and outside. What once used to be the green center symbolizing (linguistic) harmony and divine order, now represents the outer walls of a fallen world.[11] What once used to be the primordial home, now comes to stand for the essence of the unhomely. Stillman is haunted by the ambiguities that postlapsarian language produces. Unable to repress the mass of free-floating signifiers, Stillman experiences this part of New York as the locus of linguistic uncanniness. By trying to rebuild the fallen language system, Stillman perceives the city from the temporal perspective of the past. However, the past that constantly intermingles with Stillman's present is not limited to prelapsarian times but also stands in close connection to the age of modernism. His philosophy of life follows strategies characteristic of a modernist aesthetic in that he is obsessed with the idea of establishing order to a world that for him lies in fragments. Stillman's specter of the past is therefore shaped by both, the premodern and the modern, or in other words, order and chaos.

This philosophy is also symbolized by New York's grid, an artificial framework of roads produced by rectangular blocks that was introduced to Manhattan with the Commissioner's Plan in 1811. Structurally a physical representation of the Cartesian coordinate system, the implementation of the grid not only radically eliminated the island's former topography of hills and streams, but also the histories of place that were once established by the indigenous population. As Zygmunt Bauman explains: "Grids substituted faceless, anonymous ,'nodes' for self-imposing and meaning-enforcing, dictatorial centres – with a hope to impose

---

[11] In Hebrew the word for garden (*gan*) denotes 'to fence' or 'wall off' and also the word 'paradise' as applied to the garden in Genesis, originally derives from Avestan *pairi*, meaning an "enclosed Persian pleasure garden or park" (Kent par.3).

an artificially and artfully designed homogenous uniform space upon the chaos of nature and historical contingencies" (209).

This rationalization of 'wilderness' was literally smoothing the way for a city that was soon to become the most visual representation of the nation's striving for progress: the phallocentric space of white capitalism. In "The Grid as City Plan," Peter Marcuse points out that the grid's major function was to accelerate economic growth through the real estate industry and that the systematic parceling of the landscape had the advantage to render the urban fabric more coherent and transparent for government authorities. (cf. 289) Placing utilitarianism over aesthetic qualities, the grid was also foreshadowing the modernist architectural paradigm that form should follow function. Taking its name from "a medieval instrument of torture" (290), the gridiron form evokes not only the ruthlessness of utilitarianism (for the sake of aesthetic qualities) but also the notion of being trapped in anguish of body or mind. In the graphic adaptation of Auster's novel, Peter Stillman Jr.'s confusing monologue strictly follows the stylistic device of a nine-panel grid division resembling prison-bars that uncannily bring to mind Peter Stillman Jr.'s nine-year captivity in a windowless room, i. e., a place in which disorientation is induced by darkness (see Illustration 4).

Just like the tower of Babel, symbolizing both the unity and the confusion of languages, the grid also comes to stand for the strange synchronicity of order and disorder. For the walking subject, New York's network of streets is seldom perceived as an orderly structure, but rather as a chaotic assemblage of heterogeneous blocks, or a multiplicity of little different worlds. As Rem Koolhaas remarks in *Delirious New York*: "The Grid defines a new balance between control and decontrol in which the city can be at the same time ordered and fluid, a metropolis of rigid chaos" (20). Accordingly, the grid shares the same conceptual features with the labyrinth that, as Paul Basu argues, are grounded on structural paradox:

> The labyrinth [...] simultaneously represents order and disorder, clarity and confusion, integration and disintegration, unity and multiplicity, artistry and chaos. This duplicity is deeply perspectival; to the "maze-walker" immersed in the structure's passages, the labyrinth is constricted, fragmented, and confusing, whereas to the "maze-viewer," able to rise above the convoluted chaos and perceive its pattern, the dazzling artistry of the labyrinth is made apparent in all its admirable complexity. (49)

"Wer die Stadt lesen kann, kann nicht gleichzeitig in ihr gehen," writes Dorothea Löbbermann, alluding to Michel de Certeau's famous essay "Walking the City," which came out one year prior to the publication of *City of Glass*. In the essay, de Certeau comments on a line displayed on a poster he noticed on the 110th floor of the World Trade Center: "*It's hard to be down when you're up*" (180). Indeed, positioning oneself in urban space along the vertical axis entails an often confusing change of perspective and agency, so that, for example, with the act of

22

Illustration 4: Visualization of spatialized past; taken from Paul Auster. *City of Glass*. Adapted by Paul Karasik and David Mazzucchelli. London: Faber and Faber Limited, 2004.

ascending a tower or skyscraper, the pedestrian leaves social space to become inflicted with "the pleasure of 'seeing the whole'" (ibid. 152) and thus with authority. As de Certeau writes:

> To be lifted to the summit of the World Trade Center is to be lifted out of the city's grasp. One's body is no longer clasped by the streets that turn and return it according to an anonymous law; nor is it possessed, whether as player or played, by the rumble of so many differences and by the nervousness of New York traffic. When one goes up there, he leaves behind the mass that carries off and mixes up in itself any identity of authors or spectators. An Icarus flying above these waters, he can ignore the devices of Daedalus in mobile and endless labyrinths far below. (180)

However, even if the panoramic view from above temporarily frees the viewer from the chaotic space of lived urban experience on the streets below and transforms the city into a 'readable' and coherent whole, the notion of an ordered and graspable city will, in reality, always turn out to be an illusion. Trapped in a hyperreality, or rather, a vertical labyrinth in which all points of reference have been lost, Quinn wonders: "Was it possible to be at the top and at the bottom at the same time?" (118) thus, echoing a paradoxon similar to the one articulated by Michel de Certeau. His state of fundamental disorientation (and homelessness) is an indication of the fact that he has lost his stable position in urban space. However, Quinn poses this ontological question while transforming into a homeless, thus indicating his predicament of being "[l]ost, not only in the city, but within himself as well" (4).

In a similar fashion, the reader looking down onto the novel is in a god-like position and thus inflicted with a certain authority. This authority lies in the individual reader's ability to participate in the process of resolving the mystery, to symbolically yarn Adriane's thread in order to find his/her way out of the textual maze. The postmodern paradigm to make the reader as important as the protagonist, the narrator or the (flesh-and-blood) author suggests a collapse of hierarchies and a disruption of linear succession. Accordingly, all instances involved in the literary work exist simultaneously and are denied a fixed position in the communication process. Stable models of communication, therefore, collapse in the same vein as the Tower of Babel leaving behind only a leap of fragments, the unordered remnants of what was once known as diegesis and poiesis.

CONCLUSION

City of Glass displays and constructs a chronotope that fosters an uncanny state of mind. By deliberately subverting stable boundaries between reality and fiction, the past and the present, the self and the other, the modern and the postmodern, it renders the familiar strange. The uncanny is a defining feature of the modern period in which the art of defamiliarization and disturbance, most evidently exemplified by Surrealism, tried to capture the alienating experiences and insecurities brought forth by (urban) modernity. For example, the popularization of the photographic image and the telegraph at the end of the 19th century made possible the ghostly manifestation of "disembodied voices [...] and images" (Collins and Jervis 6), or the urban crowd, resembling an inanimate mass driven and choreographed by an unseen force, to many newcomers, represented a source of unease.

Yet it is not until the second half of the 20th century that these uncanny forces threaten to replace our natural or anthropological surroundings. Robotics, animation, virtual realities, and the ever-increasing speed with which messages can be sent, altered, or deleted have produced a parallel universe of the uncanny in which everyone has his/her virtual double and in which the dimensions of the real and the unreal, order and chaos can no longer be separated. Paul Auster's *City of Glass* exemplifies this world in the sense that it points to the spatio-temporal shifts that the age of postmodernity has brought forward. The novel's architexture highlights the complexities of representation and also the uncertainties and threats that representation in the digital age provokes. Contemporary writers invite techniques of the uncanny, as they most adequately describe a familiar world which in the latter half of the 20th century has become more and more strange and *other*. As Alice Jardine explains: "[Postmodernist writers] have denaturalized the world that humanism naturalized, a world whose anthropology and anthro-centrism no longer make sense. It is a strange new world they have invented, a world that is *unheimlich*. And such strangeness has necessitated speaking and writing in new and strange ways" (24). Auster's *City of Glass* shatters the notion of the detective novel in the same vein as Cervantes' Don Quixote shatters the notion of the chivalric romance. In making the familiar strikingly unfamiliar and the known unknown, both writers construct a hauntology in the Derridean sense that, grounded on paradox, cast on a spell on the reader, who happily engages in an endless quest for meaning in the depths of space, time and representation.

WORKS CITED

Auster, Paul. *City of Glass*. 1985. *The New York Trilogy*. London and Boston, MA: Faber and Faber, 2004. 3-133. Print.

—. *City of Glass*. Adapted by Paul Karasik and David Mazzucchelli. London: Faber and Faber, 2004. Print.

Bakhtin, Mikhail. *The Dialogic Imagination: Four Essays by M.M. Bakhtin*. Ed. Michael Holquist. Trans. Caryl Emerson and Michael Holquist. Austin, TX: U of Texas P, 1981. Print.

Basu, Paul. "The Labyrinthine Aesthetic in Contemporary Museum Design." *Paul Basu: Reader in Material Culture and Museum Studies*. 1 September. 1999. Web. 2 October 2009.

Bauman, Zygmunt. *Life in Fragments: Essays in Postmodern Morality*. Oxford, MA: Blackwell, 1995. Print.

Bergson, Henri. *Time and Free Will: An Essay on the Immediate Data of Consciousness*. 1910. Mineola, NY: Dover, 2001. Print.

Brooker, Peter. *New York Fictions: Modernity, Postmodernism, The New Modern*. London and New York, NY: Longman, 1996. Print.

Cixous, Hélène. "Fiction and Its Phantoms: A Reading of Freud's 'Das Unheimliche'." *New Literary History* 7.3 (1976): 525-548. Print.

Collins, Jo, and John Jervis. "Introduction." *Uncanny Modernity: Cultural Theories, Modern Anxieties*. Eds. Jo Collins and John Jervis. Basingstoke and New York, NY: Palgrave MacMillan, 2008. 1-9. Print.

de Certeau, Michel. "Spatial Stories." 1988. *What Is Architecture?* Ed. Andrew Ballantyne. London: Routledge, 2002. 72-88. Print.

—. "Walking the City." 1984. *The Cultural Studies Reader*. Ed. Simon During. New York, NY: Routledge, 1993. 151-160. Print.

Derrida, Jacques. *Of Grammatology*. 1967. Baltimore, MD: Johns Hopkins UP, 2001.

—. *Psyche: Inventions of the Other*. Vol.1. 1998. Stanford, CA: Stanford UP, 2007. Print.

—, and Barbara Johnson. *Dissemination*. 1972. London and New York, NY: Continuum, 1981. Print.

Dolar, Mladen. "'I Shall Be with You on Your Wedding-Night': Lacan and the Uncanny." *October* 58 (1991): 5-23. Print.

Ellis, Eugenia Virginia. "City of Dreams: Virtual Space/Public Space." *Writing Urbanism*. Eds. Douglas Kelbough and Kit Krankel McCullough. New York, NY: Routledge, 2008. 372-383. Print.

Foucault, Michel. "Of Other Spaces." 1967. Trans. Jay Miskowiec. *Foucault, Info*. n.p. n.d. Web. 2 Okt. 2009.

—. "What Is an Author?" 1969. *Language, Counter Memory, Practice: Selected Essays and Interviews*. Ed. Donald F. Bouchard. Ithaca, NY: Cornell UP, 1977. 113-139. Print.

Förster, Kim. "Literarische Landschaften: Über die Repräsentation von (urbanen) Räumen in Paul Auster's *The New York Trilogy*." *Postmodern New York City: Transfiguring Spaces – Raum Transformationen*. Heidelberg: Winter, 2003. 247-303. Print.

Freud, Sigmund. "The Uncanny." *The Uncanny*. New York, NY: Penguin, 2003.123-162. Print.

Harvey, David. *The Condition of Postmodernity: An Enquiry into the Origins of Cultural Change*. 1989. Malden, MA, and Oxford, MA: Blackwell, 1990. Print.

Herzogenrath, Bernd. *An Art of Desire: Reading Paul Auster*. Amsterdam: Rodopi, 1999. Print.

Holquist, Michael. "Glossary." *The Dialogic Imagination: Four Essays by Michael Bakhtin*. Austin, TX: U of Texas P, 1981. 423-434. Print.

Huyssen, Andreas. "Present Pasts: Media, Politics, Amnesia." *Public Culture* 12.1 (2000): 21-38. Print.

Jameson, Fredric. *Postmodernism or, The Cultural Logic of Late Capitalism*. Durham, NC: Duke UP, 1991. Print.

Jentsch, Ernst. "On the Psychology of the Uncanny." *Angelaki: A New Journal in Philosophy, Literature, and the Social Sciences* 2.4 (1996): 7-21. Print.

Kent, Robin. "The Garden of Eden." *Architecture RK Conversation.* n.p. n.d. Web. 2 October. 2009.

Koolhaas, Rem. *Delirious New York: A Retroactive Manifesto for Manhattan.* New York, NY: Monacelli, 1997. Print.

Löbbermann, Dorothea. "Weg(be)schreibungen, Ortserkundungen: Transients in der amerikanischen Stadt." *Topographien der Moderne.* Ed. Robert Stockhammer. Munich: Fink, 2005. 263-285. Print.

Masschelein, Anneleen. *Between Animism and Animation: The Challenges of the Uncanny as (Un)concept in the Twentieth and Twenty-first Century.* ICI Berlin. Institute for Cultural Inquiry. 8 April 2009. Keynote Address.

Merleau-Ponty, Maurice. *Phenomenology of Perception.* 1945. London and New York, NY: Routledge, 1958. Print.

Marcuse, Peter. "The Grid as City Plan: New York City and Laissez-Faire Planning in the Nineteenth Century." *Planning Perspectives* 2 (1987): 287-310. Print.

Sennett, Richard. *The Conscience of the Eye: The Design and Social Life of Cities.* New York, NY, and London: Norton, 1990. Print.

Smethurst, Paul. *The Postmodern Chronotope: Reading Space and Time in Contemporary Fiction.* Amsterdam and New York, NY: Rodopi, 2000. Print.

Wolfreys, Julian. "The Urban Uncanny: The City, the Subject, and Ghostly Modernity." *Uncanny Modernity: Cultural Theories, Modern Anxieties.* Eds. Jo Collins and John Jervis. Basingstoke and New York, NY: Palgrave Macmillan, 2008. 168-180. Print.

Part III

Polymorphous Subjectivities

Polymorphous Subjectivities: An Introduction

Susanne Hamscha

The subject is an essential category of modern thought, and one that has been considerably questioned by postmodern thinkers. Subjectivity has long been a site of conflict in debates on representation, ideology, identity, and politics, but it has increasingly come under pressure in postmodern critical theory, not least because of the critiques launched against humanist notions of the subject by Gender and Queer Theory, feminism, and postcolonialism. With the advent of postmodernity, the humanist conception of the subject as a unified self with a stable 'core' identity gave way to an understanding of the subject as fragmented and decentered. According to Fredric Jameson, the epistemological shift from modernity to postmodernity thus entails the metaphorical "'death' of the subject," by which he understands the end of "the bourgeois monad or ego or individual" (15). However, Jameson's assertion is not to be taken at face value. The subject has not vanished in postmodernity; it has only become more elusive and more difficult to grasp.

For postmodernists, the subject is a transformable, multifaceted, fragmented – in short: polymorphous – being that is in a continual state of negotiating between several subject positions, rather than a coherent and unified self. The loss of coherence and unity is, however, not lamented. The postmodern "looks for breaks," as Jameson argues (ix), and celebrates the productive potential that lies within incoherence, fragmentation, and discontinuity. While the decentering of the subject unhinges the notion of a stable identity, it also opens up the possibility of new articulations "around particular nodal points," as Ernesto Laclau suggests (40), allowing for the formation of new identities and the production of new subjects. Subjectivity, one must necessarily conclude, is always contingent on context and situation; it is an effect of power and discourse. In *Discipline and Punish*, Michel Foucault repeatedly returns to the contrast between the illusion of the autonomous subject and the reality of regulatory norms and technologies of power which constantly enforce conformity. The formation of one's "psyche, subjectivity, personality, consciousness" is, according to Foucault, the result of "methods of punishment, supervision, and constraint" (29). This insight leads Foucault to suggest the necessity of the "destruction of the subject as pseudosovereign" (*Language* 222). Put differently, Foucault pronounces the subject dead.

Foucault's account of the subject sounds grimmer than it is, however. "Where there is power, there is resistance," Foucault writes in *History of Sexuality*. "These points of resistance are present everywhere in the power network [...] by definition, they can only exist in the strategic field of power relations" (95-96). Foucault leaves the question as to how exactly resistance operates more or less unanswered, but we can find some clues in the work of Jacques Derrida and Judith Butler. Taking their cue from speech act theory, and in particular the work of J. L. Austin, both Derrida and Butler argue that identities are performatively constructed. For Austin, a performative refers to cases in which "the issuing of the utterance is the performing of an action" (6). A performative utterance is thus an illocutionary speech act: it is both deed and effect at the same time. "I hereby declare you husband and wife" is a prime example of a performative utterance. Utterances like these are not merely conventional but, as Austin says, "ritual or ceremonial" (19), hence repeated in time and not restricted to the moment of their uttering. In her definition of performativity, then, Butler follows Austin and Derrida, who replaced the term "ritual" by "iterability" and thus established a structural model of repetition. Derrida sees both world and stage as characterized by a pervasive theatricality where individual, collective, and institutional identities are iteratively constructed through the repetition of complex citational processes (18). In the first chapter of *Gender Trouble*, Butler introduces the concept of performativity when she states that "gender proves to be performative – that is, constituting the identity it is purported to be. […] There is no gender identity behind the expressions of gender; that identity is performatively constituted by the very 'expressions' that are said to be its results" (33).

Butler's argument can also be applied to identity categories other than gender; identity, as Butler argues, is a signifying practice, a rule-generated process that relies on the consistent repetition of rules that "condition and restrict culturally intelligible practices of identity" (184). The subject, Butler explains, is consequently produced "within practices of signification" (ibid.), but it is "not determined by the rules through which it is generated because signification is not a founding act" (185). In other words, reiteration can always go either way: it can be normative or subversive, it can repeat the rule or it can undermine the rule by means of, for instance, parody, pastiche, irony, or deliberate ambiguity.

Butler's theories have been very influential in the fields of Gender Studies, Body Studies, Feminist Theory, and – maybe most importantly – Queer Theory. Queer Theory is a set of ideas based around the idea that identities are not fixed and do not determine who we are. It proposes that we deliberately challenge all notions of a fixed identity, in varied and non-predictable ways, which is why Queer Theory provides us with the tools to analyze postmodern, polymorphous subjectivities most effectively. Just as the postmodern, so does Queer Theory look for breaks: "queer," as Annamarie Jagose states, "focuses on mismatches between sex, gender, and desire" (3), and Eve Kosofsky Sedgwick suggests that Queer Theory can consequently be understood as postmodernism applied to all "identity-constituting, identity-fracturing discourses" (9) which structure one's positionality in this world.

As this volume's three contributions on "Polymorphous Subjectivities" all demonstrate, Queer Theory conceives of identity as a continuum, with smooth, fluent transitions between different states of being, suggesting a fluid notion of (sexual) identity that calls into question all categories, oppositions, and equations upon which the conventional notions of identity rely. This conception of identity correlates with a postmodern understanding of identity as a project of continual renegotiation and disruption. Postmodern thought is characterized by the notion that identity is the product of the social, cultural, political, and technological context within which a subject is located. Therefore, identity is a transformable structure, which is open to endless redefinitions and reinventions of subjectivity. In other words, the postmodernist project of destabilizing seemingly fixed categories finds its strongest ally in Queer Theory, which aims at the subversion of normative regimes and the deconstruction of cultural conventions.

My own essay, "Losing Nemo, Finding Alternatives," argues for the usefulness of Queer Theory in reconceptualizing subjectivity in a postmodern world. Following Lee Edelman, I conceive of queerness not as an identity, but rather as a dynamic "zone of possibilities" (114), as a positionality that counters heteronormative "repro-ideology" (Warner 10). The positioning of queer subjects against normative practices and structures, I argue, "allows for a wide variety of possibilities for re-imagining and re-structuring, for instance, subjectivity, models of kinship, and forms of community" (161). I put queer theory into practice by reading the animated feature *Finding Nemo* (2003) as a queer film. *Finding Nemo* depicts rather unconventional family models and unusual ways of being which resist the heteronormative ideology of reproduction and teleological conceptions of space and time and makes a case for the productivity of practical kinship relations and a circular time-space continuum. I conclude that *Finding Nemo*, by encouraging us to "design alternative ways of being, form queer alliances, and acknowledge that there are multiple valid, legitimate, and productive ways in which social relations can be organized" (176), provides a glimpse at a more pluralistic, more diversified, and more hopeful world.

In the second essay of this section, "A Squeeze of the Hand," Christoph Hartner performs a queer reading of Herman Melville's novel *Moby-Dick*, arguing that from a contemporary, postmodern perspective the novel seems to abound in queer references and thus lends itself particularly well to a queer reading. In the mid-nineteenth century, homosexuality was not yet an established identity category, which is why referring to *Moby-Dick* as a 'gay novel' would be problematic. However, as Christoph points out, the prominence that Ishmael's eroticization of the (exotic) male body and his fascination with the male physique occupies can hardly be ignored. To be sure, this display of homosexual eroticism is part of the homo-social tradition of the genre that Melville writes in. "What is new," as Christoph notes, "and has been interpreted as an invention of Melville, is the fact that not only the female body is being eroticized but also that of the male" (192), which may induce contemporary readers to interpret Ishmael as a gay character. But the queering potential of Ishmael goes beyond the fascination with the male body and homoerotic episodes such as the infamous sperm-squeezing scene, as Christoph points out. Ishmael "plays with the fluidity of identities, refuses to describe anything as clearly masculine or feminine, heterosexual or homosexual, black or white, good or bad, prose or drama" (ibid.), which makes *Moby-Dick* not only a very queer but also a very postmodern(ist) text.

Leopold Lippert's essay "Negotiating Queer Social Negativity and Humanism in *Shortbus*," finally, takes issue with queer social negativity, a controversial notion which is heatedly debated by Queer Theorists. Leo discusses recent theoretical writings on queer social negativity and traces the ways in which the movie *Shortbus* (2006) acknowledges this phenomenon. He also demonstrates, however, that *Shortbus* "proposes alternative, and indeed utopian, approaches to queer community, sociality, and existence" (195), thus presenting an understanding of sociality that constantly negotiates the contradictions and ruptures of postmodern lives, on the one hand, and the need for human commonality, on the other. Leo's discussion of *Shortbus*, in other words, builds a bridge between 'queer social negativity,' that is, the representation of homosexuality as unproductive, antisocial, and death-driven, and the notion of a 'wiser humanism,' which, as Jill Dolan has it, cherishes multiplicity and difference, thus connecting humans across traditional forms of sociality (22). While *Shortbus* scrutinizes "the antisocial impetus and the emotional and social costs of queer relativism and self-indulgence" (205), as Leo concludes, its fervent assertion on a revitalized humanism also uncovers the complications and challenges of late postmodernity, demonstrating that neither queer social negativity nor a wiser humanism can aptly capture the complexities of a queer positionality.

WORKS CITED

Austin, J. L. *How To Do Things With Words*. Cambridge, MA: Harvard UP, 1975. Print.

Butler, Judith. *Gender Trouble*. New York, NY: Routledge, 1990. Print.

Derrida, Jacques. "Signature Event Context." 1977. *Limited Inc*. Ed. Gerald Graff. Evanston, IL: Northwestern UP, 1988. 1-23. Print.

Dolan, Jill. *Utopia in Performance: Finding Hope at the Theater*. Ann Arbor, MI: U of Michigan P, 2005. Print.

Edelman, Lee. *Homographesis: Essays in Gay Literary and Cultural Theory*. New York, NY: Routledge, 1994. Print.

Foucault, Michel. *Discipline and Punish*. 1975. Trans. Alan Sheridan. New York, NY: Vintage, 1995. Print.

—. *The History of Sexuality: An Introduction*. 1976. London: Penguin, 1998. Print.

—. *Language, Counter-Memory, Practice*. Ed. Donald Bouchard. Trans. Sherry Simon. Ithaca, NY: Cornell UP, 1977. Print.

Jagose, Annamarie. *Queer Theory: An Introduction*. New York, NY: NYU P, 1997. Print.

Jameson, Fredric. *Postmodernism, Or, the Cultural Logic of Late Capitalism*. Durham, NC: Duke UP, 1991. Print.

Laclau, Ernesto. *New Reflections on the Revolution of Our Time*. London: Verso, 1997. Print.

Sedgwick, Eve Kosofsky. *Tendencies*. Durham, NC: Duke UP, 1993. Print.

Warner, Michael. "Introduction: Fear of A Queer Planet." *Social Text* 29 (1991): 3-17. Print.

LOSING NEMO, FINDING ALTERNATIVES: QUEER THEORY AND THE POSTMODERN SUBJECT

SUSANNE HAMSCHA

> Dory: [*singing*]
> Just keep swimming. Just keep swimming. Just keep swimming, swimming, swimming. What do we do? We swim, swim.
>
> Marlin:
> Dory, no singing.
>
> Dory: [*continuing*]
> Ha, ha, ha, ha, ho. I love to swim. When you want to swim you want to swim.
>
> *Finding Nemo*

Let me begin this paper with a proposition. I want to suggest that the postmodern subject is always a queer subject. This might seem like a bold statement to make, but, as I will show in what follows, Queer Theory proves to be enormously useful in reconceptualizing subjectivity in a postmodern world and in resolving the inconsistencies tearing at the postmodern subject. This presumption implies, of course, that Queer Theory is not (as is often falsely assumed) solely concerned with issues of sexuality and gender. Queer Theory's main venture is rather the general transcendence of all binary oppositions and categorical thinking; Queer Theory conceives of identity as a continuum, with smooth, fluent transitions between different states of being. It suggests, in other words, a fluid notion of (sexual) identity that calls into question all categories, oppositions, and equations upon which the conventional notions of identity rely. This conception correlates with a postmodern understanding of identity as a project of continual renegotiation and disruption. Postmodern thought is marked by an "increasing sense that identity is produced by the social, cultural, and technological context from which it emerges" (Malpas 79). Identity, Simon Malpas explains, "therefore becomes a historically mutable structure that remains open to redefinition and transformation in the future" (ibid.).

The objective of my paper is to show that the postmodernist project of destabilizing seemingly fixed and natural categories can find a strong ally in Queer Theory, which provides the tools to subvert normative regimes and deconstruct cultural conventions. For this purpose, I will first endeavor to define 'queerness,' which proves to be a difficult undertaking, as the term actually resists definition. Secondly, I will outline the agenda of Queer Theory and its implications on our understanding of identity and subjectivity. Thirdly, I will put theory into practice and propose a queer reading of the Pixar film *Finding Nemo* (2003) in order to show in what ways postmodern thought can be relocated through Queer Theory. The focus of the analysis of this film will be on kinship relations on the one hand, and on reconfigurations of subjectivity in a queer time and place on the other. More specifically, I will suggest that Nemo, after having been separated from his father Marlin, forms queer alliances which subvert traditional kinship structures and legitimate alternative ways of belonging. Marlin, in turn, enters into a coalition with Dory, a rather odd little fish that lacks short-term memory and cannot remember from one minute to the next where she came from and where she is headed. Having no recollection of the past and no aspiration for the future, Dory defies the sequential logics of time, her sense of subjectivity being fundamentally situated in the fleeting moment of the now. Forced to constantly re-negotiate and re-define not only her own identity, but also her relations with everyone she meets, Dory's identity is virtually indefinable and can always only be reflective of her momentary state of being. "When you want to swim you want to swim," she happily declares; this statement is paradigmatic for Dory, as it demonstrates that her subjectivity, her needs, and her desires are transient and firmly grounded in the now.

As my reading of *Finding Nemo* will show, Queer Theory proposes to conceive of identity as being performatively constituted and to conceptualize subjectivity as ever-changing positionalities. Queer Theory thus provides effective ways and means to account for the inherent fragmentariness and permanent dislocation of postmodern subjects, which suggests that postmodernism indeed fosters a queer state of mind.

WHAT DO QUEERS WANT?

"What do queers want?" Michael Warner asks at the outset of *Fear of a Queer Planet*, one of the earliest and most influential collections on queer politics and social theory ("Introduction" vii). It should be taken for granted that what they want is "not just sex," as Warner answers his own question, because "queers live as queers [...] in contexts other than sex" (ibid.). Identity politics, questions of citizenship and nationality, issues of kinship and belonging, and cultural representation and recognition are as much at the heart of a queer agenda as sexuality. According to Warner, Queer Theory has the task to elaborate on the question of what queers want and is, consequently, not only concerned with sex and sexual identities. To be sure, Queer Theory has evolved out of the fields of Gender Studies, Gay and Lesbian Studies, and Feminist Theory; but to use 'queer' as an umbrella term for gay, lesbian, bisexual, transgender, and transsexual would be restrictive and, quite simply, wrong.[1] Neither is queer merely a 'hip' synonym for gay and lesbian, even though it is frequently used that way in order to "give someone's speech or writing a certain contemporary patina" (Doty 7).[2] While homosexuality is generally conceptualized as the opposite of heterosexuality, queerness rather has to be seen as analogous to heterosexuality (cf. Doty 79). In other words, queer is the flipside of straight; it is an alternative space that runs parallel to the dominant culture, which may be occupied by straight and non-straight people alike. To be queer, as David Halperin suggests, is to be "at odds with the normal, the legitimate, the dominant" (62), but this subject position does not automatically denote any sexual preferences, practices, or pleasures. In other words, 'queer' does not describe a sexual identity, but refers to a subversive positionality against the normative that allows for a wide variety of possibilities for re-imagining and re-structuring, for instance, subjectivity, models of kinship, and forms of community. If one wanted to establish a binary, then 'queerness' would probably be the opposite to 'heteronormativity,' which describes the "pervasive and invisible" default positionality in modern societies (Warner, "Fear" 3). Heteronormativity, as Warner argues, has "a totalizing tendency" that can only be undermined and overcome "by actively imagining a necessarily and desirably queer world" ("Fear" 8). Such a world, Warner fantasizes, would not be dominated by "repro ideology" ("Fear" 10), that is by the misleading rationale in which it is asserted that if everyone were queer (and as such non-reproductive), humankind would die out. This logic is misleading because, of course, there are gay and lesbian parents, because people who have gay sex may – occasionally or regularly – also have straight sex, and because straight sex is not always reproductive. In fact, straight sex more often than not is not supposed to be reproductive. If modern societies, whose "limit and horizon is productive futurism," con-

---

1 One of the earliest collections of essays on Queer Theory is a special edition of *differences*, edited by Teresa de Lauretis and published in 1991. Significantly, de Lauretis' introduction to the volume is entitled "Queer Theory: Lesbian and Gay Sexualities," which suggests that she subsumes 'lesbian' and 'gay' under the term 'queer.' However, in her essay, she then problematizes the relation between 'queer,' 'lesbian and gay,' and 'homosexual,' arguing that in recent years, the somewhat off-putting 'homosexual' was replaced by 'gay,' which again gave way to the more inclusive phrasing of 'lesbian and gay.' 'Queer,' in turn, is intended 'to mark a certain critical distance' from the aforementioned terms and to problematize the 'ideological liabilities' they carry with them (de Lauretis iv-v).

2 See also Annamarie Jagose, who writes that "[i]n recent years, 'queer' has come to be used differently, sometimes as an umbrella term for a coalition of culturally marginal sexual self-identifications and at other times to describe a nascent theoretical model which has developed out of more traditional lesbian and gay studies" (1).

ceived of queerness as the embodiment of the "death drive," as Edelman has it, people would have to rule all sexual acts that do not result in reproduction as queer (*No Future* 27). Warner's example of "repro ideology" illustrates very well why the term 'queer' is so contested and so difficult to pin down. Clearly, queerness transcends sexual orientation and, subsequently, to be queer means to hold a certain ideological position rather than to 'have' a specific identity.

Positionality and identity are easily confused, but I believe that it is crucial to sharply distinguish between these two notions. As a category that is constantly in the process of formation, 'queer' resists all attempts of stabilization and exploits the incoherencies of hegemonic culture (cf. Jagose 2-3). If one concedes that, as a consequence, "[*t*]*here is nothing particular to which it* [queer] *necessarily refers*" (Halperin 62), then, Halperin suggests, queer can best be described as a non-identity, rather than as an identity in the conventional sense. However, if we regard 'queerness' not as a (non-) identity but as a position, then the vagueness inherent in the term 'queer,' which may at some times seem unsatisfactory, becomes one of its biggest strengths. The indeterminacy, transformability, and elasticity of 'queer' strongly suggest a conception of queerness as a continuum or "a zone of possibilities," as Edelman calls it (*Homographesis* 114). Such a conception of a queer continuum arguably provides the greatest possible frame of identification, because it allows individuals to inhabit a queer space and to identify with a queer ideology without having to identify as homo-/hetero-/bi-/transsexual.[3] Being constantly in flux, 'queer' consequently does not and cannot take any specific, concrete materiality. Its resistance to dominant discourses must therefore be relational instead of oppositional; or, to put it differently, 'queer' denaturalizes the normal through internal subversion rather than through the formation of a discourse that runs counter to normative regimes. The queer subject, it follows, inhabits a privileged position, as a queer positionality actually

---

[3] The notion of a queer continuum recalls Adrienne Rich's notion of the "lesbian continuum," which she coined in her famous essay "Compulsory Heterosexuality and the Lesbian Continuum." In this essay, Rich argues that heterosexuality has to be seen as a political institution and is thus only one of many options that women have in structuring their lives. She encourages female identification as a means to imagine alternatives to heterosexuality, by way of which she introduces the "lesbian continuum": "I mean the term *lesbian continuum* to include a range—through each woman's life and throughout history—of woman-identified experience, not simply the fact that has had or consciously desired genital sexual experience with another woman. If we expand it to embrace many more forms of primary intensity between and among women, including the sharing of a rich, inner life, the bonding against male tyranny, the giving and receiving of practical and political support, [...] we begin to reach breadths of female history and psychology which have lain out of reach as a consequence of limited, mostly clinical, definitions of *lesbianism*" (Rich 239). A similar argument can be made, I believe, for compulsory heteronormativity and the queer continuum.

enables the envisioning of alternative "relations among sexual behaviors, erotic identities, constructions of gender, forms of knowledge, regimes of enunciation, logics of representation, modes of self-constitution, and practices of community," which radically redefines and restructures "relations among power, truth, and desire" (Halperin 62).

WHAT DOES QUEER THEORY WANT?

What does Queer Theory want? This might then be the logical follow-up question to my attempt of defining a notoriously indefinable term. The answer to this question, as the quote above by David Halperin suggests, lies essentially in the restructuring of power relations. Power, in the Foucauldian sense, "is everywhere [...] because it comes from everywhere" (Foucault 93). Power is omnipresent and is produced "from one moment to the next," as it emerges out of relations and situations (ibid.). As a "multiplicity of force relations," power is thus the organizing principle that determines which ways of being are legitimate, or normal, and which are illegitimate, or abnormal (Foucault 92).

As power is omnipresent and all-pervasive, resistance, as Foucault argues, "is never in a position of exteriority to power" (95), but rather resides *within* the web of power relations, in the form of mobile and transitory points that traverse social stratifications. In other words, resistance is always already inherent in normative regimes and describes the search for alternatives to dominant structures. Queerness, as I have pointed out above, signifies a position of resistance that seeks to reconfigure the dominant societal order by imagining an alternative space in which commonly 'illegitimate' ways of being are legitimized and given due recognition. Queer Theory, then, provides the ways and means to theorize that position of resistance.

Since 'queerness' is a positionality with no definite referent working against clear-cut identity categories, Queer Theory can hardly be said to be the theory of anything in particular, as Lauren Berlant and Michael Warner point out. Queer Theory "cannot be assimilated to a single discourse, let alone a propositional program," as they state, but it has gained ground in a variety of disciplines (343). Significantly, it flourished most visibly in those academic fields "where expert service to the state has been least familiar and where theory has consequently meant unsettlement rather than systematization" (Berlant and Warner 348). Defined by its resistance to systematize the world and its contestation of hegemonic discourses, Queer Theory can be utilized to describe and analyze "a wide range of impulses and cultural expressions" that reach beyond the boundaries of sexualities and gender (Doty 2).

Without any doubt, the primary challenge posed by Queer Theory is to dominant conceptions of the relations between sex, gender, sexuality, and identity. Gay and Lesbian Studies and Feminist Theory have, in their respective attempts to reconfigure and de-naturalize these relations, remained stuck in binary oppositions. Thus, 'homosexuality' remained the fundamental Other of the normative 'heterosexuality,' and 'woman' that of 'man.' While Gay and Lesbian Studies and Feminist Theory successfully severed the ties between sex, gender, and sexuality, the ties of these notions to identity were preserved and retained their descriptive force. Queer Theory, however, attempts to politicize sex, gender, and sexuality in a way that divorces identity from any seemingly stable points of reference, thus resisting tendencies to categorize, evaluate, and naturalize different ways of being. The presumptions underlying such a project must be that first, identity is not determined by nature/biology but is a cultural construct; second, identity is thus always in the process of forming itself, a work-in-progress that can never be completed; and third, because identity is constantly re-constructed and re-negotiated, one needs to conceive of identity as something that is *done* rather than as something that one has. In short, Queer Theory presumes that identity is performative.

QUEER THEORY AND THE POSTMODERN SUBJECT

The premise that identity is performatively constituted firmly grounds Queer Theory within current postmodern thought. For postmodernists, as Stuart Sim explains, "the subject is a fragmented being who has no essential core of identity, and is to be regarded as a process in a continual state of dissolution rather than a fixed identity or self that endures change over time" (334). If the subject is fragmented and has no definite center, then its existence must consequently be purely relational and determined by its momentary positionality.[4] In other words, the subject is not a self-enclosed, autarchic being, but it constitutes itself again and again through performative acts.

[4] See also Kevin Hart, who states that "[the] fragmentary […] has no hidden center around which it revolves, for each fragment exists only in relation with others" (72). David Harvey makes an argument for postmodernism's strong affinity for the fragment when he writes: "I begin with what appears to be the most startling fact about postmodernism: its total acceptance of the ephemerality, fragmentation, discontinuity, and the chaotic that formed the one half of Baudelaire's conception of modernity. But postmodernism responds to the fact of that in a very particular way. It does not try to transcend it, or counteract it, or even to define the 'eternal and immutable' elements that might lie within it. Postmodernism swims, even wallows, in the fragmentary and the chaotic currents of change as if that is all there is" (44).

Judith Butler's *Gender Trouble* (1990) is probably the study that was most influential in propagating the notion of performativity and the constructedness of sex and gender. In *Gender Trouble*, Butler proposes that heterosexuality is naturalized through regulatory regimes which reproduce normative relations between sex, gender, and desire. The flipside of this proposition is that "certain kinds of 'identities' cannot 'exist' – that is, those in which gender does not follow from sex and those in which the practices of desire do not 'follow' from either sex or gender" (17). It is only through these exclusionary principles that gender identity becomes intelligible. Instead of attempting to naturalize same-sex desire and liberating it from its marginal position, Butler seeks to contest the truth of gender itself, arguing that the deconstruction of all gender identity is ultimately more effective in achieving legitimation of 'deviant' sexualities. Butler thus reconfigures gender as a cultural fiction; it has to be understood as a performance, or construction, that becomes naturalized by means of endless repetition. "The action of gender," as Judith Butler argues, "requires a performance that is repeated" (140). Gender therefore has no essence, but "various acts of gender create the idea of gender, and without those acts, there would be no gender at all. Gender is, thus, a construction that regularly conceals its genesis" (ibid.). There is nothing authentic, original, or even natural about gender, but it is rather "an identity tenuously constituted in time, instituted in an exterior space through a *stylized repetition of acts*" (ibid.).[5]

Heterosexuality, which passes as the normal, natural sexuality and is therefore never in need of explaining itself, is a discursive production, Butler suggests. Or, to put it differently, it is not the foundation of the sex/gender system (which purports to merely describe heterosexuality), but it is its *effect*. Without the notion of homosexuality as its alleged 'copy,' however, heterosexuality could not set itself up as the 'authentic' and 'natural' sexuality. Heterosexuality thus presupposes homosexuality and depends on its existence as an imitation to be able to affirm its own originality (Butler, "Imitation" 22). The binary of original and copy be-

5 In response to critics of her theories, who understood gender as willfully performed, Butler emphasizes in her later book *Bodies That Matter* (1993) that "performativity is neither free play nor theatrical self representation; nor can it be simply equated with performance" (95). Gender is not like clothing that can be put on and off at will, or as it suits an individual in any given situation, but it is constrained and regulated: "Performativity cannot be understood outside of a process of iterability, a regularized and constrained repetition of norms. And this repetition is not performed *by* a subject; this repetition is what enables a subject and constitutes the temporal condition for the subject. This iterability implies that 'performance' is not a singular 'act' or event, but a ritualized production, a ritual force of prohibition and taboo, with the threat of ostracism and even death controlling and compelling the shape of the production, but not, I will insist, determining it fully in advance" (95).

gins to crumble when the performative repetition of normative gender identities fails and queer genders are produced. Both homosexuality and heterosexuality, then, have to be understood as the effect of signifying practices. As Halperin explains, "'homosexual,' like 'woman,' is not a name that refers to a 'natural kind' of thing. It's a discursive, and homophobic, construction that has come to be misrecognized as an object under the epistemological regime known as realism" (45). While Gay and Lesbian Studies may proclaim 'pride' and encourage people to 'come out,' gay and lesbian activists rely on and affirm unifying identity categories and repeatedly undermine their own cause by reasserting their status of otherness.

Queer Theory, although undoubtedly deeply anchored in the study of sexualities, has successfully transplanted its project of denaturalization also on other "axes of identification" (Jagose 99). According to Rosemary Hennessy, queer is both "anti-assimilationist and anti-separatist," thus marking

> an effort to speak from and to the differences and silences that have been suppressed by the homo-hetero binary, an effort to unpack the monolithic identities "lesbian" and "gay," including the intricate ways lesbian and gay sexualities are inflected by heterosexuality, race, gender, and ethnicity. (86-87)

Eve Sedgwick makes a similar, but even stronger, claim in her study *Tendencies*, in which she observes that recent work on the term 'queer'

> spins the term outward along dimensions that can't be subsumed under gender and sexuality at all: the ways that race, ethnicity, postcolonial nationality criss-cross with these *and other* identity-constituting, identity-fracturing discourses, for example. Intellectuals and artists of color whose sexual self-definition includes "queer" [...] are using the leverage of "queer" to do a new kind of justice to the fractal intricacies of language, skin, migration, state. Thereby the gravity (I mean the *gravitas*, the meaning, but also the *center* of gravity) of the term "queer" itself deepens and shifts. (9)

Hennessy and Sedgwick's remarks suggest that 'queer' is a concept that can only be meaningfully employed within the framework of postmodern thought. As I have mentioned above, the notion of queerness relies on an understanding of subjects as fragmented and of identities as being performed. Thus, there are significant overlaps between the fundamentals of postmodern thought and the agenda of Queer Theory. Indeed, all theoretical debates of 'queer' over the last two decades have to a great extent involved talk about a 'postmodernization of sex' in signaling a dissolution of transparent and solid categories, which entails a "loss of faith in any compelling grand narrative of sexuality" (Plummer 520). Queer Theory, as Kenneth Plummer proposes, can therefore also be understood as "poststructuralism (and postmodernism) applied to sexualities and gender" (ibid.). What is more, Queer Theory can be understood as postmodernism applied to all "identity-constituting, identity-fracturing discourses," as Sedgwick puts it (9), which structure one's positionality in this world.

LOSING NEMO, FINDING ALTERNATIVES

Having thus outlined the agenda of Queer Theory, I want to make another proposition. I want to suggest that *Finding Nemo* (2003) is a postmodern queer film. Again, this might seem like a bold proposition to make, but, as a matter of fact, this innocent kid's flick is one of the queerest movies produced in recent years.[6] Nemo is a film about unconventional ways of being, unconventional family/kinship structures, and unconventional ways of perceiving one's subjectivity and one's relations to others. The "unconventionality" depicted in this movie is nothing short of radical: in Nemo, "normal," straight relationships end in death, suggesting that nuclear family structures are doomed to failure; the relationships that prevail and propose valuable alternatives to "repro-sexuality" are the queer ones which, paradoxically enough, have no future.

Finding Nemo is an "odd little feature" (Halberstam, "Boys" 111) which tells the story of a clown-fish family that is tragically ripped apart by a hungry Barracuda in the first few minutes of the film. The mother fish perishes together with almost all of her eggs, leaving behind her henceforth very anxious partner, Marlin, and one offspring, Nemo. The film then cuts to Nemo's first day at school: Marlin, still traumatized by the Barracuda-attack, has become an overprotective father to Nemo. Marlin is paranoid about his son's safety not only because Nemo is his only family left, but also because Nemo is slightly disabled (his right pectoral fin is very small) and – so Marlin believes – thus cannot take proper care of himself. Nemo, however, grows tired of his father's nervous and hysterical at-

---

6 I concur with Judith Halberstam that much radical potential resides in cartoons and animated movies primarily targeted at kids. Halberstam mentions *Shrek*, *Wallace and Gromit*, *Over the Hedge*, *Monsters, Inc.*, and *SpongeBob Squarepants* as prime examples of children's movies that feature characters with ambiguous genders, or homosocial characters, or non-conventional kinship structures (cf. Halberstam, "Pixarvolt" and Nielsen, "Pop Culture and Queer Fish"). However, one of the most memorable homosocial Disney couples is missing from Halberstam's list, namely Timon and Pumbaa from *The Lion King* (1994). Timon, a wise-cracking meerkat, and Pumbaa, a simple-minded warthog, seem like an unlikely pair, but their inter-species relationship weathers all storms and is the only long-lasting relationship in this film. They both have no family or community they belong to, but they have clearly found love and friendship in each other. Eventually, Timon and Pumbaa find a surrogate-family in Simba (the Lion King), his female partner Nala, and their enlarged family. Even though Timon and Pumbaa are clearly the odd ones out amidst a pride of lions, they are acknowledged as equals and thus transform from the quintessential outcasts to fully integrated members of the lion community.

tempts to guard him from all dangers of the ocean and, in a moment of rebellion that should prove his capability, he swims off into the open sea, only to be caught by a diver and placed into a fishbowl in a dentist's office. Marlin immediately begins a frantic, mad search for his missing son, which leads him all the way to Sydney, Australia. On his way through the ocean, Marlin repeatedly finds himself in dangerous, life-threatening situations from which he can only escape by overcoming his own fears and by accepting the help of Dory, a quirky blue fish he crosses paths with shortly after Nemo's abduction. Eventually, Nemo can free himself from the dentist's fishbowl and is reunited with his father, but the dramatic events have changed their little family in significant ways.

The plot of *Finding Nemo* sounds straight enough, so why suggest that it is a queer film? To rephrase the question: What can be gained by reading *Finding Nemo* through the lens of Queer Theory? As my analysis will show, a queer reading of this film serves as an excellent example to highlight the connections and similar agendas between Queer Theory and Postmodern Theory. In fact, the film's focus on postmodern subjectivity can only fully be grasped when read in connection with queerness. It is important to note at this point that, as Doty explains, "queer readings and positions can become modified or change over time as people, cultures, and politics change" (8). This suggests that queerness does not reside in the text, but is produced in and through exchanges between a text, its readers, and the ways in which they connect this text to the world they know. The label 'queer' can thus never be applied to the essence of a text (cf. Sullivan 192); it can only be ascribed to a process, to a move through which the reader assumes a queer positionality and seeks to put an alternative space on the map, cutting away from the space inhabited by an all-pervasive heteronormativity. A queer reading, in other words, presents a viable alternative to a straight reading, which is consequently left as only one of several possible readings. At the same time, heteronormativity is exposed as only one of several positions one can take in reading this world and is thus dismantled as *the* one and only natural positionality.

Finding Nemo is rich with queer characters, ranging from homosocial, vegetarian sharks[7] to a forgetful blue regal tang, and a gender-confused clownfish. No, I do not suggest that Nemo is a transsexual; however, his father might just as well be one. Most viewers probably perceive Marlin as a single father, who is strug-

---

[7] It is interesting to note that the DreamWorks animation *Shark Tale* also features a vegetarian shark, Lenny, who is coded as a queer character. Lenny is scared to 'come out' as a vegetarian to his father, Don Lino, the leader of a mob of criminally-inclined sharks and a true predator. When he learns that Lenny is a vegetarian and dresses up as a dolphin (a metaphor for drag?), Don Lino is angry and mad, but eventually he makes up with his son.

gling to raise his only son. However, *Nemo* secretly harbors a narrative of transformation that is nothing short of queer. As Joan Roughgarden explains in her study *Evolution's Rainbow*, clownfish are hermaphroditic, born with active male and dormant female reproductive organs. If his partner is removed, the "remaining male turns into a female," and mates with the largest juvenile male (33). To be sure, after his partner is killed, Marlin assumes a role that has traditionally been associated with femininity: he becomes a clucking hen, is overprotective and at times hysteric. The lack of a mother is at no point addressed in the film[8], and also Marlin's loss of a female partner is not much of an issue, even though the future comes to a halt when Nemo's mother and her eggs die. Reproductivity and a traditional family structure are no longer secured, but Marlin adapts to the situation by performing both the role of a father and a mother, constantly shifting between his two roles as the situation demands.

Futurity is once again threatened, however, when Nemo is netted by a diver, and this threat can only be warded off as Nemo redefines the concepts of kinship and belonging. Finding a surrogate family in his fellow captivated fish in the dentist's tank, Nemo learns that a 'family' is not necessarily tied together by blood. To be sure, the fish may have formed a familial bond purely out of necessity, but the other inhabitants of the tank constitute a kind of family nevertheless. They have formed a queer alliance, or "practical kinship," in Bourdieu's terms, which is defined by the calling in of favors and debts, the utilization of connections, and an individual's immediate needs (cf. Freeman 308). Bound together by being in the same oppressive situation and sharing a common goal they hope to reach (liberation, that is), these inhabitants of the tank have developed a sense of responsibility for one another which deems it unimaginable that part of their group may be left behind in the dentist's tank, or one fish may gain freedom at the expense of the others. They are a very close-knit and caring community who look out for each other and accept each other with all their flaws and inadequacies (one of them suffers from delusions, another is a germophobe, and yet another shows tendencies of compulsive behavior). Nemo becomes a full member of the fish's 'tankhood' through an initiation ritual which officially marks him as one who shares their fate of being held captive. His acceptance into the tankhood allows Nemo to conceive of his fellow fish as his surrogate family and

---

8 Interestingly enough, *Finding Nemo* does not depict a single straight, nuclear family, but is flooded by (single) fathers. On Nemo's first day at school, Marlin meets three male acquaintances, which all seem to be the primary caretakers of their respective children. Also Crush, the turtle who helps Marlin and Dory find their way to Sydney, seems to raise his children by himself – at least there is no mentioning of his kids' mother, nor any other hint towards the existence of a female turtle in his family (cf. Frankel 76).

redefine the concept of kinship. Of course, his kinship relations have never conformed to the nuclear family model, but his separation from Marlin forces him to bond with perfect strangers. In order to develop a feeling of belonging to the community, Nemo has to define kinship as a set of practices rather than as biological relations, which "emerge to address fundamental forms of human dependency" (Butler, "Kinship" 14-15). To distinguish between practical and biological kinship is thus irrelevant, or even futile, as both forms of kinship follow the same principles. Kinship "consists of relationships renewed" (Freeman 308), of relationships constantly reactivated and mobilized for future use. Kinships are solidified by time spent together and experiences shared by various individuals, regardless of their heritage and their genes. The queer alliance that Nemo and the fish of the tankhood form is not radically different from a nuclear family, or marked as fundamentally other. Their alliance may have an expiration date and dissolve once they have accomplished their goals, but that does not make their bond less valid, less legitimate, or less significant than biological relations.

Besides sharing the fate of captivity, it is the stigmatization as an outcast that binds Nemo and the other fish together. Out in the ocean, Nemo was repeatedly told that he was inadequate and incapable because of his small pectoral fin. Amidst his new family members, who are all different in one way or another, Nemo experiences a feeling of normalcy for the first time in his life. As he realizes that what defines 'normal' really lies in the eye of the beholder and that it is impossible "to think of oneself as normal without thinking that some other kind of person is pathological" (Warner, *Normal* 60), he refutes the desire to be normal and comes to accept his otherness. As Michael Warner reminds us, however, "normal and pathological are not the only options" one has in defining oneself (*Normal* 59). Indeed, measuring "the worth of their relations and their way of life by the yardstick of normalcy" is "social suicide" (ibid.). Instead, Warner opts for positioning oneself as queer and embracing one's otherness as a "healthy variation" (*Normal* 60), which is precisely what Nemo eventually does. Interacting with others in a "queer culture," to use Warner's term, Nemo learns to put the normal into perspective and comes to understand that normalcy is an empty category that is not worth striving for, because "everyone deviates from the norm in some context or other" (*Normal* 70).

FORGETFUL FISH; OR, IN A QUEER TIME AND PLACE

Another "healthy variation" from the norm is Dory, Marlin's faithful companion in the search for Nemo. At the outset of my paper, I already implied that Dory is the most visibly queer character in *Finding Nemo*. Judith Halberstam emphasizes that Ellen DeGeneres, who voices Dory, is very much of a lesbian – she calls her the "very queer Ellen DeGeneres" ("Forgetting" 322) – as if one were able to infer Dory's queerness from Ellen's sexuality.[9] However, by drawing such quick conclusions, one easily misses the enormous potential that characters like Dory have in imagining alternative ways of being and knowing that cannot be measured by the infamous "yardstick of normalcy" (Warner, *Normal* 59).

Dory first appears in *Finding Nemo* when she literally bumps into Marlin only minutes after the diver captures Nemo. A completely hysterical and anxious Marlin accepts Dory's offer to help him on his search, which soon proves to be counterproductive. Dory suffers from short term memory loss and keeps forgetting why she and Marlin are swimming to Australia. Her "odd sense of time," as Halberstam explains, "scrambles all temporal interactions" ("Boys" 112) and adds a layer to the narrative which probably strikes most viewers as humorous and absurd. When she explains her problem to Marlin, for instance, Dory tells him that short-term memory loss runs in the family, but then again she comments that she cannot remember her family – so how can she be sure? Forever "exile[d] in the present tense" (ibid.), Dory's subjectivity does not bear any ties to the past (i. e. her heritage) and none of her actions are geared towards the future (i. e. reproduction). Inhabiting a queer space, Dory thus offers "fascinating insights into queer time, […] queer knowledge […] and anti-familial kinship" (ibid.).

Queer time, as Halberstam explains, emerges from the AIDS crisis, which severely diminished the horizons of possibility for the gay community and placed an emphasis on the here and now (*Queer* 2). Queer time has therefore frequently been aligned with consumption, risk, disease, and death, as opposed to a 'straight' time that is associated with the promise of futurity and longevity.[10] There is, however, another facet of queer time, as Halberstam remarks, which is all too often overlooked: Queer time is also about "the potentiality of a life unscripted by the conventions of family, inheritance, and child rearing" (ibid.). Dory embodies that potentiality, as her subjectivity and her perception of the world around her are structured "according to logics that lie outside of those paradigmatic markers of life experience – namely, birth, marriage, reproduction, and death" (ibid.), which generates an alternative temporality that may not be

---

9 See also the announcement of a Gender Studies conference, in which Halberstam's lecture on *Finding Nemo* is advertised as follows: "In her analytical reading the character Dory (voiced by lesbian celebrity Ellen Degeneres), a blue tang suffering from short-term memory loss who helps clown fish Marlin search for his son Nemo […]" (A.M.B., "The Future of Feminism"). Note how a point is made out of Ellen DeGeneres' sexuality, while the actors who dub Marlin and Nemo are not even mentioned.

10 For more details on this point, see Leo Bersani, "Is the Rectum a Grave?" and Lee Edelman, *No Future*, esp. 1-31.

*re*productive but is productive nonetheless. The conception of a queer time can only be meaningfully employed within a frame of postmodern thought, because postmodernism carries with it an opportunity "to rethink the practice of cultural production, its hierarchies and power dynamics, its tendency to resist or capitulate" (*Queer* 6). Queer time thus emerges as a meaningful model of temporality once one seizes this opportunity and resists the temporal logics of reproduction, family, and longevity. Of course, a queer adjustment in the way we conceive of time also necessitates new conceptions of space. Queer space refers to the space that queers inhabit and in which they engage to form productive relations and a counterpublic that is organized according to non-normative logics of community, identity, and embodiment (cf. ibid.).

Normative, teleological conceptions of the time-space continuum rely on memory, on a knowledge of the past and an awareness of one's embeddedness within a social structure. According to such a conception, the question where one comes from and where one is headed significantly defines one's identity. The present, in other words, is inextricably linked to the past and the future. *Finding Nemo*, then, introduces a queer space-time continuum, which is encoded in Dory's forgetfulness. Forgetting is the flipside of memory, as "memory is a process that depends crucially upon forgetting," as Joseph Roach states (2). What is more, memory is generally aligned with knowledge and power, whereas forgetting is synonymous with failure and inferiority. While memory is productive, because it constantly reproduces the past and thus shapes present and future, forgetting (similar to queerness) symbolizes the death of futurity and is essentially destructive. *Finding Nemo* challenges this conception of the memory/forgetting dyad and explores the positive potential of forgetting. Forgetting, as Marlin has to concede towards the end of the film, when he believes Nemo to be dead, can indeed be a blessing. Still haunted by the memories of the deadly Barracuda attack, he cannot bear the thought of a future without his son. His deep desire to forget in order to be able to imagine a future recalls Nietzsche's argument that there can be "no happiness, no cheerfulness, no hope, no pride, no real present, without forgetfulness" (35). Dory, in contrast, is not burdened by memories or haunted by her past. Past and future are of no relevance to her, as her existence is firmly rooted in the now and is, in fact, a constant process of renegotiating her own identity and her relations with everyone she encounters. Put differently, time, in its conventional conception, cannot adequately describe Dory's specific situatedness. The present is, because of its ephemeral and fleeting character, essentially a non-time that only exists in passing and seemingly lacks meaning if severed from past and future, if divorced from origin and telos. Dory's "ephemeral sense of knowledge and her continuous sense of a lack of context" (Halberstam, "Boys" 112) necessitate an investment in the moment and an adaptability to new situations in order to be able to make meaning. Dory finds herself in a new situation in virtually every moment of every day. There is no essence to her identity; in good postmodern fashion, it is produced time and again in an endless series of performative acts, and can 'only' be reflective of her momentary state of being in a specific context. When she wants to swim, she swims, and when she decides to accompany Marlin, she does so because she sees herself as Marlin's 'little helper' in that particular moment.

Even though Dory is essentially unattached, she does not follow her immediate needs and desires in a hedonistic fashion; her actions are always regulated by her relation to Marlin and by the queer coalition they have formed. Dory and Marlin are a peculiar pair indeed: Dory aids Marlin without desiring him or expecting some kind of retribution, she accompanies Marlin on a journey that – to her – has no specific goal, and she helps to repair the familial bonds between Marlin and Nemo without knowing the specifics of their relationship (cf. ibid.). Similar to the bond of the fish in the dentist's tank, Marlin and Dory's queer coalition is a practical kinship that is first and foremost based on dependency. To Dory, who has no memories of her biological family whatsoever, Marlin is as much next of kin as her 'real' family would be. Marlin functions as father/brother to Dory, his continuous presence, the fact that he "sticks with her," as she puts it, infusing her with a feeling of safety and security. Marlin, in turn, 'utilizes' Dory for his own means. While he is inhibited by his knowledge of the dangers that lurk in every corner of the ocean, Dory's exile in the present is marked by insouciance and relentless hope. Whereas Marlin is repeatedly on the brink of giving up, because the past has taught him to always expect the worst, Dory's optimism cannot be shaken. She does not remember why she and Marlin are swimming to Sydney and whom they are trying to find, but that does not matter. In a queer time and place, hope functions as the foil to reproductivity. As Dory does not comply with the rules of teleological time and the reproductive imperative, she is situated outside the social order, in the anti-social realm of negativity and destruction (cf. Edelman, "Ever After" 469-70). In order to redefine her existence as positive and productive, she needs to produce new queer social imaginaries, in which futurity is not secured by reproduction but hope. Queerness is, in other words, not the "social order's death drive," as Edelman (*No Future* 3) polemically proposes, but it is, in fact, the realm of ultimate hopefulness. It figures as a state of being which is, ideally, not regulated by normative regimes but characterized by endless possibilities in which social relations can be meaningfully organized. Whatever their goal may be, Dory is clearly confident that she and Marlin will reach it. If necessary, they simply have to redefine it. Nemo may be lost, but they will surely find an alternative, as long as they just keep swimming.

NOW WHAT? – BRINGING IT ALL BACK HOME

Finding Nemo ends with the fish of the tankhood finally escaping from the dentist's aquarium. When the dentist has to clean the tank and puts the inhabitants of the tank into plastic bags, they seize the moment to roll out of the window, across the street, and into the harbor. The final shot shows them swimming on the surface of the ocean in their plastic bags from which there is yet again no possibility to escape. "Now what?" one of them asks – what are they to do now that they have found a way out of the tank only to put themselves into another situation that restricts them in their freedom?

"Now what?" is also the question with which I want to conclude this paper. What (if anything) can we take home from a queer reading of *Finding Nemo*? Does Queer Theory as a form of postmodern theory provide us with tools and methods that are not only useful in reflecting on the world around us, but that can also bring about actual political and social change? Or does it promise us ways of liberation from hegemonic discourses only to leave us stuck in a plastic bag? In recent years, 'kinship' has been a buzzword in debates on equal rights and issues such as same-sex marriage and the adoption right for same-sex couples. The title of Judith Butler's essay "Is Kinship Always Already Heterosexual?" sums up what is at stake in such debates. Too often, Butler states, marriage and kinship become confounded in popular opinion, "when we hear not only that marriage is and ought to remain a heterosexual institution and bond but also that kinship does not work, or does not qualify as kinship, unless it assumes a recognizable family form" (Butler, "Kinship" 14). Marriage, according to such a world-view, is the institution that should secure the structure of the nuclear family and organize sexuality in the service of reproductivity. If same-sex marriage, the non-reproductive evil twin of straight marriage, were legalized, then reproduction would no longer be regulated by the state and the Child, the common fear seems to be, would have to be put on the list of endangered species. The Child, as Edelman persuasively argues, "remains the perpetual horizon of every acknowledged politics" (Edelman, *No Future* 3). The legitimacy of relationships, but also political and social recognition, is thus tied to one's willingness to reproduce, to "fight for the children" and thus for the future (cf. ibid.). But can this stance on (same-sex) marriage be upheld in the face of the breakdown of the nuclear family? How far should the state's regulation of sexuality and desire go, how far do we *want* it to go?[11]

By redefining kinship and releasing it from the iron grip of repro-sexuality, relationships of various kinds which do not conform to the nuclear family model may achieve recognition and legitimacy. Human dependency, not reproduction, should be the force that structures kinship. Child rearing, providing emotional support to loved ones, taking care during times of illness – these are not hetero or homo acts but *human* acts which can be performed just as well by biological relatives as by surrogates. A film like *Finding Nemo*, then, does have a real political agenda as it raises people's awareness that growing up outside of nuclear family structures and forming alternative alliances is not 'abnormal' but just a different, queer way of being. I refute the assumption that assuming a queer rather than a heteronormative position and engaging in non-reproductive relationships means following and giving in to the death drive. As I have shown in this paper, the productivity of queer relationships has to be located outside of the cycle of reproduction. Dory may never *have* a family, but she *saves* one and thus contributes her share to securing the future. The fish of the tankhood will never produce offspring, but they instill a faith and self-reliance in Nemo that will define his future significantly. Queers, in other words, may not reproduce their own biological offspring, but they can nevertheless participate in the future in productive ways.

As the discussions on same-sex marriage are reaching fever pitch in the U.S. and in many European countries, the project of Queer Theory to destabilize and de-naturalize long-established conceptions of identity, sexuality, and embodiment is more important than ever. To conceive of all identity categories as performatively constituted and regulated by normative regimes is only the first step. The second step must be the active resistance to the acceptance of heternormativ-

---

11 Same-sex marriage is a very controversial issue, also within the LGBT community. In November 2003, the Massachusetts Supreme Court ruled that same-sex couples were entitled to marriage rights – a decision which deeply divided the United States and sparked a worldwide debate on same-sex marriage. In 2004, initiatives to ban same-sex marriage were passed in eleven state ballots; most recently, in November 2008, the ban of same-sex marriage in California caused an uproar, leading to protests and demonstrations all across the state. The most pressing question concerning same-sex marriage within the LGBT community is how desirable marriage really is. Is same-sex marriage simply a matter of equal rights, and thus an essential human right that is being withheld from a part of the population? Or is marriage a patriarchal, heterosexist institution, which would force same-sex couples to conform "to a script that is essentially heterosexual" (Meeks and Stein 137) and should thus be rejected altogether? Queer and feminist critics often point out the politics of normalization and assimilation that lie at the heart of the debates within the LGBT community. Do same-sex couples want to be more "normal" and assimilate to heterosexual forms of being, or is such a move fundamentally counterproductive to queer politics? For more information on this discussion, see Meeks and Stein.

ity as the norm and the willingness to adopt a queer positionality. We can take our cues from Nemo and Dory and design alternative ways of being, form queer alliances, and acknowledge that there are multiple valid, legitimate, and productive ways in which social relations can be organized. And maybe we will find that a queer world is not necessarily a better, but surely a more hopeful world.

WORKS CITED

A.M.B. "The Future of Feminism." *University of Chicago Magazine* 96.4 (April 2004): n. pag. Web. 19 March 2009.

Berlant, Lauren, and Michael Warner. "What Does Queer Theory Teach Us About X?" *PMLA* 110 (1995): 343-349. Print.

Bersani, Leo. "Is the Rectum a Grave?" *October* 43 (1987): 197-222. Print.

Butler, Judith. *Gender Trouble*. New York, NY: Routledge, 1990. Print.

—. "Imitation and Gender Insubordination". *Inside/Out.: Lesbian Theories, Gay Theories*. Ed. Diana Fuss. New York, NY: Routledge, 1991. 13-31. Print.

—. *Bodies That Matter: On the Discursive Limits of "Sex"*. New York, NY: Routledge, 1993. Print.

—. "Is Kinship Always Already Heterosexual?" *differences* 13.1 (2002): 14-44. Print.

De Lauretis, Teresa. "Queer Theory: Lesbian and Gay Sexualities." *differences* 3.2 (1991): iii-xviii. Print.

Doty, Alexander. *Making Things Perfectly Queer: Interpreting Mass Culture*. Minneapolis, MN: U of Minnesota P, 1993. Print.

Edelman, Lee. *Homographesis: Essays in Gay Literary and Cultural Theory*. New York, NY: Routledge, 1994. Print.

—. *No Future: Queer Theory and the Death Drive*. Durham, NC: Duke UP, 2004. Print.

—. "Ever After: History, Negativity, and the Social." *South Atlantic Quarterly* 106.3 (2007): 469-476. Print.

Finding Nemo. Dir. and Writ. Andrew Stanton. Perf. Albert Brooks, Ellen DeGeneres, Alexander Gould, Willem Defoe, Geoffrey Rush, et al. (voices). 2003. Walt Disney Pictures, 2003. DVD.

Foucault, Michel. *The History of Sexuality: An Introduction*. London: Penguin, 1998. Print.

Frankel, Laurie. "Finding Nemo." *Film and History* 34.1 (2004): 75-76. Print.

Freeman, Elizabeth. "Queer Belongings: Kinship Theory and Queer Theory." *A Companion to Lesbian, Gay, Bisexual, Transgender, and Queer Studies*. Ed. George E. Haggerty and Molly McGarry. New York, NY: Blackwell, 2007. 295-314. Print.

Halberstam, Judith. *In a Queer Time and Place*. New York, NY: NYU P, 2005. Print.

—. "Boys will be Bois? Or, Transgender Feminism and Forgetful Fish." *Intersections Between Feminist and Queer Theory*. Eds. Diane Richardson et al. London: Palgrave, 2006. 97-115. Print.

—. "Forgetting Family: Queer Alternatives to Oedipal Relations." *A Companion to Lesbian, Gay, Bisexual, Transgender, and Queer Studies*. Eds. George E. Haggerty and Molly McGarry. New York, NY: Blackwell, 2007. 315-324. Print.

—. "Pixarvolt: Animation and Revolt." *FlowTV* 6.06 (2007): n. pag. Web. 19 March 2009.

Halperin, David. *Saint Foucault: Towards a Gay Hagiography*. Oxford, MA: Oxford UP, 1995. Print.

Hart, Kevin. *Postmodernism*. Oxford, MA: Oneworld, 2004. Print.

Harvey, David. *The Condition of Postmodernity: An Enquiry into the Origins of Cultural Change*. Oxford, MA: Blackwell, 1989. Print.

Hennessy, Rosemary. "Queer Theory, Left Politics." *Rethinking Marxism* 7.3 (1994): 85-111. Print.

Jagose, Annemarie. *Queer Theory: An Introduction*. New York, NY: NYU P, 1997. Print.

Malpas, Simon. *The Postmodern*. New York, NY: Routledge, 2005. Print.

Meeks, Chet, and Arlene Stein. "Refiguring the Family: Towards a Post-Queer Politics of Gay and Lesbian Marriage." *Intersections between Feminist and Queer Theory*. Eds. Diane Richardson et al. London: Palgrave, 2006. 136-155. Print.

Nielsen, Annette. "Pop Culture and Queer Fish." *Web Magazine FORUM for Gender and Culture* (2005): n. pag. Web. 19 March, 2009.

Nietzsche, Friedrich. *The Genealogy of Morals*. Trans. Horace Barnett Samuel. New York, NY: Dover, 2003. Print.

Plummer, Kenneth. "Queers, Bodies, and Postmodern Sexualities: A Note on Revisiting the 'Sexual' in Symbolic Interactionism." *Qualitative Sociology* 26.4 (2003): 515-530. Print.

Roach, Joseph. *Cities of the Dead: Circum-Atlantic Performance*. New York, NY: Columbia UP, 1996. Print.

Roughgarden, Joan. *Evolution's Rainbow: Diversity, Gender, and Sexuality in Nature and People*. Berkeley, CA: U of California P, 2004. Print.

Rich, Adrienne. "Compulsory Heterosexuality and the Lesbian Continuum." *The Lesbian and Gay Studies Reader*. Eds. Henry Abelove, Michèle A. Barale, and David Halperin. New York, NY: Routledge, 1993. 227-254. Print.

Sedgwick, Eve Kosofsky. *Tendencies*. Durham, NC: Duke UP, 1993. Print.

Shark Tale. Dir. Bibo Bergeron and Vicky Jenson. Writ. Michael J. Wilson and Rob Petterman. Perf. Will Smith, Robert De Niro, Renée Zellweger, Jack Black, Angelina Jolie, et al. (voices). 2004. DreamWorks Animation, 2005. DVD.

Sim, Stuart, ed. *The Routledge Companion to Postmodernism*. London: Routledge, 2001. Print.

Sullivan, Nikki. *A Critical Introduction to Queer Theory*. New York, NY: NYU P, 2003. Print.

The Lion King. Dir. Roger Allers and Rob Minkoff. Writ. Irene Mecchi, Jonathan Roberts, and Linda Woolverton. Perf. Jonathan Taylor Thomas, Matthew Broderick, Jeremy Irons, James Earl Jones, Nathan Lane, Moira Kelly, et al. (voices). 1994. Walt Disney Pictures, 1994. DVD.

Warner, Michael. "Introduction: Fear of A Queer Planet." *Social Text* 29 (1991): 3-17. Print.

—. "Introduction." *Fear of a Queer Planet: Queer Politics and Social Theory*. Ed. Michael Warner. Minneapolis, MN: U of Minnesota P, 1993. vii-xxxi. Print.

—. *The Trouble with Normal: Sex, Politics, and the Ethics of Queer Life*. New York, NY: The Free Press, 1999. Print.

A SQUEEZE OF THE HAND: A QUEER READING OF *MOBY-DICK*

CHRISTOPH HARTNER

Moby-Dick is an open text, one that is not limited to one ultimately true reading, but that offers a variety of possible interpretations. Herman Melville had gone far beyond the literary borders of his time when he crafted a highly ambiguous work that alluded to a wide array of themes, motifs, and styles which repulsed many of his contemporaries. However, it is also what has kept readers and scholars interested in the novel up until today – and will in the future. One way of approaching Melville's classic is to read it through a pink lens; indeed, I will claim that as a postmodern queer scholar there is really no other way to read this novel. Refuted by many as a brainchild that destroyed the identitarian efforts that were put forth by the Gay and Lesbian Movement, queerness has proven to be a potent tool for understanding sexuality in a postmodern world. *Moby-Dick* is a postmodern novel in the same way that queerness is a postmodern concept: They both do not try to achieve holistic meaning but celebrate the psychological fragmentation and organic fluidity of (postmodern) subjectivity. Constant re-evaluation is what keeps both *Moby-Dick* and queerness alive and kicking. By analytically combining the two in this paper, I hope to be pumping fresh blood into their kicking legs.

THE ANTISOCIAL TURN IN QUEER THEORY

Recent work in Queer Theory under the influence of Leo Bersani's definition of sex as anti-communitarian, self-shattering, and anti-identitarian produces a counter-intuitive but crucial shift in thinking away from projects of redemption, reconstruction, restoration and reclamation and towards what can only be called an anti-social, negative, and anti-relational theory of sexuality. In a lecture she gave at Vienna University, Judith Halberstam called this shift "counter-intuitive," because it upends our understanding of the interconnectedness of intimacy, romance, and social contact and replaces it with a very harsh but radically realistic recognition of both the selfishness of sex and its destructive power. Rather than a life force connecting pleasure to life, survival, and futurity, sex – and particularly homosexual sex – presents a death drive that undoes the self, releases it from the drive for mastery and coherence and resolution: "The value of sexuality itself," writes Bersani, "is to demean the seriousness of efforts to redeem it" (27). Judith Halberstam describes this theory as a refusal to acknowledge the queer community as something that is able to offer identification and a sense of belonging. She claims that the purpose of the queer is to criticize, because queer is the negative in a positive, heteronormative procreative society. Queerness is the end, the border – it stands in the way of optimistic heteronormativity. David Halperin states that "queer is by definition whatever is at odds with the normal, the legitimate, the dominant. There is nothing in particular to which it necessarily refers. It is an identity without an essence" (61-62).

In his highly sarcastic and polemic book *No Future: Queer Theory and the Death Drive* (2004), Lee Edelman claims that queerness is the ultimate refusal of the heteronormative reproductive futurism, the drive to reproduce and thus live on in the future. Edelman sees the Child as the primary symbol of this reproductive futurism. The Child is the society's phantasma of a hope that is projected into the future but never comes true. Queerness/Homosexuality is by many conservative forces called the anti-human. For instance, the former mayor of Lourdes called homosexuals "those who care nothing for the future [...] the gravediggers of society," and Father John Miller said "gay activity is wholeheartedly determined to do battle against human life" (qtd. in Edelman 37). Edelman suggests that homosexuals should not resist this heteronormative equation of homosexuality with death, sterility, and the anti-social, but that they should embrace it. They should not want to be included into the norm but rather see themselves as constant disrupters of the norm and thus as a structural force, affecting the social order as such. It is not that homosexuals should give up the struggle for rights, but for this to be the limit of homosexual aspiration would be a total capitulation to the social order.

The figure who refuses the future is not the homosexual per se, but what Edelman calls (in a Lacanian neologism) the *sinthomosexual*. Sinthomes are signs that stand for nothing, a pure sign that does not stop to write itself and is thus characterized through its radical singularity and questions the symbolic order as such. The sinthomosexual becomes the substitute for a position that has given up the faith that a 'final signifier' will give sense to the future. Instead of waiting for the fulfillment of the ever changing desires, sinthomosexuality enjoys the "unthinkable jouissance [physical or intellectual pleasure, delight, or ecstasy] that would put an end to fantasy – and, with it, to futurity – by reducing the assurance of meaning in fantasy's promise of continuity to the meaningless circulation and repetitions of the drive" (39). By resisting interpretation, the sinthome embodies the unsymbolizable rest of reality and thus the hope for a future wholeness of society. This is in stark contrast to the theories of Judith Butler, who assumes that a more inclusive definition of the human is possible or at least desirable. Queer is simply that which cannot be included in any allegedly closed wholeness. Despite the fact that Edelman has not much positive to say about homosexual parenting, his theory cannot be read as a refusal of children as such. Quite the contrary, his analysis also tries to save children from the Cult of the Child, in which they are tyrannized by the Future that they are held to represent. At the bottom of his theory stands the opinion that "[q]ueerness can never define an identity; it can only ever disturb one" (17).

COMING OUT OF CIVILIZATION

"Call me Ishmael!" (21) With this opening line, the narrator of *Moby-Dick* establishes his position outside the world of civilization. He is named after the biblical outcast from the Book of Genesis and does everything in his (narrative) power to position himself in relation to nature rather than to the society that he comes from. There is "nothing particular to interest" (ibid.) him on shore; quite to the contrary, the civilized world produces a "damp, drizzly November" (ibid.) in his soul. He decides to go to sea, a world that is led not by the rules of civilization but by those of nature.

This urge to enter the natural world Ishmael claims to share with many others: "If they but knew it, almost all men in their degree, some time or other, cherish very nearly the same feelings toward the ocean with me" (ibid.). This statement also establishes Ishmael's view on 'true' manhood that involves the idea of leaving civilization behind to conquer the world of nature. In order to fulfill this urge to dive into the natural world, Ishmael 'comes out' of the civilized world, travels "the streets [that] take you waterward" (ibid.) and thus enters what Gloria Anzaldùa in her groundbreaking work *La Frontera: The New Mestiza* termed "Borderlands," meaning spaces where two or more cultures collide and occupy the same territory. In the case of *Moby-Dick*, the heteronormative, white, civilized world collides with the sexually and ethnically open natural world in the borderland of the harbor towns of Manhatto, New Bedford, and Nantucket. The borderland is inhabited by what Anzaldùa calls "Los Atroversados" – "those who live in the borderlands [...], caught between two colliding cultures, this queer group of 'outcasts' emerges from attempts to separate, definitively, 'us' from 'them'" (McRuer 116).

> Posted like silent sentinels all around the town, stand thousands upon thousands of mortal men fixed in ocean reveries. Some leaning against the spiles; some seated upon the pier-heads; some looking over the bulwarks of ships from China; some high aloft in the rigging, as if striving to get still better seaward peep. [...] But look! here come more crowds pacing straight for the water and seemingly bound for a dive. Strange! Nothing will contempt them but the extremest limit of the land; loitering under the shady lee of yonder warehouses will not suffice. No. They must get just as nigh the water as they possible can without falling in. And there they stand – miles of them – leagues. Inlanders all, they come from lanes and alleys, streets and

> avenues – north, east, south and west. Yet here they all unite. Tell me, does the magnetic virtue of the needles of the compasses of all those ships. (*Moby-Dick* 21-22)

The ocean is perceived as the place where otherness is completely accepted because difference is seen as a part of nature. Many people like Ishmael want to reach this ideal world, or if they cannot reach it, at least be as close as they can. The borderland is a space where the basic norms of the civilized world are still present and valid, but the mere closeness to the ocean offers at least the possibility of crossing the border to the natural state of things. In New Bedford and Nantucket the borders of nature and society have become blurred and have created a space of their own, a space where borders of race, gender, and sexuality can be transgressed. In that sense, Melville's harbor-towns are early examples of the larger cities that started to arise with the emergence of industrialization in the second half of the 19th century and which have been described by Mitchell Moss as providing a surrounding that was "tolerant of cultural innovation and deviation from conventional modes of working and living" (par. 15).

"HEAVENS! LOOK AT THAT TOMAHAWK!" THE SENSATION OF FLESH

From the very beginning of the novel, Ishmael is described not as a lady's man but as a man's man in the queerest sense of the word. As a character, he surrounds himself only with men, and as a narrator he hardly mentions women at all and develops a conspicuous fascination for the male physique. Even before his highly eroticized description of his encounters with Queequeg, Ishmael exhibits an admiration of the male body. Upon first putting his eyes on his future shipmate Bulkington, for instance, Ishmael remarks: "He stood full six feet in height, with noble shoulders, and a chest like a coffer-dam. I have seldom seen such a brawn in a man" (34). Later aboard the *Pequod*, Ishmael frequently describes other shipmates in terms of their physique. It is not that he is not interested in their personality; however, his first and foremost fascination seems to be with the bodies of those men. The muscled, hyper-masculine sailors seem to represent what Ishmael is looking for as far as ideals of masculinity are concerned: bodies shaped by the contact with nature. They are real men and do not represent the over-civilized form of masculinity that Ishmael obviously wishes to escape from. It is only his "strong moral principle" (21) that keeps him from "deliberately stepping into the street and methodically knocking people's hats off" (ibid.). Ishmael is sick of the hat-wearing masculinity that civilization requires him to subordinate to, and thus his fascination for the male physique is also a symbolic admiration for the *savoir vivre* that is defined through the escape from civilization and direct contact with nature, a contact that also alters the shape of the body.

Most clearly, this fascination for the male body is expressed in Ishmael's descriptions of Queequeg. During their first encounter, Ishmael closely watches Queequeg's "business of undressing" (40) and minutely describes the details of the harpooner's body: It comes like a relief to Ishmael when Queequeg "at last showed his chest and arms" (ibid.), all of which are covered with tattoos. Ishmael quite obviously adores Queequeg's body; his routines with his "wooden idol" (41) and, not to forget, the tomahawk. Through Ishmael's phallic descriptions of Queequeg's religious regalia of his indigenous heritage, it seems as if they too become parts of Queequeg's body, just like his cultural background is literally embedded in his body through the tattoos. Queequeg's physical appearance becomes an expression of his cultural otherness and his link to nature.

'Eat the meat' is a phrase that can frequently be found in contemporary erotic or pornographic contexts – mostly, but not exclusively, gay – as a command of a male sexual partner to his counterpart (male or female) to perform oral sex. The way in which sexuality and a cannibalistic sensation of flesh is intermingled in this phrase might not be obvious to a modern reader. However, as Caleb Crain claims in his article "Lovers of Human Flesh: Homosexuality and Cannibalism in Melville's Novels," there seems to be a certain tradition of linking those two concepts, a tradition that Melville participated in as well.

Adventure stories, especially those of sea-voyages, were a common literary genre at Melville's time. One reason for their popularity was the fact that those stories allowed for the human otherness of exotic cultures to be discussed. Of special interest in stories of sea-voyages were the peculiarities of the savages that the adventurers encountered during their travels. Frequent savages in the stories of Melville and his time were the inhabitants of the South Seas (like Queequeg), who were frequently described to be infamous for two things: their cannibalism and their promiscuity (including same-sex activity). Those two features of otherness were main factors that drew readers to such stories. The savages were perceived as both fascinating and repulsive. Thus, through this double bind of horror and attraction, cannibalism and promiscuous (homo)sexuality were strangely united in the role of the savage of the South Seas. Melville, having sailed the South Seas himself and having (like most of his contemporaries) read (and written) a great number of those adventure stories, was definitely aware of those (at his time still somewhat unspeakable) secrets of the savages of the South Seas and was thus, as Crain puts it, "free to play with these associations" (32).

This double bind of horror and attraction is also expressed when Ishmael first encounters Queequeg. Ishmael has a fit of hysteria and panic, yet at the same time he cannot stop himself from watching Queequeg and, according to Crain, Ishmael is "not in control of his own actions" (32) any more. Ishmael expresses the fear that he might not be able to sleep "in [his] own skin" (34). He, on the one hand, is scared to lose his identity, his life, yet on the other hand is also what Crain calls a typical "solitary and self-reliant American of the 19th century who desperately wants to lose the self" (34).

Of course, there never exists a real danger for Ishmael that Queequeg might actually kill and eat him, because in the culture of the South Seas, cannibalism was part of a strictly regulated code of cultural traditions and was practiced only on very specific religious occasions as part of a human sacrifice to the gods. But as a part of Ishmael's approximation to a more natural masculinity, he has to face his fears of otherness to finally be able to overcome them. After his initial fit of panic, Ishmael realizes that Queequeg is "on the whole a clean, comely looking cannibal" (43) and that he "[b]etter sleep with a sober cannibal than a drunken Christian" (ibid.).

Especially in this first encounter between Ishmael and Queequeg, cannibalism serves as a trope of difference and as a threat to the autonomous self. For working-class men, sharing a bed was a common event in Melville's time, but one that was more and more becoming terrorized by what Eve Kosofsky Sedgwick has termed "homosexual panic," denoting the situation in which a man while becoming aware of attraction to another man resorts to paranoia. Attraction, thus, can easily turn into revulsion and even violence (cf. 83-85). Although Melville's time did not yet have a concept of homosexuality, Sedgwick claims that homophobia did exist in the fear of being labeled as not belonging to the norm, as the Other. This fear of becoming part of the Other is clearly expressed in the character of Ishmael, and especially in his fight with himself prior to and during his first encounter with Queequeg. The homosexual panic of Ishmael is expressed through a fear of cannibalism, a fear of figuratively being eaten up by the Other. Because Ishmael cannot express his fears of homosexuality directly (simply because he lacks the terminology for this 20th century concept), he unconsciously translates them onto fears of cannibalism. Robert K. Martin argues: "Learning to undo ethnocentric fears [of cannibalism] includes overcoming the fear of sharing bed, even if that means admitting the possibility of sexuality" ("Melville and Sexuality" 193).

Once Ishmael has overcome those fears, he literally becomes one with the natural Other that Queequeg represents. He enjoys the best night of sleep of his whole life and wakes up the next morning finding "Queequeg's arm thrown over me in the most loving and affectionate manner. You had almost thought I had been his wife" (43). Ishmael, being newlywed to this otherness of the natural world, still expresses doubts and fears about his liaison with Queequeg, but ultimately enjoys it a great deal. He literally lets himself be 'eaten up' by the "bridegroom clasp" (45) of the savage and seems to have overcome his fear of not "sleeping in his own skin" (34): "Methinks my body is but the lees of my better being. In fact take my body who will, take it I say, it is not me" (53-54). The fear of cannibalism is replaced by an enjoyment of the freedom that an association with savage masculinity brings.

Ishmael even joins in Queequeg's cannibalistic tradition by developing what I would call a cannibalistic 'gaze.' Ishmael's fascination with the male physique becomes more radical and more devious. At breakfast after his first night with Queequeg, Ishmael observes: "The bar-room was now full of the boarders who had been dropping in the night previous, and whom I had not as yet had a good look at" (47). Ishmael expands his role as the self-described "looker on" (33) of the male company that he keeps and develops a visual hunger for male bodies, which he frequently describes in terms of food: "This young fellow's healthy cheek is like a sun-toasted pear in hue, and would seem to smell almost as musky" (47). In this example, the man Ishmael gazes at becomes an over-ripe fruit of nature, a delicacy that invites to be devoured. The cannibalistic nature of Ishmael's gaze symbolizes Ishmael's transition from the civilized to the uncivilized world. While in much of the other works of Melville, as Crain claims, the linking of homosexuality and cannibalism results in a love that devours and ultimately destroys, *Moby-Dick* presents an alternative to this pessimistic imagery, because "instead of a homosexual love that is cannibalistic, there is a cannibal love that is homosexual" (45).

Queequeg, who remains Ishmael's main object of gazing, serves as a sort of bridge between the civilized and the natural world. Ishmael describes him as "a creature in the transition state – neither caterpillar nor butterfly" (46) – and thus offers the perfect ground of identification for Ishmael's own transition. According to Martin's book Hero, Captain, and Stranger, Queequeg serves as a means of Ishmael's transformation from his cowardly culture-bound self to a figure of cooperation and sharing. The 'unity of otherness' (racial, cultural, religious, sexual) in the character of the savage is part of Ishmael's fascination for Queequeg in *Moby-Dick* as well. Queequeg is not a man who tries to reach the standards of 19th century manhood, but lives by his own rules and regulations. He has not given up his natural urges (as expressed in his cannibalism) for a civilized society. Thus, Queequeg becomes Ishmael's loophole out of Western Society and a bridge to the natural world of the sea that no relation with a civilized man could have offered: "In a countryman, this sudden flame of friendship would have seemed far too premature, a thing to be much distrusted; but in this simple savage these old rules would not apply" (67).

"A SQUEEZE OF THE HAND" THE EROTICISM OF A COMMON FATE

Despite Melville's description of Ishmael and Queequeg as a loving couple, there are certain limitations to their relationship that are communicated very clearly. Their blissful, eroticized friendship is possible only in the borderland of New Bedford and Nantucket, and the sexual/romantic side of their friendship can be enacted only in the enclosed space of the bedroom they share. Once they enter the ship, Ishmael and Queequeg are separated by forces that come both from the inside and the outside of their relationship.

First and foremost, once Ishmael, as a narrator, is on board the *Pequod*, his interest shifts away from Queequeg to the world of the whaling business. Queequeg has fulfilled his job as a bridge to the natural world and becomes one of the shipmates. The eroticized friendship between Ishmael and Queequeg is replaced by the affectionate male togetherness of the workers on board the whaling ship. At times Ishmael still exhibits a cannibalistic gaze towards his fellow crewman, but the eroticizing of the exotic male body is backgrounded by what Woods calls "the eroticism of dynamic masculinity, expressed and fulfilled in physical action" (297-298). Ishmael's descriptions move away from the phallic nature of Queequeg's cultural regalia to the phallicism that Ishmael sees in the work on board the *Pequod* and in the nature of the whale. For a contemporary reader, many of those descriptions read like examinations of the nature of sexuality as such, and a modern queer reader may find in Ishmael's explanatory approach to the White Whale many similarities to the different explanatory approaches (be they supportive or suppressive) to homosexuality and queerness.

For instance, Ishmael uses physiognomy and phrenology (judging human characters from facial features and from the shape of the skull) to describe the whale and try to find out more about his character. As a modern queer reader, such an attempt reminds of historical studies that have been done with and about people that exhibited some form of racial or sexual otherness. For a long time it was believed, for instance, that homosexual men could be recognized by the fact that their ring-finger was longer than their index-finger, which was read as a sign for an increased amount of female hormones in the body (cf. Katz 33-57). Ishmael also devotes an entire chapter to the description of the whale's penis, which was also an early method for trying to find a way to point out sexual otherness by bodily features.

The phallocentrism that Ishmael exhibits in both his descriptions of the whale and of the work on board the whaling ship leads to a strange form of eroticizing of the whaling business. The violence that is directed towards the whale is accentuated with a strange sexuality, because Ishmael portrays all of the tools for a whale hunt as phallic: For instance, the penetrative nature of the killing of a whale with a harpoon is frequently described by Ishmael as a quasi-sexual act, or the whole chapter "Pitchpoling" is dedicated to an eroticized description of the way in which Queequeg oils his boat, so that it will slide into the ocean more smoothly.

Ishmael eroticizes not only the tools for whale hunting by presenting them as phallic symbols, but also the common work of the shipman on board the *Pequod*. This peculiarity of Ishmael's narration culminates in the chapter "A Squeeze of the Hand," in which Ishmael gives an account of the manual processing of spermaceti. Gregory Woods claims that in this chapter "work and leisure merge to the extent that the men's efficient working relations and their affection are functionally indistinguishable from each other" (164). Work, thus, is literally transformed into sexuality:

> It was our business to squeeze these lumps back into fluid. A sweet and unctuous duty! [...] After having my hands in it for only a few minutes, my fingers felt like eels, and began, as it were, to serpentine and spiralize.
> [...] I declare to you, that for the time I lived as in a musky meadow; I forgot all about our horrible oath; in that inexpressible sperm, I washed my hands and my heart of it; I almost began to credit the old Paracelsan superstition that sperm is of rare virtue in allaying the heat of anger: while bathing in that bath, I felt divinely free from all ill-will, or petulance [*sic!*], or malice, of any sort whatsoever.
> Squeeze! squeeze! squeeze! all the morning long; I squeezed that sperm till I myself almost melted into it; I squeezed that sperm till a strange sort of insanity came over me; and I found myself unwittingly squeezing my co-laborers' hands in it, mistaking their hands for the gentle globules. Such an abounding, affectionate, friendly, loving feeling did this avocation beget; that at last I was continually squeezing their hands, and looking up into their eyes sentimentally; as much as to say, – Oh! my dear fellow beings, why should we longer cherish any social acerbities, or know the slightest ill-humor or envy! Come; let us squeeze hands all round; nay, let us all squeeze ourselves into each other; let us squeeze ourselves universally into the very milk and sperm of kindness.
> Would that I could keep squeezing that sperm for ever! For now, since by many prolonged, repeated experiences, I have perceived that in all cases man must eventually lower, or at least shift, his conceit of attainable felicity; not placing it anywhere in the intellect or the fancy; but in the wife, the heart, the bed, the table, the saddle, the fire-side, the country; now that I have perceived all this, I am ready to squeeze case eternally. In thoughts of the visions of the night, I saw long rows of angels in paradise, each with his hands in a jar of spermaceti. (397-398)

Other than the penetrative nature of the sexualized violence that is directed towards the whales, the sexuality among the men can only be described as masturbative. Gregory Woods reads the scene as "a pornographic description of a circle-jerk, a rhapsodic episode of mutual masturbation" (297-298) and Robert K. Martin even points out that every positive description of sexuality in Melville is a depiction of male masturbation, frequently mutual (cf. *Hero, Captain, and*

Stranger 58-62). However one wants to read the scene in comparison to other sexual episodes in the work of Melville, the sperm-squeezing scene is one of the most unabashedly homoerotic episodes in 19th century literature, and one that seems almost impossible not to read as queer.

The combination of direct contact with his shipmates and hands-on connection to nature results in an orgasmic fulfillment of all of Ishmael's wishes and expectations for his escape from civilization. Never is Ishmael's dream of the all-male conquest of nature closer to becoming real than when he and his shipmates are elbow-deep in whale sperm. However, this feeling of almost-perfection is possible only because it is a "momentary suspension of the real" (Martin, "Melville and Sexuality" 195). Squeezing the whale sperm with his shipmates, Ishmael finds himself transported to a pastoral scene of a "musky meadow" (397) and is so caught up in the erotic sensation that he is able to forget the "horrible oath" (398) of vengeance obtained by Ahab. For just a moment Ishmael and the shipmates are able to forget their doomed quest for Moby Dick. But despite the fact that it is only a momentary suspension of the real, the sperm-squeezing scene does offer an alternative. Martin argues:

> Melville is too much of a cynic about human nature and too honest about the realities of economics of labor to let this vision last, but he is also too much of a radical dreamer not to entertain the possibility of such a transformative sexuality in which men enjoy each other and, at least temporarily, abandon their place in the order of work. ("Melville and Sexuality" 195)

Immediately after the masturbative episode of sperm-squeezing comes to an end, Ishmael (as if having a bad conscience about what he did) talks about women and the security of the land. Finally, he ends the chapter with a description of the dangers of processing whale-fat in the blubber-room:

> This spade is sharp as hone can make it; the spademan's feet are shoeless; the thing he stands on will sometimes irresistibly slide away from him, like a sledge. If he cuts off one of his own toes, or one of his assistants', would you be very much astonished? Toes are scarce among veteran blubber-room men. (400)

To a contemporary reader, to end a description of fulfilling homosexual sexuality with expressing the fear of negative effects on the body (an amputation), brings to mind the prevalent (and absurd) assumption that (too much) non-procreative sex (especially masturbation) can lead to blindness or other forms of sickness. Ishmael enjoys the momentary (sexual) freedom from Ahab's domination, but quickly thereafter returns to his subordinated status on board the *Pequod*.

The loss of control over his own body that Ishmael experiences during the sperm-squeezing scene is, in fact, similar to the way he and the other shipman completely lose themselves under the leadership of Ahab. Their bodies are his to use, they surrender themselves completely to their patriarchal leader – literally until death does them part. Only Starbuck dares to express criticism of Ahab's mad quest, but finally he too does not take any steps to prevent the fate of the *Pequod.* The sperm-squeezing scene is the only moment on board the *Pequod* during which the sailors are masters of their own body. Thus, the episode also represents the only attempt to break out of Ahab's kingship and to achieve democratic camaraderie. It is a sexual rebellion against the mad industrial machinery Ahab puts them in.

Crain claims that in the world Melville describes, "physical intimacy between men was inextricable from power" (41). As powerful as the sexual rebellion against Ahab in the sperm-squeezing scene may be, his power over the shipmates is stronger. The positive, communal loss of control that they experience through sexuality is only temporary. Ahab quickly gains back his power over their bodies and minds. This power finally becomes so strong that in the chapter "The Needle" he is even able to 'invert' their compasses, and the trip no longer relies on any nautical instruments any more, but solely on Ahab.

So there is, if you will, a certain cannibalistic nature to Ahab's power over the crew. He 'eats up' their minds and turns their bodies into tools of his quest. Under his doomed regime the sailors are not only de-individualized but also symbolically incorporealized. But the cannibalistic (in the sense of body-devouring) nature of Ahab's quest affects not only the shipmates but also eats away at the captain himself. He once describes his obsession with the White Whale as "a vulture [that] feeds upon that heart forever" (202). Thus, the cannibalism that is presented in the narration of Ishmael serves two very different means: on the one hand, cannibalism serves as a metaphor for the shared otherness of Queequeg and Ishmael that cannot be expressed in (homo)sexual terms (as explained above), but on the other hand, it is yet another metaphor for the fact that Ahab's quest is doomed to end in death and thus eats away on the bodies and souls of the men involved.

THE QUEER ANTI-SOCIAL NATURE OF AHAB'S QUEST

"No Future" is not only the title of Lee Edelman's polemic way of getting even with the reproductive futurism of the heteronormative world, but could also be seen as a theme of *Moby-Dick*. From the very beginning of the novel, the deadly fate of the *Pequod* and its shipmates is sealed. The Child that Edelman sees as the ultimate emblem for a hopeful future appears only in the vague memories that Ahab has of his family, in the lunatic form of Pip, and in the necessary survival of the narrator Ishmael. Neither offers any space for projecting hope into the future. Edelman's equation of queerness with death, sterility, and the antisocial is not hard to find in *Moby-Dick* as well: Ishmael's love for Queequeg is expressed mainly in terms related to cannibalism and thus to death; the sperm-squeezing scene is masturbatory and thus completely sterile, non-procreative; and the all-male society that is established on board the *Pequod* is not compatible with the society of the land, purely utopian, and serves no greater social function.

Thus, the queerness that is portrayed in *Moby-Dick* clearly disrupts the optimistic futurity and represents the negative in a positive, heteronormative, procreative society. Ahab wants to hunt down the immortal Moby Dick, who represents this reproductive futurism. As the proto-whale and the archetype of all whales, Moby Dick is the ultimate symbol of procreative futurism and thus makes Ahab aware of his own mortality. But rather than seeing his own children as a way to live forever, he tries to hunt down procreative futurism as such – and fails. Only once is Starbuck able to get Ahab to talk about his children, but not even that thought is able to turn Ahab's maniacal quest around. Ahab's fatal obsession with the White Whale is questioned too infrequently and too inconsequentially. Nobody ever really tries to put an end to the quest, quite in contrast, many men seem to join Ahab's death drive and find excitement, enjoyment, and fulfillment in it. They do so despite all the warnings and despite the fact that the object of Ahab's obsession is never really tangible, more myth than reality. Ahab is able to keep his men on his side with all means possible, but his quest to hunt down Moby Dick and to become a god by killing a god ultimately fails.

More successful in his rebellion against heteronormative futurism, I would like to argue, is Ishmael. Both as a narrator and as a character he enjoys the "unthinkable jouissance that would put an end to fantasy – and, with it, to futurity – by reducing the assurance of meaning in fantasy's promise of continuity to the meaningless circulation and repetitions of the drive" (Edelman 39), which Edelman sees as a pivotal characteristic of what he has termed the sinthomosexual. Quite similar to a sinthome, Ishmael represents an empty sign that does not stop to write itself. His very first utterance as a narrator, "Call me Ishmael" (21), establishes him as someone who constantly invents himself anew: He is an 'Atroversado' when he enters the borderland of the harbor-towns, a cannibalistic savage when he is in love with Queequeg, a shipmate once he enters the *Pequod*, etc. As a narrator, Ishmael constantly rewrites himself and thus completely resists interpretation as a character. He plays with the norms of whatever society he is in and whatever company he keeps, and queers them. Ishmael eroticizes every situation that he gets into and every encounter that he makes. The borderland, the exotic brown man, the democratic workmanship on board the *Pequod*, the natural world of the whales, or even Ahab's deathly quest for Moby Dick – all of those aspects Ishmael somehow manages to eroticize in his narration: from his adoration of Queequeg's tomahawk to an entire chapter dedicated to the penis of the whale, Ishmael's narrative is full of highly eroticized phallic symbols. Ishmael thus queers the whole novel, because as a narrator he does not allow for any clear identities to arise. His erotic view of the world surrounding him makes him queer not only in the sense of not fitting into the sexual norm, but also because he fulfills Edelman's ultimate definition of queerness as never being able to define an identity, but only to disturb one (17).

For Ishmael, however, being the disturber that he is means that ultimately he cannot become a full member of the closed wholeness of the crew of the *Pequod*. At best, as the sperm-squeezing scene suggests, he can temporarily unite with the community surrounding him through his ability to eroticize even the simplest of handy-work. But as a character, Ishmael can never really become an integral part of the community of the shipmates.

In the end, however, this status as an outsider is the reason for Ishmael's survival. As a *sinthomosexual*, a trickster-like disturber of norms, Ishmael manages to queer even the deathly doom of the *Pequod* and to survive. It thus seems only logical that it is Queequeg's coffin, as a symbolic reminder of an earlier queer breaking of the norm, which enables Ishmael to flee the sinking ship. Queequeg has been his bridge from the civilized to the natural world and in the end serves as a bridge back.

MOBY-DICK – A QUEER NOVEL?

As a contemporary reader it seems almost impossible not to perceive many of the episodes in *Moby-Dick* as clearly anti-heterosexual and/or homosocial and/or even homosexual, and to read some characters as being queer. The first question that thus arises when reading the novel as a modern queer scholar, is why the novel's open-hearted depiction of male-male intimacy, love and sexuality did not cause more of an uproar? Leslie Fiedler offers an explanation in his landmark publication *Love and Death in the American Novel*, where he claims that back in Melville's time, episodes such as the love between Ishmael and Queequeg were still read as "pure marriages of males, sexless and holy" and that, quite to the contrary, "male-male love was seen as the symbol of innocence itself" (69). Fiedler even presents episodes like the love between Ishmael and Queequeg as a sort of counter-paradise in which it is not the arrival of the snake that confuses the innocent state of the love of Adam and Eve, but where the arrival of Eve disturbs the original harmony between Adam and the snake. In the context of *Moby-Dick*, this way of reading paradise would imply that Ishmael (Adam) and Queequeg (the snake) are able to lead a harmonic relationship until the queenly Ahab (Eve) arrives on the scene with his obsessive quest to become godlike and fully understand the mysteries of paradisiacal nature.

Despite the fact that Eve Kosofsky Sedgwick has proven that homosexual panic did exist prior to the scientific category of the homosexual, one cannot conclude that Melville tried to make same-sex sexuality an explicit theme of *Moby-Dick*. The homosexual eroticism that is so clearly present in the novel is part of the homo-social tradition of the genre that Melville writes in. What is new though, and has been interpreted as an invention of Melville, is the fact that not only the female body is being eroticized but also that of the male. Ishmael, being the initiator of this eroticized same-sex game, thus reads like a gay character for a contemporary queer reader. Yet, as I have argued above, it is simply impossible to read Ishmael as identifiable with any category, let alone gay. Leo Bersani points out that Melville's characters have no sexual objectivity at all and that although there are many signifiers for homosexual desire, he questions the presence of a homosexual signified. He sees in the homoerotic episodes of *Moby-Dick* a peculiarity of American literature: a psychologically inconsequential homosexuality (145-146). The homoeroticism, as Bersani claims, serves as a possible alternative to the egoistic quest of Ahab on the one hand, and as a symbol of the dream of an all-male utopian counter-society on the other, and thus has very restricted areas in which it can work.

As I have argued above, however, the queering potential of Ishmael goes much further than those homoerotic episodes that Bersani and most other queer scholars that have dealt with Melville's *Moby-Dick* before me suggest. While all of the previous queer readings of the novel have acknowledged the homoeroticism and queerness of some of the episodes within the story, but refused to see *Moby-Dick* as a queer text per se, I would like to suggest that for a contemporary queer reader, Melville's classic is just that: a queer text. Ishmael, as Melville's narrator, does anything in his power to queer the story that he tells and the genre that he writes in. He plays with the fluidity of identities, refuses to describe anything as clearly masculine or feminine, heterosexual or homosexual, black or white, good or bad, prose or drama. In that sense, *Moby-Dick* is not only quite queer, but also very postmodernist in its approach. Too often does Melville in *Moby-Dick* show sympathy for otherness, too often are his argumentations a bit queer, too often does Ishmael manage to eroticize even the simplest scene, and too often is sexuality directed at anything *but* a woman. As a contemporary queer scholar there is no other way than to not get academically aroused by the novel.

WORKS CITED

Anzaldùa, Gloria. *La Frontera: The New Mestiza*. San Francisco, CA: Aunt Lute, 1987. Print.

Bersani, Leo. *The Culture of Redemption*. Cambridge, MA: Harvard UP, 1990. Print.

Butler, Judith. *Gender Trouble: Feminism and the Subversion of Identity*. London: Routledge, 1990. Print.
Crain, Caleb. "Lovers of Flesh: Homosexuality and Cannibalism in Melville's Novels." *American Literature* 66.1 (1994): 25-53. Print.
Edelman, Lee. *No Future: Queer Theory and the Death Drive*. Durham, NC: Duke UP, 2004. Print.
Halberstam, Judith. *The Anti-Social Turn in Queer Theory*. University of Vienna. 23 March 2007. Lecture.
Halperin, David E. *Saint Foucault: Towards a Gay Hagiography*. Oxford: Oxford UP, 2003. Print.
Katz, Jonathan. *The Invention of Heterosexuality*. New York, NY: Dutton, 1995. Print.
Martin, Robert K. *Hero, Captain, and Stranger: Male Friendship, Social Critique, and Literary Form in the Sea Novels of Herman Melville*. Chapel Hill, NC: U of North Carolina P, 1986. Print.
—. "Melville and Sexuality." *The Cambridge Companion to Herman Melville*. Ed. Robert S. Levine. New York, NY: Cambridge UP, 1998. 186-201. Print.
McRuer, Robert. *The Queer Renaissance: Contemporary American Literature and the Reinvention of Lesbian and Gay Identities*. New York, NY: NYU P, 1997. Print.
Melville, Herman. *Moby-Dick; or, The Whale*. 1851. London: Penguin, 1994. Print
Moss, Mitchell. "Reinventing the Central City as a Place to Live and Work." *Mitchell L. Moss Online*, Mitchell L. Moss, 1997. Web. 10 March 2010.
Sedgwick, Eve Kosofsky. *Between Men: English Literature and Male Homosocial Desire*. New York, NY: Columbia UP, 1985. Print.
—. *Tendencies*. London: Routledge, 1994. Print.
Woods, Gregory. *The History of Gay Literature – The Male Tradition*. New Haven, CT: Yale UP, 1998. Print.

NEGOTIATING POSTMODERNITY AND QUEER UTOPIANISM IN *SHORTBUS*

LEOPOLD LIPPERT

James, young, urban, and not-so-professional, is sitting naked on the living room floor of his Brooklyn apartment. Acrobatically contorting his body, James is eagerly trying to give himself a blowjob. The arduous curling seems more desperate than sensual, and when James finally orgasms, he immediately starts to cry, finding himself solitary and emotionally empty. This scene, opening John Cameron Mitchell's 2006 movie *Shortbus*, makes an incredibly candid representation of *queer social negativity*, a phenomenon that has been debated fiercely among Queer Theorists over the last few years. Queer social negativity, in a nutshell, denotes the "representation of homosexuality as sterile, unproductive, antifamily, and death-driven," as Queer Studies scholar Tim Dean (827) explains. Queerness, thus, puts into crisis a particular "grand narrative" (Lyotard, xxiii) of modernity, that of desire, the life-giving spirit of any formation of sociality, sustainability, and progress. When James ejaculates into his own mouth, he turns desire upon itself; he swallows up the collective fantasies of procreation and life, and instead chooses to take queer pleasure in the excessive superabundance of human waste.

In the following, I will survey recent theoretical writings on queer social negativity, and attempt to trace the ways in which *Shortbus*, a cinematic representation of queer urban life in the early 21st century, acknowledges the phenomenon. I will, however, also show how *Shortbus* proposes alternative, and indeed utopian, approaches to queer community, sociality, and existence. *Shortbus*, I argue, stands symptomatic for what Jill Dolan calls a "wiser humanism," (22) an understanding of sociality that recognizes the contradictions and ruptures of postmodern lives, and yet articulates the need for "human commonality despite the vagaries of difference" (171). Reading *Shortbus* along the lines of both queer social negativity and Dolan's wiser humanism, my subsequent analysis will have a particular focus on two aspects of the film: the re-membering of AIDS and the re-inscription of the urban community during a blackout in New York City.[1]

---

1 Parts of this argument have already appeared, under a different pretext, in my *Utopian Contemporaries: Queer Temporality and America*. Saarbrücken: VDM, 2009.

ADVOCATES OF ABORTION: THEORIZING QUEER SOCIAL NEGATIVITY

Lee Edelman's seditious polemic, *No Future: Queer Theory and the Death Drive* (2004), opens with the allegation that "the queer comes to figure the bar to every realization of futurity, the resistance, internal to the social, to every social structure or form" (4). Queerness, thus, is imagined outside socially feasible forms of belonging, kinship, and citizenship and, as such, "responsible for the undoing of social organization, collective reality, and, inevitably, life itself" (13). Although a structurally indispensable antagonist of procreative sociality, the figure of the queer poses an existential threat to a social order built on desire and reproduction. Instead, queerness is associated with excess, surplus, and amoral self-indulgence, with a pervasive social negativity that refuses to partake in the "marriage of identity to futurity in order to realize the social subject" (14). Detrimental to the reproductive cycles of any viable form of social structuring, queerness undoes chronology and teleology; it frustrates the seemingly inalienable cultural narratives of identity, meaning, and collective self-realization, and promises *no future* instead. The queer, then, serves as a perpetual reminder of a disastrous antisocial, a deadly specter haunting the futurist triad of self, children, and family.

The idea of a queer social negativity has its historical roots in the 1980s, when the AIDS crisis firmly installed the discursive connection between (male) homosexuality and the deadly HI virus. As a cultural metaphor, essayist Susan Sontag points out, AIDS is "linked to an imputation of guilt" (112): Affecting a comparably high number of gay men, the disease has been regarded a "punishment for living unhealthy lives" (113) and as "plague-like, a moral judgment on society" (148). A prototypically queer illness, Sontag shows, AIDS poses a severe threat to the futurist desires of sociality, as it turns the "vision of linear progress [...] into a vision of disaster" (177). AIDS deprives queerness of its future, of its social viability, and relocates it to an antisocial realm that is merely premortal, imbued with death and immanently damaging to the reproductive fantasies of all social networks.

In a(n) (in)famous article published during the peak of the AIDS crisis in the United States, cultural theorist Leo Bersani inquires, "Is the Rectum a Grave?," and observes the "heterosexual association of anal sex with [...] self-annihilation" (222). Already in the late 1980s, he recognizes the death drive with which queerness has been equated ever since. For Bersani, the rectum, as an indicator of sexual surplus, displays a "potential for death" and violently shatters the "sacrosanct value of selfhood" (222). AIDS, as a queer prop, symbolizes the deadly stop sign that threatens to bring the future to a halt and with it the whole teleological venture of human sociality.

For Edelman, the only viable political strategy is self-conscious affirmation. "Rather than rejecting, with liberal discourse," he claims, "this ascription of negativity to the queer, we might, I argue, do better to consider accepting and even embracing it" (4). Instead of pursuing assimilationist or inclusionist politics that overlook the structural inevitability of a *queer negativity* in any social order, he candidly recommends to articulate "at last the words for which we're condemned should we speak them or not: that we are the advocates of abortion" (31). Queers, Edelman suggests, should actively adopt the position of social negativity and thereby trouble, or queer, for that matter, a network of social relations that has offered no mode of existence for queerness in the first place; queers, he insists, should celebrate their opposition to family, social belonging, and life, as they are always already denied survival within any community, or any social organization as such.

SHORTBUS: "A SALON FOR THE GIFTED AND CHALLENGED"

As an exemplary vehicle to travel a postmodern landscape in which the ideas of queer social negativity are acted out, John Cameron Mitchell's 2006 film *Shortbus* will be the focus of this article. The film represents a cinematic endeavor that has been instantly recognized as outstanding. Nathan Lee, for instance, raves about the "hotties of indeterminate gender" and claims that "[n]o movie has illustrated a broader spectrum of contemporary sexual identity" (71). In a similar vein, Todd McCarthy, writing for the entertainment industry magazine *Variety*, attests a "vibrant vibe" to *Shortbus*, and finds that the film displays an "intense curiosity and generous spirit" (34). Premiering in late 2006, *Shortbus* achieved additional notoriety for its sexual explicitness. The frank and matter-of-fact depiction of unsimulated sex scenes, however, seems "too playful, too witty, and too little intent on engendering arousal to be porn," (48) as Linda Williams maintains. Sex, in *Shortbus*, is not captured for instant gratification; on the contrary, it functions as a metaphor for community and emotional trust.

The narrative of *Shortbus* unfolds in a New York City ravaged but also reinvigorated by the terrorist attacks of September 11, 2001. A "classic ensemble movie" (Curlovich 49), *Shortbus* introduces its audience to the strangely intertwined lives of its central characters. Connected through their regular visits to the Brooklyn sex club Shortbus, they all strive to solve their particular sexual problems, difficulties that turn out to be complications of emotional sensitivity as well: Sofia (Sook-Yin Lee) and Rob (Raphael Barker), a married couple with a stylish flat in Midtown, find themselves unable to connect sexually, as Sofia remains "pre-orgasmic" despite her desperate attempts to experience sexual climax; James (Paul Dawson), who was already referred to, and Jamie (PJ DeBoy), partners for five years, want to open up their relationship and begin a sexual liaison with boyish Ceth (Jay Brannan); dominatrix Severin (Lindsay Beamish), a professional sex worker, although fluent in her sadistic craft, is despairingly craving for "real human interaction"; and a peculiar senior citizen (Alan Mandell), who introduces himself as former mayor of New York, still worries about his inadequate response to the 1980s AIDS crisis.

All these characters eagerly seek and gradually find relief in host Justin Bond's Shortbus, "a salon," as he puts it, "for the gifted and challenged," or, as reviewer Nathan Lee holds, a "home to the damaged souls, flaming creatures and assorted sexpot superfreaks of the post-gay New York City bohemia" (71). During a final gathering set against the backdrop of the 2003 blackout in New York, the plot lines are resolved: To the soothing acoustic sounds of an improvised string orchestra and the solemn voice of Justin Bond, everyone begins to touch one another gently and lovingly, tenderly engaging in a soft caressing of their fellow human beings. The film ends as Sofia reaches her first orgasm ever, an immediate consequence of the benevolent powers of the emerging queer community, and a moment so overflowing with creative energy that the lights suddenly go back on in the city.

My subsequent reading of *Shortbus* will show how the tropes of queer social negativity appear in the film, and how their fatal impact is renegotiated, re-membered, as it were, foreshadowing a "wiser humanism" (Dolan 22) that makes thinkable specifically queer modes of belonging. In her 2005 book *Utopia in Performance: Finding Hope at the Theater*, performance scholar Jill Dolan outlines what such a wiser humanism would entail. Living in a time in which humanism has been "driven to disrepair and disrepute by the cynicism of late capitalist globalism" (21), Dolan finds it utterly necessary to envisage a "reenvisioned humanism [that] is contextual, situational, and specific, nothing at all like the totalizing signifier it once described" (22). Dolan's idea of humanity cherishes the multiplicities, the ruptures, the complexities, and the particularities of postmodern identity, yet it contains an unconcealed promotion of common human values, "like the need for survival and for love, for compassion, and for hope" (ibid.). A wiser humanism, then, would strive for human connectivity that transcends conventional forms of sociality, those based on difference and desire.

"HOME CAN BE VERY UNFORGIVING": RE-MEMBERING AIDS

The following section will elucidate in particular how AIDS, the deadly disease that has been affecting the United States since the early 1980s, is relieved of its social negativity and its highly destructive associations with homosexuality. In *Shortbus*, I argue, memories of AIDS are revised, and with them the socially negative representation of queerness in public discourse.

A preliminary to the re-membering of AIDS and the concomitant renegotiation of queer social negativity is an encounter between youngish urbanite Ceth (Jay Brannan) and an older gentleman (Alan Mandell) who claims that he "used to be the mayor of New York." A thinly veiled fictional doppelganger, the old man evokes the personality and historical legacy of Ed Koch, mayor of New York City from 1978 to 1989. As Koch was in charge of the city during much of the 1980s, his time in office coincided with the apex of the AIDS crisis in the United States. The ex-mayor's appearance in *Shortbus*, as perplexing as it might be at first glance, in fact employs an established performance device. Koch's double reifies what theater historian Joseph Roach describes as "effigy," a mechanism that may "produce memory through surrogation[2]" (36). For Roach, the effigy "fills by means of surrogation a vacancy created by the absence of an original. Beyond ostensibly inanimate effigies fashioned from wood or cloth," he continues, "there are more elusive but more powerful effigies fashioned from flesh" (ibid.). Because effigies, says Roach, "hold open a place in memory into which many different people may step according to circumstances and occasions" (ibid.), they harbor enormous potential for cultural transformation. Stepping into the empty space left by the historical Ed Koch, his replica in *Shortbus* certainly functions as such an effigy in the flesh.

Performing Ed Koch in effigy, the mayor of *Shortbus* begins a thoughtful conversation with Ceth. They sit down on a sofa and, after some obligatory double entendres, the mayor begins to relate the story of his search for absolution. "New York is where everyone comes to be forgiven," he affirms poignantly and supports his belief by the observation that "New Yorkers are permeable. Therefore, we're sane." Despondently, however, he must inform his young companion that "consequently, we're the target of the impermeable, and the insane." Having been attacked fiercely in the course of his political life, the mayor had to realize that "home can be very unforgiving." With a sometime cracking voice, he continues to recount the sad role he played during the peak of AIDS in New York in the 1980s. "People said that I didn't do enough to help prevent the AIDS crisis because I was in the closet," the Koch effigy tells Ceth, and yet he insists,

---

[2] Developed from the word *surrogate*, "surrogation" may be conceptualized as a process that involves cultural substitution through performance and that makes transparent "how culture reproduces and re-creates itself" (Roach 2). Roach further points out that "the process of surrogation does not begin or end but continues as actual or perceived vacancies occur in the network of relations that constitutes the social fabric" (2).

"that's not true. I did the best I could." At last, the mayor confesses that he "was scared, and impermeable," and, with a concluding sigh of resignation, he finally admits that "everybody knew so little then. I know even less now."

The Koch effigy's remarkable evocation of AIDS acknowledges the cultural need to still remember the disease and its social ramifications. His quasi-monologue seems particularly significant in the light of what David Román points out in his *Performance in America*.[3] "Soon after the 1996 international AIDS conference in Vancouver," he observes, "there was a great deal of talk in the United States about the end of AIDS, and much of it implied that the need to talk about AIDS had ended as well" (49). Analyzing the sudden ubiquity of "end-of-AIDS pronouncements" (56), Román discerns a discourse that "seems to have rendered invisible the social, cultural, and medical problems that structured this moment in the late 1990s in AIDS history" (56). Confronted with the cultural obscuration of the epidemic, Román argues for renewed remembering, for a resumed valorization of AIDS memory. Román, who elsewhere describes "memory as an active agent of creating meaning," ("Remembering," 283) calls for a revision of "the past so that we might generate both new understandings of what has transpired and what still yet needs to be done (ibid.). When the *Shortbus*-mayor begins to talk about AIDS, he participates in that project, insisting on reanimating a contagion that has been temporarily consigned to oblivion.

The conversation between Ceth and the mayor, despite its references to AIDS in the past tense, sets out to remember the disease, to rework mainstream AIDS knowledges (queer social negativity, that is), and to create alternative meanings in the process. When the mayor in effigy describes AIDS as a "crisis," he is evoking a heavily ideological set of discourses that has associated AIDS with antisocial queerness and its destructive, even lethal, powers. Alluding to the "crisis," the mayor of *Shortbus* brings to mind theories that regard AIDS as a "visitation specially aimed at (and deservedly incurred by) Western homosexuals" (Sontag, 149). For Susan Sontag, whose influential *AIDS and Its Metaphors* supplies a succinct account of the cultural symbolism that has surrounded the disease since the 1980s, "AIDS is understood in a premodern way, as a disease incurred by people both as individuals and as members of a 'risk group'" (134). AIDS thus "revives the archaic idea of a tainted community that illness has judged" (ibid.), a group of people that consists, for Ed Koch, of the (male) homosexual population of New York. Craving for political success, Koch painstaking-

---

[3] Román, whose 1998 book *Acts of Intervention* already investigated how AIDS has shaped public memory, devotes a whole chapter of his *Performance in America*, ironically entitled "Not about AIDS," to recent AIDS (non-)discourses.

ly avoided any contact with such a tainted community, so as not to appear contaminated in any sense.

For Jean Comaroff, the repercussions of AIDS are even more far-reaching, as she regards the disease inextricably linked with the social negativities of postmodernity at large. In a 2007 article for the journal *Public Culture*, Comaroff states that "AIDS also casts a premodern pall over the emancipated pleasures, the amoral, free-wheeling desires that animated advanced consumer societies" (197). Eventually recognizing the queerness of the postmodern condition, she realizes how AIDS, because of its queer negativity, interferes with the familial futurity of the social project. "If 'family values' are the all-purpose glue meant to ensure social and moral reproduction under these conditions" (199), Comaroff argues, then "AIDS has been read as a quintessential sign of all that imperils a civilized future-in-the-world, an iconic social pathology" (199).

For the historical Ed Koch, any association with such discourses interfered with his political ambitions. The dilemma he was faced with is summed up very aptly in a play by Larry Kramer, vocal AIDS activist and playwright. In *The Normal Heart*, a character called Emma, a physician, announces that New York has got "a mayor who's a bachelor and I assume afraid of being perceived as too friendly to anyone gay. And who is also out to protect a billion-dollar-a-year tourist industry. He's not about to tell the world there's an epidemic menacing his city" (24). For Koch, the only viable strategy was silence, a disastrous speechlessness that only intensified the discursive explosion that equaled queer social negativity and AIDS.

Through the body of his effigy, however, Ed Koch attempts to re-member and reassemble AIDS discourse. Entering negotiations with Ceth, certainly a member of an alleged – to use a term as misleading as it is potentially dangerous – post-AIDS generation, the Koch effigy undertakes the creation of new collective memory. As the mayor finishes his remarkable apology and has conceded his fears, Ceth reaches over and briefly kisses him on the mouth, momentarily vindicating him of guilt and thereby altering AIDS memory. The kiss is juxtaposed with scenes of a beautifully arranged orgy in the nearby Sex not Bombs-room. This cinematic amalgamation creatively establishes a link between Koch's absolution from queer negativity and the joyful sexual acts next door. Sex and queer erotic pleasure, in *Shortbus*, are no longer regarded as unhealthy or detrimental, but as intensely pleasurable implements for the design and practice of a wiser community of human beings. Still feeling the need to talk about AIDS, the film refuses to consign to oblivion the disease and the people still suffering from its devastating consequences. What *Shortbus* chooses to forget, however, are the discursive clusters that have loaded AIDS with social negativity and queer destruction. In the moment of their kiss, Ceth and the faux mayor actively re-imagine America and the AIDS epidemic that has ravaged it. Ed Koch's sins are kissed away in effigy, while queer sex is related to social positivity, human warmth, and community, not to annihilation and death. Koch and Ceth gather new meaning as they invent more inclusive understandings of humanity, do away with queer social negativity, and anticipate a communion of love, pleasure, and forgiveness.

"WE ALL GET IT IN THE END": REVISING HUMANISM

The last section of this paper provides a close reading of the blackout that concludes the film's narrative. The short-lived suspension of power, I claim, makes possible a renegotiation of both the network of queer characters in *Shortbus* and New York as public space. In order to better understand the impact of the film's closing scenes, I find it necessary to first survey the problems of community and social negativity that the film tackles. A particularly striking example, the opening sequence of *Shortbus* may work as an antithesis to the utopian convention during the blackout. By way of contrast, therefore, I want to juxtapose the first scenes of the movie with its conclusion, and concomitantly reveal the ways in which queer negativity is removed from the social fabric of *Shortbus*.

At the outset of the movie, most of its characters lack in what the mayor would probably call 'permeability,' a social openness that would enable them to bond satisfactorily with other people. Instead, they have opted for lives of solitary unease, for ridiculous attempts to achieve sexual pleasure, and for antisocial desires that destroy any sense of community and sustainability. As *Shortbus* opens, its characters put themselves in opposition to futurity, sociality, and, most tragically, life itself.

The film starts with a slow movement of the camera, which is gently floating into a digitally animated replica of New York City, and which starts to introduce the dramatis personae of *Shortbus*, wittily revealing character through sexual acts. First, the audience is acquainted with James and his peculiar way to give/get a blowjob. The antisocial dimensions of his auto-fellatio are increased by the fact that James has been staging this scene for a suicide tape. Recording himself on video, he is in the process of creating memory, a material trace to leave behind for his lover Jamie. Swinging along with the airy pulse of film's jazzy soundtrack, queer social negativity materializes in the body of James, who is suicidal and selfish. James, this introductory sequence seems to convey, represents a fatal detriment to sustainability and the social.

James' blowjob is intercut with a sequence of scenes that presents dominatrix Severin[4], a professional sex worker who is entertaining a client. In a high-rise building adjacent to New York's Ground Zero, the steady cracking of Severin's whip sexually arouses a young man. For the dominatrix, who would normally live in a cold and sterile basement, her desensitizing job "*is* real life." Asked by the john about her "thoughts on procreation," Severin insists, "I wanna do it by myself, in the dark, like a worm." An egocentric threat to reproduction and family, Severin's anti-sociality mirrors that of James. Although they both feel the need to have, as Severin later puts it, "a real human interaction sometimes," they prove unable to commit emotionally and impede the humanist project of a queer community.

Still zigzagging over the digital New York City, the camera finally settles down to the house of Sofia and Rob, a married couple that lives in a fashionable flat in midtown Manhattan, right next to Central Park. Sofia and Rob are having sex, and their attempts at lovemaking seem particularly acrobatic and inventive. Their spectacular contortions, however, turn out to be ridiculously meaningless efforts to connect with each other. Despite their numerous pathetic undertakings, Sofia has never had an orgasm with Rob; in fact, she has never had an orgasm at all. For Sofia, as she will tell an all-female group later, sex is "a great workout," but, she has to admit, it sometimes "feels like […] somebody is gonna kill me and I just have to, you know, smile and pretend to enjoy it, yeah, and that way I can survive." Sofia and Rob's initial intercourse is only the beginning of Sofia's hopeless project to achieve an orgasm, by all means an innovative endeavor. Unable to be permeated emotionally, however, Sofia's sexual enterprise falls short of its audacious objectives. Instead, she partakes in the social negativity that surrounds the queerness of the film's characters. The sequence, thus, highlights the queer inability to build sustainable relationships and leaves the main characters in *Shortbus* solitary and emotionally reclusive.

In the following, I want to contrast the apathetic opening of *Shortbus* with the final sequence of the film, which portrays a queer moment that is capable of transforming social negativity into an imaginative blueprint of community. In the moment of blackout, the characters of *Shortbus* creatively reassemble America. Performing acoustically in the candlelit sex club, mistress Justin Bond leads a string ensemble and a brass marching band in a final eruption of joy and com-

---

4 Severin is the name of the main character in Leopold von Sacher-Masoch's 1870 novella *Venus in Furs*, a book in which masochistic sexual fantasies are celebrated. The fact that von Sacher-Masoch's Severin is a man who derives pleasure from being treated degradingly, while the Severin of *Shortbus* is a female dominatrix, is indicative of the film's queer playing with signifiers.

munity, an exuberant celebration that eventually relights even Lady Liberty's torch.

At a crucial point in the narrative, the social negativity of the characters escalates so rapidly that it causes an overload of negative feeling, a superabundance that is eventually literalized by an overload of New York's electrical grid. The power outage leaves behind an empty urban space, a precariously vulnerable tabula rasa from which new circuits of community and citizenship may emanate. The blackout moment in *Shortbus* is a direct reference to an actual power failure that affected New York City in the summer of 2003. In *Village Voice*, John Cameron Mitchell, the director of *Shortbus*, states that the film was

> all about the spirit of the blackout – that feeling we had that night is what I wanted to show. You turn off your cell phone and look into each other's eyes and realize you're alive and you're in New York. *Shortbus* is a love song. (qtd. in Romano 94)

In the concluding sequence, this spirit of queer possibility is reiterated, while the social negativity that has accumulated throughout the movie is dispersed. When the lights go out in *Shortbus*, all the cast members assemble in the Brooklyn sex club for one last time. Host Justin Bond has already lit the house with candles, and gleefully welcomes his community with the calm and soothing sounds of a small and improvised string orchestra. In the warm glimmer of myriad candles, Bond begins his peaceful chant. "We all bear the scars, we all feign a laugh," he intones as the club is slowly filling with patrons. As the song progresses, more and more people revel in the gentle atmosphere of the *Shortbus*, and when Bond finally sings that "we all get it in the end," the utopian powers of the queer community begin to work.

Gradually, and without any sign of hurry, the Shortbus community turns to one another. Lovingly, they start to touch, hug, embrace, and kiss. Consciously ignoring the heteronormative directives regarding gender and sexual orientation, the people of *Shortbus* show their all-embracing love without restrictions. James, who luckily has survived a suicide attempt, is reunited with Jamie, and they kiss passionately; Ceth finds a momentary partner in Caleb (Peter Stickles), the man who saved James's life, and they also start to caress each other; Severin, although sitting alone, seems to enjoy the delightful company as well; Justin Bond, despite being preoccupied with singing, even finds the time to lasciviously lick the mayor's face; and Sofia, eventually, becomes intimate with a particular heterosexual couple she has spied on and envied throughout the film.

For a last merry-go-round, the musicians of the Hungry March Band suddenly enter the Shortbus, repeating the last chorus of Justin Bond's song and luring everyone into an exuberant celebration of community. In the hopeful buzz of music, dance, and love, Sofia finally achieves an orgasm, and, in the end, it is the orgasmic energy of the queer communion that brings back electricity to New

York. Celebrating their queer sociality, the people of *Shortbus* fill the blank spaces of the darkened city with a new understanding of belonging and kinship. Sofia, Severin, James, Jamie, Ceth, Justin Bond, the mayor in effigy, and many others anticipate the utopian promise of a queer family; they begin to reinvent the kinship structures that tie humanity together and remove the heavy burden of negativity from queerness.

In the foregoing reflections, I have endeavored a reading of *Shortbus* that meanders between the theoretical concepts of queer social negativity and Jill Dolan's wiser humanism. Although the film literally takes great pains in scrutinizing the antisocial impetus and the emotional and social costs of queer relativism and self-indulgence, its insistence on a reinvigorated humanism, on what Dolan would describe as "an erotics of connection and commonality" (20), is particularly revealing about the complications and challenges of late postmodernity. The mere celebration of social instability, diffusion, and negativity no longer holds; and to Edelman's assertion that "there are no *queers* in that future as there can be no future for queers" (30), the *Shortbus* community may simply respond their wiser tune – "we all get it in the end."

WORKS CITED

Bersani, Leo. "Is the Rectum a Grave?" *October* 43 (1987): 197-222. Print.

Comaroff, Jean. "Beyond Bare Life: AIDS, (Bio)Politics, and the Neoliberal Order." *Public Culture* 19.1 (2007): 197-219. Print.

Curlovich, John Michael. "The Sex Film Project (USA)." *Gay and Lesbian Review* 14.1 (2007): 49. Print.

Dean, Tim. "The Antisocial Homosexual." *PMLA* 121.3 (2006): 826-828. Print.

Dolan, Jill. *Utopia in Performance: Finding Hope at the Theater*. Ann Arbor, MI: U of Michigan P, 2005. Print.

Edelman, Lee. *No Future: Queer Theory and the Death Drive*. Durham, NC: Duke UP, 2004. Print.

Kramer, Larry. *The Normal Heart and The Destiny of Me*. 1985/1993. New York, NY: Grove, 2000. Print.

Lee, Nathan. "Shortbus." *Film Comment* 42.5 (2006): 70-71. Print.

Lyotard, Jean-François. *The Postmodern Condition: A Report on Knowledge*. 1979. Trans. Geoff Bennington and Brian Massumi. Minneapolis, MN: U of Minnesota P, 1984. Print.

McCarthy, Todd. "Shortbus." *Variety* 29 May-4 June 2006: 33-34. Print.

Roach, Joseph. *Cities of the Dead: Circum-Atlantic Performance*. New York, NY: Columbia UP, 1996. Print.

Román, David. *Acts of Intervention: Performance, Gay Culture, and AIDS*. Bloomington, IN: Indiana UP, 1998. Print.

—. *Performance in America*: Contemporary U.S. Culture and the Performing Arts. Durham, NC: Duke UP, 2005. Print.

—. "Remembering AIDS: A Reconsideration of the Film Longtime Companion." *GLQ: A Journal of Lesbian and Gay Studies* 12.2 (2006): 281-301. Print.

Romano, Tricia. "Riding the Shortbus." *Village Voice* 4-10 Oct. 2006: 94. Print.

Sacher-Masoch, Leopold von. *Venus in Furs*. 1870. Trans. Joachim Neugroschel. New York, NY: Penguin, 2000. Print.

Shortbus. Dir. John Cameron Mitchell. Perf. Sook-Yin Lee, Paul Dawson, Jay Brannan, PJ DeBoy, Lindsay Beamish, Alan Mandell, Peter Stickles, and Raphael Barker. 2006. Fortissimo Films, 2006. DVD.

Sontag, Susan. *Illness as Metaphor and AIDS and Its Metaphors*. New York, NY: Picador, 1990. Print.

Williams, Linda. "Shortbus." *Cineaste* 32.2 (2007): 47-49. Print.

Part IV
Transamérica

TRANSAMÉRICA: A LONG JOURNEY THROUGH AND BEYOND THE AMERICAS

GUNDO RIAL Y COSTAS

The Transamérica is one of the longest stretches of railway in the whole world which connects the very rear ends of the Americas. Although it does not exist in real life it alludes to the transcontinental highway Panamericana, as well as to the discarded plans of a Pan American Railway in the second half of the 19th century. The metaphor is thought to condense existing imaginaries about the different types of railroads in the Americas. A vast number of rail connections on the continent covers local, regional, and transnational distances. Randomly choosing some of the possible tracks, one instantly perceives the large variety of interconnections, with the Trans Andean railways and the Federal Rail Network linking different destinations in South America, and the Northern Pacific Railroad and the Canadian Railroads covering transnational regions in North America.

The idea behind the metaphor of Transamérica is the seemingly paradoxical combination of connecting and contrasting some of the richest with some of the poorest parts of the world. Up to a certain point, the metaphorical image of the railway can be applied to the transnational movements represented in the texts which sometimes unite spaces through straddling the (Mexican-U. S.) border. They connect people with their often transnational life stories in literature and telenovelas. The represented imaginaries picture the dangers of new forced migrations while they break up old definitions and replace them by new ones, in North America and Latin America, including the Caribbean.

Yet, the Transamérica is only a tentative image, for some of the points to be made here this metaphor will not be sufficient: it might even be misleading because it refers to already hegemonically defined discourses and debates. This is because the concept of the railway has to be considered in the context of the advent of modernity, often linked to severe, frequently cruel, processes of exclusion and discrimination. The mass murder of the native population in the USA as well as the displacement and segregation of hundreds of thousands of people who lost their jobs and their hope for a better life in Rio de Janeiro are only two examples out of a vast and sad collection of historic events that are connected to the introduction of the railroad.

The metaphor of the Transamérica may further be thought to be of limited character, trapped in the materiality of its nodal points in the lifeworld. Although there is a large number of dots, stops, and stations penetrating and staining the fabric of the imaginary map of the Americas drawn by us, one still has to remark that some of the corners of these sections, such as Canada, the very rear basin of the Caribbean, Central America, and Patagonia are beyond its reach.

In addition, as all the texts of this section refer to new spatial logics of the everyday which go beyond the real and well-trodden routes, we may leave the *Transamérica* metaphor behind and take new paths. They may also refer to the accelerated circulation of people, images, and practices going beyond the spatial confinements of the Americas, opening up imagined spaces through literary narratives or through the practice of world construction through the acts of reading or transnational networks. Through these global flows[1] accompanied by the quirkiness of its disjunctures and bumps, the ways and stretches referred to in the essays of this section become much more complex, intertwined, as they construct a dynamic network. They are constantly overlapping, featuring our present world at large which transcends a possible cartographic mapping in a 'real route' of a railway.

All of the texts are linked by an invisible yet palpable and tear-resistant ribbon. It is one that is made of an interwoven fabric with a signature that covers the spaces of the Americas. Apart from sometimes broken English, it also bears writings in Spanish and Portuguese, although we have to admit the absence of Indigeneous languages whose splendour and cultural complexity shall at least be evoked here in this presence through absence. Despite the regrettable absence, one may still speak of a relative plurality of some of the voices of this continent which link the different adventurous, often risky and dramatic tales of deterritorialization. Triggered and caused by ever newly emerging and developing flows of migrations they have led and are still leading to new forms of cultural contact as they contribute to create new imagined and imaginary homelands. At the same time, they help to construct a plurilingual, multidiverse, or even postethnic[2] America, which shall be referred to as 'Transamérica' here.

After this rather long journey off the beaten rail tracks, let us return to our preliminary metaphor. Instead of focusing only on the notion of the railway, we shall shift the focus to the prefix 'trans' in order to rely on its connecting versatility[3]. Certainly, another (overdetermined) stress shall be placed on the accented

---

1 I am very much indebted to the work of Arjun Appadurai for inspiration, as well as to a personal communication by him after the conference "Beyond Multiculturalism" in the House of the Cultures of the World (HKW) in Berlin (June 2009).

2 See David Hollinger. *Postethnic America: Beyond Multiculturalism.* 1995. New York, NY: Basic Books, 2008.

3 Obviously, there are still a good deal more connections which might be drawn, like the ones concerning (trans)gender. They are even referred to with the same metaphor in a road movie (*Transamerica*, 2005) about the life of a transsexual in the USA.

"é" in 'Transamérica' in order to emphasize its Hispano- as well as its Luso-Brazilian elements which correspond to the respective writing of 'América' in Spanish and Portuguese.

Marcel Vejmelka opens this section with his paradigmatic contribution "Yoknapatawpha Between the Deep South and the West Indies: The Dynamics of Transculturation in William Faulkner's *Absalom, Absalom!* and *Go Down, Moses*" by defining the concept of transculturation through the writings of Cuban anthropologist Fernando Ortiz, complemented by ideas of Uruguayan critic Angel Rama. Grounded in this theoretical approach, he thoroughly investigates William Faulkner's novels *Absolom, Absolom!* and *Go Down, Moses* and proposes a way in which these works can be read as vital contributions to the construction of a transculturated and transculturating America.

With "The Chronotopos in the (Postmodern) Novel of the Americas: Towards a Transareal Topology of the Local," Pablo Valdivia Orozco discusses the space of the Americas with a very clever and inspiring analysis of Mikhail Bakhtin's concept of the chronotope and its relational time-space compressions. On this basis, Pablo creatively develops a new literary theoretical approach of a topology of the novel. It originates in the transgression inherent in languages and their specific condition as being of a transplanted nature in the Americas. This is subsequently evidenced through examples from two American writers, Gabriel García Márquez and Sandra Cisneros.

My own essay entitled "Revisiting Spivak: Does the Subaltern Speak in and through Telenovelas?" ventures into the possible depths of Brazilian telenovelas, often erroneously regarded as shallow territory. Discussing the polysemic meaning of Gayatri Spivak's concept of the subaltern, I attempt to disentangle the complexity of this term as well as its passage to the Americas by further investigating traces of the subaltern or of subaltern positions in the more recent Brazilian telenovelas *O Rei do Gado* and *América*.

The three contributions provide a varied segment of the multi-faceted narratives of the Americas, as they (border)cross clear-cut classifications and link Anglo, Hispano, and Luso America in an innovative way. It remains to be seen whether this will also be echoed in the lifeworld and not only restricted to fictional accounts as presented here. Finally, one should bear in mind that the texts are in a constant and dynamic dialogue with the others in this volume.

The focus is placed on a debordered and plural America whose cultural production is not limited to Anglo America but aware of the necessity of Latin American contributions that are too often silenced. Therefore, this section also functions as a bright free-floating buoy in the still rather gray North American sea of fiction. The latter is of a specific relevance as the supposedly smaller Latin American brothers' and sisters' voices, no matter whether born and raised in the northern or the southern part, are often silenced. In respective public debates and discussions they are often not heard, despite the Chicanos', Latinos', Afro-Americans', American Natives' and Asians' important contributions in this respect. The existing canon formation in the USA has still a strong focus on traditional cultural production.

We shall therefore try to highlight the cultural products of this other (Trans)América with a clear graphic marker that can also work on other levels, as a kind of cultural flashlight. Hence, the following essays are not intended to be marginal complements to the mainly North American canon, but rather equally valid and essential contributions to the study of the Americas. They are directly linked, often symbiotically connected with the others on a rhetorical, spatial, thematic, and epistemological level, indicating the effects of cultural globalization.

Despite the order of the essays, this section is also a result of an on-going ping pong dialogue of friendship and familiar resemblance with Ana Reynaud, which is partially reflected by her lively and thoughtful epilogue. Concocted in a Witt(genstein)y way, Ana emphasizes the relevance of the everyday in a particular manner as she muses about the fictional representations of its artifacts, its sense and its nonsense in a swift, Hermes-like fashion. Hence, these streams of thought colorfully reflect on our contributions by underlining the power of the translocal, no matter whether this is in Rio de Janeiro, the Deep South, on the Mexican border, or in New York.

YOKNAPATAWPHA BETWEEN THE DEEP SOUTH AND THE WEST INDIES: THE DYNAMICS OF TRANSCULTURATION IN WILLIAM FAULKNER'S *ABSALOM, ABSALOM!* AND *GO DOWN, MOSES*

MARCEL VEJMELKA

FERNANDO ORTIZ: THE COUNTERPOINT OF TRANSCULTURATION

In 1940, in his *Contrapunteo cubano del tabaco y el azúcar*, the anthropologist Fernando Ortiz proposed a reading of Cuba's socio-cultural formation based on the interactions and entanglements of two fundamental elements of the island's colonial economy: tobacco and sugar:

> Out of the agricultural and industrial development of these amazing plants were to come those economic interests which foreign traders would twist and weave for centuries to form the web of our country's history, the motives of its leaders, and, at one and the same time, the shackles and the support of its people. (Ortiz, "Cuban counterpoint" 4)

The processes of cultural encounters and conflicts Ortiz describes in his essay are synthesized in his concept of *transculturation* as mutual transformation and new reconfiguration of cultural elements within the interactions that form the basis of colonialism and migration. Transculturation is a term opposed to hegemonic conceptions like 'acculturation,' strengthening the inevitable transformation of all parts involved in a cultural encounter, conflict or interaction. Ortiz introduced it only in a short note, but almost immediately it was adopted as a key concept within Latin American cultural theory in the second half of the 20th century. Ortiz explains:

> I have chosen the word transculturation to express the highly varied phenomena that have come about in Cuba as a result of the extremely complex transmutations of culture that have taken place here, and without a knowledge of which it is impossible to understand the evolutions of the Cuban folk, either in the economic or in the institutional, legal, ethical, religious, artistic, linguistic, psychological, sexual, or other aspects of its life. (98)

Tobacco represents, for Ortiz, a genuinely American plant, with a whole tradition of religious, ritual and medical uses and meanings. From the encounter between Indigenous populations in the Americas and European colonialists, in a process of transculturation, tobacco and smoking culture as we know it today was constituted. In the tobacco plantations, Ortiz perceives a living presence of the Indigenous traditions and cultures related to this plant and its uses. Thus, for Ortiz, tobacco symbolizes the re-valorization of an "authentically traditional" product of Cuban (and American) transculturation, a cultural element that shows the marks and traces of its origins and transformations.

Sugar cane, on the contrary, was imported to the Americas by the first European discoverers and literally 'transplanted' to the New World, where the sugar plantations soon became a fundamental element of colonial economy. An economic machinery and a mechanical system which spread from the Caribbean throughout the American hemisphere, and which marked the historical process of colonial America during several centuries. Fundamentally relying on slave labor, sugar production symbolizes for Ortiz the violent destruction of Indigenous and African cultures for the sake of extraction, exploration and economic gains.

The economy of the sugar plantation has become a central aspect of American cultural theory. More or less at the same time as Ortiz, the Brazilian sociologist Gilberto Freyre, in his pioneering *Casa-grande & senzala*, published in 1933, studied the significance of sugar plantations in Brazil's Northeast for the formation of its hybrid society and its conceptions of race and class. In the US, the anthropologist Charles Wagley set the comparative study of different plantation regions in the Americas within his methodological framework of American subcultures during the 1950s and 60s.[1] Particularly in the Caribbean, the plantation has experienced an exceptional career as key concept and metaphor in cultural theory. In his book *La isla que se repite*, published in 1998, Cuban poet and intellectual Antonio Benítez Rojo followed Ortiz' scheme of the plantation in economic and technical evolution, adopting its superior stage of the *ingenio* – the radically industrialized and automated sugar plantation – for his reading of Caribbean cultures within the framework of chaos theory and fractal logics. Finally, in his *Le discours antillais*, the Martinican poet and philosopher Edouard Glissant, before the background of his relational poetics, interprets the logics of the "plantation system" as a central force in the historical processes and cultural dynamics of "creolization."

---

1 "We distinguish nine significant Latin American subculture types. They are called 'subcultures' because they are variations of a larger cultural tradition and represent the way of life o significant segments of the Latin American population. They are called 'types' because their content differs according to the environment, history, and distinctive local traditions of the nation or subregion in which they are found" (Wagley 83). These types are 1) Tribal Indian; 2) Modern Indian; 3) Peasant; 4) Engenho Plantation; 5) Usina Plantation; 6) Town; 7) Metropolitan Upper Class; 8) Metropolitan Middle Class, and 9) Urban Proletariat (83-84).

The counterpoint of tobacco and sugar stages clearly the complex configurations of transculturation and its radical poles of 'positive' (harmonic and creative) as well as 'negative' (violent and mechanical) cultural transmutations. Ortiz critically reconstructs the cultural and social history of Cuba, the Caribbean and – regarding the fundamental logics of New World colonialism – the Americas. The logics of the plantation – be it sugar or cotton, later on coffee, cocoa or bananas – fundamentally shapes and determines the formation of regional cultures in the Americas. Due to the complex composition of the *Cuban Counterpoint*[2] and the ambiguity of Ortiz' conception of transculturation between national and global dynamics, its critical reception is marked by the difficulties of its immediate application to the analysis of concrete phenomena. Nevertheless, the challenges of this dynamic concept also bear extraordinary potentials, as the Argentinean-Mexican critic Liliana Weinberg points out[3]:

> Due to the multiple contexts where the concept of transculturation can be applied and recontextualized, and in some cases even re-semanticised (although there is a core of the concept that remains constant, that never means confusion and hybrid indistinction, but *asimmetry, conflictivity, dynamics, complexity and creativity*), it is not as simple as some might think; it is not simple to obtain a single and definite meaning of the term that was conceived precisely for the sake of its dynamic capacity of re-adaption and re-signification. (34)

Articulating this innovative dialog between the history of sugar production and that of tobacco cultivation in Cuba, i. e. between the logics of slavery-based economy and the dynamics of cultural encounters, Ortiz shows that (Latin) American culture as a whole is to be understood as a result of complex and overlapping transculturating processes. Not only the Indigenous populations or the African slaves in the Americas were "deculturated" by being expelled from their homelands, cut off from their traditions and believes, and afterwards "reculturated" – Christianized and 'civilized' – as a means of controlled integration into the colonizer's cultural system, but also the colonizers themselves –despite their conviction of being exclusively acting upon this New World – were instantly affected by multiple transformations caused by the interactions with the indigen-

---

2 The *Contrapunteo* consists of the main essay (72 pages in my edition), followed by 25 numbered "additional chapters" with a total of 384 pages. The main essay explores the formal liberties and literary potentials of its genre, performing a dialogical narration – a genuinely Cuban meaning of the term "contrapunteo" – of his theme. The "additional chapters" serve for theoretical and methodological explanations and historical digressions. The English translation contains only 12 of the original 25 "additional chapters."

3 See also Spitta (6-15) and Rojas.

ous and African cultures they forced under their rule.[4] The same applies to miscegenation, which is no longer perceived as a unidirectional process, or 'deterioration,' of white blood or 'whitening' of non-white subjects, but as a multidirectional constitution of new and mixed ethnic configurations without a fixed center.[5]

Another important aspect of Ortiz' concept is its focus on creativity. New cultural configurations and manifestations emerging from the violent encounter between conquerors and colonized, slaveholders and slaves, always carry the mark of their origin, but they also open up new spaces of meaning and agency. This creative potential of transculturation should be linked intimately to more recent proposals of dealing with cultural hybridity, as they were formulated by Homi Bhabha in *The Location of Culture* in the realm of Anglophone Postcolonial Studies and by Nestor García Canclini in *Culturas híbridas* in the Latin American context.[6]

ÁNGEL RAMA: TOWARDS NARRATIVE TRANSCULTURATION

In the 1970s, the Uruguayan critic Ángel Rama adapted and applied Ortiz's idea of transculturation to the study of Latin American literatures in their socioeconomic contexts during the 19th and 20th centuries. With his term of *narrative transculturation* he suggested a fundamental contextualization of literary works and history within the dynamics of colonial and post-colonial societies. In this way, he follows and continues the dialectics of global and national perspectives

---

4 A telling example of this process is the already mentioned history of Western smoking culture. Another example with suggestive links to the application of transculturation to the North American context is given by Freyre in his study on Northeastern Brazilian sugar plantations: In the blurred zone between the planter's mansion and the slaves' huts, colored nannies became segregated parts of the 'family,' taking care of the 'white' children, familiarizing them from the very beginnings of their lives with African chants, tales, food and habits. One immediately remembers William Faulkner's intense paternalistic affection for his family's servant "Mummy" Caroline Barr, to whom he dedicated *Go Down, Moses* – see also his "Funeral Sermon for Mummy Caroline Barr" – and whose portrait can be read in several of his literary nannies.

5 Ortiz illustrates this aspect with the metaphor of 'ajiaco,' a traditional Cuban stew that unites elements from Europe, Africa and the island's Indigenous populations ("Los factores humanos"; Catoira).

6 Bhabha focuses on the "location of cultures" and their agents, proposing his famous "third space" as a "space in-between" where new enunciations by new cultural agents not allocated to determined and fixed cultural constellations become possible. With his "hybrid cultures," Canclini shifts from cultural mixtures on national or ethnic levels to the increasingly blurred boundaries between popular cultures and so called high culture, proposing as an analytical instrument the concept of "cultural reconversion," envisioning the complex processes of reconfiguration and transformation within the postmodern and globalized dynamics of culture.

on cultural formations, which becomes especially clear in his frequently asserted intent to contribute to the fortification of a hemispheric "Latin American literature and culture" (Rama, *La novela*). At the same time, his approach to literature bears a radical mobility, regarding its location in time, space and society, that is being explored in new readings of his critical thought within the context of Postcolonial, Postmodern and Subaltern Studies which go beyond the traditional range of 'Latin America' (see Kraniauskas; La Campa, *Latin Americanism* 121-147).

Rama parts from the conflict between tradition and modernization in the formation of a cultural autonomy in Latin America. Facing a heavy burden of Iberian cultural legacy, beginning with the languages inherited from Spain and Portugal, and the structural weakness of the recent national entities that rose from independence, the idea of internationalism and supranational cultural concepts became central in the conceptions of Latin America. In the cultural and literary realm, within this tension of external influences and internal forces, the tendency to see peculiarity expressed in the 'local color' of regionalist works was confronted with the need to accompany the multifold modernization of literary language, structure and worldview – which for Rama, inspired by Vittorio Lanternari's scheme of cultural vulnerability, rigidity and plasticity, are the key aspects of a transcultured and transculturating literary expression (Rama, "Literature and Culture" 134-135).

> Transculturation is a force that acts with ease as much on its own particular heritage, in accordance with its developmental situation, as on external contributions. It is precisely this capacity to elaborate with originality, a feature that may be found anywhere in the territory, but most clearly in the remotest strata of the interior regions, which demonstrates, despite difficult historical circumstances, that the process of transculturation belongs to a creative and lively society. (136)

In the confrontation with this problem of Latin American self-conception, Rama extended the cultural dynamics of Ortiz's concept by the spatial dimension of "cultural regions" (*comarcas or áreas culturales*), territories of cultural coherence, whose configuration combines the presence of different indigenous cultures, administrative units of the colonies and finally the dialectics of global modernization and resisting popular cultures.

> On a second, more robust and valid level, Latin America's diversity is confirmed by the existence of cultural regions. [...] These regions can also encompass various neighboring countries or within them cut out regions of common characteristics, establishing a map whose borders do not adjust to those of the independent nations. This second map of Latin America is more truthful than the official one, whose

> borders were at most determined by the old administrative divisions of the Colonies and, to a no less degree, by the contingencies of national or international political life. (Rama, *Transculturación narrativa* 57-58[7])

Rama's cultural regions superpose and entangle several temporal, spatial and cultural orders set in motion. His alternative map of the Americas, drawn from configurations of cultural history, does not simply superpose two cultural layers (one Indigenous or African, the other European; one colonized, the other colonizing). The interwoven layers of this map contain the temporal dimension of historical processes that are never fixed or definite. The regional units, delineated according to central cultural features, are in constant transformation and interact mutually within the field of local, regional and global forces (Rama, "Literature and Culture" 138). Thus, the concept of culture in the Americas is set in temporal and spatial motion; it registers periods of discoveries, conquest and colonization, of economic exploration and exploitation, the extermination of Indigenous, African and popular cultures, their resistance as well as their strategies of adaptation. This conception is the basis which enables its structural transposition to other geographical and historical spaces, as proposed here within the cultural territories of the Americas:

> This map is organized by two crossing centerlines: the one we could consider the horizontal line, which manifests itself in the time-space occupied by societies (Indigenous communities, regions of livestock farming, cities, national spaces etc.), and the vertical one that crosses them according to socio-economic configurations, imposing on any of these societies the re-organization of their time-space in conformity with social stratification, types of occupation and work etc. (Rama, *Transculturación narrativa* 244)

In a similar way as did Ortiz, Rama underlines the importance of the creative stance in the conceptions of transculturation, which become crucial in the realm of literature, where the achievement of a truly autonomous literary expression for Latin American reality would represent a "narrative transculturation" in the most extensive sense, as a transculturated literature and also a literature of transculturation:

> Through the prism of transculturation one can also perceive a creative task, part of the neoculturation Fernando Ortiz speaks of, a neoculturation operating simultaneously on both cultural sources in contact with each other. There would be, of course, losses, selections, rediscoveries, and incorporations. These four operations are concomitant and all are resolved within the overall restructuring of the cultural system, which is the highest creative function achieved in the transculturating process. (Rama, "Literature and Culture" 140)

---

7 All translations mine.

The three basic problems "narrative transculturation" has to confront are the language(s), the structure, and the worldview implemented in a literary text. Language has to achieve a certain identity with its regional object, without explicitly othering regional and unlettered linguistic expressions, or reducing it to a picturesque alterity. As literary discourse, it is inevitably part of the modern rationalization of narrative and representation, but by its particular fashion, this language is capable of "restoring a regional vision of the world" (142-143). In terms of literary structure, there exists the even greater difficulty of bridging the gap between traditional and oral forms of narrative and modern literary discourse. The solution Rama believes to be the most powerful lies in a sort of subversion of modernist techniques by a "retreat into traditionalist cultural sources" (143) and popular narrative structures. The worldview, finally, concerns the problem of how to overcome the Euro-centered models of reality, cognition and its representation while taking part in one of its fundamental means of expression, which is literature. On the example of the conception of reality and myth, Rama analyzes how Latin American writers from the Vanguards to the new regionalists developed different worldviews that to a different degree drew upon European models of myth and rationality:

> [T]he transculturators facilitate the expansion of new mythic tales, removing them from their ambiguous and powerful background as precise and enigmatic creations. [...] In truth, such a response overcomes modernization with unexpected intensity, with a breadth that few modern writers were capable of achieving. "Mythic thinking" will oppose the use of "literary myths." (151)

The central representatives of this narrative transculturation in the second half of the 20th century are, for example, the Peruvian José María Arguedas, from the Andean cultural region, the Mexican Juan Rulfo, Gabriel García Márquez from the Caribbean coast of Colombia, João Guimarães Rosa as an example for the intra-national region of the Brazilian sertão, but also an apparently 'universal' writer such as Juan Carlos Onetti, who in his literary work recreated the reality of the Río de la Plata. Taking into account the importance of regional cultures for all of these writers, and remembering also that at least three of them – García Márquez, Rulfo, and Onetti – were declared admirers and 'followers' of the US-southerner William Faulkner, the application of transculturation as an analytical category to his work becomes almost a manifest step. Within this context, the analysis of William Faulkner represents an especially apt example of the hemispheric dimensions of transculturation as a conception of cultural formation as well as one of the literary and cultural reflection contained in his representation of the Deep South.

Even more so as the bridge of Faulkner's Latin American reception was not constructed by chance: He was read and adopted not as a US writer, but as a southern writer, approaching the historical experiences of South America with that of the US South (see Fayen; Aboul-Ela). Contemplating the shared history and hybrid condition of both souths within the Caribbean and hemispheric dynamics of the Americas before the US Civil War, Southern planters and slaveholders appear as members of the same caste of New World landlords as their Caribbean or Brazilian fellows (Pratt Guterl 447). The US South can be analyzed as part of "Plantation America" (Wagley) or the Caribbean "Plantation system" (Glissant, *Le discours antillais*), a supranational vision to be overlaid with that of the South representing an infra-national cultural region within the US. The problematic of cultural autonomy and its expression in the two souths – one (South America) confronted with the hegemonic impulses of international metropolises even before its nations became politically independent, the other (the US South) 'internally' colonized after the Civil War – is also a shared one. A common hemispheric space in cultural configurations and literary responses, where the work of William Faulkner occupies a singular and central position: "Yoknapathawpha County does not just share a border with the Caribbean, it shares a history as well" (Cohn 166).

ABSALOM, ABSALOM! THOMAS SUTPEN'S IMPOSSIBLE 'DESIGN'

This shared history and common Caribbean space is re-traced by Edouard Glissant in his approach to Faulkner and the Deep South, which is staged as a travelogue that opens with Glissant's crossing from the archipelago to the mainland, from the Caribbean coast of the US to Faulkner's mansion in Rowan Oak, Oxford, Mississippi (*Faulkner*). Traversing, in a similar way, Faulkner's novels, stories and themes, Glissant points to a central aspect of writing before the background of narrative transculturation:

> At the same time, we can see that, while accumulating narratives and short stories, patiently constructing some novels from his short-story material, or writing others in fits and fevers, Faulkner "sweeps" the country's horizons, particularly aware of what he must say about two generic types (for whom he takes narrative responsibility): poor White farmers and Blacks. […] The language of these interwoven interior monologues does not abandon the realm of peasant speech or relinquish the grandeur of epic interrogation. (44-45)

Transculturating processes enter linguistic and literary representation on the level of narrative techniques, interacting with their contents in form of themes and protagonists. As Ángel Rama commented on processes of narrative transculturation, in Faulkner's work there is a complex fusion of traditional expressions and elements with modern narrative techniques. In his characteristic interior monologues, forms of oral story telling penetrate in the realm of the written code, different regional and ethnic worldviews are contrasted and combined in the juxtaposition of narrating voices and their perspectives. For Glissant, the central topic of *Absalom, Absalom!* – first published in 1936 – is the condensation and simultaneity of the South's historical guilt that is envisioned as an individual and collective fate, symbolized in the duality of incest and miscegenation which haunts the genealogical 'design' of the *arriviste* cotton planter Thomas Sutpen, whose natural son with a Haitian mulatto pretends to marry his legitimate daughter with a white Yoknapatawpha lady:

> In Faulkner's *Absalom, Absalom!* the *historical desire* extends generally to the primordial trace (the foundation) of the Sutpen family, and particularly to the origin of the protagonist called Bon. So, if this last one is a negro, his pretension to the possession of Judith Sutpen is calamitous; but one will discover that he is maybe *also* her brother (her miscegenated half-brother). The primordial incest strikes *back*. One sees clearly that it is a desire (the knowledge of an origin, of the origin) whose elucidation will be fatal. (Glissant, *Le discours antillais* 256)

Thomas Sutpen, who was born in Virginia into a family of poor White farm workers and who in Haiti became rich and powerful as overseer of a sugar plantation, is obsessed with the foundation and perpetuation of a dynasty of his own. He married his first wife in Haiti, not knowing – or at least he claims so – that the sugar planter's daughter, supposedly of Spanish descent, was a *métisse*. When his first son Charles Bon is born, he rejects this mixed offspring, leaves his wife and returns to the US. He settles in Jefferson, starts a cotton plantation, marries Ellen Coldfield, and with her has a daughter, Judith, and another son, Henry, his 'legitimate' heir and the fulfillment of his 'design' for a genealogy. His two families and sons differentiate and also merge two spaces that are constitutive of the US South: the white planter's society on the continent and the racially mixed reality of the Caribbean, marked by the "perversion of original descent," as Glissant suggests: "How could he place himself in the center of what he is, now that his legitimacy appears uncertain to him? That way, a collectivity can doubt of itself, lose itself within its vertigo" (*Faulkner* 257-258). The obsessive combat against the awareness of this perverted original descent, of the real origin in contrast and contradiction to its idealized and mystified imagination, this imaginary of an 'original sin' and thereof resulting 'doomed fate' of the Deep South's socio-economic constitution – as incorporated by Thomas Sutpen – forms the center around which Faulkner's fictitious county of Yoknapatawpha is constructed.

> What I learned was that there was a place called the West Indies to which poor men went in ships and became rich, it didn't matter how, so long as that man was clever and courageous: the latter of which I believed that I possessed, the former of which I believed that, if it were to be learned by energy and will in the school of endeavor and experience, I should learn. (Faulkner, *Absalom, Absalom!* 200)

Thomas Sutpen came to spend ten years in Haiti (1823-33), acculturating himself partially to the social and cultural reality on the island, or more exactly becoming 'transculturated' in a mixture of conscious and unconscious, or involuntary, transformations. Consciously, he learns French and Patois, he adjusts himself to the social order of Haitian plantation society, but he fails to realize the implications of an independent nation born out of the first successful revolution of African slaves in the Americas. Haitian society at Sutpen's time was a regime of Creole landlords oppressing slave-like Creole and black peasants on their plantations, a fact that should have shown him the impossibility of his purist 'design' of that island. Sutpen also seems not to realize that he decides to return to the US at a point where he can no longer return to his former self. He has become a stranger in the South, and the inhabitants of Yoknapatawpha inevitably perceive him as an "uncanny" menace for their "American innocence" (La Campa, "Mimicry and the Uncanny"). His 'alterity' in the Jeffersonians' perception is symbolized in the African slaves he takes with him to the US to work on his cotton plantation. These slaves most probably were traded directly and illegally from Africa to Haiti, they communicate with Sutpen in Haitian Patois, which no one in Jefferson understands or even recognizes: "The negroes could speak no English yet and doubtless there were more than Akers who did not know that the language in which they and Sutpen communicated was a sort of French and not some dark and fatal tongue of their own" (Faulkner, *Absalom, Absalom!* 29).

Sutpen now incorporates everything that Jefferson and the Deep South's slaveholder society need to ignore or forget in order to maintain their self-mystification as a "paternalistic and idyllic" social regime. For this reason, all transmitting instances of his life – several Jeffersonian voices – pretend to ignore what Sutpen was doing exactly in Haiti, how he became rich and where he bought the slaves for his plantation. The collectivity of the South is thus taking a certain part in his second project for a dynastic design, which is also an attempt of forgetting his first "failure:"

> Sutpen is a conqueror in Haiti, fathering a design out of the mixture of Spanish, French, and African blood. This mating gratifies the need for labor and the lust for wealth, then is set aside, forgotten when the sacraments of gentrification begin. Sutpen's white wife Ellen represents the respectability that is founded on obliviousness to material reality; her only responsibility is to etherealize money whose source does not bear recollection. (Matthews 255)

But Sutpen's first wife follows him to the US, raising their son Charles Bon in New Orleans, the most Creole and Caribbean city in the South. In 1859, Charles Bon gets to know his half-brother Henry at the University of Mississippi in Oxford. He gets engaged to Judith and discloses himself to Henry as his miscegenated half-brother, who in the southerner's logic is perceived as a Negro. Thomas Sutpen explains to Henry the need to avoid the marriage between Charles

Bon and Judith at any cost: "*He must not marry her, Henry. His mother's father told me that her mother had been a Spanish woman. I believed him; it was not until after he was born that I found out that his mother was part negro*" (Faulkner, *Absalom, Absalom!* 292). No word on the presumable threat of incest, Thomas Sutpen is exclusively obsessed with his fear of miscegenation. After this demand to kill his half-brother, Henry breaks free from his father, renouncing his inheritance and the design of a Sutpen dynasty. The family drama merges into the national context of the beginning Civil War, amplifying its symbolic meanings to the cultural constitution and self-image of the Old South by confronting the violent process of US nation building.[8] Henry, who fights in the Confederate army together with Charles Bon, hopes that at least one of them will die in the war, thus relieving him from the decision. But Henry's conflict is intensified as he is wounded in battle and saved by Charles Bon. After the war, when Charles Bon about to marry Judith, Henry tells him of their father's demand, and Bon is the first to explicitly comment on the fact that the incestuous dimension of his love is not relevant for the Sutpens:

> *So it's the miscegenation, not the incest, which you cant bear.* [...] *And he sent me no word? He did not ask you to send me to him? No word to me, no word at all?* [...] *He would not have needed to ask it, require it, of me. I would have offered it. I would have said, I will never see her again, before he could have asked it of me. He did not have to do this, Henry. He didn't need to tell you I am a nigger to stop me. He could have stopped me without that, Henry.* (293)

Henry shoots Bon before he can marry Judith, then he disappears. By avoiding the 'contamination' of his 'design,' Sutpen has lost his only male heir, and also his second wife Ellen dies. He desperately initiates another attempt, but Ellen's sister Rosa does not accept his condition to marry her only after having given birth to a boy. Sutpen then impregnates Milly, the granddaughter of his white tenant Wash Jones. He renounces to marry her when the child is born a girl, and is killed by her grandfather. Years later, when Henry Sutpen returns to his father's mansion Sutpen's Hundred, his mulatto half-sister Clytie, fearing that Rosa Coldfield and Quentin Compson – who come to the plantation in order to help Henry – will call the police, sets fire to the house, where she and Henry die.

---

8 Here, the image of the house is transposed from Sutpen's anachronistic mansion – Sutpen's Hundred, the material expression of his will to dynasty – to Abraham Lincoln's metaphor of the nation as a common house of north and south. "A house divided against itself cannot stand," as he formulated in his famous speech in 1858, opposes the socio-economic community of the US to the self-perception of southern slaveholder elite as a society and culture of its own. I thank my Americanist colleague Martin Lüthe for his valuable comments on the cultural contexts of the US Civil War.

The only survivor of the Sutpen family is Jim Bond – son of Charles Etienne de Saint Velery Bon, the natural son of Charles Bon with an "octoroon mistress" from New Orleans, who was raised by Judith and Clytie: "[…] and he, Jim Bond, the scion, the last of his race, seeing it too now and howling with human reason now since now even he could have known what he was howling about" (309).

The potential for conflict of Yoknapatawpha's collective 'knowing not-knowing' is condensed within the figure of Quentin Compson III – the last first-born son and destined heir of one of Jefferson's foundational dynasties, who in a long conversation with his roommate Shreve at Harvard University reconstructs the different voices – his father's, his grandfather's, his aunt Rosa's – that reconstructed the history of Thomas Sutpen. He feels an urge and need to tell this story, which at the same time is a task imposed upon him by the historical guilt of "his" South, a decisive element of his narrative voice because the reader knows from the beginning that Quentin is telling this story only a few weeks before his suicide in June 1910, which 'already' occurred in the novel *The Sound and the Fury*.

> I suggest that privileged Southerners of the Compson caste found refuge in such knowing not-knowing, in a language that displayed historical realities without granting them visibility. The "something" that "is missing" when Mr. Compson brings the words together, I contend he already knows: it is the whole story of the new-world plantation that makes Sutpen's career from Haiti to Jefferson entirely legible as a story of colonial crime–Amerindian genocide, slave trade, human chattel, bigamy, rape, incest, the loveless outrage of the land. (Matthews 256-257)

Quentin's account and 'recreation' of Charles Bon is contaminated by his own fear of miscegenation and incest, which are menacing the social order that he represents as the final stage of the "original white southerner" (Ladd 147), but which he also denies by his own incestuous love for his sister Candace in *The Sound and the Fury*. Following Barbara Ladd's interpretation, miscegenation and incest are synonyms for Quentin, as they are for his contemporary post-war South, so that he interprets his own acts as "morally black" and sees himself as a "white nigger:"

> It is a powerful equation when read in terms of Quentin's narrative of race and sex, where the monster who must be destroyed, the figure who "owns the terror", is both black and brother, despite the rhetoric that would deny that relationship; in other words, it is a dramatization of the white racist's most nightmarish vision of his future under the new dispensation. (152)

Quentin himself does not know how to deal with these dramas and imaginaries, which he is reflecting through the distance of his narration, but from which he also cannot withdraw. He incorporates the South that he experiences as his personal conflict and within the tragic and absurd failure of Thomas Sutpen's obsession with a genealogical design. At the end of the novel, at the end of Quentin's self-reflective account on Sutpen, his room-mate Shreve comments:

> "You've got one nigger left. One nigger Sutpen left. Of course you cant catch him and you dont even always see him and you never will be able to use him. But you've got him there still. You still hear him at night sometimes. Dont you?"
> "[...] Now I want you to tell me just one thing more. Why do you hate the South?"
> "I dont hate it," Quentin said, quickly, at once, immediately; "I dont hate it," he said. *I dont hate it* he thought, panting in the cold air, the iron New England dark: *I dont. I dont! I dont hate it! I dont hate it!* (Faulkner, *Absalom, Absalom!* 310-311)

Because for Quentin, whose perspective continues within the past of the Old South, the enduring presence of Thomas Sutpen's last and miscegenated descendant symbolizes exactly the doom of his own caste and culture:

> That Charles Bon should, in following his U.S. father (and Martinican grandfather) into the frontier wilderness of Mississippi [...], eventuate in the figure of Jim Bond, the "one nigger Sutpen left", whose howling in that wilderness has no direction, cannot be traced toward New Orleans, toward the West Indies, nor finally eastward toward Europe–no direction, in fact, except inward–is the final reclamation of a damning history by Quentin Compson, as he himself lies displaced and shivering in a "cold known land." (Ladd 154)

GO DOWN, MOSES
IKE MCCASLIN AND THE IMPOSSIBLE RETURN TO AN 'ORIGIN'

The representations of Yoknapatawpha's indigenous habitants form a correspondence and, simultaneously, a contrast to the dynastic and racist self-conception of southern planters, as represented exemplarily by the white parvenu Thomas Sutpen, and complete the contradictory picture of cultures and transculturation in Faulkner's writings. In the first part of *Go Down, Moses*, the Chickasaw appear as a remembered and at the same time mystified collectivity that incorporates the 'prehistoric' times of North America's south before its discovery and conquest by the Europeans. This remote and unknown past is leaving its traces in the present, where they interact within the historically configured issue of ethnic and cultural miscegenation. Two central protagonists in Faulkner's universe of Yoknapatawpha are, in this respect, Sam Fathers and Isaac "Ike" McCaslin.

The Chickasaw people are by Faulkner portrayed as more flexible and pragmatic than their white counterparts, who gradually expropriate and marginalize them in the course of history.[9] Their genealogy is reconstructed from the early times of coexistence with the arriving white settlers, arranging themselves from the beginning with the new circumstances of this cultural encounter. The first chief to actively embrace the consequences of the forced transculturation of his people by colonization is Ikkemotubbe, also called Du Homme and later – in a suggestive phonetic 'assimilation' and symbolic inversion of the French name – "Doom." He and his heirs are shown in a progressive process of miscegenation with both white and black men and women, within a narrative ambiguity between a positive contrast to the racially obsessed white planters and a paternalistic vision of increasing physical and moral degeneration (Faulkner, "Red Leaves" 321). In the recent past and present of Yoknapatawpha, the old Sam Fathers represents the final stage of this Indigenous genealogy and transculturation: he does not belong to any ethnic group; the whites consider him a Negro, the black as "mixed blood," and only the Chickasaw seem to reserve him an undetermined and unproblematic place within their social and ethnic order. For the white planters, who gave him the name of Sam Fathers,[10] he also represents a mythic and prehistoric link to nature and wilderness, an aspect that is treated in *Go Down, Moses* when he interacts with members of the McCaslin family, another foundational dynasty of Jefferson. Young Isaac McCaslin learns from his 16 years elder cousin Carothers McCaslin Edmonds about this old servant of their family:

> He was a wild man. When he was born, all his blood on both sides, except the little white part, knew things that had been tamed out of our blood so long ago that we have not only forgotten them, we have to live together in herds to protect ourselves from our own sources. He was the direct son not only of a warrior but of a chief. Then he grew up and began to learn things, and all of a sudden one day he found out that he had been betrayed, the blood of the warriors and chiefs had been betrayed. (Faulkner, *Go Down, Moses* 124)

In Carothers' understanding, Sam's origins from the relationship between the culturally already transformed, but ethnically pure, Chickasaw chief "Doom"

9 As occurs in Faulkner's complex and conflictive relation to and representation of Blacks (see, for example, the central characters of Dilsey in *The Sound and the Fury*, or Lucas Beauchamp in *Intruder in the Dust*), the indigenous protagonists oscillate between critical counterparts, paternalistic parodies and mere idealization, cf. Gage; Horsford.

10 In the beginning of "A Justice," the once again narrator Quentin Compson explains: "He lived with the Negroes and they—the white people; the Negroes called him a blue-gum—called him a Negro. But he wasn't a Negro. That's what I'm going to tell about" (Faulkner, "A Justice" 343). And Sam Fathers himself describes his position: "'These Niggers,' he said. 'They call me Uncle Blue-Gum. And the white folks, they call me Sam Fathers.'
'Isn't that your name?' I said.
'No. Not in the old days. I remember'" (344).

and a "quadroon" slave, mixing Indian blood with both white and black parts, represents an inevitable existential conflict: "[...] himself his own battleground, the scene of his own vanquishment and the mausoleum of his defeat. His cage aint us" (124-125). Inverting this legitimizing white master's perspective, Sam Fathers appears as a result of complex miscegenation and therefore a guardian of different and even opposed historical experiences:

> Of African and Indian descent, Sam Fathers represents the archetypical *ancêtre* who [...] links the spiritual and physical realms of existence and acts as a mediator between the past and present. Sam Father's role as an ancestor is twofold in that he possesses the ancestral memory of his Indian past as well as the experience of the injustices of the enslavements of Africans. (Anderson 98)

Sam Fathers – whose name now also reveals his symbolic meaning – does not suffer from his ethnic and cultural condition. On the contrary, he transmits his knowledge of nature and man, of different ethnicities and cultures, and of transculturation to the younger generations. His most apt disciple in this regard is young Isaac McCaslin, who later as old "Uncle Ike" will occupy a similar place in the Yoknapatawpha society. Ike admires Sam's particularities, which normally are perceived as deviant or threatening alterity. Their intimate relationship evolves with the bear hunt in the woods. There, the hunting is portrayed as a space of interaction between civilization and wilderness, modernity and tradition, between Jefferson's historicity and "Old Ben's" (the hunted bear) realm of myth; a space where Isaac is initiated by his cultural mentor Sam Fathers.[11]

Isaac learns how to move in the woods, to understand some of the transcendental dimensions of hunting and to become partially one with nature while waiting for the bear. But this ideal of innocent integration of man into nature is necessarily as precarious as is the transcultural ideal incorporated by Sam Fathers. This becomes evident by the fact that Boon Hogganbeck, another mixed Chickasaw's descendant, but not from an aristocratic line, who generally renounces his Indian side and considers himself white (Faulkner, *Go Down, Moses* 126), in the end kills the mythic bear Old Ben in a way that goes against all traditions of good and respectful hunting.

From that point onwards, the fear of miscegenation and incest, of this doubled threat to the foundations of white self-perception in the Deep South appears: As an adult, Ike McCalsin discovers and reads the old ledgers of his family. By deciphering short notes and laconic figures, he learns that his grandfather had

---

11 It is not by accident that the ritualistic hunting parties have their base in General de Spain's camp, on the former grounds of Sutpen's Hundred, propriety and symbol of Thomas Sutpen's racially purist project of a genealogy.

bought the young slave Eunice in New Orleans and made her his mistress, impregnating her with his daughter Tomasina, called "Tomy," and marrying her formally to his slave Thucydus. The grandfather also turned his natural daughter into his mistress, fathering in her his son Terrel. Under these circumstances, Eunice drowned herself, while Tomy died in childbed. Even without being officially recognized, self-confident Terrel or "Tomey's Turl" considered himself half-brother of Buddy and Buck McCaslin, Isaac's father and uncle, who in their awareness of the shame and guilt their father had committed, implicitly accepted all his vindications. So, Terrel became the founder of an alternative and uncomfortable branch of the McCaslin dynasty – the Beauchamps, initiated by incest and miscegenation.[12]

Ike is confronted with the historical guilt of his family, the foundations of his own identity and socio-economic position, as part of Yoknapatawpha's foundational dynasties, white landowners and proud southerners (Anderson 104). Through the ledgers, he reconstructs the never openly admitted deeds of his forefathers, the true and complete tradition he represents, and, in contrast to young Quentin Compson, who only through suicide manages to flee from the guilt of his origins and history, liberates himself in life from this historical burden – even if only individually and to a certain degree:

> In deciphering the scrawled, nearly illegible entries of his semiliterate father and uncle, Ike, like the patient in analysis, learns to interpret the writing, the traces of past desires. Unlike Sutpen or old Carothers, Ike does not deny his past; and unlike Quentin he avoids the merging with those past desires. Ike literally "remembers" a past which belongs to him and his family. (King 197)

But neither Issac McCaslin nor the Deep South he incorporates can completely escape from the vicious circle of incest and miscegenation, from the fear of fundamental threats to their very identity and existence. At the end of his life, old Uncle Ike joins the younger men in the hunting parties, trying (unsuccessfully) to transmit something of what he has learned from Sam Fathers, reconstructing the former woods in face of the last remaining 'wilderness' of the present. One day, when he is waiting alone in the hunting camp, a young woman appears and ex-

---

12 His proud son Lucas Beauchamp will have his part in the McCaslin heritage paid out and leave the plantation. In *Intruder in the Dust*, where Lucas is wrongly accused of having murdered a white man, he demands to be treated as a member of the (white and respected) McCaslin family: "'I aint a Edmonds. I dont belong to these new folks. I belong to the old lot. I'm a McCaslin.'" (Faulkner, *Intruder in the Dust* 297), while the collective narrative voice admits: "[...] every white man in that whole section of the county had been thinking about him for years: *We got to make him be a nigger first. He's got to admit he's a nigger. Then maybe we will accept him as he seems to intend to be accepted*" (296). On the "white" and "black" genealogies of the McCaslins, see King.

plains that her newborn baby's father is the son of Ike's cousin McCaslin Edmonds. Ike immediately, and only by her features, realizes that the woman is of mixed descent, and once again the combination of incest and miscegenation proves to be the central and most powerful threat to white self-fashioning in Faulkner's South. Even a person as experienced and transculturated as Ike McCaslin is horrified by the sight of a "Negro" entering his genealogical order, forgetting instantly his own painful recovery of his family's past. But he is brutally reminded that this "quadroon" or "octoroon" child is only repeating and continuing the history of the McCaslins when the woman explains to be of the Beauchamp line:

> Now he understood what it was she had brought into the tent with her, what old Isham had already told him by sending the youth to bring her in to him—the pale lips, the skin pallid and dead-looking yet not ill, the dark and tragic and foreknowing eyes. *Maybe in a thousand or two thousand years in America, he thought. But not now! Not now!* He cried, not loud, in a voice of amazement, pity, and outrage: "You're a nigger!"
> "Yes," she said. "James Beauchamp—you called him Tennie's Jim though he had a name—was my grandfather. I said you were Uncle Isaac." (Faulkner, *Go Down, Moses* 266)

So Ike only momentarily falls back into his forefathers' patterns of interpretation and action. His first terror already reveals an awareness that differentiates between southern society and his individual perception, and on this individual level he overcomes the mechanic horror that characterized a Thomas Sutpen or his grandfather Carothers McCaslin Edmonds and that internally destroyed young Quentin Compson. Even if he does not free himself entirely from the racist and purist thought of his caste[13], in this moment he becomes capable of feeling tenderness and admiration for the force and magic of transculturation within his own family, as he has always felt towards Sam Fathers, the tales of the Chickasaw, the hunting. In his old eyes, the young woman and her son symbolize the hope that they – and with them the Deep South as a whole – might escape from the fate of inherited and perpetuated guilt:

> He didn't grasp it, he merely touched it—the gnarled, bloodless, bone-light bone-dry old man's fingers touching for a second the smooth young flesh where the strong old blood ran after its long journey back to home. "Tennie's Jim," he said.

---

[13] "However, Ike's choice only displaces his confinement within the system he deems unjust and cursed. Rather than freeing himself of the curse, he remains indirectly bound to the 'tamed land' and all it represents by becoming financially dependent upon the cousin to whom he relinquishes the plantation. And, as the reader discovers in 'Delta Autumn,' Ike's consciousness of the injustice of the racial system does not allow him to overcome his own personal racism" (Anderson 99-100).

> "Tennie's Jim." He drew the hand back beneath the blanket again; he said harshly now: "It's a boy, I reckon. They usually are, except that one that was its own mother too."
> "Yes," she said. "It's a boy." (267)

CONCLUSION

In his essay "On Fear; Deep South in Labor: Mississippi," published in 1956, William Faulkner analyses the Mississippians', the Southerners', and finally also his own personal existential "fear" of abolishing racial boundaries and segregations in the US. This extra-literary comment on what, within his literary work, is portrayed as Sutpen's obsessive fear of miscegenation and Ike McCaslin's painful confrontation with it, underlines the unquestionable processes and realities of transculturation in the US South as a central problem and object in Faulkner's work. As his protagonists and Yoknapatawpha's collectivity, Faulkner – their "sole owner and proprietor" – shows his awareness of its inevitability and of the futileness of trying to deny it against all evidence. This position is described by Faulkner in his essay "Mississippi," in a way that sums up the relation of his entire work to his Deep South: "Loving all of it [Mississippi, the South] even while he had to hate some of it because he knows now that you dont love because: you love despite; not for the virtues, but for the faults" ("Mississippi" 42-43).

Quentin Compson, who did not manage to "love" the South and whose negation of "hating it" at the end of *Absalom, Absalom!* expresses desperation and resignation, condenses and radicalizes this fear of Yoknapatawpha's white habitants in face of their possible black or colored heritage or origin, which would question – and which permanently challenges – their need for a secure and legitimate descent, unsettling the grounds of their cultural identity. In these very terms Edouard Glissant describes the historical experience and the suffering of slavery that, in the first stance, remains as a presence within the fundamental condition of the slaves' descendants (*Le discours antillais* 41). But the same mechanism is working on the side of the former slaveholders and their sons, in whose thought this trace and guilt always becomes present. Before this background, the order of rationality that apprehends historical movements and recognizes them in the movements of the present, represents a threat for those cultural conceptions of the Self and the Other that are based on the deceptive security suggested by an imaginary of unambiguous and homogeneous cultures.[14] For the legitimizing "origins" of white planters in North America's south, the danger of "miscegenated blood" consists in being dragged into the vortex of severed and excluded roots, into which they – the historical caste of white colonizers – have forced those Others, their "opposites," through slavery and the displacement from Africa to the Americas (42).

This whole complex is represented in *Absalom, Absalom!*, where Thomas Sutpen's drama between incest, racism and the fear of hybridity forms the constellation of the inner entanglement within the American context. The rejection is so radical that the own son is killed in order to save the racist design, but transculturating processes in the Northern American hemisphere prove to be inevitable and undeniable. The only survivor in the end is a descendant of Caribbean and US-American slaves, perpetuating the threat in the perception of the white masters, while at the same time carrying into the open spaces of the Mississippi woods the vision of a new but also historically experienced form of hybridity. Quentin Compson is a part yet also an opposite of this allegory, confronting his inherited guilt in his role as narrator, admitting and denying this guilt, finally being destroyed by it or escaping from it by his suicide. Isaac McCaslin is not destroyed by this fear, he is forced and also partially willing to admit and acknowledge it. Under the force of cultural experience and reality, he becomes the most capable representative of Faulkner's literary universe, of not only facing the historical guilt of his culture, but also of embracing the fact of transculturation – understood as ethnic and cultural hybridity – and of turning it productive – at least rudimentarily.

William Faulkner was not a "transculturator" in the sense Ángel Rama described his Latin American fellow writers in the second half of the 20th century; too deeply was he rooted within his Old South with all its guilt and contradictions, resolutely "loving it for the faults." But his literary work, originating from this conflictive love, with its thematic, narrative and linguistic penetration into the deepest and darkest layers of the Deep South, is – despite and even against Faulkner himself, and in a very similar way as the life of Isaac McCaslin – a transculturated and transculturating one.

---

14 In the case of the US self-image as an ethnically and culturally homogeneous nation, representing the whole of so-called 'Western culture,' the arguments of Samuel S. Huntington are only one and quite recent – but also internationally successful – example of that fear.

WORKS CITED

Aboul-Ela, Hosam M. *Other South: Faulkner, Coloniality, and the Mariátegui Tradition*. Pittsburgh, Pa.: University of Pittsburgh Press, 2004. Print.

Anderson, Debra L. *Decolonizing the Text. Glissantian Readings in Caribbean and African-American Literatures*. New York, NY: Lang, 1995. Print.

Benítez Rojo, Antonio. *La isla que se repite: El Caribe y la perspectiva posmoderna*. Edición definitiva. Barcelona: Casiopea, 1998. Print (English translation: *The Repeating Island: The Caribbean and the Postmodern Perspective*. Trans. James Maraniss. Durham, NC: Duke University Press, 1992. Print).

Bhabha, Homi K. *The Location of Culture*. London: Routledge, 1994. Print.

Catoira, Patricia. "Transculturación à la Ajiaco: A Recipe for Modernity." *Cuban Counterpoints: The Legacy of Fernando Ortiz*. Eds. Mauricio Augusto Font and Alfonso W. Quiroz. Lanham, MD: Lexington Books, 2005: 181-192. Print.

Cohn, Deborah. "'He was one of us': The Representation of William Faulkner and the U.S. South by Latin American Authors." *Comparative Literature Studies* 34.2 (1997): 149-169. Print.

Faulkner, William. *The Sound and the Fury*. 1929. "The Sound and the Fury." *Novels 1926 - 1929*. Eds. Joseph Blotner and Noel Polk. New York, NY: Library of America, 2006: 877-1144. Print.

—. "Red Leaves." 1930. *Collected Stories of William Faulkner*. New York, NY: Vintage, 1995: 313–342. Print.

—. "A Justice." 1931. *Collected Stories of William Faulkner*. New York, NY: Vintage, 1995: 343–360. Print.

—. *Absalom, Absalom!* 1936. "Absalom, Absalom!" *Novels 1936 - 1940*. Eds. Joseph Blotner and Noel Polk. New York, NY: Library of America, 1990: 1-316. Print.

—. *Go Down, Moses*. 1942. "Go Down, Moses." *Novels 1942 - 1954*. Ed. Joseph Blotner. New York, NY: Library of America, 1994: 1-282. Print.

—. *Intruder in the Dust*. 1948. "Intruder in the Dust." *Novels 1942 - 1954*. Ed. Joseph Blotner. New York, NY: Library of America, 1994: 283-470. Print.

—. "Funeral Sermon for Mummy Caroline Barr, February 4, 1940." *Essays, Speeches & Public Letters*. 2nd Edition. Ed. James B. Meriwether. New York, NY: Modern Library, 2004: 117-118. Print.

—. "Mississippi." *Essays, Speeches & Public Letters*. 2nd Edition. Ed. James B. Meriwether. New York, NY: Modern Library, 2004: 11-43. Print.

—. "On Fear: Deep South in Labor: Mississippi." *Essays, Speeches & Public Letters*. 2nd Edition. Ed. James B. Meriwether. New York, NY: Modern Library, 2004: 92-106. Print.

Fayen, Tanya T. *In Search of the Latin American Faulkner*. Lanham, MD: University Press of America, 1995. Print.

Freyre, Gilberto. "Casa-grande & senzala. Formação da família brasileira sob o regime da economia patriarcal." *Intérpretes do Brasil*. Coordeneção, seleção de livros e prefácio de Silviano Santiago. 3 vols. Rio de Janeiro: Nova Aguilar, 2002: 121-646. Print (*The Masters and the Slaves: A Study in the Development of Brazilian Civilization*. Trans. Samuel Putnam. 2nd English Language Edition. New York, NY: Knopf, 1956. Print).

Gage, Duane. "William Faulkner's Indians." *American Indian Quarterly* 1.1 (1974): 27-33. Print.

García Canclini, Néstor. *Culturas híbridas: Estrategias para entrar y salir de la modernidad.* 1989. México: Grijalbo, 2004. Print (*Hybrid Cultures: Strategies for Entering and Leaving Modernity.* Trans. Christopher L. Chiappari. Minneapolis, MN: University of Minnesota Press, 1995. Print).

Glissant, Édouard. *Faulkner, Mississipi.* Paris: Gallimard, 1998. Print (*Faulkner, Mississippi.* Trans. Barbara B. Lewis and Thomas C. Spear. Chicago, IL: University of Chicago Press, 2000. Print).

—. *Le discours antillais.* 1981. Paris: Gallimard, 2002. Print (*Caribbean Discourse: Selected Essays.* Trans. J. Michael Dash. Charlottesville, VA: University of Virginia Press, 1989. Print).

Horsford, Howard C. "Faulkner's (Mostly) Unreal Indians in Early Mississippi History." *American Literature* 64.2 (1992): 311-330. Print.

Huntington, Samuel S. *Who are We? The Challenges to America's National Identity.* New York, NY: Simon & Schuster, 2004. Print.

King, Richard H. "Working Through: Faulkner's *Go Down, Moses.*" *William Faulkner.* Ed. Harold Bloom. New York, NY: Chelsea House, 1986: 193–205. Print.

Kraniauskas, John. "Hybridity in a Transnational Frame: Latin Americanist and Postcolonial Perspectives on Cultural Studies." *The Latin American Cultural Studies Reader.* Eds. Ana del Sarto, Alicia Ríos, and Abril Trigo. Durham, NC: Duke University Press, 2004: 736-759. Print.

La Campa, Román de. *Latin Americanism.* Minneapolis, MN: University of Minnesota Press, 1999. Print.

—. "Mimicry and the Uncanny in Caribbean Discourse." *The Latin American Cultural Studies Reader.* Eds. Ana del Sarto, Alicia Ríos, and Abril Trigo. Durham, NC: Duke University Press, 2004: 535-560. Print.

Ladd, Barbara. *Nationalism and the Color Line in George W. Cable, Mark Twain, and William Faulkner.* Baton Rouge, LA: Louisiana State University Press, 1996. Print.

Matthews, John T. "Recalling the West Indies: From Yoknapatawpha to Haiti and Back." *American Literary History* 16.2 (2004): 238-262. Print.

Ortiz, Fernando. "Los factores humanos de la cubanidad." *Etnia y sociedad.* Selección, notas y prólogo de Isaac Barreal. La Habana: Editorial de Ciencias Sociales, 1993: 1-20. Print.

—. *Contrapunteo cubano del tabaco y el azúcar (Advertencia de sus contrastes agrarios, económicos, históricos y sociales, su etnografía y su transculturación).* 1940. Madrid: CubaEspaña, 1999. Print (*Cuban Counterpoint: Tobacco and Sugar.* Trans. Harriet de Onís. Durham, NC: Duke University Press, 1995. Print).

Pratt Guterl, Matthew. "'I Went to the West Indies': Race, Place, and the Antebellum South." *American Literary History* 18.3 (2006): 446-467. Print.

Rama, Ángel. "Literature and Culture." Trans. Christine McIntyre. *The Latin American Cultural Studies Reader.* Eds. Ana del Sarto, Alicia Ríos, and Abril Trigo. Durham, NC: Duke University Press, 2004: 120-152. Print.

—. *Transculturación Narrativa en América Latina.* 1982. 4th Edition. México: Siglo XXI, 2004. Print.

—. *La novela en América Latina: Panoramas 1920-1980.* Santiago de Chile: Ediciones Universidad Alberto Hurtado, 2008. Print.

—. "Los procesos de transculturación en la narrativa latinoamericana." *La novela en América Latina: Panoramas 1920-1980.* Santiago de Chile: Ediciones Universidad Alberto Hurtado, 2008: 227-258. Print.

Rojas, Rafael. "Transculturation and nationalism." *Cuban Counterpoints: The Legacy of Fernando Ortiz*. Eds. Mauricio Augusto Font and Alfonso W. Quiroz. Lanham, Md: Lexington Books, 2005: 65-72. Print.

Spitta, Silvia. *Between Two Waters. Narratives of Transculturation in Latin America*. Houston, TX: Rice University Press, 1995. Print.

Wagley, Charles. "A Typology of Latin American Subcultures." *The Latin American Tradition: Essays on the Unity and Diversity of Latin American Culture*. New York, London: Columbia University Press, 1968: 81-117. Print.

Weinberg, Liliana. "Ensayo y transculturación." *Cuadernos Americanos* 96 (1996): 31-47. Print.

THE CHRONOTOPOS IN THE (POSTMODERN) NOVEL OF THE AMÉRICAS: TOWARDS A TRANSAREAL TOPOLOGY OF THE LOCAL

PABLO VALDIVIA OROZCO

CHRONOTOPE: A DISCUSSION

As discussed in *The Dialogic Imagination*, Bakhtin's theory of the chronotope is surely one of the most central texts in postmodern literary theory dealing with the interdependence of literary space and time. In this paper, I want to highlight a significant shift in his theory that unfortunately has not been taken into consideration in most of the works that make use of his concept.[1] Contrary to established definitions which interpret the chronotope as diegetic time-space-relation, that is, as a relation *within* a given plot, I propose to read the chronotope as a model of interaction between different chronotopes. Special emphasis will be put on the fact that the interaction goes beyond the text in its physical and its conceptual sense precisely because the reader tries to re-create the different relationships within a text.

In the first version of his theory of the chronotope, written in the late 1930s, Bakhtin claims to be inspired by Einstein's theory of relativity when he argues that the term is intended to be "almost a metaphor (but not entirely)" for the "inseparability of time and space" (84). The metaphor, not only in this case, goes beyond its explication concerning the indissolubility of time and space; the theory of relativity does not only consider the relation between space and time, but also the role of the observer and his or her standpoint. When applying the metaphor to the field of literary criticism, this role can only be ascribed to the reader, given that the text cannot relate itself to a certain perspective. Taking this additional element into account necessarily leads to a conception that has to consider several chronotopes in interaction, since we cannot assume one fixed and single observing view, or, respectively, an ideal reader position from which all other chronotopes can be approached without any bias.

In the afterword from 1973, Bakhtin makes this point explicit, arguably under the influence of the Konstanz reception theory (Wegner 1359).[2] The fact that

---

[1] One paradigmatic example is Smethurst's *Postmodern Chronotope*.

[2] The Konstanz reception theory, mainly known through the works of Wolfgang Iser and Hans-Robert Jauß, discusses the role of the reader as a structural element of literary texts. Beginning

there is only little attention paid to this epilog may be due to the fact that it includes no concrete analysis of texts but is strictly theoretical. Nevertheless, this is a crucial text, since it presents a theory of the chronotope that goes beyond a formalism that reduces itself to a diegetic description. In the course of my argument, I will thus not so much alter Bakhtin's theory but rather highlight an intention that is already significant in the first version, yet is reduced to a sort of historical semantics of literary poetics: "The chronotope as a formally constitutive category determines to a significant degree the image of man in literature as well. The image of man is always intrinsically chronotopic" (85).

Accordingly, Bakhtin does not merely react to at the times current debates like the ones on reception theory, but emphasizes some aspects of his earlier version. Only in a footnote, Bakhtin writes:

> Here we employ the Kantian evaluation of the importance of these forms in the cognitive process, but differ from Kant in taking them as 'transcendental', but as forms of the most immediate reality. We shall attempt to show the role these forms play in the process of concrete artistic cognition (artistic visualization) under conditions obtaining in the genre of the novel. (ibid.)

The anthropological dimension goes beyond Bakhtin's study of different chronotopes as part of the history and genesis of the novel. The Kantian paradigm of an *a priori* existence of time and space in human cognition is more than a literary problem, although literature (and with it, literary theory) offers a valuable reflection on this topic and, even more, a privileged access to a question we can never face because its implications always influence our thinking. The chronotope now turns out to be a condition of human existence and cognition where places are constructed through their interactions and crossings in time. This more general understanding of the chronotope already implies a certain metahistorical hypothesis about our world and the way we perceive and conceive it. At this stage of the argument, I may only highlight the multiplicity of different chronotopes as a certain awareness of more than just one context.

The first consequence of this broader vision is that the chronotopic cognition itself is already effective in literary communication in the sense that the identification of a chronotope already presupposes the effect of another chronotope. The chronotope's borders are therefore not an intrinsic quality of the chronotope itself, but rather an effect of a *relational difference*. In contrast to a strictly diegetic application of the term, I therefore propose to understand the chronotope beyond a conceptual metaphor for the temporal dynamic in a given spatial formation of a

their work in the late 1960s, it is important to consider that their theories, especially in the case of Jauß, imply a hermeneutic reflection. Sense, therefore, is the central category.

story. This strictly *topographic* conception of the latter would make it impossible to consider crucial aspects in Bakhtin's theory, which I will develop as a theory of a topology of the novel. Topology – in contrast to a strict topography – refers less to the order *within* a space than to the organization of relations, such as inside and outside or transgressive movements as overlappings and crossings. The change in descriptive vocabulary thus also implies a shift in focus. By insisting on the fact that a chronotope has to be read in order to be defined, the term transcends any possible limitation to a mere aesthetics of production. Very similar to Peircean semiosis (it is no accident that both Peirce and Bakhtin were profound experts in Kantian philosophy), Bakhtin concludes that a chronotope is understood only by another chronotope:

> Within the limits of a single world [...] we may notice a number of different chronotopes and complex interactions among them [...]. Chronotopes are mutually inclusive, they co-exist, they may be interwoven with, repace or oppose one another, contradict one another or find themselves in ever more complex interrelationships. [...] The general characteristic of these interactions is that they are dialogical [...]. But this dialogue cannot enter into the world represented in the work, nor into any of the chronotopes represented in it; it is outside the world represented, although not outside the work as a whole. It (this dialogue) enters the world of the author, of the performer, and the world of the listeners and readers. And all theses worlds are chronotopic as well. (252)

Another crucial term in Bakhtin's literary theory that is much more established in today's critical vocabulary is connected to this relational logic: dialogicity. The eminent importance of this link consists in recalling that the chronotope is first of all a literary term and should not be reduced to a cognitive concept or read as a theory of human cognition as such. That is to say: Instead of explaining how human beings conceive their world, the question is insofar a more historical one as the chronotope translates a dialogical principle of poetic diction, namely that of novelistic prose, that has not always been there and that presupposes a decentralization of language or, in Bakthin's own passionate words, "a certain linguistic homelessness of literary consciousness" (251).

It can be argued that this decisive implication in the theory of the chronotope refers to an interaction between the different time-space relations and especially to their overlap with the chronotope of the reader that, most importantly, has to bridge some kind of distance, be it cultural, temporal or spatial. Without any doubt, the distance is thought mainly in spatial terms, highlighting once again that the chronotope (and not the topochronos) does not refer to the relation of time and space as such, but to the question of how time is experienced in certain and, in this case, fragmented spaces:

> Of course these real people, the authors and the listeners or readers, may be (and often are) located in differing time-spaces, sometimes separated from each other by

> centuries and by great spatial distances, but nevertheless they are located in a real, unitary and ay yet incomplete historical world set off by a sharp and categorical boundary from the represented world in the text. Therefore we may call this world the world that creates the text for all its aspects – the reality reflected in the text, the authors creating the text, the performers of the text (if they exist) and finally the listeners or readers who recreate and in so doing renew the text – participate equally in the chronotopes of our world (which serve as the source of representation) emerge the reflected and created chronotopes of the world represented in the work (in the text). (253)

It is through this dialogue with the text that a further chronotope emerges: the chronotope of the author. In order to avoid a psychological reconstruction of the empirical author (a further indication of how the concept shifts from the aesthetics of production to reception theory), Bakhtin refrains from discussing the third chronotope in relation to psychology or history. Rather, this third chronotope articulates itself in the materiality of the text. The importance of this at first sight surprising reference is underlined by the fact that Bakhtin clearly distinguishes the material text from the composition of the text:

> How are the chronotopes of the author and the listener or reader presented to us? First and foremost, we experience them in the external material being of the work and in its purely external composition. But this material of the work is not dead, it is speaking, signifying (it involves signs); we not only see and perceive it, but in it we can always hear voices even while reading silently to ourselves). We are represented with a text occupying a certain specific place in space; that is, it is localized; our creation of it, our acquaintance with it occurs through time. The text as such never appears as a dead thing; beginning with any text – and sometimes passing through a lengthy series of mediating links – we always arrive, in the final analysis, at the human voice, which is to say we come up against the human being. (252)

As Bakhtin first refers to the materiality of the text and only then to its "voice," or 'spirit,' one can detect a figuration of a certain position towards the history of the text, which is further highlighted by Bakhtin's recurring insistence on distance. If something is communicated first by its materiality, it is because there is no continuous tradition of its meaning. The distance to which Bakthin refers here is not a natural state nor a free implication, but rather a general linguistic condition in a society that is in contact with more than one history and language, i. e., a society whose language has become homeless. In an earlier text, translated as *The Discourse of the Novel*, Bakhtin puts special emphasis on this sort of 'contact':

> Even a community torn by social struggle – if it remains isolated and sealed-off as a national entity – will be insufficient social soil for relativization of literary-language consciousness at the deepest level, for its re-tuning into a new prosaic key. […] A deeply involved participation in alien cultures and languages (one is impossible without the other) inevitably leads to an awareness of the dissociation between language and intentions, language and thought, language and expression. (368-369)

Already anticipating what will be discussed as a foundational experience in the Americas, Bakhtin, in a very discrete, but nonetheless decisive manner, includes another setting that will find its paradigmatic case in the experience of colonization. It seems hard to formulate a more concise definition of the colonial linguistic situation than experiencing the language of the authority as "another's language" (370):

> The situation is analogous in those cases where a single and unitary language is at the same time another's language. What inevitably happens is a decay and collapse of the religious, political and ideological authority connected with that language. It is during this decay that the decentered language consciousness of prose art ripens, finding its support in the social heteroglossia of national languages that are actually spoken. (ibid.)

THE AMERICAS AND THE POSTMODERN

The main hypothesis of my following argument here is that the American experience, and especially its translation into postmodern novels, cannot only be read against this theoretical backdrop, but offers a poignant expression of it.

Over the last 30 years, postmodern cultural and literary theory has had a tremendous impact on national literary theory and also, even if less visible, on disciplinary regimes like national or monolingual philology. One of the many categories that have been affected by the new and not so new paradigms of a world globalized by migration, transnational mediascapes, and technologies is surely the concept of locality. In Latin American cultural critique (not the same as the much later formation of Latin American Cultural Studies), not only has the literary canon been questioned, but so have the interactions in cultural practices. Urban popular culture, as the Mexican cultural critic Carlos Monsiváis argues, has become (apart from the simultaneously internationalized Latin American novel) one of the most striking examples of the translocality and –nationality of (Latin) American cultures. Instead, the specificity of locality turned out to be an intersection that combines local, national, regional, continental, and transareal references in complex interactions. We can thus see how the functioning of the chronotope "as the primary means for materializing time in space" (Bakhtin 250) might serve as a model for the postmodern condition of today's cultures and localities in the sense that this materialization is radically relational.

The fact that these paradigms become more visible with the focus on a postmodern locality should not lead to the assumption that they imply a limitation to postmodernity. In a certain sense, the linguistic condition of these paradigms does not start with modernity, but already with the colonial beginnings of the

Americas. This historical perspective, of course, is postmodern and postcolonial critique in its best sense.

In order to explain where the colonial beginning of modernity translates itself to a linguistic condition, one has to locate the "linguistic homelessness" (Bakhtin 369) within an American setting. As mentioned above, the colonial experience might be a paradigmatic case, where the language and its territory do not coincide. This split, as Bakhtin argued, implies a "heteroglossia" where every denotation is threatened by a radically relational linguistic practice.

To affirm that the history of the Americas is to be conceived as a cultural area that defines itself by a difference in simultaneity and relation would be obvious. Instead of taking this property as a separating feature on whose basis the Americas are to be differentiated from the Old World, it seems to be more interesting to investigate how this experience translates into the linguistic condition of our pluri-chronotopic world and world cognition. In other words: It seems more promising to read this condition as a linguistic condition.

The experience of living in more than just one world – something that Bakhtin discussed with the chronotopes of the novel – is a key concept in several discourses. Following Blumenberg, it constitutes not only the implicit pact of the novel, but equally exposes the notion of reality (*Wirklichkeitsbegriff*) in modernity (*Neuzeit*) (67). This figure of several contexts can be retold and retraced within the colonial experience and it is there, where the importance of the American experience becomes obvious. Instead of describing the "decentralization" of language in relatively abstract terms, we find ourselves confronted with a kind of primordial scene (*Ur-Szene*) in an almost entirely Freudian sense.

Echoing Bakhtin's theory of the complex interactions between various chronotopes and its presupposition of a decentered linguistic consciousness, the Mexican writer Octavio Paz narrates a history of the linguistic situation in Latin America in his Nobel Prize Lecture that focuses on the American experience:

> Languages are vast realities that transcend those political and historical entities we call nations. The European languages we speak in the Americas illustrate this. The special position of our literatures when compared to those of England, Spain, Portugal and France depends precisely on this fundamental fact: they are literatures written in transplanted tongues. Languages are born and grow from the native soil, nourished by a common history. The European languages were rooted out from their native soil and their own tradition, and then planted in an unknown and unnamed world: they took root in the new lands and, as they grew within the societies of America, they were transformed. They are the same plant yet also a different plant. [...] To understand more clearly the special position of writers in the Americas, we should think of the dialogue maintained by Japanese, Chinese or Arabic writers with the different literatures of Europe. It is a dialogue that cuts across multiple languages and civilizations. Our dialogue, on the other hand, takes place within the same language.

The globalization of languages (studied by intellectuals such as Serge Gruzinski, Walter Mignolo, and Ottmar Ette) does not only permit linguistic transplantation, but the birth of a language on a foreign ground. It is in this situation that the enigmatic figure of a dialogue "within the same language" becomes more evident.[3] For Paz, the foundational narrative of modernity, a narrative that becomes explicit in postmodern fiction, is not the loss of an evident world or the loss of an absolute authority, but the moment where language could be nothing else but a transforming translation. The Peruvian intellectual Julio Ortega rephrased this experience as follows:

> The day after the conquest, the postcolonial world began in the scripts of translation. In partials versions and overlaid readings of the event, the New World subject who had to speak and read in the language of the Old World was already an interpreter, and from that moment onward translation would define this modern subject of the Americas. (39)

This strong emphasis on a linguistic situation is one of the main reasons why I propose to develop the concept of a transareal locality from the inside of literary theory. My hypothesis is that literature, as a globally created and locally distinguishing sign system, paradigmatically presupposes a locality that is already transareal. Our conception of literary aesthetics, and especially of the poetics of the novel, already contains terms and models of spatial formations which are impossible to conceive of in a strictly local way. Still, they imply the possibility of transgression or rather repeat the always deferring translations which stood at the beginning of the 'New World subject.'

What makes postmodern novels so interesting is the fact that they discuss local legacies under conditions where the local cannot be regarded as naturally given, but often as violently constituted. Although already present in early colonial works of the Americas, it is in postmodernist fiction that this linguistic condition becomes an explicit and metaliterary device. *Caramelo* by Sandra Cisneros and *Cien años de Soledad* by Gabriel García Márquez treat cultural differences and cultural memories in specific transcultural settings, that is: moments of transgression which make a certain translational reflection and activity necessary. It is no coincidence that both authors more or less explicitly refer to the abovementioned primordial scene: In Sandra Cisneros' novel, a "Chronology" is attached in which the history of US American migration begins with the first encounter between the Mexican emperor Moctezuma II and the Conquistador Hernán Cortés. García Márquez repeats the experience of a New World by

---

[3] In the Spanish original, the expression used is "en el interior" ("a dialogue in the interior of the same language").

describing his famous Macondo as a world that "was so recent that many things lacked names, and in order to indicate them it was necessary to point" (*Cien años* 1).

This metalinguistic reflection is also present in relation to the writing itself in a way that structurally mimics what Bakhtin defined as the complex relations between different chronotopes. The places of writing, on the one hand, and the places of the stories, on the other hand, represent two different chronotopes that are related by their authors' translational movement. Although this aspect can - to a certain extent – be found in all literature(s) in the sense that literary fiction always presupposes a kind of transgression, it surely is the dispositive of cultural difference that leads to a situation where the (cultural) self-localization of the authors (and their writing, respectively) and the diegetic worlds of their stories seem to diverge. The main task of these works is, consequently, a constant translation of their place. 'Here,' in these novels, is anything but a clear deictic expression. It is more likely to be the place where a possible transgression is insinuated, a place of constant oscillation, a place where language reveals its relational logic.

Of course, given the limited space, this paper cannot offer a profound analysis of the authors' complete works. What I propose instead is a set of two short exemplary studies that primarily focus on the beginnings and the endings of the novels. This is justified by the fact that the beginning and the end of a text perform transgressive movements: The beginning refers to the reader's 'entrance' into the diegetic world; the end to the reader's 'exit.' As Bakhtin claims, these are "sharp and categorical" (253) boundaries, implying transgressions that are not continuously mediated, but marked by a rupture. Not surprisingly, what the respective beginnings of *Cien años* and *Caramelo* do have in common is that they situate the story in relation to their writing as an already read text; that is, they relate the story to something that is not just extra-diegetic, but logically outside the story. This combination of inner and outer references justifies the use of the word 'topology' which – in contrast to topography – does not relate to a certain spatial order, but rather to an organization of inner and outer localizations and to the moments of their transgression (see Günzel). It is no coincidence that especially the novel becomes a fertile ground for this discussion, since the novel is a form that constantly reflects the simultaneity of its inner and outer relations, its inner diegetic logic and its outer logics, like generic norms or history.

To conceive of 'literary localities,' especially in the postmodern novel of the Americas and against the backdrop of a "linguistic homelessness," requires taking into consideration the exterior position from which writing is possible, and the exterior position of the reader. Although this relational aspect is a literary feature that obviously is not exclusive to the postmodern novel of the Americas, it is in these kinds of novels that this feature is translated into a cultural history and condition. The transgressive notion of the chronotope serves as a conceptual metaphor for a specific way of human existence and cognition that structurally translates the historical genesis of a (post)colonial (post)modernity.

'HERE' AND 'THERE': RELATIONAL CHRONOTOPES IN *CARAMELO*

In Sandra Cisneros' novel *Caramelo*, the beginning implies a multiple deferral. There is no sentence that leads the reader immediately into the novel's diegetic space. Instead, it opens with a dedication, an opening bilingual epigraph, a disclaimer, and, finally, as part of the first chapter, a second epigraph, a quotation of a song by Augustín Lara, which is immediately commented on by the narrative voice marked in italics. The first sentence after these paratexts alludes to a further displacement: "We are little in the photograph above Father's bed. We were little in Acapulco. We will always be little. For him we are just as we were then" (3). Only then the narrative voice adopts an internal focalization by describing the trip to Acapulco where the photo has been taken and for which it functions as a "remembrance" (ibid.). One is thus facing a problematic border. If we consider that the first sentence already puts emphasis on the narrative feature of multiple perspectives, the border between narrative text and paratext is everything but evident. The multiple beginnings serve as multiple frames that question the existence of a 'proper' beginning.

Given this multiplicity, it seems more promising to relate these paratexts to a more efficient distinction than the one made by opposing story and discourse. Only then one might get rid of the aporetic question of which paratexts are part of the story and which are part of the discourse. This problem is also apparent in another central narratological category: the question of perspectivity. In Cisneros' text, perspective (itself a spatial term and not, as Bal argues, a mainly visual term) is not only an effect of the discourse's arrangement that is reflected in the internal logic of the story, but a constant interrogation of at least two different perspectival forces in the text. The focalizer (more in Bal's sense and less in Genette's sense), in this case, is somehow split between the focus the proper narrative logic produces (that is, the narrative discourse itself) and the focus it pretends to recreate, i. e., the main perspective of the story, or, the constantly quoting voice of Lala, the main character.

Confronted with this predicament, one should recall the logic of the chronotopos as a strictly relational organization of inside and outside. This relation does not exist in a fixed way and is not entirely made up by the text. This relational aspect has a special, but not exclusive, importance for novels that are usually considered as working in an inter- and transcultural context. Especially when the nexus between "language and intentions, language and thought, language and expression" (Bakhtin 368-369) is conceived as a nexus that has been destabilized from its very beginning, the notion of the chronotopos turns out to be extremely complex: What kind of time is bound to what kind of space? Cisneros designs chronotopes that already presuppose another chronotope to fulfill their interrelation. This continuous splitting through the constant reference to an Other designates divisions apparent in language and culture as such. This split needs a further, external or 'cultural,' dimension to be understood properly and is structurally based on the complex interactions between different chronotopes.

In Cisneros' text, this interaction between different chronotopoi becomes immediately obvious through her use of narrative voice, which does not only have to consider a character's perspective ("for him"), but also a medial focalizer ("in the photograph"), and finally a temporal perspective ("then"). The most important point here is that all these instances are obviously not identical with one narratorial perspective. By combining various perspectives, the narrative voice finally produces not a totalizing view, but a further perspective from which this multiple configuration is possible. From this perspective, the varied beginnings, paratexts, footnotes, and citations anticipate the linguistic situation of a narrator who is not subject to a fixed order, but the personified hub of many voices. They all contribute to the production of a specific narrative that must not be mistaken for the author's origin or locality. Instead, the place constructed by the narrator does everything to assign that this place is a place of a possible transgression.

My first hypothesis concerning this transgressive narrative locality is that this configuration of multiple sources and citations is the narrative 'here.' This 'here' is thus not only the necessary starting point of every narration but also the marker of an already implied transgression. So, what happens to the 'here' in the text?

The first time the word 'here' is used, it seems to be more of a 'there' given the fact that it refers to the locality of the photograph: "Here are the Acapulco waters lapping behind us, and here we are sitting on the lip of land water. [...] Here is Father squinting that same squint I always make when I'm photographed" (ibid.). The photograph, itself a framed representation and therefore including a border, is hanging above the bed of the narrator's father. So the narrative voice is already performing a migratory movement by saying "here," triggered by the photo, while the photo itself, as we get to know later, is located in Chicago. 'Here' seems to be the place someone points to, a movement that normally requires a 'there.' The second time 'here' is mentioned, it names a place of absence:

> I'm not here. They've forgotten about me when the photographer walking along the beach proposes a portrait, un recuerdo, a remembrance literally. No one notices I'm off by myself building sand houses. [...] Then everyone realizes the portrait is incomplete. It's as if I didn't exist. (4)

"Here," first of all, is not the immediate location of the narrator, but the other place to which her narration is directed. In that sense, it is also 'not here.' The 'here' ('there') of the photograph is the 'not here' ('here') of the narrative voice. At the same time, what is really present during the process of reading is not the photo, but the narrative voice. In that sense, 'not here' is 'here.' Precisely because the narrator does not exist on the photo, she can assume another kind of existence. This absence is obviously the position the narrator has in common with the photographer. It gives her the privilege (and the symbolically male power position) to read the picture in a certain way, or putting it in Lacanian terms: to have a story and not be it.

At the end of the novel, a further connotation of the narrative 'here' is suggested:

> This is the family photo from our trip to Acapulco when we were little. But I'm not here [...] Same as always, they forgot about me. –What are you talking about? You weren't making sand castles, Lala. You want the truth? You were mad, and that's why when we called you over, you wouldn't come. (429)

The very beginning of the narration becomes a topic, turning, so to say, the narrative situation inside out, thereby drawing the reader's awareness to the moment and the act of narrating. The narrative outside ('there') is converted to a 'here' of the narrative discourse by a dialogical situation.

In summary, at least three relational nodes have to be considered in the context of the word 'here': the 'here' of the narrated setting (Acapulco), the 'here' from where this setting is commented on and narrated within the story (Chicago), and finally the 'here' of the narrating act itself (the logically external locus of enunciation) that presupposes and performs the dialogical principle that Bakhtin considered as the basis for the understanding of the chronotopic interrelations. This principle, as applied at the end of the novel, is related to the migration experience, an experience that paradigmatically questions a natural nexus between time and space:

> And I don't know how it is with anyone else, but for me, [...], that time and that place, are all bound together in a country I am homesick for, that doesn't exist anymore. That never existed. A country I invented. Like all emigrants between here and there. (433)

It is this complex chronotopos of the invented country that, in the end, organizes the different 'heres' and 'theres' and that illustrates how the chronotopos implies its own transgression.

MACONDO'S OVERLAPPING

The beginning of García Márquez' *Cien Años de Soledad* (1967) is totally different from the one in *Caramelo* in that it apparently features an omniscient narrator who starts his narration right away:

> Many years later facing the firing squad, Colonel Aureliano Buendía was to remember that distant afternoon when his father took him to discover ice. At that time Macondo was a village of twenty adobe houses, built on the bank of a river of clear water that ran along a bed of polished stones, which were white and enormous, like prehistoric eggs. (3)[4]

The first sentence reveals a position that seems to be overlooking the whole story, while the second one is a sentence that sounds almost like the beginning of a fairy tale. The hypothesis I want to work out in the following paragraphs is that the place or also the Macondo chronotope are narrated and understood from two different logics. On the one hand, there is the intrinsic logic of the story that is displaced by the second sentence. Macondo is a place that is constructed within the text and limited by the frontiers the text indicates. On the other hand, there is an extrinsic logic of the text, as the story does not unfold chronologically but is already available as a whole; as a story that is already written. The border that is essential here is not the diegetic frontier, but the frontier between the text and the reader. This doubling is repeated at the end of the novel. This strategy can also be found in Bakhtin's theory of the chronotope.

In order to make things more obvious, I want to discuss an immanent reading of the chronotope that comes to fatal conclusions. In "Cronotopía y Modernidad en *Cien años de soledad*" Araújo Fontalvo argues: "The importance of the chronotopic level depends on the affirmation that the conception of time is rigorously correlative to the conception of the world" (par. 1)[5]. Consequently, what a literary critic has to do is to retrace the genesis, bloom and decay of a literary "microuniverso" (par. 4). Afterwards, this micro-universe can be understood as following various allegorical readings that are characteristic of a different modernity. Following this reading, modernity is considered to be an external force that, if applied to Latin America, would lead to the failure of true progress ("falta de

---

4 "Muchos años después, frente al pelotón de fusilamiento, el coronel Aureliano Buendía había de recordar aquella tarde remota en que su padre lo llevó a conocer el hielo. Macondo era entonces una aldea de veinte casas de barro y cañabrava construidas a la orilla de un río de aguas diáfanas que se precipitaban por un lecho de piedras pulidas, blancas y enormes como huevos prehistóricos." All of the following translations are mine.

5 "La importancia del nivel cronotópico radica en la constatación de que la concepción del tiempo es rigurosamente correlativa con la concepción del mundo."

auténtico progreso"; par. 14) and, as an external force, destroys Macondo's chronotope of the idyll ("cronotopo del idilio"; par. 12), making any natural development impossible.

Macondo is not the closed and hardly reachable town located in an impenetrable jungle. In fact, it has two different frontiers. On the one hand, there is the strictly diegetic frontier representing the limits of Macondo that in the process of modernization has become less strict. On the other hand, within the house of the Buendía family, there is a frontier which is marked by the laboratory of the gypsy Melquíades. In this room, reading texts is the main activity. It is thus no surprise that the revelatory moment of the last Buendía finally decoding Malquíades' manuscripts occurs in that room. The readers of that novel, therefore, read of a reader reading as if the manuscripts were a speaking mirror. What Aureliano Babilonia reads is the history of the Buendía family, in other words, a text that easily could be confounded with the actual text of the novel. Thus, the text anticipates its own reading and at the same time implies the reading of its diegetic reader. It is a text that shows awareness of itself as already written. This multiple meta-referential ending, understood as the node of narrative locality, exposes the radically relational logic of the narrative discourse.

While in the first example of Cisneros' 'here,' the reader had to deal with a locality between the narrated and the narration itself, whose narrative performance configured different 'heres' surrounded by various 'nows,' the 'here' in question now refers to the limits of the locality of the diegesis. Locality presupposes the consideration of different outsides of a text. Outside of Macondo refers at least to two different frontiers: a diegetic one and a metaliterary one. The locality of the Macondo chronotope is then the result of the interaction between its outsides; the diegetic limits of Macondo and the moment of its reading. Just as the last of the Buendías becomes a reader of himself, the reader becomes the heir of the story. This reading of the Macondo chronotope does not raise the question if the idyll is the right model for Macondo, but rather which kind of interactions take place when an external reader, by reading, confronts his world with the worlds he or she has just read. This question has to be raised against the deep conviction of García Márquez that we construct our lives based on stories we are willing to inherit.

To return to the discussion of modernity that was implicit in the "chronotope of the idyll," one can state that although a critique of a normative conception of modernity is still necessary and urgent, it is far too short-sighted to see just an external western force in modernity. The inequality of power relations does not imply that there have been no interactions in this surely asymmetric relation between what is usually called 'western modernity' and the rest. Modernity is not something that acts against the colonized regions of this world forcing mankind to search for paradise lost, but also something that has been constituted in an asymmetric exchange and interaction with the colonies (see Randeria; Mignolo).

Why is this critique pertinent here? A narrow conception of the chronotope corresponds to a narrow conception of modernity. This is why Araújo Fontalvo identifies the chronotope of the idyll with the author's intention: "the positioning of García Márquez: to reexamine the model of modernity that has been imposed on Latin America" (par. 14)[6]. A different reading of García Márquez' Macondo presupposes that the challenge of (post)modernity is not whether there is a good and different (post)modernity, but – and the clearly postmodernist aesthetic of García Márquez' novel supports this argument – rather the question if and how histories of origin can translate themselves into (post)modernity. This is the reason why the anthropological dimension of the chronotope theory becomes especially interesting in a context of cultural memory. Literature, understood as a globally grown and transculturally coded symbolic system, is insofar a paradigmatic case as it hardly qualifies for being an immediate and even original representation of a local past. On the contrary, a literary representation is never an immediate representation of the narrated place, but already implies to conceive of even the most local and idyllic chronotope as already mediated and interconnected. In that sense, saying 'here' means for García Márquez and Plinio Apuleyo Mendoza that this other world ("el otro mundo") becomes part of our 'here,' transforming our 'here' into a complete reality ("toda la realidad") (127). This reality is complete as a totality. Totality was the deadly result of the decoding of the last Buendía, who allegorizes the risks of a closed chronotope. In contrast, 'complete' indicates the insight that Bakhtin already formulated in his theory of the chronotopos: A model describing the way in which the linguistically homeless human experiences the nexus of time and space that is never complete in itself but only through its dialogue with the outside world.

CONCLUSION

To allege that (literary) narrations do not only contain a certain story or content, but also a proper logic of their form is surely a commonplace in modern and postmodern literary and aesthetic theory. As not only revealed by Iser's theory, modern mimesis has to be considered also as a performance, because the mimet-

6 "[…] la toma de posición de García Márquez: examinar de nuevo el modelo de modernidad que se ha impuesto en Latinoamérica."

ic forms do not have an intrinsic relation to their signified nor do they have an immediate one to their referent. The novel can thus be considered as a genre that is, unlike the epic, basically translocal, or, to be more precise, a genre that enunciates its localities within an already translocal enunciation in an already displaced language. In this sense, the novel, and especially the theory of the chronotope, can be considered as a linguistic paradigm of a world that is decentered and in which histories are strictly relational. Literature and literary theory can serve as a laboratory of our ability to handle these multiple chronotopes.

For this purpose, the postmodern novel of the Americas is a crucial object of inquiry. Its reflection on and of the chronotope are not to be considered a radical break with earlier or other poetical practices. Rather, it seems as if the postmodern novel of the Americas makes explicit some aspects of spatial formation, which are foundational for the genre and its poetics. This is the case because the Americas have had to deal with a linguistic situation which Octavio Paz called the "transplantation of languages" since their very beginning. Starting from this paradigm, I have suggested rethinking the chronotopes of the novel in the same discontinuous ways as we conceive of languages, especially after their colonial globalization. Because of those crossings and mainly because of the implied negotiations of inner and outer relations, this space should preferably be called the topology of the novel and thus focus more on the movements than on fixed constellations. In sum, one may paraphrase these arguments in the formula that the space of the novel is the space of its own transgression and the relations it makes possible and necessary by this transgression. If the chronotope mainly refers to the "materialization of time in space," then decentered language serves as temporal complement and historical index in the sense that this deferring tells the history of how different (social, cultural, etc.) spaces materialize in the present of language. This crisscrossing is both the reason why it is worth reshaping the chronotope in a context of postmodern literary theory and a mandate to develop transdisciplinary approaches which trace the different demands and strategies of transgression.

WORKS CITED

Araújo Fontalvo, Orlando. "Cronotopía y Modernidad en Cien años de soledad." *Espéculo: Revista de estudios literarios* 23 (2003): n. pag. Web. March 15, 2010.

Bakhtin, Mikhail M. *The Dialogic Imagination: Four Essays.* Ed. Michael Holquist. Trans. Caryl Emerson and Michael Holquist. Austin, TX: U of Texas P, 1981.

Blumenberg, Hans. "Wirklichkeitsbegriff und Möglichkeit des Romans." *Nachahmung und Illusion.* Ed. H. R. Jauß. Munich: Fink, 1967. 9-26. Print.

Cisneros, Sandra. *Caramelo: Or puro cuento.* London: Bloomsbury, 2002. Print.

Dünne, Jörg, ed. *Raumtheorie: Grundlagentexte aus Philosophie und Kulturwissenschaften*. Frankfurt/Main: Suhrkamp, 2006. Print.
Ette, Ottmar. *ZwischenWeltenSchreiben: Literaturen ohne festen Wohnsitz*. Berlin: Kadmos, 2005. Print.
García Márquez, Gabriel. *Cien años de soledad*. 1967. Buenos Aires: Edición Suramericana. 2002. Print.
—. "La realidad escondida." *Una jornada en Macondo*. Hannes Wallrafen. Bogotá: Villegas Editores, 1992. 1-3. Print.
—, and Plinio Apuleyo Mendoza. *El Olor de la guayaba*. Barcelona: Bruguera, 1982. Print.
Günzel, Stephan, ed. *Topologie. Zur Raumbeschreibung in den Kultur- und Medienwissenschaften*. Bielefeld: transcript, 2008. Print.
Iser, Wolfgang. *Das Fiktive und das Imaginäre: Perspektiven literarischer Anthropologie*. Frankfurt/Main: Suhrkamp, 1993. Print.
Mignolo, Walter D. *Local Histories/Global Designs: Coloniality, Subaltern Knowledges, and Border Thinking*. Princeton, NJ: Princeton UP, 2000. Print.
Ortega, Julio. "Transatlantic Translations." *PMLA* 118.1 (2003): 25-40. Print.
Paz, Octavio. "In Search of the Present." *Nobelprize.org*. Nobel Foundation, 8 December 1990. Web. 2 February 2010.
Randeria, Shalini. *Geschichte und verwobene Moderne*. Berlin: Schiller, 1999. Print.
Smethurst, Paul. *The Postmodern Chronotope: Reading Space and Time in Contemporary Fiction*. Amsterdam: Rodopi, 2000. Print.
Wegner, Michael. "Die Zeit im Raum. Zur Chronotopostheorie Michail Bakhtins." *Weimarer Beiträge* 35.8 (1989): 1357-1367. Print.

Revisiting Spivak: Does the Subaltern Speak In and Through Telenovelas?

Gundo Rial y Costas

The tempest-tossed, fragmented, moving and moved landscapes of (post)modernity offer a large quantity of theoretical approaches with respective terminologies in order to conceive these scenes. One of the perspectives which might help to understand the world of (post)modernity is the concept of the *subaltern*. Of arguably polysemic nature, Gayatri Spivak defines the subaltern as identity in difference, and further that no unrepresentable subaltern subject can know and speak for itself ("Can the Subaltern Speak" 285). As such, it is discursively constructed, while it achieves definition through processes of exclusion. In the following, I will locate it within the context of its emergence by also retracing a possible archeology, including different processes of appropriations, shifts, and generalizations.

In addition to the investigation of the concept along with its different signifying practices, I shall also follow the question of one of its main discursive formations, the one about whether the subaltern does actually speak or not. In dialogue with the aforementioned landscapes, a cultural cartography will be elaborated with a spatial and temporal location of the different conceptualizations. Thus, I will start with the early usage of the term, its appropriation by Antonio Gramsci, later adaptations by the Subaltern Study Group in India, the passage to the Americas, and finally place the main emphasis on Gayatri Spivak's articulations. Then, the focus will shift from India to the Americas by showing in how far the Latin American Subaltern Studies Group grounded their project on Spivak's and Guha's conceptions, along with the claims that were articulated with this conceptual relocation. Moving in a last step to the southern part of the Americas, I will question in how far the subaltern actually finds a space to speak in Brazilian telenovelas, the most influential media product in Latin America. I shall therefore discuss two of these audiovisual narratives, *O Rei do Gado* (*The Cattle King*, 1996, Benedito Rui Barbosa) and *América* (2005, Glória Perez), both of which have been in the spotlight of (inter)national critique.

Although usually rather silenced in these narratives, in *O Rei do Gado*, there is the medial representation of members of the MST (Movement Without Land) in Brazil, a social movement of subaltern people without land who occupy unused territories. *América*, the second example, tells the stories of mostly poor Brazilian migrants who try to realize their American dream by illegally entering the USA through sometimes lethal passages.

A POSSIBLE ARCHEOLOGY OF THE SUBALTERN

The origins of the subaltern lead to first usages in 18th century military circles, referring to officers who possess a rank lower than captain. With a considerable difference of more than a century the concept found its way to the Americas. Such an early foregrounding in history is relevant in order to understand the usage of the term in the early 20th century. This long leap in history shall be permitted, as the signifier subaltern was fixed to its signified, with obviously varying referents depending on the structure of the military referred to.

Antonio Gramsci, imprisoned in the 1920s for alleged subversive political activism, contributed to a resignification of the term and opened up discussions in many different academic disciplines as well as in left-wing circles that soon reached global importance. As Gramsci's writings were under strict censorship[1] restricting the use of certain compromising left-wing semantics, he had to elaborate a code for a wide range of particularly Marxist terms. One of the forbidden terms, 'the proletariat,' was thus replaced by 'the subaltern' (Spivak, "Power/Knowledge" 141), denoting the Italian working class and thus also the binary division between the rather rich North and the rather poor south of Italy.

Several decades later, in the late 1970s, the Indian historian Ranajit Guha adapted Gramsci's concept for the politics of his left-wing study group. Through an epistemological approach that applied a 'strategic essentialism,' the Subaltern Study Group registered the voices of rural peasants in South India, which earlier had not found entry into official historiography. That way, exclusive elitism in South Asian Studies was questioned (Guha, "Preface" vii) from 'below.' Several of the approaches of the group around Guha were grounded in Gramsci's idea of the subaltern as a hegemonic product consolidating the 'national' and the 'popular.' However, the Italian scholar's concept of the subaltern was applied to Indian society in an occasionally simplified and essentializing manner. Its rough equivalents 'popular,' 'mass,' and 'lower class' were directly transposed to the Indian caste context with a generalizing reference to tribal and low-caste agricultural laborers, landholding peasants, and laborers in plantations, mines, and industries (Sarkar 273).

The academic group's extensive research, which also contested the ambiguities of the concept (Guha, "Historiography" 5), resulted in six volumes of se-

---

1 Antonio Gramsci documented his central thoughts in so-called *Quaderni di carcere* (*Prison Notebooks*), which were constantly checked for compromising ideological content by the prison director (cf. Gramsci *Erziehung* A5). "Subaltern" is frequently written in inverted comas, which contributes to its marking as a code (cf. *Gefängnishefte* 110).

lected writings which focused on the social diversity manifested in differences concerning regional or national caste or subaltern people (Sarkar 274). In the latter half of the 1980s, the group's most productive period which criticized the remains of British colonial rule, collaboration with Gayatri Spivak was initiated.

GAYATRI SPIVAK AND HER CONCEPTIONS OF THE SUBALTERN

In the following, I shall try to reconstruct the way in which Spivak has continually tried to reconceptualize the subaltern while enquiring about the possibilities to 'speak' for social actors in subaltern situations. The main reference point is the monumental 1988 essay "Can the Subaltern Speak?," whose central argument can be traced back to early attempts in the magazine *Wedge*[2]. These opening words, which were eliminated from subsequent rewritings, however, provide *avant la lettre* crucial insights for the understanding of Spivak's concept:

> An understanding of contemporary relations of power and of the Western intellectual's role within them requires an examination of the intersection of a theory of representation and the political economy of global capitalism. A theory of representation points, on the one hand, to the domain of *ideology, meaning, and subjectivity*, and, on the other hand, to the domain of *politics, the state, and the law*. (Spivak, "Can the Subaltern Speak" 271; emphasis mine)

The quotation above highlights Spivak's Marxist commitment, combined with a poststructuralist curiosity to explore representation. In addition to the aforementioned triads of 'ideology,' 'meaning,' and 'subjectivity,' as well as 'politics,' 'the state,' and 'the law,' she employs a third one: power, desire, and interest, originally intended as the title of the piece (ibid.). This third triad provides the framework for Spivak's reasoning, while the discussion of the subaltern is engendered through the relations amongst the three different aspects.

Let me start with a discussion of the main ideas with a special focus on the subaltern. Spivak firstly draws a relation between the critique of subject positions by European philosophers and the non-representation of the so-called 'Third World Subject.' In a commentary on Foucault and Deleuze, Spivak highlights their usage of essentialized concepts, such as 'Asia' ("Can the Subaltern Speak" 272). The following critique of Deleuze ("Can the Subaltern Speak" 275) introduces one of the main elements of the essay: the two meanings of 'represent,' in the philosophical and the political sense. Drawing on Karl Marx, Spivak exempl-

---

[2] There, Spivak was not yet aware of the pragmatic magnitude of the verb used for her questioning, as the author referred to "Can the subaltern talk?" and not "Can the Subaltern speak?"

ifies how the German scholar differentiated between 'darstellen' (represent) and 'vertreten' (represent). The polysemy of meaning was ignored in its original translation into English, one denoting to 'speak about' and the other to 'speak for': "I have dwelt so long on this passage in Marx, because it spells out the inner dynamics of *Vertretung*, or representation in the political context. Representation in the economic context is *Darstellung*, the philosophical concept of representation as staging, or indeed, signification, which relates to the divided subject in an indirect way" ("Can the Subaltern Speak" 278).

According to Spivak, radical textual practice should include the double meaning of representations rather than reintroduce the individual subject through totalizing concepts of power and desire ("Can the Subaltern Speak" 279). She proposes a possible counter-argument from Hindu law, substantially influenced by English colonial rule, the latter being foreclosed to the central question: "On the other side of the international division of labor from socialized capital, inside *and* outside the circuit of the epistemic violence of imperialist law and education supplementing an earlier economic text, *can the subaltern speak*?" ("Can the Subaltern Speak" 283).

Gramsci's idea of the intellectual's position within the process of the subaltern's cultural movement into hegemony is complemented by a possible integration of female agency. It serves to link the conceptions to the Subaltern Study Group's definition of the subaltern and its attempt to critically rethink colonial Indian historiography. In this respect, Spivak's linkage between the triad of power, desire, and interest and the subaltern becomes obvious. This is manifested by the discussion of Guha's definition of the subaltern as a heterogeneous group[3] which consists of people from the margins or 'silenced centre,' such as the illiterate peasantry, tribals, and the urban subproletariat.

Spivak stresses the heterogeneous and relational functions of the different groups, also the 'ideal' subaltern one which, depending on the constellation, might change its status. Its identity is hence constituted through difference. She continues with the following observation: "For the 'true' subaltern group, whose identity is its difference, there is no unrepresentable subaltern subject that can know and speak itself; the intellectual is not to abstain from representation" ("Can the Subaltern Speak" 285). Spivak finds theoretical support in Derrida's deconstructionist approaches[4] in order to discuss the understanding of (colonial)

---

3 The other three groups are subsumed under the concept of 'elite' and are further categorized: firstly there are the foreign groups; the second one consists of indigenous groups in whole India; and the third one includes dominant groups on a regional/local level (Spivak, *Subaltern* 283).

4 See also her preface to her translation of *On Grammatology* (Derrida lxxi).

subject constructions through an "appeal" or "call" to the "quite-other," which is located within oneself, and not attempting to let the other speak for herself ("Can the Subaltern Speak" 294).

Spivak finally tries to consolidate the theoretical foregrounding with an example from Hindu law about wife burning and its abolition by the English colonizers. The focus is placed on the constitution of the subaltern woman: "Can the subaltern speak? What must the elite do to watch out for the continuing construction of the subaltern? The question of 'woman' seems most problematic in this context" ("Can the Subaltern Speak" 294). Adopting a Freudian psychoanalytic approach that follows the axiom "White men are saving brown women from brown men" ("Can the Subaltern Speak" 297), Spivak elucidates the disappearance of the subaltern woman's voice within the dynamics of a specific cultural practice. The 'protection' of women by the English colonial rulers thus becomes a signifier for the establishment of a '*good* society' in which wife burning is turned into crime, thus crossing the frontier between the private and public.

Spivak delves into an analysis of the Hindu ritual of *sati*[5], of wife burning, and its abolishment in colonial India. Hindu conservatives wanted to continue the ritual while the British colonial rulers wanted to abolish it. Spivak investigates the way in which the English colonizers reported on the ritual, and the way in which the Indians did. By referring back to historical texts, Spivak makes obvious that no place was allotted to the female subaltern subject from which it could speak. In addition, the figure of the woman disappears into a displaced figuration of the 'third-world' woman ("Can the Subaltern Speak" 307).

This example is further backed by the life history of Bhuvaneswari Bhadur, a Hindi activist who was ordered to commit a political murder. As she could not persuade herself to carry it out, she decided to commit suicide. She killed herself during her menstruation time, a period in which the sati could not be executed, because she did not want this act to be interpreted as a form of sati due to an illegitimate passion. After her death, her motif was silenced and the death described as a case of illicit love ("Can the Subaltern Speak" 308).

The life story of Bhadur elucidates Spivak's question whether the subaltern can speak or not, as it negates this possibility. I attempt to isolate some of the most relevant points by the author for a possible practical application of this approach. First, I propose to define the subaltern as a relational and dynamic term which depends on the situation and on the place of enunciation. Second, although according to Spivak the subaltern cannot speak, the author admits ten

5 This ritual from Hindu religion was employed when the husband had died and the widow, in order to have a spiritual continuation, had to go on the pyre and immolate herself.

years later possibilities of speaking[6], which might be investigated in order to analyze where and when these enunciations can occur. Third, Spivak's questioning of the intellectual's position through the double meaning of 'represent' provides a methodological toolbox, since this reasoning may be applied to the questioning of hegemonic relations and mechanisms at work when analyzing any form of cultural phenomena. Following such an approach, one should enquire "Who is actually represented?" and "Who is represented by whom?" in order to find out the mechanisms for agency construction by also going beyond the written or the audiovisual text.

SUBALTERN STUDIES IN THE AMERICAS

Spivak's essay spurred widespread reactions. In order to provide an idea of its multi-faceted and multi-disciplinary debates, I shall give a brief overview of some of the most relevant ones: A special issue of *ACOLIT* wondered "Can the 'Subaltern' be Read?" while Maggio's "Can the Subaltern be Heard?" discussed the reception and the role of the critic in the global context, Medovoi's "Can the Subaltern Vote?" questioned the political meaning of representation, Grandin's "Can the Subaltern be Seen?" investigated the photographic representation of the K'iche in Guatemala at the beginning of the 20th century. Finally, the volume *Spricht die Subalterne Deutsch?* (*Does the Subaltern Speak German?*) specifically linked the subaltern to the German academic and cultural context. The debates, often led simultaneously in different (media) spaces, were not bound to specific regions. Reflecting the disjuncture of these global reception processes, particularly The Latin American Subaltern Studies Group proves to be an example which elucidates the incorporation of elements found in Spivak's, Guha's, and Gramsci's concepts.

With a clear reference to a certain type of "strategic essentialism," the Latin American Subaltern Studies Group was originally based on the ideas of the Subaltern Study Group, with the intention of visualizing the lives of the subaltern. Initiated in the early 1990s in the USA, it was based on an essentialist postulate advocating the poor and their right to acknowledgement (Rodríguez 3). Accompanied by Gramsci's subdivision of nation-popular, these studies also constituted a radical critique of elite cultures. The founding manifesto of the Latin American

[6] See particularly her rewriting of 1999 and integration within the essay "History," in which she says that it was an "inadvisable remark" to state that the subaltern cannot speak (Spivak *Postcolonial* 308) and that "subaltern is reserved for the decolonized space" (310).

Studies Group by Beverley, Sanchinés, and Mignolo reveals a major problem in the contemporary circulation of knowledge. Firstly, albeit the group is composed of mostly US scholars with a Latin American background, it personifies a certain form of centralization of knowledge which reflects certain positions of colonialism.[7] Secondly, routes of cultural globalization, along with its peculiar form of representation processes, are manifest in the conflation of several theoretical approaches, as in the case of the three p's (Postcolonial, Postmodern, and Poststructuralist Studies) which is also due to the heritage of Latin American Cultural Studies, which has, since its beginnings, been conceived rather as a form of practice than as a theory.

When taking a look at the founding statement, one can observe different receptions of the ideas of the subaltern in Latin American Studies, including the displacement of revolutionary projects, the processes of redemocratization, the new dynamics created by the effects of the mass media, and the transnational economic reconfigurations: "The subaltern is conceived as a subject that emerges across, or at the intersections of, a spectrum of academic disciplines ranging from the philosophical critique of metaphysics to contemporary literary and cultural theory, to history and social sciences" ("Founding Statement" 3).

The fact that Latin America has a long history of conceiving 'nation' and 'the national' as non-popular, all-inclusive terms is of special relevance in this context. Albeit the concept was not in academic usage before the 1980s, popular discourses in Latin America have a long tradition of tackling similar issues. It goes back to the dialectics of colonial oppression followed by the articulation of a *crítica cultural*. The processes are further reflected by corresponding semantics with a long tradition in Latin American social theory, going back to the pedagogic of the oppressed[8]. A founding definition is subsequently articulated with a clear political and social commitment:

A heightened sensitivity to the complexities of social difference and, on the other, the composition of a plural, but bounded, space or platform of research and discussion in which everyone has a place. Traditional configurations of democracy and the nation-state have barred subaltern social classes and groups from actively participating both in the political process and in the constitution of

[7] Due to continuing processes of colonialism, Latin American Studies do not have a long history in Latin America, because there is no tradition in studying the continent (see Mignolo *Idea*). Only in the last few decades, Latin American Studies Centres were founded, as at the Universidade de São Paulo. They are an 'invention' from the USA developed in postwar years (see Mignolo *Local*).

[8] On some occasions, Spivak herself uses 'oppressed' instead of 'subaltern' (see "Can the Subaltern Speak," especially 274-279).

academically authorized knowledge, and have not recognized their potential contributions as a pool of human capital, except by default ("Founding Statement" 5).

According to Mignolo, the general intention of the group was to allot a space to the representation of subaltern groups insofar as the subaltern has to be conceived of as a perspective rather than a category ("Subaltern"). One can state that the general conception was one which aimed at linking these forms of studies in exploring the limits of the state:

> To represent subalternity in Latin America, in whatever form it takes wherever it appears to find the blank space where it speaks as a sociopolitical subject, requires us to explore the margins of the state. Our premise, again, is the nation, as a conceptual space, is not identical to the nation as state. Our initial concepts are therefore more geographical than institutional. ("Founding Statement" 9)

Apart from the central socio-political commitment, the subaltern's dissemination into the area of Latin American Studies has been clearly noted, expanding its semantic reach to such an extent that even languages such as Spanish or Portuguese are referred to as subaltern, or whole regions or countries. This leads to a general diffusion of the concept, or a dilution, as Spivak stated in a lecture in 2004. That is why one shall regard the subaltern rather as a textual practice grounded within the dynamics of its object. It also seems as if the role of the intellectual's essentializing subject position is less strictly treated in Latin American Subaltern Studies. This might be explained through the success of the genre of *testimonio literature* and its evaluation as a supposedly authentic subaltern document.

DOES THE SUBALTERN SPEAK IN AND THROUGH TELENOVELAS?

Telenovelas are audiovisual narratives of Latin American origin with a closed structure that run for six to eight months. They are either structured around one usually female protagonist or feature a multiplot narrative with several main characters. With a long tradition, going back to the French feuilleton novel and the *radionovela*, these forms of audiovisual narratives look back at more than half a century of successful media history. Curious enough, the Latin American Subaltern Study Group called the telenovela the new reference medium in Latin America ("Founding Statement" 9), even though telenovelas are produced by large media conglomerates, often with a global reach, and embedded within neoliberal market logics. As they, and here I shall exclusively refer to its Brazilian representatives, are often so successful that they occupy the prime-time slots on TV, theses have been articulated highlighting their supposed 'anti-imperialistic,' or subaltern, forms (see Mato). However, this is a rather romanticized view of left-wing North American scholars who do not interpret (media) reality according to its discursive position with respect to culture and power.

Telenovelas are Brazil's top export product, often produced by TV Globo, one of the largest media conglomerates on the globe. TV Globo adheres to a strict hierarchic and neoliberal policy and therefore does not have subaltern potential in terms of its structure. Yet, despite its hierarchic neoliberal production places that imply the frequent exclusion of some marginalized groups, such as blacks, one might detect traces of the subaltern in its narratives.

Usually, scholars place the Brazilian subaltern in the context of cultural resistance through the articulation of alternative and traditional cultural practices, such as Afro-Brazilian Maracatú music, the oral literary traditions of the Cordel, or the Afro-blocks in the Carneval in Salvador (Peres 116). However, one might also find other possible traces of the subaltern by watching TV Globo. TV Globo is notorious for its long tradition, with a dubious and dark history during the military dictatorship (Leal Filho 42); it is also famous for frequently including images of Brazil's beautiful landscapes in its telenovelas and nearly exclusively using white actors, rarely referring to the realities of Brazilian life. Yet, following de Certeau's musings on strategies (78), it becomes obvious that every system bears space for 'loopholes.' Albeit these forms of representation often seem to integrate rather polished or manipulated fragments from 'real' life, occasionally they also depict different imageries.

In order to understand the inclusion of fragments of subalterns into the telenovelas, one may pose an anthropological question about their authors and the field in which they are placed. Equipped with a power which is only comparable to the European auteur cinema, they are actively involved in decision-making on the highest level, and are therefore a vital part of the genesis of a telenovela. The complex relations of these processes are illustrated by two incidents that concern the production of *América*. The first one shows the great authority of the telenovela author: after a month, when the telenovela had not reached the required target figures, scriptwriter Glória Pérez ordered the substitution of the director.

The second example highlights the complicated and complex networks of influence and hierarchy in this theatre of representation: in the last episode, two of the male actors were supposed to French-kiss, but this gay kiss was censored without the knowledge of the author, who had insisted on airing this scene. Against this background, one has to conceive the different processes at work when a telenovela is broadcast together with the complex forms of communication, as the author continues writing the plot every week, almost in real time, different from homologue productions in Hispano America. As the achievement of inserting and staging elements of the 'real' is one of the most desirable objectives of a telenovela, and as that effect should yield an accordingly high number of spectators, sometimes life histories of subalterns or subaltern positions are integrated into the plot.

O Rei do Gado: The Subaltern and Social Movements

O Rei do Gado repeatedly tried to represent the MST (*Movimento Sem Terra*), the movement of people without land. In order to understand the possible meanings of these depictions, one needs to understand their position in Brazilian history. In Brazil, a country without efficient agrarian reform, the distribution of territory is extremely unjust. Since the 1930s and during the processes of modernization, rurally based farmers lost their land and started to reclaim it. The reclaiming of the land found its manifestation in illegal appropriations. The first reported cases dating back to the late 1970s changed into more organized ones after the foundation of the movement in 1987. Against this background, Rui Barbosa conceived of a telenovela which draws upon these economic disparities. One narrative thread follows the story of Italian immigrants working on the coffee plantations on the outskirts of São Paulo. In a second thread, a big landowner falls in love with a member of the MST. The final thread chronicles the life story of a couple who are members of the MST. This couple, which frequently appeared on other TV shows, criticized their own representation in the telenovela. For example, they complained about replacing the movement's representative color of green for red[9]. Shot during the era of heavy confrontation between the movement and the military force, it contributed to the increase o the movement's popularity (see Hammond).

One might ask how far the two conditions of Spivak's concept of 'representation' are fulfilled. It can be argued that there exists a form of representation, in the sense of portraying, through the subalterns' way of representation, as in similar adoptions of clothing styles, forms of speech, and social interaction with almost an excess of the real. Therefore, one may follow the Brazilian sociologist Sérgio Costa, who speaks about the instrumentalization of politics by telenovelas and of the instrumentalization of telenovelas by politics (14). In this respect, one should further differentiate between the representation of specific subaltern subjects or subject positions and that of a whole group, the MST, as subaltern,

9 Parallel to the screening of the telenovela, general media interest was spurred about the subaltern integrants of the group, as e.g. the case of Débora Rodrigues, a truck driver, who even posed nude for *Playboy*, after the consensus of the MST group, with a big media echo condensed in the headline of the widely read magazine *Veja*: "Without land, without clothes" (cf. Machado-Borges 124-125).

whose analysis might trick one into homogeneization. In addition, one should further enquire about the integration of 'frequency' into a possible analytic grid – does the subaltern constantly speak in the representation, or only briefly? And what is the actual effect of the representation?

The second meaning, as in the political representation, will be rather negated. And still, despite its representation in a fictional narrative and a hegemonic medium, in some episodes the fictional members of the movement were given the opportunity to utter their wishes for land and other claims regarding certain politics on agriculture. This considerably increased popularity (Hamburger 142). On the other hand, one cannot talk about a continuous process of this aspect, even if the roles were conceived by the scriptwriter; following a specific narrative pattern, the positive effects of the media representation were not echoed by sustainable politics. Regarding the Latin American Subaltern Study Group's definition, it might be argued that a certain reconstruction of the subaltern peasants' life was achieved and, at least to a certain extent, the political message of the movement was conveyed.

Maybe one could add a further dimension, namely the one of personal interest and solidarity. Frequently, this resembles the effect of peer identification. The growing popularity of the MST that followed the broadcasting and subsequent continuation of the series bears testimony to this phenomenon. It might function as a key element in the analysis of the subaltern as far as the effects that such constructions achieve among the spectators or readers are concerned. This means that the production of media images may contribute to (positively!) influence the construction of people's social imaginaries (Soares de Souza 87) including ones which represent the subaltern.

AMÉRICA: MIGRANTS AS SUBALTERNS AND THE AESTHETICIZATION OF SUBALTERNS

América, a more recent example, was written by Glória Pérez in 2005 and broadcast in the same year. It enjoyed astounding popular success but received ambivalent reception from critics. In this telenovela, several interesting constellations are at hand which might initiate a fruitful dialogue with the concept of the subaltern. The series is a transnational migration saga in which the realization of dreams constitutes the main theme. This is exemplified by leaving the country and emigrating to the USA, as does the protagonist Sol, or staying and settling in Brazil, as does Sol's boyfriend Tião. These different conceptions of life are contrasted and complemented by a wide range of parallel narrative threads, with almost a hundred different characters who all attempt to realize their dreams.

In *América*, the representation of the subaltern is expressed in a particularly interesting form: following Spivak, it can be described as dynamic and relational, and as identity-in-differential producing, as exemplified by the protagonist Sol. Starting with Sol's childhood, *América* recounts her life in a shanty town in Rio de Janeiro, emphasizing the demolishment of her barrack-like house built without permission. As Sol's family loses everything and is forced to live on the margin of society, this can be described as a form of temporary subaltern representation. It is only of a temporary or even sudden character, as the spectators learn in the course of the telenovela that the man who was ordered to demolish their barrack had hosted her family in his humble house in the lower-middle class region of Vila Isabel in North Rio de Janeiro.

But even though the subaltern is seen from a different perspective, its dynamic nature is at work: as Sol decides to emigrate to the USA in order to realize her childhood dream, she is denied a visa and has to contract a coyote to illegally immigrate into the USA. As a consequence, she loses her status as a citizen and turns into a subaltern migrant. This new phase of life is represented by the audiovisual narrative through the hardships and dangers during the collaboration with the coyote, the trip from Brazil to Mexico, and the passage through the desert into the USA. She also has to come to terms with her status as an illegal and unemployed subject. The latter culminates in disappointments of leading a new life in which she has to work as a cleaner, sausage vendor, go-go dancer, and even become a test person for drug experiments. As Sol does not have any access to medical service and is without a social security number, she is also not permitted to go to the hospital when she falls ill. In order to regularize her status, turning from a subaltern illegal immigrant into an immigrant being granted the right to stay in the country, the protagonist decides to obtain the Green Card through a set-up marriage and has to resign from her romantic dream of marrying the love of her life. Yet, the vulnerability of her in-between status continues after her marriage through controls by migration officials, who disturb her private sphere with unannounced visits.

In *América*, illegal migration or, respectively, being subaltern becomes the major theme. Sol's destiny, which is left open at the end when she regains her 'normal' status and is deported to Brazil together with her North American husband and their baby, is complemented by the ones of other people sharing a similar fate. There are even spaces where their destinies meet, such as the Miami pension of the Mexican exile Consuelo, where many of the undocumented migrants live while sharing their experiences as underdogs. Discriminations against skin color, precarious linguistic skills, and different cultural matrixes are not only frequent topics of conversation at the pension, but also lived through practices in the daily routines of the subaltern subjects. Following the principle of pars pro toto as representing all Latin Americans' illegal lives' (hi)stories in the USA, this audiovisual narrative – although grounded in the matrix of melodrama – opens up new ways for the representation of the subaltern. The authenticity of several aspects of the passage as well as the life in the new homeland are exemplified through an interesting process of representation and translation.

The subaltern and its imprints can also be reconstructed by tracing the constitution of the process from the subaltern subjects in the lifeworld to the creative process in script writing. The author of *América*, Glória Pérez, discovered her interest in migration issues when she was on vacation in the USA, where she started to record interviews with Latin Americans living there illegally. She further contracted José Carlos Sebe Bom Meihi, a professor of oral history specializing in Brazilian migration to the USA who had himself border-crossed. His book called *Brasil Fora de si* (*Brazil out of itself*), which includes more than 700 interviews with mostly undocumented Brazilians living in the USA, served as the major source and inspiration for Perez to develop some of her subaltern characters. The migrants' pension in Miami, the go-go dancing girls, and the taxi driving Brazilian immigrant Jota are all characters or places which the author extracted from Bom Meihi's recounts.

In this context, the question of representation turns into a complex poststructuralist one, indicating the intertwined nature of representational processes: the accounts by subaltern migrants were either recorded by the script writer or the anthropologist and then integrated into an already existing narrative sketch. As the telenovela continued, the author found support by actively engaging in dialogues with Brazilians living in the US diaspora through the internet and integrated suggestions from the online community into the narrative.[10]

The link between desire, power, and interest might be elucidated with the following example from *América*: In the 109th episode, Ed, a North American who has not yet declared his love to the Brazilian Sol, is visited by a friend in his apartment in Miami. In the scene, in which the friend finds a book on Ed's desk, the abovementioned *Brasil fora de si*, Ed is asked to read the title from the spine of the book[11]: "*Brasil outside itself*! Are you interested in Brazilians?" Ed answers: "I wanted to understand this phenomenon better [...] this increase of the number of Brazilians who want to get into the USA [...]." The friend insists: "Do you want to understand Brazil better or this Brazilian woman who you married?"

---

10 See Pérez' social network site on *Orkut*: www.orkut.com

11 The translation from Brazilian Portuguese is mine.

In the conversation several forms of meaning production are at play: firstly, there is the link between a supposed representation of the subaltern migrant(s) and the way she entered the fictitious world of the telenovela. Then, there is the conflation of fiction and the 'real' through the material insertion of the book by the anthropologist, which is also linked to economic aspects as it functions as a contextualization of the migrants' story and an extra-compositional point of reference. It is also tied to economic interest, because it is a very cunning form of product placement. Further, and within the narrative, is the oppressed desire of Ed, sublimated by "getting to know Sol" through the reading about her culture, materialized by the book, since the physical and biblical form of knowing is not allowed, because he is committed to another woman. Power is working at various levels: firstly, there is the power of the author's gesture towards the anthropologist by offering his book the medial space for product placement, which would usually cost a fortune. Therefore, and in order to understand the intrinsic and complex processes at work here, one should take a look at the way in which the book was merchandised and sold in Brazil. The cover, consisting of a paper ribbon which reproduced the design of the logo of the telenovela, said "A saga dos Brasileiros na América" ("The saga of the Brazilians in America"), while it further provided the information that the anthropologist was Pérez' counselor for the telenovela. Secondly, there is also a double power structure at work within the narrative: the silencing and taking away of Sol's personal identity by referring to her as "the Brazilian woman," as well as the fact that she is also at Ed's mercy as the wedding was only set-up; but Sol depends on this status in order to get her Green Card. This refers to the third manifestation of a power constellation: the depiction of irregular migrants in the USA as subaltern.

To conclude, one may call attention to another case of subaltern articulations in *América*. This is a constellation in which one of the most cherished Brazilian actors, Marianna Ximenez, is portrayed as a young rebellious teenage girl called Raissa. The telenovela playwright intended to illustrate the rich and spoiled girl's rebellion by representing her as a *funkeira*, a member of the subcultural movement of *baile funk*, a music and dance from the favelas, the shanty towns in Brazil. The baile funk is originally the expression of the poor, mostly black, youths from the more than 700 favelas in Rio de Janeiro, and can therefore be termed a form of subaltern expression. However, in the past few years the music has reached mainstream acceptance due to its commercialization. Thus, Glória Perez, the scriptwriter, reenacts a form of peripheric representation by staging some of the chapters in the shanty town which culminates in Raissa's wedding at a baile funk party.

As the popularity amongst the Brazilian public was high, this narrative thread was extended and the famous funk DJ Marlboro and MC Tati Quebra Barraco appeared in *América*. This constellation shows a supposedly marginal or subaltern movement that is stereotypically instrumentalized as a vehicle for expressing the forbidden. This is further essentialized by the scriptwriter, who uses this world of the marginalized in order to oppose it to the rich upper class life of Raissa's parents. At the same time, there is a visualization of this movement, the musicians appear as themselves in the narrative, and verbal expressions from funk music are used by the actors and circulate nationwide. Nevertheless, one has to admit that the DJs use their supposedly subaltern positions in order to propagate their music and cash in on it, while the people from the communities only appear as extras in the dance scenes.

Therefore, one might speak about a certain type of aestheticization of subaltern expressions. This has to be seen in the wider context of desire and interest of the culture industry, which cashes in on any kind of (stereo)type worthwhile for possible identifications. That the negotiation of the subaltern is of an ambivalent nature becomes evident with two respective examples: the first one is the closing party of *América*, an event staged after the end of filming a telenovela. It is always in the centre of media attention, it may even be described as the last episode of every telenovela, as TV, newspapers, and magazines report extensively about it. Against the odds to invite a DJ who would play more traditional music, DJ Marlboro was invited to play funk, thus indirectly consolidating this form of music, particularly as the present actors imitated all the typical dance moves from the favelas. The second example, however, speaks in favor of an exclusion of this music movement, as manifested by the official CDs for the telenovela, where the funk tunes were omitted without further comments by its producers.

CONCLUSION

I have attempted to discuss the complex nature of the concept of the subaltern and its embedding within the context of possible forms of agency grounded in a wider context of desire, power, and interest. The first coding of the concept by Antonio Gramsci in a situation of need and pain seems to continue nowadays, as the subaltern has encountered several re-interpretations and re-readings, often cryptic in nature.

The different forms of representation, as suggested by Spivak, may also be regarded as having metaphoric value, because their meanings are never fixed, at least not in Spivak's poststructuralist approaches. They are helpful in order to grasp the inner dynamics of agency and to deconstruct essentialist positions. Spivak herself does this through a harsh critique of Deleuze and Foucault by recurring to Marx and Derrida, and finally by referring to a concrete example from India in which the female subaltern subject was silenced.

Hence, it was revealed that the debate and research about the subaltern in Latin America was particularly led from the US. Approaches developed in the context were frequently linked to a 'return to the subject,' similar to the ones in the Subaltern Study Group's approaches. These theoretical considerations were based on politically committed textual practices with the intention to bestow the subaltern with an intellectual voice. That is why these positions sometimes collide with the ones taken by Spivak: between 'rescuing' the subaltern as subject (Subaltern Study Group, Latin American Study Group) and defining the subaltern as dynamic and differential space (Spivak).

Equipped with this knowledge while adopting the latter position of the subaltern as a particularly relational term that was constructed through processes of exclusion, I tried to trace possible echoes of subaltern positions in Brazilian telenovelas. Contrary to the well-trodden path of looking for cultural representations in peripheral or marginalized forms of articulation, I pointed to traces in these popular media narratives. Led by the choice of my examples, *O Rei do Gado* and *América*, I encountered revealing constellations of social movements and migrant networks which provide telling insights into the different processes of representation involved in the construction, production, and reception of these telenovelas. In this respect, at least some echoes of the voices of the subaltern could be recorded and the contours of a whole subaltern movement, as in the MST in *O Rei do Gado*, were outlined.

At the same time, the dynamic and unfixed character of this concept was questioned and negotiated. It has to be repeated that it works within a logic of liquidity, meanings are too evasive to be fixed. This liquidity (also echoed by Spivak) was exemplified by Sol's fluid position oscillating between the status of a migrant and a non-migrant in *América*.

For subsequent studies, one might incorporate the close-knit communication processes of encoding and decoding into respective research. Thus, Reception Studies could initiate a fruitful dialogue with the postcolonial/postmodern approaches of the subaltern, as they might contribute to shed more light on the intertwined discourses of domination and hegemony articulated in often stereotypical images by the mass media.

WORKS CITED

América. Telenovela, Glória Pérez, TV Globo, 2005.

Costa, Sérgio. "Der Kamp um Öffentlichkeit: Begriffe, Akteure, politische Dynamiken." *Jahrbuch Lateinamerika 28: Medien und ihre Mittel*. Eds. Karin Gabbert, Wolfgang Gabbert, and Ulrich Godeking. Münster: Westfälisches Dampfboot, 2004. 9-24. Print.

Derrida, Jacques. *On Grammatology*. 1974. Baltimore, MD: John Hopkins UP, 1997. Print de Certeau, Michel. *Die Kunst des Handelns*. 1980. Berlin: Merve,1988. Print.

Döring, Tobias, Uwe Schäfer, and Mark Stein, eds. Can the 'Subaltern' be Read? The Role of the Critic in Postcolonial Studies. *ACOLIT* 2 (1996). Print.

Gramsci, Antonio. *Gefängnishefte*. 1929. Argument: Hamburg, 1991. Print.

—. *Erziehung und Bildung*. 1929. Hamburg: Argument Verlag, 2004. Print.

Grandin, Greg. "Can the Subaltern be Seen? Photography and the Affects of Nationalism." *Hispanic American Historical Review* 84.1 (2004): 83-111. Print.

Guha, Ranajit. "On some Aspects of the Historiography of Colonial India." *Subaltern Studies I: Writings on South Asian History and Society*. Ed. Ranajit Guha. New York, NY: Oxford Unveristy Press, 1982. 1-8. Print.

—. "Preface." *Subaltern Studies II*. Ed. Ranajit Guha. New York, NY: Oxford UP, 1984. vii-viii. Print.

Hamburger, Ester. *O Brasil Antenado: A Sociedade da Telenovela*. São Paulo: Jorge Zahar, 2005. Print.

Hammond, John. "The MST and the Media: Competing Images of the Brazilian Landless Farmworkers Movement." *Latin American Politics and Society* 46.4 (2004): 61-90. Print.

Leal Filho, Laurindo. "Quarenta Anos depois, a TV Brasileira ainda guarda Marcas da Ditadura." *Revista USP* 61 (2004): 40-47. Print.

Latin American Subaltern Studies Group. "Founding Statement." *Dispositio/n* 19.46 (1994): 1-13. Print.

Machado Borges, Thais. *Only For You. Brazilians and the Telenovela Flow*. Stockholm: Almqvist & Wiksell, 2003. Print.

Maggio, Jay. "Can the Subaltern Be Heard? Political Theory, Translation, Representation, and Gayatri Chakravorty Spivak." *Alternatives: Global, Local, Political* 32.4 (2007): 419-444. Print.

Mato, Daniel. "Telenovelas: Transnacionalización de la Industia y Transformaciones del Género." *Industrias Culturales e Integración Latinoamericana*. Ed. Nestor Garcia Canclin. México: Grijalbo, 1999. 229-257. Print.

Medovoi, Leerom, et al. "Can the Subaltern Vote?" *Socialist Review* 20.3 (1990): 133-149. Print.

Mignolo, Walter. "Are Subaltern Studies Postmodern or Postcolonial? The Politics and Sensibilities of Geo-Cultural Locations." *Dispositio/n* 19.46 (1994): 45-73. Print.

—. *Local Histories, Global Designs*. New York, NY: Routledge, 2000. Print.

—. *The Idea of Latin America*. Oxford: Blackwell, 2005. Print.

O Rei do Gado. Telenovela, Benedito Rui Barbosa, TV Globo,1996.

Peres, P. "Subaltern Spaces in Brazil." *Dispositio/n* 19.46 (1996): 113-126. Print.

Rodríguez, Ileana. "Reading Subalterns Across Texts, Disciplines, and Theories: From Representation to Recognition." *The Latin American Subaltern Studies Reader*. Ed. Ileana Rodríguez. Durham, NC: Duke UP, 2001. 1-33. Print.

Sarkar, Sumit. "The Conditions and Nature of Subaltern Militancy: Bengal from Swadeshi to Non-Co-operation." Guha, Ranajit. *Subaltern Studies I. Writings on South Asian History and Society*. Ed. Ranajit Guha. New York, NY: Oxford UP, 1982. 271-320. Print.

Sebe Bom Meihi, José. *Brasil Fora de Si*. São Paulo: Planeta, 2004. Print.

Soares di Souza, Licia. *Televisão e Cultura: Análise Semiótica da Ficcção Seriada*. Salvador de Bahia, 2003. Print.

Spivak, Gayatri Chakravorty. "Can the Subaltern Talk? Speculations of Widow Sacrifice." *Wedge* 7/8 (1982): 120-130. Print.

—. "Can the Subaltern Speak?" *Marxism and the Interpretation of Culture*. Ed. Cary Nelson. Urbana, IL: U of Illinois P, 1987. 271-313. Print.

—. "More on Power/Knowledge." 1992. *The Spivak Reader: Selected Work of Gayatri Chakravorty Spivak*. Eds. Donna Landry and Gerald M. MacLean. New York, NY: Routledge, 1996. Print.

—. *A Critique of Postcolonial Reason: Toward a Vanishing Present*. Cambridge, MA: Harvard UP, 1999. Print.

—. "The Trajectory of the Subaltern in My Work." 2004. *YouTube*. Google, Inc., 7 February 2008. Web. March 15, 2010.

Steyerl, Hito, and Encarnación Gutiérrez Rodríguez, eds. *Spricht die Subalterne Deutsch? Migration und postkoloniale Kritik*. Münster: Unrast, 2003. Print.

After THOUGHTS

FROM COPACABANA: VARENIKES, KEBABS, A TURTLE, AND A PIGEON

ANA TERESA JARDIM REYNAUD

The invitation to write the afterword to *Landscapes of Postmodernity* comes when I have moved back, to Rio de Janeiro, to Copacabana, the neighborhood where I spent my life as a child and young adult. Between my early contact with the cultural ambience and the everyday life of this South American sea-resort and my recent moving back, I have accumulated years spent in Europe, a Ph.D. in Media Studies at Sussex University, and the experience of teaching at home and abroad. And I find that the return to Copacabana coincides with a desire to experiment with the form of the essay, and I tell this to Gundo, Petra, Walter, and Michael, to whom I explain rather guiltily that I'm in no mood for a more rigorously structured academic piece right now. But it's not solely the nonchalance brought about by the proximity of the tropical beach sea that's affecting me. I think I'm overcome by a recurring sensation of puzzlement regarding things I experience and see in my daily contact with the world I live in, and with academic work. Knowledge, learning, living, it all feels very fragmented and changing very fast to me as I try to keep some sort of grip of it all, trying to avoid on one hand a sense of apocalypse and on the other a forced, cool optimism.

At the university, my eager 20 year undergraduates do not wish to read theoretical texts and find all the references they think they need on the web. They are not interested in the past, in any form of it. They are not even interested in pop culture produced over the last years. They seem immersed in an all-expansive present, formed by everyday experiences, be they virtual or real. They just don't seem to understand my worries that I need to keep alive the exercise of trying to connect the threads between manifestations of thought and cultural practices in their trajectories in time up to now. In my darkest moments I suspect my students seriously doubt that I have something to tell them, and they don't seem to be very keen to hear. They want to talk, express themselves – but not to me. It's to their peers they wish to talk to, to others who are experiencing everyday life in a way similar way (no matter if spatially distant or scattered).

Henry Jenkins talks about this curious conflating of the power of the media producer and the power of the consumer. He explains that it is not so important to discuss the media in Media Studies now, since new media will not simply replace old media but will rather learn to interact with it in a complex relationship he calls "convergence culture." Jenkins explains that this is not a technological revolution; it is a cultural shift, dependent on the active participation of the consumers working in a social dynamic.

I find Jenkins' explanations timely and well conceived, but I still feel baffled. There seems indeed to be plenty of information around, on *Wikipedia*, on blogs, on the collective creation of games, on *YouTube*. But is there knowledge? Knowledge seems to me to be less cumulative and more constructed through careful, authorized dialogue. It has been traditionally built through hierarchic channels, the school being the primary one, to the obvious cost of more equal and ample access. Trying to analyze this massive production of information and the splitting it entails (peers read by peers, groups by groups) can be a very complex task if we try to think about it without condescending to an ingratiating populism or trying to keep trendy at any cost. This immense horizontal web of exchanges and information, where sometimes angry opinions replace debate and everyone is a producer of content, sounds like a cacophonic and somehow alienated body of noise and images that have no degree of substance or depth. Jenkins suggests that collectively the participants will gather knowledge they would not be able to get alone. As an example, he mentions a map that needs deciphering in the TV series *Lost*. The fans gather around it on the internet and solve the puzzle. But what prize is there to be extracted from such operation? What's the relevance of the map of *Lost*?

And that brings me back to this book, to this collection of articles which try in competent and engaging ways to (re-)locate key concepts of postmodern thought. Which seems to me a very timely strategy, since I sometimes feel that theory can be now – as never before – ecologically endangered. That's why the relocating is so crucial; and be it an attempt at revising post-structuralism, or trying to explore new spaces (and perceptions of spaces) that are being created and presented to us (and by us), or trying to address the ever delicate problem of changing subjectivities and identities, or finally casting a look, a glance at the other sides of the Atlantic, it is being done here with the exact measure of pushing and keeping the boundaries. These texts try to address the perplexities, uncertainties, slippery terrains we are called upon to thread now, while building newer frames of perception and thinking. These frames are crafted as useful tools and born out of fruitful conversations and intersections between theories, approaches, and subjects. And this tentative, yet very serious take on theory reminds me of the Wittgensteinian goal (which he declared non-scientific in its method) not to build a site but to see before himself, "transparent, the basis of some possible constructions."

So, writing from this side of the Atlantic and with the partial responsibility of a final word, I will explore two ideas trying to keep up with re-locating as a method. They are the idea of culture and of the everyday, and I'll re-read them very specifically and briefly, or rather I'll feel their pulse here and now.

The idea of culture – a staple to Cultural Studies, the initial revolutionary notion of seeing ways of living as cultures (a working-class culture, for instance, which possessed its own sensibilities, patterns, ways of functioning and expressing itself, ways which were not literate but rather lived) – has remained with us (though not unproblematically). Cultural Studies has, over the years, suffered from the burden of populism, of Marxist orthodoxy, but on the other hand, it has so strongly influenced society that only now we are beginning to question the rather schematic take on the categories of the alternative, of the subcultural, as sites of struggle. We start to realize that what is popular doesn't always spell resistance, and that the extreme identity quest could lead to a certain isolation.

I'd like to evoke a phenomenon I've been noting, and one that intrigues me. I feel that to a certain extent culture has become self-explanatory.

The reasons for that are linked with late capitalism, which has found in culture the ultimate commodity. It can be sold; it blurs class boundaries since people are willing to "learn" about others, it is global in its interest for the multicultural. But local cultures are now self-defined in order that they can be sold – and not only to the "Other," but also on the local market, to the local life. In Copacabana, for instance, you can walk around a few blocks and learn and experience a little bit of the world of the elderly, of the favelas, of the traditional Jewish and the Middle-East communities, of sports, and of the artisans, prostitutes and transsexuals whose work address that other crucial group, the tourists. The interesting thing is that there is a new category of tourists, different from the ones that came earlier in search of the exotic. The young tourists who walk about and go to the beach and are interested in capoeira and have knowledge of Rio's most hip cultural scene are here for the culture. They are here for this self-explicit, self-constructed impermanent culture that they are taking part in promoting and bringing to life.

For us, from Rio, a seaside resort in hard times of financial economic crisis, the organization of urban space around culture is one way out of bankruptcy. The interest in the other, the interest in life, in how other people live and in how we live – which was supported and produced by Cultural Studies – has imploded and found its own (and not always scholarly) means of expressing itself.

I am not critical about this phenomenon. I'm observing it with the glad eye of an ethnographer who feels her job has passed on to the hands of the non-expert. I'm queuing in a shop in Copacabana and an Anglo-Saxon couple in front of me wears caps with OHIO embroidered in them. The Brazilian woman paying for her goods in front of them pays in endless installments (a Brazilian habit born out of necessity which has become a style of consumption). "It's their culture," they comment knowingly to each other. They heard about it, they observed it, they know. It's not difficult now to translate across cultures.

None of this is new, and it has been brought up in a pioneer way by Wittgenstein, who suggested that depending on one's environment, one's physical needs and desires, one's emotions, one's sensory capacities, and so on, different concepts will be more natural or useful to us. Words, gestures, expressions come alive, as it were, only within a language game, a culture, a form of life.

As I walk around Copacabana, I see the elderly try to get better access to wheelchairs and better health treatment from the neighborhood health units and popular drugstores. People in the favela are trying to open the places where they live not only to visitation ("favela tours") but to exchanges and more interactive projects with the outside communities down the hills. The sex-workers are probably seeking regulation and safety, too, but what I note most is the attempt of the artisans in promoting an original production that is consistently based on the notion of recycling. Actually, the whole neighborhood is naturally inclined to the idea of a sustainable economic practice, since the former more upscale families who still live here and are now visibly less affluent sell their bric-a-brac on a regular basis. Instead of restaurants à la carte and buffets, Copacabana has invented a myriad of "by the kilo" bistros that are the ultimate cheap solution to waste. You eat and pay for what is weighed in your plate, no less, no more (Varenikes and kebabs weigh the same and are served side by side). I approach the beach. In front of the Copacabana Palace Grand Hotel stand the Rainbow flags, announcing the embracing of diversity and its rights. But it is the new economies of exchange, in their tiny ways, the undercurrent of new modulations in the way of thinking and speaking, that I find the radical, hopeful experiences. I don't think they fit into the metaphor of the widely spread web and its equivalences. These punctual interventions are not ice-skating in the surface but neither are they going deep into the texture of post-modern life and thought. Maybe a better image could be found in fishing, which lots of people still do on this urban beach. Go deep here and there, when you need, for a little while, see what you can get.

The second idea I'd like to think about here is the everyday. Roger Silverstone, my former teacher (and someone who has left us much too early), wrote *Television and Everyday Life* in 1994. I've been thinking about him while walking about my newly found Copacabana. Roger was curious, open, and re-reading his book I had the pleasure of rediscovering his sophisticated and very solid theorizing and the grace of his writing. I wished to re-read Roger because I had been puzzled by what I perceived as another change brought about, this time by *YouTube*: an interest in "life" presented with the least degree of mediation. In *YouTube*, little trivial flashes of expressed subjectivities barely separated by language and culture, manage to circulate, communicate, and provoke a keen and general interest. Rather than engaging with the representation of life – such as fiction films, for instance – there is an appetite in the viewers for portraits of people and situations that seem immediate. These viewings seem to allow for an enlargement of experience that is not burdened with didacticism but rather feeds on the desire to tap into common, informal knowledge. We could almost say that life has become momentarily more interesting than the more contrived and elaborated forms of representation of life.

Last week I was at the university, trying to get my undergraduate students interested in reading a (light) theoretical text. It is about the influence of the gothic novel on films like *X-Men*, which I don't like but which I'm using to try to communicate with my students. My student Luana, who is a very active and notorious graffiti designer, seems distracted and agitated. She finally confesses she hasn't slept all night, glued to *YouTube*. And she saw something she now can't stop talking about. It was footage of a big turtle coming out of the water and being bothered by a pigeon flying around it. The turtle, to everyone's surprise, swiftly catches the pigeon mid-air, suddenly becoming a hunter. I can't understand the fascination, but there it is, undeniable and contagious as she now retells her impression of the scene and makes the other students want to see it too.

She is clever, and this Animal Planet clip seems so tedious and boring to me. What is the attraction? What's the charm? I'd rather see anything that was produced through human agency and interference. Like a movie, even a bad one. What has gone wrong? Could it be that my students are suffering from a hangover of art/entertainment? Was it the fault of too much art?

And that's how I resorted to Roger Silverstone, to see what he was thinking back in 1994, when television was the medium that asked to be studied and properly understood. In his last chapter he says he doesn't expect to produce a theory of everyday life. "Post-modernism has taught us, if nothing else, that the time for such an undertaking is now past. But I do want to try and offer a route through some of the paradoxes" (160). He wants to link television and everyday life because, after Stephen Heath, he finds a seamless equivalence of television with everyday life in its extensiveness, expansiveness, instability, interminability, and ubiquity. He goes on to remind us of the approach defined by the post-Lukacsian critiques of the Frankfurt School, by versions of French Marxism, such as those of Lefebvre, Bourdieu and Foucault, as well as by the mass society critics of the 1950s, all of whom see in everyday life an expression of a defeated politics, politics mistaking play for power. And he also refers to Michel de Certeau (and representatives of the new populism) who linked everyday life with the sphere of the popular, seeing the popular as a site of opposition, and who saw in everyday life the possibilities for a transcending, if albeit limited politics, real in its consequences; a politics in which play is power. These views, affirms Roger, represent and preserve a dichotomous approach to the study of everyday life which tends to preserve and reinforce the equivalent, dystopian and utopian, dichotomies of common sense. These dichotomies can no longer be sustained. Against this he wants to interpose "a hopefully more measured approach, an approach based on an understanding of the dynamic and uneven politics of everyday life; an approach based both in cultural critique and empirical research" (161). He finds in Winnicott and his notion of the transitional object the metaphor that serves him.

> Everyday culture is in this sense, [...] transitional. Everyday life appears in practice, [...] and the terms of that paradox – the found object and the created object – the imposed meanings and the selected meanings – the controlled behaviors and the free – the meaningless and the meaningful – the passive and the active – are in constant tension. (164)

Silverstone saw that what he called the ordinariness of everyday life, its taken-for-grantedness, is not homogeneous. Not only is it profoundly differentiated by virtue of culture – ethnic, religious, class, national or gendered culture - but it is also uneven in its formal quality. What I'd like to retain, though, is the idea he urges upon us – that of Agency. It would be the capacity for historically situated reflexive and purposive behavior. And I wonder where agency will relocate itself in the endless stream of clips of *YouTube*, and how the passive/active, consumer/producer dichotomies will try to resolve themselves in the next years.

I come across a rather long passage by Wittgenstein with which I'd like to conclude:

> Engelmann told me that when he rummages round at home in a drawer full of his own manuscripts, they strike him as so splendid that he thinks it would be worth making them available to other people. (He says it's the same when he is reading through letters from his dead relations.) But when he imagines publishing a selection of them the whole business loses its charm and value and becomes impossible. I said that was like the following case: Nothing could be more remarkable than seeing a man who thinks he is unobserved performing some quite simple everyday activity. Let us imagine a theatre: the curtains go up and we see a man alone in his room, walking up and down, lightning a cigarette, sitting down, etc, so that suddenly we are observing a human being from outside in a way that ordinarily we can never observe ourselves; it would be like watching a chapter of biography with our own eyes, – surely this would be uncanny and wonderful at the same time. We should be observing something more wonderful than anything a playwright could arrange to be acted or spoken on the stage: life itself. But then we do see this everyday without its making the slightest impression on us! True enough, but we do not see it from that point of view. Well, when E. looks at what he has written and finds it marvelous (even though he would not care to publish any of the pieces individually), he is seeing his life as a work of art created by God and, as such, it is certainly worth contemplating, as is every life and everything whatever. But only an artist can so represent an individual thing as to make it appear to us like a work of art; it is right that those manuscripts should lose their value when looked at singly

> and specially when regarded disinterestedly, i. e. by someone who doesn't feel enthusiastic about them in advance. A work of art forces us - as one might say – to see it in the right perspective but, in the absence of art, the object is just a fragment of nature like any other; we may exalt it through our enthusiasm but that does not give anyone else the right to confront us with it. (I keep thinking of one of those snapshots of a piece of scenery which is of interest for the man who took it because he was there himself and experienced something; but someone else will quite justifiably look at it coldly, in so far as it is ever justifiable to look at something coldly).
> But it seems to me too that there is a way of capturing the world sub specie aeterni other than through the work of the artist. Thought has such a way – so I believe – it is as though it flies above the world and leaves us as it is – observing it from above, in flight.

So my impression is that much could be gained from making everyone a producer of content. Still, we will need to find a way to meddle with things again in order to see them as they are. And the articles in this volume are doing just that.

WORKS CITED

Silverstone, Roger. *Television and Everyday Life*. London: Routledge, 1994. Print.
Wittgenstein, Ludwig. *Culture and Value*. Chicago, IL: U of Chicago P, 1977. Print.

CONTRIBUTORS

PETRA ECKHARD is an Assistant Professor (pre-doc) at the Department of American Studies at the University of Graz, Austria, where she is teaching courses in American Literature. Her fields of research include 20th century American literature and culture, postmodern urban theory, the city in literature (especially New York), gothic fiction & representations of the uncanny, and graphic narratives. She is currently finishing her dissertation entitled "The Goth/am Chronotopes: Time, Space, and the Uncanny in Postmodern New York Fiction" and co-editing the proceedings of the 2009 AAAS conference, *Contact Spaces of American Culture*, which is to be published in 2011.

MICHAEL FUCHS earned his Magister in English and American Studies from the University of Graz in spring 2007. In 2008, a revision of his diploma thesis was published as *The Simpsons: Postmodernism, Postmodernity, and America's Most Animated Family*. Currently an Assistant Professor (pre-doc) at the Department of American Studies, University of Graz, Michael is closing in on finishing his Ph.D. thesis on meta-reference in horror movies. His research interests are eclectic; at the moment, he is working on topics as varied as reflexivity in feature pornography, the recent reemergence of Nazisploitation cinema, the TV series *Supernatural*, the cult-stardom of Bruce Campbell, and professional wrestling and the American working class as well as co-editing a volume on American icons. As a sideline, Michael is one of the managing directors of a real estate and transaction services company.

SUSANNE HAMSCHA is a Ph.D. candidate at the Graduate School of North American Studies (FU Berlin). She studied English and American Studies at the University of Vienna and at the University of Massachusetts at Amherst, where she was a fellow in the Graduate Certificate in Advanced Feminist Studies. Her M.A. thesis, "The Body-in-Pieces," is concerned with the significance of the fragmented body in the fiction of Djuna Barnes, Rebecca Brown, and Jeanette Winterson. In her dissertation, "The Fiction of America: Performing the Cultural Imaginary in American Literature and Culture," she analyzes how the 'Americanness' of American culture is performatively constituted in nineteenth-century American literature and contemporary pop culture. Her research interests include the American Renaissance, American modernism, feminist literature, popular culture, film studies, and gender theory.

CHRISTOPH HARTNER, born 1980 in Judenburg, Upper Styria (Austria), studied English and Media at Karl-Franzens-Universität in Graz. He received the Excellence in English and American Studies Award for his thesis on "The Construction of Queer and Two-Spirit Identity in Literature" and is curently working as a freelance journalist in arts and literature.

WALTER W. HÖLBLING is Professor of U. S. Literature and Culture at the American Studies Department at Karl-Franzens-University in Graz, Austria. Among the books he wrote and co-edited are *Fiktionen vom Krieg im neueren amerikanischen Roman* (1987), *Utopian Thought in American Literature* (1988), *The European Emigrant Experience in the U. S. A.* (1992), *U. S. Documentary Films on World War II and Vietnam* (1993), *'Nature's Nation' Revisited: American Concepts of Nature from Wonder to Ecological Crisis* (2003), *What Is American?* (2004), *US Icons and Iconicity* (2006), and a volume of student essays, *Theories Applied to Texts: For Students, By Students* (2007). Together with his friend Gabriele Pötscher, he has also published two volumes of poetry in English, *Love Lust Loss* (2003) and *Think Twice* (2006).

ANA TERESA JARDIM REYNAUD earned her Ph.D. from Sussex University, Great Britain. Her thesis was about Brazilian Videoart and most of it has been published as articles in Brazilian and international periodicals and magazines. She teaches at Universidade Federal do Estado do Rio de Janeiro (UNIRIO). Ana is also a fiction writer and has published several collections of short stories. Currently, she is finishing a teenage illustrated novel about the neighborhood of Copacabana in Rio de Janeiro.

CORNELIA KLECKER graduated from the University of Innsbruck in English and American Studies as well as Comparative Literature. Her diploma thesis "Skip and Rewind: When Time Gets out of Line in Mainstream Film" discusses the phenomenon of the frequent use of non-linear narrative in contemporary popular film. Presently, she is employed at the Department of American Studies at the University of Innsbruck and is working on her Ph.D. thesis about mind-tricking narrative in contemporary mainstream film.

LEOPOLD LIPPERT holds an M.A. in English and American Studies from the University of Vienna (2008) and is currently writing a dissertation on the 'Americanness' of Austrian cultural practice. A revised version of his diploma thesis was published as *Utopian Contemporaries: Queer Temporality and America* in 2009. His research interests include 20th and 21st century American culture, Performance Studies and American drama, Queer Theory, and transnational American Studies.

MICHAEL PHILLIPS is a Ph.D. candidate at the Department of American Studies, University of Graz, where he serves as a lecturer at the Department of English and the School of Social and Economic Sciences. After graduating *magna cum laude* from the University of Pennsylvania, Michael took a hiatus from academia to live and work in various countries before settling down in Austria to complete his Masters Degree with a focus on narrative identity construction in postmodern fiction. In his Ph.D. thesis, he is exploring the representation of iconic music stars in various cinematic genres and how these images help construct subject positions for various groups within the audience. Together with Klaus Rieser and Michael Fuchs, he is currently editing a volume on American icons. Mike's research interests include postmodern literature, American icons, rock music, and film studies.

SIMONE PUFF is an Assistant Professor (pre-doc) at the Department of English and American Studies at Klagenfurt University in Austria, where she teaches classes in American Literature and Cultural Studies. She is currently interested in African American Studies, particularly in black women writers, black feminisms, and intersecting oppressions. Simone's Ph.D. project in progress addresses contemporary aspects of colorism; discrimination based on skin color within Black America. With her interdisciplinary thesis on the Black Feminist Movement, which is based on a research stay at Syracuse University, she earned two master's degrees from Klagenfurt University. Simone Puff is the treasurer and a member of the Austrian Association for American Studies and co-editor of the association's 2008 conference proceedings entitled *Almighty Dollar* (LIT Verlag, forthcoming 2010).

GUNDO RIAL Y COSTAS is a Ph.D. candidate in Latin American Studies at Freie Universität Berlin, where he is working on cultural transformation processes in the Americas. He has also studied Latin American Studies at King's College London and anthropology in Mérida, Mexico. Gundo has contributed essays to the following publications: *Mercosul/Mercosur: Dynamik der Grenzen und kulturelle Integration* (BKV, 2007), *Differenz und Herrschaft in den Amerikas* (transcript, 2009), *Sociedades Desiguais: Genero, Cidadania e Identidade* (Nova Harmonia, 2009), *Brasilien Heute* (with Costa, Sérgio; Vervuert, 2010; forthcoming), and *Aesthetic Practices and Politics in Media, Music, and Art: Performing Migration* (Routledge, 2010; forthcoming).

MICHAEL ROZENDAL is Assistant Professor of Rhetoric and Composition at the University of San Francisco who received his Ph.D. from the University at Buffalo and his M.A. from Stanford. As a Fulbright Professor in Germany during the

2008-2009 academic year, he had the pleasure to work with Austria's Young Americanists at the inception of this volume. His ongoing research on 1930s America explores the interactions between social and formal radicalism, modernist and proletarian writing in the period's vibrant print culture. He has lectured and taught on postmodernism, modernism, and contemporary political rhetoric.

PABLO VALDIVIA OROZCO holds an M.A. in Latin American and Communication Studies. Between 2005 and 2008, he was a scholarship holder in the DFG (German Science Fund)-funded research project "Lebensformen und Lebenswissen" (forms and knowledge of life). Since 2009, he has been an Assistant Professor at the University of Potsdam. Pablo has published several articles, among others in *Dynamisierte Räume: Zur Theorie der Bewegung in den romanischen Kulturen* (2009), *Literaturwissenschaft als Lebenswissenschaft* (Narr, 2009), *Transchile* (Vervuert, 2010), and *Happy Days: Lebenswissen nach Cavell* (Fink, 2010).

MARCEL VEJMELKA earned his Ph.D. in Latin American Studies from Freie Universität Berlin in 2004. In 2007-08, he was postdoctoral fellow at the International Graduate Centre for the Study of Culture at the University of Gießen. Currently, he is an assistant professor at the Department of Spanish and Portuguese at University of Mainz, Germany. Marcel's publications include *Kreuzwege: Querungen* (tranvía, 2005), *Welt des Sertão / Sertão der Welt* (co-ed.; tranvía, 2007), *A obra de Jorge Amado nas Alemanhas oriental e ocidental: suas recepções e traduces* (Casa de Palavras, 2008), and *Amazônia – região universal e teatro do mundo* (co-ed; Globo, 2010).

INDEX

E

F

G

H

I

J

K

L

M

N

O

P